Workshop on Challenges & Perspectives in Creating Large Language Models

Dublin, Ireland
27 May 2022

ISBN: 978-1-7138-6727-2

Printed from e-media with permission by:

Curran Associates, Inc.
57 Morehouse Lane
Red Hook, NY 12571

Some format issues inherent in the e-media version may also appear in this print version.

Printed with permission by Curran Associates, Inc. (2023)

For permission requests, please contact the Association for Computational Linguistics at the address below.

Association for Computational Linguistics
209 N. Eighth Street
Stroudsburg, Pennsylvania 18360

Phone: 1-570-476-8006
Fax: 1-570-476-0860

acl@aclweb.org

Additional copies of this publication are available from:

Curran Associates, Inc.
57 Morehouse Lane
Red Hook, NY 12571 USA
Phone: 845-758-0400
Fax: 845-758-2633
Email: curran@proceedings.com
Web: www.proceedings.com

2022

Challenges & Perspectives in Creating Large Language Models

Proceedings of the Workshop

May 27, 2022

The organizers gratefully acknowledge the support from the following sponsors.

Sponsor

NAVER LABS Europe

Introduction

Two years after the appearance of GPT-3, large language models seem to have taken over NLP. Their capabilities, limitations, societal impact and the potential new applications they unlocked have been discussed and debated at length. A handful of replication studies have been published since then, confirming some of the initial findings and discovering new limitations. This workshop aims to gather researchers and practitioners involved in the creation of these models in order to:

1. Share ideas on the next directions of research in this field, including—but not limited to—grounding, multi-modal models, continuous updates and reasoning capabilities.

2. Share best-practices, brainstorm solutions to identified limitations and discuss challenges, such as infrastructure, data, ethical & legal frameworks, evaluation, training efficiency, etc.

This workshop is organized by the BigScience[1] initiative and will also serve as the closing session of this one year-long initiative aimed at developing a multilingual large language model, which is gathering 1.000+ researchers from more than 60 countries and 250 institutions and research labs. Its goal is to investigate the creation of a large scale dataset and model from a very wide diversity of angles.

[1] https://bigscience.huggingface.co/

Organizing Committee

Organization Committee

Angela Fan, Meta AI
Matthias Gallé, Naver Labs Europe
Suzana Ilić, HuggingFace
Thomas Wolf, HuggingFace

Steering Committee

Yoav Goldberg, Bar Ilan University & Allen Institute for Artificial Intelligence
Percy Lang, Stanford University
Margaret Mitchell, HuggingFace & Ethical AI LLC
Alice Oh, KAIST
Alexander Rush, Cornell University

Program Committee

Program Chairs

Angela Fan, Facebook
Matthias Gallé, Naver Labs Europee
Suzana Ilic, HuggingFace
Thomas Wolf, HuggingFace

Table of Contents

Program

Friday, May 27, 2022

12:30 - 11:00	*Poster Session*
14:00 - 15:00	*BigScience*
15:00 - 15:20	*Data Governance*
15:20 - 15:40	*Data*
15:40 - 16:00	*Modeling*
16:00 - 16:20	*Prompt Engineering*
16:20 - 16:40	*Evaluation*

Lifelong Pretraining: Continually Adapting Language Models to Emerging Corpora

Xisen Jin[†1] **Dejiao Zhang**[2] **Henghui Zhu**[2] **Wei Xiao**[2]
Shang-Wen Li[‡2] **Xiaokai Wei**[2] **Andrew Arnold**[2] **Xiang Ren**[1]
[1]University of Southern California [2]AWS AI Labs
{xisenjin,xiangren}@usc.edu
{dejiaoz, henghui, weixiaow, shangwenl, xiaokaiw, anarnld}
@amazon.com

Abstract

Pretrained language models (PTLMs) are typically learned over a large, static corpus and further fine-tuned for various downstream tasks. However, when deployed in the real world, a PTLM-based model must deal with data distributions that deviate from what the PTLM was initially trained on. In this paper, we study a *lifelong language model pretraining* challenge where a PTLM is continually updated so as to adapt to emerging data. Over a domain-incremental research paper stream and a chronologically-ordered tweet stream, we incrementally pretrain a PTLM with different continual learning algorithms, and keep track of the downstream task performance (after fine-tuning). We evaluate PTLM's ability to adapt to new corpora while retaining learned knowledge in earlier corpora. Our experiments show distillation-based approaches to be most effective in retaining downstream performance in earlier domains. The algorithms also improve knowledge transfer, allowing models to achieve better downstream performance over the latest data, and improve temporal generalization when distribution gaps exist between training and evaluation because of time. We believe our problem formulation, methods, and analysis will inspire future studies towards continual pretraining of language models.

1 Introduction

Pretrained language models (PTLMs) have achieved remarkable performance on benchmark datasets for a range of NLP tasks (Liu et al., 2019b; Brown et al., 2020). However, when deployed in the wild, NLP systems must deal with emerging data that have constantly shifting data distribution, different from the text corpora they were initially pretrained on — for example, when new data domains are introduced (upper part of Fig. 1) (Gururangan et al., 2020), or when the language uses and vocabulary change over time (lower part of Fig. 1) (Lazaridou et al., 2021). Fine-tuning from a static and possibly "outdated" PTLM may limit the model performance on downstream tasks, as the PTLM may no longer provide an effective model initialization (Beltagy et al., 2019; Müller et al., 2020). Here we look to understand whether continuously adapting a PTLM to emerging data can yield gains on various downstream tasks, and how to achieve better downstream performance for such lifelong PTLM adaptation.

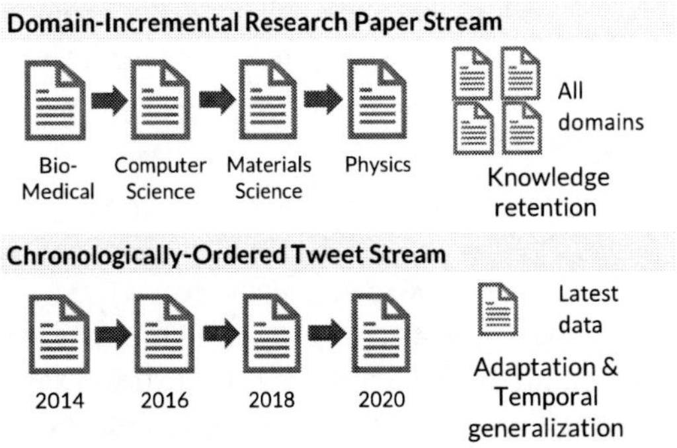

Figure 1: Two data streams created for studying lifelong language model pre-training. We focus on evaluating knowledge retention on the domain-incremental research papers stream; we focus on adaptation to the latest data and temporal generalization on the chronologically ordered tweet stream.

A number of recent works make attempts on adapting PTLMs to a new data domain. Gururangan et al. (2020); Yao et al. (2021) adapt language models to corpora of different genres and topics and observe performance improvement in domain-specific downstream tasks. Arumae et al. (2020) further show that by regularizing the parameters of PTLMs, the downstream tasks performance on the general domain can be preserved. Another line of works focuses on temporal domain shift (Hombaiah et al., 2021), which analyzes the effect of pretraining over up-to-date data to the downstream tasks. Röttger and Pierrehumbert (2021) further study vocabulary composition approaches for improving adaptation to up-to-date corpora. However,

Proceedings of BigScience Episode #5 – Workshop on Challenges & Perspectives in Creating Large Language Models, pages 1 - 16
May 27, 2022

these work focus their study on adapting PTLM to a single new domain; while in practice, corpora from distinct domains and time stamps may emerge sequentially. Whether one can maintain a single, up-to-date PTLM remains an open problem. Related to this, Lazaridou et al. (2021) study adaptation of PTLMs over temporal data streams, but solely focus on language modeling instead of fine-tuning performance. It is also important to understand multiple aspects of the utility of lifelong PTLM pretraining, such as knowledge retention over all the seen data, and study what methods can improve the utility of PTLMs in such a continual pretraining process.

In this paper, we formulate a *Lifelong Language Model Pretraining* task to simulate practical scenarios of maintaining and adapting a PTLM over emerging corpora, create a testbed (along with pretraining data streams and downstream tasks) for studying continual pretraining algorithms, and present a systematic evaluation protocol for measuring the progress made on this challenging problem (see Figure 2 for an illustration). We consider two types of text corpus sequences when constructing pretraining data streams, each of which simulates a representative use case and that has slightly different focuses on the evaluation: continuously learning a single model that is applicable to both old and new domains; and improving the model's ability to handle latest data. Specifically, we construct 1) a domain-incremental text stream that consists of academic papers published in four research fields, and 2) a temporal tweet stream that consists of tweets collected from four different years. By conducting systematic experiments on these two data streams, we look to answer a series of analysis questions: 1) whether continual pretraining retains fine-tuning performance over earlier corpora compared to traditional offline pretraining, 2) whether pretraining improves downstream performance on the latest data, and 3) whether pretraining improves temporal generalization where training and evaluation have distribution gaps because of time.

To address the research questions above, we conduct a systematic evaluation of existing continual learning (CL) algorithms, spanning over model-expansion based, memory-based, and distillation-based approaches. Our results show distillation-based approaches are most effective in knowledge retention in the research paper stream, while simultaneously improve adaptation to latest data and temporal generalization in the tweet stream. We believe our problem formulation, evaluation setup, methods and analysis can inspire more future work on continual pretraining of language models.

2 Problem Formulation

Here we present the problem formulation for lifelong pretraining of PTLM, provide details about the data stream construction process and downstream tasks, and introduce the evaluation protocol.

2.1 Lifelong Pretraining of PTLMs

We consider the scenario where one needs to deploy and/or maintain NLP models over a sequence of T data domains. At each time step t the model visits an unlabeled text corpus D_t from a domain with a data distribution $P(D_t)$. The data distribution $P(D_t)$ evolves as the time step t, forming a *data stream* $D_{1..T} = \{D_1, D_2, ...D_T\}$. In practice, the data domain shift can refer to the topic change of the text content (from computer science research papers to biomedical papers), or temporal evolution of the text (from past to recent tweets). The task of *lifelong pretraining of PTLM* looks to continuously adapt a language model f as the model visits (unlabeled) text corpus D_t from the data stream $D_{1..T}$, in order to provide a good model initialization for fine-tuning on downstream tasks from the same domain. With slight abuse in notations, we also use D_t to directly refer to a data domain.

Here, we assume a language model f is updated sequentially over each pretraining corpora D_t, without accessing the full earlier corpora $\{D_i\}_{i<t}$ in the data stream $D_{1..T}$. This aims to capture practical constraints such as privacy restriction for storing earlier data, or computation budget for training over all the text corpora in $D_{1..T}$. We use f_t to denote the language model right *after* updating on the domain D_t. In our study, f is a RoBERTa-base transformer (Liu et al., 2019b) and the model (f_0) is initialized with pretrained RoBERTa weights.

The utility of the PTLMs $\{f_t\}$ is evaluated based on their fine-tuned model performance on various downstream tasks. After updating on a domain D_i, the model f_i can be fine-tuned over downstream tasks from visited domains D_t where $t \leq i$. We note the set of downstream tasks related to domain D_t as $S_t = \{S_t^j\}_{j=1}^{N_t}$, assuming the number of downstream tasks is N_t. Note that in the fine-tuning stage, model f_t has no access to any of the pretraining corpus $D_{1..T}$.

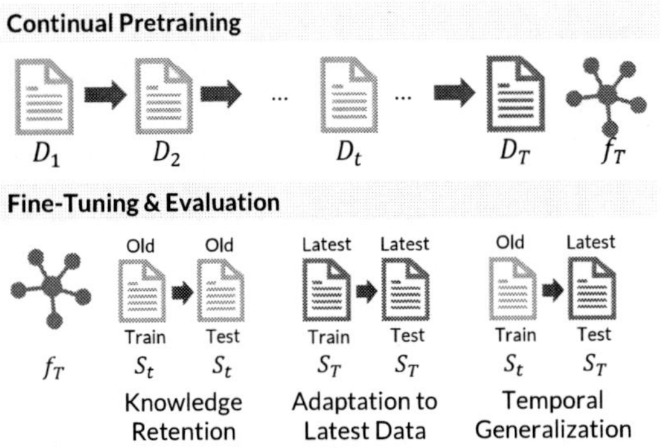

Figure 2: **Training, evaluation setups, and metrics of lifelong language model pretraining.** The model sequentially visits each corpus, and is fine-tuned on downstream datasets related to the domains of pretraining. We evaluate knowledge retention and adaptation to new data with downstream fine-tuning performance on old and latest domains respectively. Besides, we evaluate temporal generalization where training/test examples are drawn from different time steps.

2.2 Data Streams & Downstream Datasets

We construct data streams to simulate two representative scenarios of data domain shifts in practice (also see Fig. 1): one *domain-incremental* stream to simulate the sequential changes of research paper areas; and one *chronologically-ordered* stream to simulate tweets emerging over time.

Domain-incremental Paper Stream. This paper stream consists of the full text of research papers published in four research areas: biomedical, computer science, material science, and physics, filtered from the S2ORC dataset[1], which are presented sequentially to the model. For each domain, we evaluate downstream performance over two datasets. The downstream tasks span over various tasks such as relation extraction and named entity recognition, and are summarized in Table 1. We detail these datasets in Appendix D.

Chronologically-ordered Tweet Stream. This tweet data stream consists of tweets from the year 2014, 2016, 2018 and 2020, collected by the Archive Team[2] and preprocessed following Nguyen et al. (2020). These four tweet corpora are presented sequentially to the language model following the chronological order of the tweet year. For downstream tasks, we hold out 1M tweets from each year's corpus to construct multi-label hashtag prediction datasets (Gong and Zhang, 2016) and single-label emoji prediction datasets (Barbieri et al., 2018). On two datasets, we report label ranking average precision scores (a multi-label version of MRR) of models (Azeemi and Waheed, 2021) and Macro-F1 respectively. The detailed dataset construction process is included in Appendix D.

[1] We use the 20200705v1 version of the S2ORC dataset at https://github.com/allenai/s2orc

[2] https://archive.org/details/twitterstream

Domains	Downstream Datasets	Metrics
Bio-Medicine	Chemprot (Vindahl, 2016)	Micro-F1
	RCT-Sample (Dernoncourt and Lee, 2017)	Micro-F1
Comp. Science	ACL-ARC (Jurgens et al., 2018)	Macro-F1
	SciERC (Luan et al., 2018)	Macro-F1
Mat. Science	Synthesis (Mysore et al., 2019)	Macro-F1
	MNER (Olivetti et al., 2020)	Micro-F1
Physics	Keyphrase (Augenstein et al., 2017)	Macro-F1
	Hyponym (Augenstein et al., 2017)	Macro-F1

Table 1: Summary of downstream datasets relevant to each domain in the research paper stream.

2.3 Evaluation Protocol

We consider three key aspects for evaluating the utility of the language models $\{f_t\}$ that are continuously updated over the data stream $D_{1..T}$, also illustrated in Figure 2: 1) knowledge retention and transfer over the pretraining corpora seen earlier; 2) adaptation to the latest data domain, and 3) temporal generalization when training and evaluation data are from different time steps.

Knowledge Retention. A key utility of continual language model pretraining is to obtain a single model applicable to all domains. We focus on the evaluation of the ability with the domain-incremental paper stream, because for the tweet stream, the practical need of performance over outdated data is limited. Knowledge retention is measured with the downstream task performance from earlier or the current domains that the pretrained model has visited. More formally, for each pretrained model checkpoint in $\{f_i\}$, we fine-tune f_i over downstream tasks $\{S_t\}$ where $t \leq i$ and evaluate the corresponding test set performance. It is important that the models do not suffer from catastrophic forgetting (Robins, 1995), *i.e.,* significantly reduced helpfulness when f_i is fine-tuned for downstream tasks S_t from earlier domains with $t < i$.

Adaption to Latest Data Domain. In certain scenarios, performance of downstream models over the latest data domain should be emphasized. For example, classifiers in the tweet domain are usually trained and evaluated with up-to-date data for practical deployment. Formally, we focus on the downstream task performance of models fine-tuned from the final pretrained model checkpoint f_T, where the downstream tasks S_T are also from the latest domain. To succeed in these metrics, it is crucial for the model to transfer knowledge from earlier domains to the latest domain.

Temporal Generalization Ability. We consider another practical fine-tuning scenario in the tweet stream where the model is trained on outdated data and evaluated on the latest data (Rijhwani and Preotiuc-Pietro, 2020; Huang and Paul, 2018), referred to as the *temporal generalization* ability. Formally, we fine-tune the final pretrained model checkpoint f_T over the training set of downstream tasks S_t from an earlier time step ($t < T$), and evaluate on the test set of the downstream tasks S_T from the latest time step T.

3 Methods

Lifelong language model pretraining introduces novel challenges because of the large training sets and more comprehensive evaluation protocols compared to classification tasks. We establish several strong baselines, and evaluate the performance of continual learning algorithms from different categories spanning over model-expansion, memory-based, and distillation-based approaches, We illustrate the approaches in Figure 3.

3.1 Simple Baselines

We consider several simple baselines which continual learning algorithms will be compared against. `RoBERTa-base` (f_0) corresponds to not pretraining on any of the domain-specific corpora. By separately pretraining f_0 on each corpus $D_1, D_2, ...D_T$, we obtain T `Task-Specific` pretrained models. We also pretrain f_0 sequentially over $D_{1..T}$, which we refer to as `sequential pretraining`. While it allows knowledge transfer between domains compared to domain-specific models, without any continual learning algorithms, sequential pretraining is prone to catastrophic forgetting (Robins, 1995). Finally, we randomly shuffle corpora from all domains $D_{1..T}$ before pretraining, noted as `Multi-Task Learning (MTL)`. MTL corresponds to an offline training paradigm that models new corpora by re-training over all corpora seen before. The drawback is that it requires storing full data from earlier domains, and that it can be extremely costly to repetitively retrain over earlier data if new data keeps emerging.

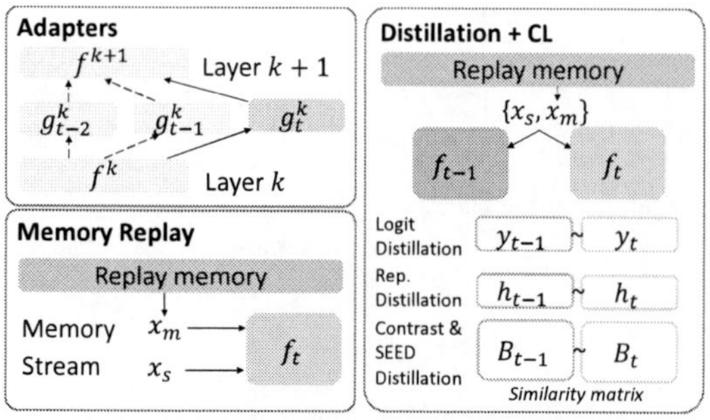

Figure 3: **Comparison of adapter, memory replay, and distillation-based continual learning algorithms.** Details of the methods are introduced in Sec. 3.

3.2 Model-expansion and Regularization-based Methods

We first introduce model-expansion based approaches, which add small trainable modules (*e.g.*, multi-layer perceptron) to the model per new domain while keeping other parts of the model frozen. The `Adapter` approach is a representative approach that learns a set of "adapter" layers $g_t = \{g_t^k\}_{k=1}^K$ for each domain D_t and each of the K transformer layers (Houlsby et al., 2019). We also experiment with a simple `Layer Expansion` approach, which learns separate top two layers of the transformer and the prediction head for each domain. We also involve a regularization-based continual learning baseline, online EWC (Schwarz et al., 2018), which directly penalize change of model parameters.

3.3 Memory Replay Methods

We also experiment with Experience Replay (ER) (Chaudhry et al., 2019), which alleviates forgetting by storing a subset of earlier examples and periodically re-training (replaying) over them. We maintain a fixed-size memory M ($100k$ examples by default) and populate the memory M each time pretraining on a domain D_t finishes with examples in the current domain. We ensure M always contains a balanced sample of examples from all seen domains $D_{1..t}$. We replay a mini-batch of examples from the memory every 10 training steps.

3.4 Distillation-based CL Methods

While knowledge distillation (KD) (Hinton et al., 2015) techniques have been studied intensively for pretrained language models (Sun et al., 2019), applying them to continual learning has been under-explored outside image classification tasks (Li and Hoiem, 2018; Rebuffi et al., 2017; Hou et al., 2018). Distillation based CL approaches store one previous model checkpoint of the model (noted as f_{t-1}) and regularize the differences between f_{t-1} and the current model f_t. We adapt several existing knowledge distillation techniques to PTLMs and utilize them for continual learning. We note, while individual distillation techniques are not original, their adaptation to CL algorithms can be novel.

We perform distillation with examples from the current domain D_t and a replay memory M (similar to ER). Despite the potential gap between D_t and the training data of f_{t-1}, the approach allows utilizing more data for distillation. Formally, each time the model receives a mini-batch of stream examples $\boldsymbol{x}_s$ or a draws mini-batch of memory examples $\boldsymbol{x}_m$ from M (both noted as $\boldsymbol{x}$), we collect certain outputs of the model (*e.g.*, output logits or intermediate representations) with f_{t-1} and f_t. We compute a distillation loss $\ell_{\text{KD}}(\boldsymbol{x}, f_{t-1}, f_t)$ that penalizes the differences between the model outputs, and jointly optimize it with the masked language modeling loss ℓ_{MLM}. The final objective is written as $\ell = \ell_{\text{MLM}} + \alpha \ell_{\text{KD}}$, where α is a hyperparameter to weight the distillation loss.

Logit Distillation. In logit distillation (Hinton et al., 2015), we collect the output logits of f_t and f_{t-1}, noted as $\boldsymbol{y}_t$ and $\boldsymbol{y}_{t-1}$ respectively. The distillation loss is computed as $D_{\text{KL}}(\boldsymbol{y}_t, \boldsymbol{y}_{t-1})$, where D_{KL} is the Kullback–Leibler divergence function.

Representation Distillation. We also consider minimizing the representational deviation of sentences between previous and current models (Sun et al., 2019; Jiao et al., 2020). We extract the representation of each word of two models, noted as $\boldsymbol{h}_{t-1}^{1:N}$ and $\boldsymbol{h}_t^{1:N}$, before the masked language modeling prediction head, where N is the length of the sentence. Then, we compute MSE loss $||\boldsymbol{h}_{t-1}^{1:N} - \boldsymbol{h}_t^{1:N}||_2^2$ as the distillation loss.

Contrastive Distillation. In addition to output logits and hidden representations, we further look into *representational similarity within a batch of examples* as additional knowledge to distill. The approach is adapted from (Cha et al., 2021), which is originally studied for supervised image classification tasks. We briefly introduce the adapted algorithm and leave the details in Appendix E. During continual pretraining, in addition to the language model pretraining objective, we add an unsupervised contrastive learning objective, namely the SimCSE (Gao et al., 2021) objective to encourage sentence representations to reflect semantic similarities between sentences. Then, we compute the intra-batch representational similarity matrices of sentence representations (*i.e.* between each pair of examples in the mini-batch) with f_{t-1} and f_t, noted as $\mathbf{B}^{t-1}$ and $\mathbf{B}^t$, and minimize the cross entropy loss $\ell_{\text{distill}} = -\frac{1}{N}\sum_{i=1}^{N}\sum_{j=1}^{N}\mathbf{B}_{ij}^{t-1}\log\mathbf{B}_{ij}^{t}$

Self-Supervised Distillation (SEED). SEED distillation proposed by (Fang et al., 2021) has a similar spirit as the contrastive distillation. The only difference is that it distills representational similarity *between the batch and a large set of other examples*. We leave the details of the algorithm in Appendix E. We further combine SEED Distillationwith logit distillation and refer to the approach as SEED-Logit Distillation.

4 Results

We summarize our findings over the created data streams. We ask whether lifelong pretraining and continual learning algorithms are effective base on our evaluation protocol proposed in Sec. 2.3.

4.1 Experiment Settings

We use the `RoBERTa-base` model (Liu et al., 2019b), initialized with RoBERTa-base weights throughout the experiments. We set the maximal sequence length to 128 and an effective training batch size of 2,048. On the research paper stream, models are trained for $8k$ steps in the first domain and $4k$ steps in the subsequent domains. On the Tweet stream, we train the models for $4k$ steps in each domain. These correspond to less than a single pass of data in each domain. See Appendix A for detailed setups.

4.2 Domain Incremental Data Stream

As we introduced in Sec. 2.2, in the domain incremental research paper stream, we expect a model f_t to perform well on all downstream tasks $S_{1..t}$ from domains $D_{1..t}$. In Table 2, we report the performance of models on all downstream tasks $S_{1..T}$ fine-tuned from the final pretraining checkpoint, f_T. We visualize more complete change of downstream task performance over different time steps of pretraining (*i.e.*,, f_1, f_2, f_3, f_4) in Fig. 4. We also report the log perplexity of masked language modeling (MLM) in Table 2 as additional information. With these results, we address the research questions below.

Task	D_1 - Biomedical			D_2 - Computer Science			D_3 - Materials Science			D_4 - Physics		
Dataset	Chemprot	RCT-Sample	MLM	ACL-ARC	SciERC	MLM	MNER	Synthesis	MLM	Keyphrase	Hyponym	MLM
Roberta-base	$82.03_{\pm 0.7}$	$78.07_{\pm 0.7}$	1.993	$64.32_{\pm 2.8}$	$79.07_{\pm 1.6}$	2.153	$83.15_{\pm 0.3}$	$91.25_{\pm 0.6}$	2.117	$66.21_{\pm 1.0}$	$67.59_{\pm 4.5}$	2.278
Sequential Pretraining	$82.09_{\pm 0.5}$	$79.60_{\pm 0.5}$	1.654	$72.73_{\pm 2.9}$	$81.43_{\pm 0.8}$	1.807	**83.99**$_{\pm 0.3}$	$92.10_{\pm 1.0}$	1.590	**67.57**$_{\pm 1.0}$	**74.68**$_{\pm 4.4}$	**1.381**
ER	$82.73_{\pm 0.3}$	$79.98_{\pm 0.3}$	1.737	$72.50_{\pm 1.0}$	$81.64_{\pm 1.1}$	1.857	**83.99**$_{\pm 0.4}$	$92.65_{\pm 0.4}$	1.621	$66.11_{\pm 1.1}$	$72.82_{\pm 4.3}$	1.391
Online EWC	$81.83_{\pm 0.2}$	$78.84_{\pm 0.5}$	1.655	$71.81_{\pm 2.6}$	$80.79_{\pm 0.5}$	1.803	$83.43_{\pm 0.4}$	$91.89_{\pm 0.5}$	1.571	$66.70_{\pm 0.6}$	$72.98_{\pm 6.0}$	1.388
Adapter	$83.30_{\pm 0.4}$	$80.41_{\pm 0.4}$	1.417	$69.32_{\pm 3.5}$	$80.22_{\pm 1.5}$	**1.633**	$83.91_{\pm 0.3}$	$91.69_{\pm 0.6}$	1.522	$66.23_{\pm 1.4}$	$69.65_{\pm 4.5}$	1.554
Layer Expansion	$83.74_{\pm 0.3}$	$81.10_{\pm 0.5}$	**1.210**	$65.17_{\pm 2.9}$	$79.35_{\pm 0.8}$	1.756	$82.48_{\pm 0.4}$	$92.33_{\pm 1.0}$	1.389	$65.70_{\pm 1.1}$	$73.34_{\pm 3.7}$	1.534
Logit-KD	$83.39_{\pm 0.4}$	**81.21**$_{\pm 0.1}$	1.392	**73.70**$_{\pm 3.4}$	$81.92_{\pm 0.8}$	1.699	$83.96_{\pm 0.3}$	$92.20_{\pm 1.0}$	**1.425**	$64.75_{\pm 1.1}$	$71.29_{\pm 3.6}$	1.460
Rep-KD	$82.34_{\pm 0.3}$	$79.59_{\pm 0.5}$	1.684	$71.17_{\pm 2.5}$	$78.78_{\pm 1.1}$	1.810	$84.13_{\pm 0.3}$	$92.02_{\pm 0.8}$	1.585	$65.96_{\pm 1.6}$	$73.93_{\pm 5.5}$	1.389
Contrast-KD	$82.29_{\pm 0.5}$	$79.92_{\pm 0.4}$	1.722	$71.15_{\pm 1.1}$	$80.49_{\pm 1.6}$	1.856	$83.26_{\pm 0.4}$	$92.62_{\pm 0.7}$	1.612	$65.95_{\pm 1.7}$	$72.26_{\pm 3.1}$	1.428
SEED-KD	$82.78_{\pm 0.3}$	$80.38_{\pm 0.4}$	1.720	$69.98_{\pm 2.4}$	$81.61_{\pm 0.7}$	1.829	$82.99_{\pm 0.4}$	$92.35_{\pm 0.7}$	1.609	$65.35_{\pm 1.0}$	$74.79_{\pm 4.1}$	1.401
SEED-Logit-KD	**83.72**$_{\pm 0.4}$	$81.05_{\pm 0.2}$	1.391	$69.90_{\pm 4.5}$	**83.03**$_{\pm 0.6}$	1.703	$83.28_{\pm 0.5}$	**92.87**$_{\pm 1.0}$	1.428	$65.96_{\pm 1.5}$	$71.92_{\pm 5.5}$	1.460
Task-Specific LM	$83.74_{\pm 0.3}$	$81.10_{\pm 0.5}$	1.210	$72.20_{\pm 2.6}$	$81.24_{\pm 1.7}$	1.629	$84.02_{\pm 0.2}$	$91.56_{\pm 0.4}$	1.418	$65.95_{\pm 1.1}$	$69.43_{\pm 4.5}$	1.426
MTL	$82.91_{\pm 1.6}$	$80.67_{\pm 0.4}$	1.289	$69.46_{\pm 1.8}$	$81.12_{\pm 0.8}$	1.616	$83.92_{\pm 0.3}$	$92.66_{\pm 0.6}$	1.355	$65.37_{\pm 1.6}$	$73.31_{\pm 5.2}$	1.418

Table 2: **Results on the Research Paper stream.** We report log perplexity of MLM and the performance of downstream models fine-tuned from the final checkpoint of the pretrained model ($t = 4$). Performance of the best performing CL algorithm is marked bold.

Does lifelong pretraining help retain knowledge across different domain corpora? We first examine whether task-specific or lifelong pretraining improves performance over domain-specific downstream tasks. Comparing Task-Specific LMs with RoBERTa-base in Table 2, we notice consistent performance improvements, especially on Biomedical and Computer Science domains (D_1, D_2). We also see Sequential Pretraining could consistently outperform RoBERTa-base. However, the comparison between Sequential Pretraining and Task Specific LMs are mixed: on D_1, D_2, D_3, Sequential Pretraining could outperform Task-Specific LMs only except MNER; while on the earliest biomedical domain (D_1), Sequential Pretraining achieves substantially lower performance. From Figure 4, we see the performance of Sequential Pretraining on Chemprot and RCT (from D_1) drops significantly from $t = 1$ to 4. The results imply lifelong pretraining allows later domains to benefit from knowledge transfer from earlier domains, but the performance on earlier domains is limited because of forgetting.

Does continual learning algorithms help retain knowledge in sequential pretraining? Next, we compare different kinds of CL algorithms and investigate the effect of CL algorithms in alleviating forgetting and improving knowledge transfer. Table 2 shows that Online-EWC slightly improves MLM perplexity compared to Sequential PT, but brings no improvement to the fine-tuning performance. We hypothesize that regularization directly in the parameter space as in Online-EWC is not effective when the parameter space is very high dimensional. Adapter improves downstream task F1 scores on the bio-medical domain (D_1) by 1.2% and 0.8%, but does not outperform Sequential Pretraining in other domains (similarly for Simple Layer Expansion approach), likely because a great portion of the model is kept frozen.

$\|M\|$, k	Chemprot	RCT	ACL-ARC	SciERC	MLM-$D_{1,2}$
$100k$, 10	82.73	79.98	72.50	81.64	1.737/1.857
$100k$, 100	82.06	78.64	71.97	81.62	1.599/1.789
$10M$, 10	82.87	79.98	71.80	81.63	1.438/1.732

Table 3: Downstream task and MLM performance of f_T under different memory sizes $|M|$ and the frequency of replay k (replaying every k steps of training) in ER.

In contrast, the memory-replay based approach (ER) allows training the full parameters of the model and has been shown to be highly effective in continual learning of classification tasks (Wang et al., 2019; Chaudhry et al., 2019). However, we surprisingly find that ER could hardly improve over Sequential Pretraining except D_1. A similar pattern can be found in the MLM perplexity. We hypothesize that the positive effect of example replay has diminished because of the overfitting to the memory examples. Table 3 summarizes the effect of tuning hyperpameters in ER. When we reduce the frequency of replay (from every 10 steps to 100 steps), the MLM performance improves, which implies reduced overfitting; however, the performance of downstream task performance does not improve. When we increase the size of the memory $|M|$ from $100k$ to $10M$, the MLM perplexity also improves; still, there are still no improvements in downstream tasks. It may imply ER itself is not an effective approach for continual pretraining.

Unlike ER, distillation approaches utilize richer information such as output logits or representation similarity to preserve past knowledge. We find either Logit KD or SEED-Logit KD to be most effective depending on the task, while Rep-KD and Contrastive-KD are less effective. The best performing distillation approach improves F1 over Sequential Pretraining on downstream tasks from

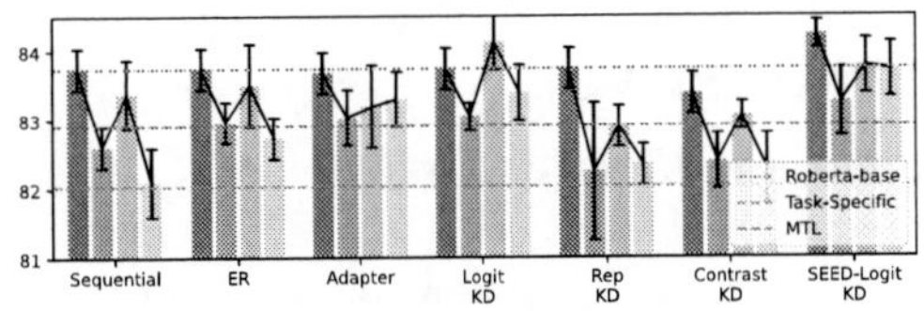

(a) Chemprot

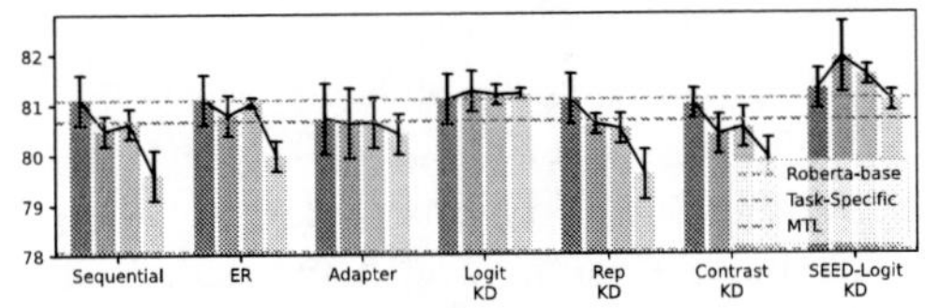

(b) RCT-Sample

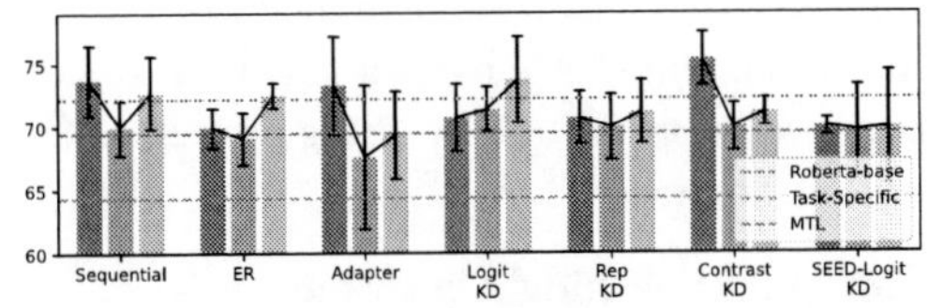

(c) ACL-ARC

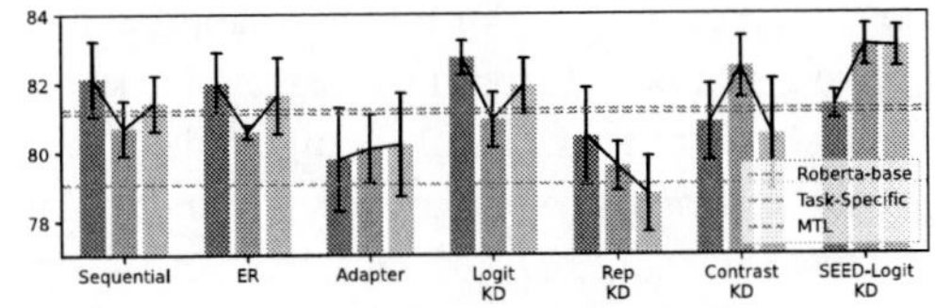

(d) SciERC

Figure 4: **Performance evolution of downstream models.** Models are fine-tuned from checkpoints of lifelong pretrained LMs at different time steps t. For Chemprot and RCT-Sample from D_1, we use $t \in \{1, 2, 3, 4\}$; while for ACL-ARC and SciERC from D_2, $t \in \{2, 3, 4\}$. Methods achieving the best performance at the end of training ($t = 4$) is highlighted.

D_1, D_2 at least by 1.0%. However, performance on D_3, D_4, which come later in the data stream, does not improve over Sequential Pretraining, possibly because the distillation loss term makes the model rigid in obtaining new knowledge.

What is the gap between lifelong pretraining and multi-task learning across all the domains? Multi-Task Learning refers to the offline training paradigm, which retrain PTLMs over all corpora ($D_{1..t}$) each time a new corpus D_t becomes available. We examine whether lifelong pretraining is comparable to multi-task pretraining in terms of performance. From Table 2 and Figure 4, we see Sequential Pretraining in general underperforms MTL except for the final domain. However, certain CL approaches, such as Logit-Distillation, could improve over MTL on all downstream tasks from the first and the second domain. We speculate the reason is that continual learning naturally provides a curriculum (Xu et al., 2020; Shi et al., 2015) to models where each individual task is easier to learn.

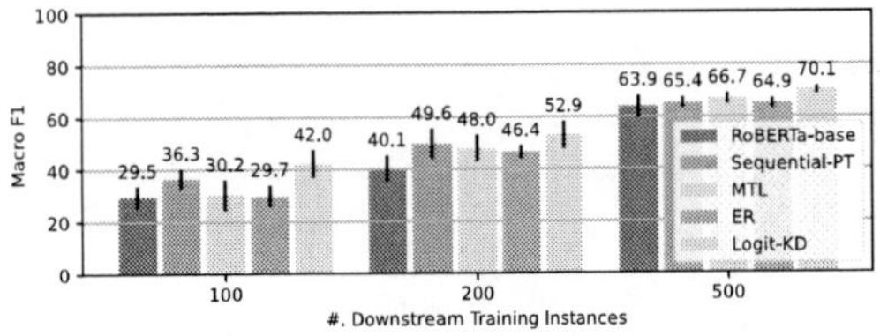

Figure 5: **Performance of downstream models with various number of training examples**, exemplified with SciERC. The models are fine-tuned from the final pretrained model (f_4).

The results have a positive implication that lifelong pretraining is not only more computationally efficient and requires less storage of past data, but may also improve the performance of pretraining.

Does lifelong pretraining make models more data efficient? In Table 5, we further examine the performance of final pretrained models under different amounts of training examples. We include full results in Appendix B. We find in general, performance improvements are more significant in the low-resource setup.

Computational Costs. We analyze computational costs of different CL algorithms and present additional experiments with controlled computational costs. We find additional computational cost is necessary for performance improvement of distillation-based CL. However, it is not possible to trade performance simply by investing more computation budget with arbitrary CL algorithms. We leave detailed discussions in Appendix F.

4.3 Temporal Data Stream

We conduct analysis on pretraining PTLM on chronologically-ordered tweet corpora, to understand whether lifelong pretraining helps adaptation to the latest data and improves temporal generalization ability. The results are summarized in Table 4.

Will LMs be outdated? We compare the performance of Task-Specific (2014) to the Task-Specific models pretrained on the year of downstream datasets (noted as Task-Specific (Latest)) and notice consistent improvements in downstream tasks in 2018 and 2020 (first two columns in Table 4). Sequential Pretraining could also outperform the Task-Specific (2014) model. It verifies that language models may get outdated, which can be addressed by task-specific or lifelong pretraining over the latest corpora.

Does lifelong pretraining help improve the downstream model's performance on latest data? We show that downstream model's performance over

Years	2018 (D_3)	2020 (D_4)	2014 (D_1) $\rightarrow$ 2020 (D_4)	2016 (D_2) $\rightarrow$ 2020 (D_4)
		Hashtag Prediction		
RoBERTa-base	$48.08_{\pm 1.0}$	$56.42_{\pm 0.2}$	$39.31_{\pm 2.7}$	$42.23_{\pm 2.7}$
Sequential PT	$56.79_{\pm 0.5}$	$59.85_{\pm 0.4}$	$44.00_{\pm 1.1}$	$49.87_{\pm 1.8}$
ER	$56.93_{\pm 0.1}$	$59.56_{\pm 1.7}$	$43.31_{\pm 0.2}$	$50.72_{\pm 0.6}$
Logit-KD	$\mathbf{58.21}_{\pm 0.5}$	$60.52_{\pm 0.2}$	$44.26_{\pm 0.9}$	$50.92_{\pm 0.8}$
Contrast-KD	$57.94_{\pm 0.4}$	$59.54_{\pm 0.3}$	$45.22_{\pm 0.1}$	$\mathbf{52.14}_{\pm 1.1}$
SEED-KD	$56.87_{\pm 0.2}$	$59.71_{\pm 0.2}$	$43.39_{\pm 0.4}$	$49.62_{\pm 1.0}$
SEED-Logit-KD	$57.75_{\pm 0.4}$	$\mathbf{60.74}_{\pm 0.6}$	$\mathbf{45.35}_{\pm 0.6}$	$51.56_{\pm 0.7}$
Task-Specific (2014)	$56.16_{\pm 0.6}$	$59.59_{\pm 0.3}$	$44.34_{\pm 0.6}$	$49.26_{\pm 0.7}$
Task-Specific (Latest)	$56.61_{\pm 0.4}$	$59.87_{\pm 0.6}$	$43.44_{\pm 0.5}$	$49.41_{\pm 1.1}$
MTL	$57.89_{\pm 0.4}$	$59.95_{\pm 0.3}$	$44.04_{\pm 0.3}$	$50.37_{\pm 0.3}$
		Emoji Prediction		
RoBERTa-base	$25.71_{\pm 0.1}$	$24.42_{\pm 0.2}$	$12.02_{\pm 0.4}$	$13.24_{\pm 0.2}$
Sequential PT	$29.30_{\pm 0.1}$	$27.69_{\pm 0.1}$	$14.20_{\pm 0.2}$	$16.08_{\pm 1.4}$
ER	$29.50_{\pm 0.1}$	$27.75_{\pm 0.1}$	$14.36_{\pm 0.4}$	$16.82_{\pm 0.3}$
Logit-KD	$29.77_{\pm 0.1}$	$27.80_{\pm 0.1}$	$14.20_{\pm 0.3}$	$16.28_{\pm 1.1}$
Contrast-KD	$29.48_{\pm 0.2}$	$27.72_{\pm 0.3}$	$\mathbf{14.42}_{\pm 0.3}$	$\mathbf{17.52}_{\pm 0.1}$
SEED-KD	$\mathbf{30.12}_{\pm 0.1}$	$27.66_{\pm 0.1}$	$14.36_{\pm 0.1}$	$16.97_{\pm 0.4}$
SEED-Logit-KD	$29.98_{\pm 0.1}$	$\mathbf{27.84}_{\pm 0.2}$	$14.36_{\pm 0.1}$	$16.97_{\pm 0.3}$
Task-Specific (2014)	$28.94_{\pm 0.0}$	$26.98_{\pm 0.2}$	$13.39_{\pm 0.2}$	$15.14_{\pm 0.2}$
Task-Specific (Latest)	$29.06_{\pm 0.2}$	$27.19_{\pm 0.1}$	$13.00_{\pm 0.2}$	$14.48_{\pm 0.3}$
MTL	$29.52_{\pm 0.2}$	$27.47_{\pm 0.0}$	$14.07_{\pm 0.2}$	$16.64_{\pm 0.2}$

Table 4: **Results on temporal data stream.** We show fine-tuning performance over years 2018 and 2020 (D_3, D_4) and the Temporal generalization from 2014 or 2016 to 2020 data ($D_1 \rightarrow D_4$, $D_2 \rightarrow D_4$) on Twitter Hashtag and Emoji prediction datasets. Models are fine-tuned from the final pre-trained model f_T. Full results are included in Appendix C.

later data (D_3, D_4) can be improved over Task-Specific models when continual learning algorithms are applied. From the first two columns of Table 4, we see Logit-KD and SEED-KD improve Hashtag prediction score over data of years 2018 and 2020. SEED-Logit KD further improves prediction F1 on Emoji prediction. Note that these findings are in contrast to the research paper stream, where CL algorithms do not improve performance in the latest domain D_4. The reason can be the higher similarity between domains in the tweet corpora making the knowledge transfer easier, which is further discussed in Appendix H.

Does lifelong pretraining improve temporal generalization? Temporal generalization evaluates downstream performance over latest test data when fine-tuned over outdated training data. We show lifelong pretraining brings clear improvement to temporal generalization. From Table 4, we see even Sequential Pretraining could improve over the model pretrained merely on the year 2020 data (Task-Specific (2020)) consistently. We find performance further improves with CL algorithms applied. SEED-Logit-KD performs best in general on crossyear hashtag prediction tasks. In crossyear emoji prediction, we find Contrast-KD and SEED-KD perform best. We also find that SEED-Logit-KD could slightly outperform Logit-KD.

5 Related Works

Domain and Temporal Adaptation of Language Models. Gururangan et al. (2020) study adaptation of PTLMs to domain-specific corpora. Arumae et al. (2020) study algorithms to mitigate forgetting in original PTLMs, but does not investigate forgetting that happens over a sequence of domains. Maronikolakis and Schütze (2021); Röttger and Pierrehumbert (2021); Luu et al. (2021) proposes sequential pretraining over domains or emerging data, but did not investigate CL algorithms. Several recent studies have demonstrated the necessity of adapting LMs over time (Lazaridou et al., 2021) while specifically focusing on factual knowledge (Dhingra et al., 2021; Jang et al., 2021).

Continual Learning Algorithms in NLP. Continual learning in NLP has mainly been studied for classification tasks. An effective approach is to utilize a number of stored past examples (de Masson d'Autume et al., 2019; Wang et al., 2020), or pseudo examples (*e.g.,* the ones generated with a PTLM (Sun et al., 2020; Kanwatchara et al., 2021)). Recent extensions of the algorithm (Chuang et al., 2020) perform knowledge distillation with generated pseudo examples. Other lines of works focus on regularization over the sentence representations (Wang et al., 2019; Huang et al., 2021; Liu et al., 2019a) or directly merging models in the parameter space (Matena and Raffel, 2021). Model expansion-based approaches (Liu et al., 2019a; Pfeiffer et al., 2021), including learning domain specific expert models (Gururangan et al., 2021), are also actively studied.

6 Conclusion

In this paper, we formulated the lifelong language model pretraining problem and constructed two data streams associated with downstream datasets. We evaluated knowledge retention, adaptation to the latest data, and temporal generalization ability of continually pretrained language models. Our experiments show distillation-based approaches being most effective in these evaluation setups. A limitation of the work is that it has not been fully addressed whether there exists a variant of distillation-based CL approach that consistently outperforms Logit-KD. Based on the current observation, we conclude the performance of different KD approaches for CL is highly task-dependent. It asks for more future works into continual learning algorithms within the proposed problem setup.

References

Kristjan Arumae, Qing Sun, and Parminder Bhatia. 2020. An empirical investigation towards efficient multi-domain language model pre-training. In *Proceedings of the 2020 Conference on Empirical Methods in Natural Language Processing (EMNLP)*, pages 4854–4864, Online. Association for Computational Linguistics.

Isabelle Augenstein, Mrinal Das, Sebastian Riedel, Lakshmi Vikraman, and Andrew McCallum. 2017. SemEval 2017 task 10: ScienceIE - extracting keyphrases and relations from scientific publications. In *Proceedings of the 11th International Workshop on Semantic Evaluation (SemEval-2017)*, pages 546–555, Vancouver, Canada. Association for Computational Linguistics.

Abdul Hameed Azeemi and Adeel Waheed. 2021. Covid-19 tweets analysis through transformer language models. *ArXiv*, abs/2103.00199.

Francesco Barbieri, Jose Camacho-Collados, Francesco Ronzano, Luis Espinosa-Anke, Miguel Ballesteros, Valerio Basile, Viviana Patti, and Horacio Saggion. 2018. SemEval 2018 task 2: Multilingual emoji prediction. In *Proceedings of The 12th International Workshop on Semantic Evaluation*, pages 24–33, New Orleans, Louisiana. Association for Computational Linguistics.

Iz Beltagy, Kyle Lo, and Arman Cohan. 2019. SciBERT: A pretrained language model for scientific text. In *Proceedings of the 2019 Conference on Empirical Methods in Natural Language Processing and the 9th International Joint Conference on Natural Language Processing (EMNLP-IJCNLP)*, pages 3615–3620, Hong Kong, China. Association for Computational Linguistics.

Tom B. Brown, Benjamin Mann, Nick Ryder, Melanie Subbiah, Jared Kaplan, Prafulla Dhariwal, Arvind Neelakantan, Pranav Shyam, Girish Sastry, Amanda Askell, Sandhini Agarwal, Ariel Herbert-Voss, Gretchen Krueger, Tom Henighan, Rewon Child, Aditya Ramesh, Daniel M. Ziegler, Jeffrey Wu, Clemens Winter, Christopher Hesse, Mark Chen, Eric Sigler, Mateusz Litwin, Scott Gray, Benjamin Chess, Jack Clark, Christopher Berner, Sam McCandlish, Alec Radford, Ilya Sutskever, and Dario Amodei. 2020. Language models are few-shot learners. In *Advances in Neural Information Processing Systems 33: Annual Conference on Neural Information Processing Systems 2020, NeurIPS 2020, December 6-12, 2020, virtual*.

Hyuntak Cha, Jaeho Lee, and Jinwoo Shin. 2021. Co2l: Contrastive continual learning. *ArXiv*, abs/2106.14413.

Arslan Chaudhry, Marcus Rohrbach, Mohamed Elhoseiny, Thalaiyasingam Ajanthan, Puneet K Dokania, Philip HS Torr, and Marc'Aurelio Ranzato. 2019. On tiny episodic memories in continual learning. *arXiv preprint arXiv:1902.10486*.

Yung-Sung Chuang, Shang-Yu Su, and Yun-Nung Chen. 2020. Lifelong language knowledge distillation. In *Proceedings of the 2020 Conference on Empirical Methods in Natural Language Processing (EMNLP)*, pages 2914–2924, Online. Association for Computational Linguistics.

Cyprien de Masson d'Autume, Sebastian Ruder, Lingpeng Kong, and Dani Yogatama. 2019. Episodic memory in lifelong language learning. In *Advances in Neural Information Processing Systems 32: Annual Conference on Neural Information Processing Systems 2019, NeurIPS 2019, December 8-14, 2019, Vancouver, BC, Canada*, pages 13122–13131.

Franck Dernoncourt and Ji Young Lee. 2017. PubMed 200k RCT: a dataset for sequential sentence classification in medical abstracts. In *Proceedings of the Eighth International Joint Conference on Natural Language Processing (Volume 2: Short Papers)*, pages 308–313, Taipei, Taiwan. Asian Federation of Natural Language Processing.

Jacob Devlin, Ming-Wei Chang, Kenton Lee, and Kristina Toutanova. 2019. BERT: Pre-training of deep bidirectional transformers for language understanding. In *Proceedings of the 2019 Conference of the North American Chapter of the Association for Computational Linguistics: Human Language Technologies, Volume 1 (Long and Short Papers)*, pages 4171–4186, Minneapolis, Minnesota. Association for Computational Linguistics.

Bhuwan Dhingra, Jeremy R. Cole, Julian Martin Eisenschlos, D. Gillick, Jacob Eisenstein, and William W. Cohen. 2021. Time-aware language models as temporal knowledge bases. *ArXiv*, abs/2106.15110.

Zhiyuan Fang, Jianfeng Wang, Lijuan Wang, L. Zhang, Yezhou Yang, and Zicheng Liu. 2021. Seed: Self-supervised distillation for visual representation. *ArXiv*, abs/2101.04731.

Tianyu Gao, Xingcheng Yao, and Danqi Chen. 2021. Simcse: Simple contrastive learning of sentence embeddings. *ArXiv*, abs/2104.08821.

Yuyun Gong and Qi Zhang. 2016. Hashtag recommendation using attention-based convolutional neural network. In *Proceedings of the Twenty-Fifth International Joint Conference on Artificial Intelligence, IJCAI 2016, New York, NY, USA, 9-15 July 2016*, pages 2782–2788. IJCAI/AAAI Press.

Suchin Gururangan, Michael Lewis, Ari Holtzman, Noah A. Smith, and Luke Zettlemoyer. 2021. Demix layers: Disentangling domains for modular language modeling. *ArXiv*, abs/2108.05036.

Suchin Gururangan, Ana Marasović, Swabha Swayamdipta, Kyle Lo, Iz Beltagy, Doug Downey, and Noah A. Smith. 2020. Don't stop pretraining: Adapt language models to domains and tasks. In *Proceedings of the 58th Annual Meeting of the Association for Computational Linguistics*, pages

8342–8360, Online. Association for Computational Linguistics.

Geoffrey E. Hinton, Oriol Vinyals, and J. Dean. 2015. Distilling the knowledge in a neural network. *ArXiv*, abs/1503.02531.

Spurthi Amba Hombaiah, Tao Chen, Mingyang Zhang, Michael Bendersky, and Marc-Alexander Najork. 2021. Dynamic language models for continuously evolving content. *Proceedings of the 27th ACM SIGKDD Conference on Knowledge Discovery & Data Mining*.

Saihui Hou, Xinyu Pan, Chen Change Loy, Zilei Wang, and Dahua Lin. 2018. Lifelong learning via progressive distillation and retrospection. In *ECCV*.

Neil Houlsby, Andrei Giurgiu, Stanislaw Jastrzebski, Bruna Morrone, Quentin de Laroussilhe, Andrea Gesmundo, Mona Attariyan, and Sylvain Gelly. 2019. Parameter-efficient transfer learning for NLP. In *Proceedings of the 36th International Conference on Machine Learning, ICML 2019, 9-15 June 2019, Long Beach, California, USA*, volume 97 of *Proceedings of Machine Learning Research*, pages 2790–2799. PMLR.

Xiaolei Huang and Michael J. Paul. 2018. Examining temporality in document classification. In *Proceedings of the 56th Annual Meeting of the Association for Computational Linguistics (Volume 2: Short Papers)*, pages 694–699, Melbourne, Australia. Association for Computational Linguistics.

Yufan Huang, Yanzhe Zhang, Jiaao Chen, Xuezhi Wang, and Diyi Yang. 2021. Continual learning for text classification with information disentanglement based regularization. In *Proceedings of the 2021 Conference of the North American Chapter of the Association for Computational Linguistics: Human Language Technologies*, pages 2736–2746, Online. Association for Computational Linguistics.

Joel Jang, Seonghyeon Ye, Sohee Yang, Joongbo Shin, Janghoon Han, Gyeonghun Kim, Stanley Jungkyu Choi, and Minjoon Seo. 2021. Towards continual knowledge learning of language models. *arXiv preprint arXiv:2110.03215*.

Xiaoqi Jiao, Yichun Yin, Lifeng Shang, Xin Jiang, Xiao Chen, Linlin Li, Fang Wang, and Qun Liu. 2020. TinyBERT: Distilling BERT for natural language understanding. In *Findings of the Association for Computational Linguistics: EMNLP 2020*, pages 4163–4174, Online. Association for Computational Linguistics.

David Jurgens, Srijan Kumar, Raine Hoover, Dan McFarland, and Dan Jurafsky. 2018. Measuring the evolution of a scientific field through citation frames. *Transactions of the Association for Computational Linguistics*, 6:391–406.

Kasidis Kanwatchara, Thanapapas Horsuwan, Piyawat Lertvittayakumjorn, Boonserm Kijsirikul, and Peerapon Vateekul. 2021. Rational LAMOL: A rationale-based lifelong learning framework. In *Proceedings of the 59th Annual Meeting of the Association for Computational Linguistics and the 11th International Joint Conference on Natural Language Processing (Volume 1: Long Papers)*, pages 2942–2953, Online. Association for Computational Linguistics.

Angeliki Lazaridou, A. Kuncoro, E. Gribovskaya, Devang Agrawal, Adam Liska, Tayfun Terzi, Mai Gimenez, Cyprien de Masson d'Autume, Sebastian Ruder, Dani Yogatama, Kris Cao, Tomás Kociský, Susannah Young, and P. Blunsom. 2021. Assessing temporal generalization in neural language models. *NeurIPS*.

Zhizhong Li and Derek Hoiem. 2018. Learning without forgetting. *IEEE Transactions on Pattern Analysis and Machine Intelligence*, 40:2935–2947.

Tianlin Liu, Lyle Ungar, and João Sedoc. 2019a. Continual learning for sentence representations using conceptors. In *Proceedings of the 2019 Conference of the North American Chapter of the Association for Computational Linguistics: Human Language Technologies, Volume 1 (Long and Short Papers)*, pages 3274–3279, Minneapolis, Minnesota. Association for Computational Linguistics.

Yinhan Liu, Myle Ott, Naman Goyal, Jingfei Du, Mandar Joshi, Danqi Chen, Omer Levy, Mike Lewis, Luke Zettlemoyer, and Veselin Stoyanov. 2019b. Roberta: A robustly optimized bert pretraining approach. *ArXiv*, abs/1907.11692.

Kyle Lo, Lucy Lu Wang, Mark Neumann, Rodney Kinney, and Daniel Weld. 2020. S2ORC: The semantic scholar open research corpus. In *Proceedings of the 58th Annual Meeting of the Association for Computational Linguistics*, pages 4969–4983, Online. Association for Computational Linguistics.

Yi Luan, Luheng He, Mari Ostendorf, and Hannaneh Hajishirzi. 2018. Multi-task identification of entities, relations, and coreference for scientific knowledge graph construction. In *Proceedings of the 2018 Conference on Empirical Methods in Natural Language Processing*, pages 3219–3232, Brussels, Belgium. Association for Computational Linguistics.

Kelvin Luu, Daniel Khashabi, Suchin Gururangan, Karishma Mandyam, and Noah A. Smith. 2021. Time waits for no one! analysis and challenges of temporal misalignment.

Antonis Maronikolakis and Hinrich Schütze. 2021. Multidomain pretrained language models for green NLP. In *Proceedings of the Second Workshop on Domain Adaptation for NLP*, pages 1–8, Kyiv, Ukraine. Association for Computational Linguistics.

Michael Matena and Colin Raffel. 2021. Merging models with fisher-weighted averaging. *ArXiv*, abs/2111.09832.

Martin Müller, Marcel Salathé, and Per Egil Kummervold. 2020. Covid-twitter-bert: A natural language processing model to analyse covid-19 content on twitter. *ArXiv*, abs/2005.07503.

Sheshera Mysore, Zachary Jensen, Edward Kim, Kevin Huang, Haw-Shiuan Chang, Emma Strubell, Jeffrey Flanigan, Andrew McCallum, and Elsa Olivetti. 2019. The materials science procedural text corpus: Annotating materials synthesis procedures with shallow semantic structures. In *Proceedings of the 13th Linguistic Annotation Workshop*, pages 56–64, Florence, Italy. Association for Computational Linguistics.

Dat Quoc Nguyen, Thanh Vu, and Anh Tuan Nguyen. 2020. BERTweet: A pre-trained language model for English tweets. In *Proceedings of the 2020 Conference on Empirical Methods in Natural Language Processing: System Demonstrations*, pages 9–14, Online. Association for Computational Linguistics.

Elsa A Olivetti, Jacqueline M Cole, Edward Kim, Olga Kononova, Gerbrand Ceder, Thomas Yong-Jin Han, and Anna M Hiszpanski. 2020. Data-driven materials research enabled by natural language processing and information extraction. *Applied Physics Reviews*, 7(4):041317.

Jonas Pfeiffer, Aishwarya Kamath, Andreas Rücklé, Kyunghyun Cho, and Iryna Gurevych. 2021. AdapterFusion: Non-destructive task composition for transfer learning. In *Proceedings of the 16th Conference of the European Chapter of the Association for Computational Linguistics: Main Volume*, pages 487–503, Online. Association for Computational Linguistics.

Sylvestre-Alvise Rebuffi, Alexander Kolesnikov, Georg Sperl, and Christoph H. Lampert. 2017. icarl: Incremental classifier and representation learning. In *2017 IEEE Conference on Computer Vision and Pattern Recognition, CVPR 2017, Honolulu, HI, USA, July 21-26, 2017*, pages 5533–5542. IEEE Computer Society.

Shruti Rijhwani and Daniel Preotiuc-Pietro. 2020. Temporally-informed analysis of named entity recognition. In *Proceedings of the 58th Annual Meeting of the Association for Computational Linguistics*, pages 7605–7617, Online. Association for Computational Linguistics.

Anthony V. Robins. 1995. Catastrophic forgetting, rehearsal and pseudorehearsal. *Connect. Sci.*, 7:123–146.

Paul Röttger and J. Pierrehumbert. 2021. Temporal adaptation of bert and performance on downstream document classification: Insights from social media. *Findings of EMNLP*.

Jonathan Schwarz, Wojciech Czarnecki, Jelena Luketina, Agnieszka Grabska-Barwinska, Yee Whye Teh, Razvan Pascanu, and Raia Hadsell. 2018. Progress & compress: A scalable framework for continual learning. In *Proceedings of the 35th International Conference on Machine Learning, ICML 2018, Stockholmsmässan, Stockholm, Sweden, July 10-15, 2018*, volume 80 of *Proceedings of Machine Learning Research*, pages 4535–4544. PMLR.

Yangyang Shi, Martha Larson, and Catholijn M. Jonker. 2015. Recurrent neural network language model adaptation with curriculum learning. *Comput. Speech Lang.*, 33:136–154.

Fan-Keng Sun, Cheng-Hao Ho, and Hung-Yi Lee. 2020. LAMOL: language modeling for lifelong language learning. In *8th International Conference on Learning Representations, ICLR 2020, Addis Ababa, Ethiopia, April 26-30, 2020*. OpenReview.net.

Siqi Sun, Yu Cheng, Zhe Gan, and Jingjing Liu. 2019. Patient knowledge distillation for BERT model compression. In *Proceedings of the 2019 Conference on Empirical Methods in Natural Language Processing and the 9th International Joint Conference on Natural Language Processing (EMNLP-IJCNLP)*, pages 4323–4332, Hong Kong, China. Association for Computational Linguistics.

Jens Vindahl. 2016. Chemprot-3.0: a global chemical biology diseases mapping.

Hong Wang, Wenhan Xiong, Mo Yu, Xiaoxiao Guo, Shiyu Chang, and William Yang Wang. 2019. Sentence embedding alignment for lifelong relation extraction. In *Proceedings of the 2019 Conference of the North American Chapter of the Association for Computational Linguistics: Human Language Technologies, Volume 1 (Long and Short Papers)*, pages 796–806, Minneapolis, Minnesota. Association for Computational Linguistics.

Zirui Wang, Sanket Vaibhav Mehta, Barnabas Poczos, and Jaime Carbonell. 2020. Efficient meta lifelong-learning with limited memory. In *Proceedings of the 2020 Conference on Empirical Methods in Natural Language Processing (EMNLP)*, pages 535–548, Online. Association for Computational Linguistics.

Benfeng Xu, Licheng Zhang, Zhendong Mao, Quan Wang, Hongtao Xie, and Yongdong Zhang. 2020. Curriculum learning for natural language understanding. In *Proceedings of the 58th Annual Meeting of the Association for Computational Linguistics*, pages 6095–6104, Online. Association for Computational Linguistics.

Yunzhi Yao, Shaohan Huang, Wenhui Wang, Li Dong, and Furu Wei. 2021. Adapt-and-distill: Developing small, fast and effective pretrained language models for domains. In *Findings of the Association for Computational Linguistics: ACL-IJCNLP 2021*, pages 460–470, Online. Association for Computational Linguistics.

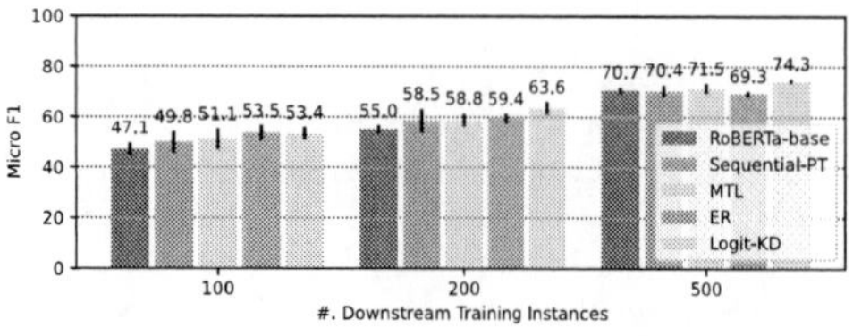

(a) Chemprot

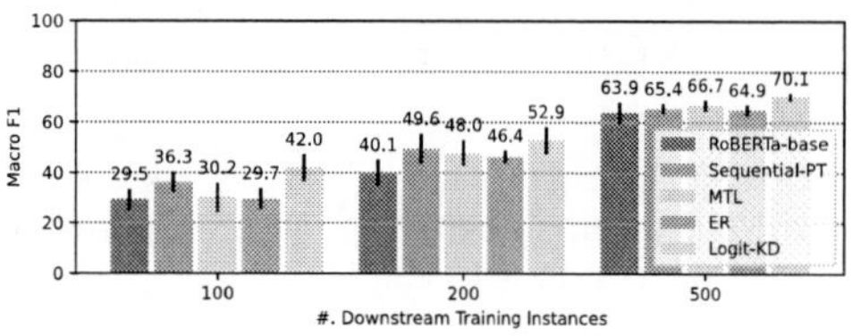

(b) SciERC

Figure 6: Performance of downstream models with various number of training examples. The models are fine-tuned from the final pretrained model (f_4).

A Detailed Experiment Settings

We use a linearly decreasing learning rate initialized with 5e-4 on the research paper stream and 3e-4 on the tweet stream. On the research paper stream, we train the model for 8,000 steps in the first task, and 4,000 steps in the subsequent tasks. On the tweet stream, we train the model for 8,000 steps in all tasks. We hold out 128,000 sentences from each corpus to evaluate MLM performance. As the size of pretraining corpora is large, during training, each training example is visited only once. We use the masked language modeling perplexity over held-out validation sets of the pretraining corpora as the metrics for hyperparameter tuning. Common hyperparameters such as learning rate and batch sizes are tuned with Task-specific models with the first task. Hyperparameters that are specific to continual learning algorithms, such as the scale of the distillation loss, is tuned using the first two domains in the stream according to the MLM performance over validation sets. The weight of the distillation term α is set as 1.0 for logit distillation and 0.1 for other distillation algorithms. By default, we replay or perform distillation with a mini-batch of examples from the replay memory every 10 training steps in ER and Distillation-based CL approaches. We use the huggingface transformers library `https://github.com/huggingface/transformers` for implementation.

B Low-Resource Fine-Tuning

Figure 6 summarizes the performance of fine-tuned models from the final model checkpoint ($t = 4$) using different amount of downstream training examples. We see on Chemprot and SciERC, the benefit of Sequential Pretraining over RoBERTa-base is more significant in low-resource fine-tuning setups. Whenever Seqential Pretraining outperforms RoBERTa-base, we notice Logit-KD could further improve over Sequential Pretraining.

Task	2014	2016	2018	2020
	Hashtag Prediction			
RoBERTa-base	56.65$_{\pm 0.6}$	45.50$_{\pm 2.1}$	48.08$_{\pm 1.0}$	56.42$_{\pm 0.2}$
Sequential PT	59.00$_{\pm 0.1}$	54.28$_{\pm 0.3}$	56.79$_{\pm 0.5}$	59.85$_{\pm 0.4}$
ER	59.00$_{\pm 0.1}$	54.90$_{\pm 0.2}$	56.93$_{\pm 0.1}$	59.56$_{\pm 1.7}$
Adapter	58.76$_{\pm 0.7}$	52.55$_{\pm 1.5}$	54.34$_{\pm 1.7}$	59.01$_{\pm 1.0}$
Logit-KD	60.93$_{\pm 0.5}$	55.96$_{\pm 0.2}$	58.21$_{\pm 0.5}$	60.52$_{\pm 0.2}$
Rep-KD	60.47$_{\pm 0.1}$	51.77$_{\pm 2.6}$	55.79$_{\pm 1.4}$	59.80$_{\pm 0.2}$
Contrast-KD	60.72$_{\pm 0.6}$	55.85$_{\pm 0.0}$	57.94$_{\pm 0.4}$	59.54$_{\pm 0.3}$
SEED-KD	58.82$_{\pm 0.4}$	54.55$_{\pm 0.5}$	56.87$_{\pm 0.2}$	59.71$_{\pm 0.2}$
SEED-Logit-KD	61.28$_{\pm 0.2}$	55.59$_{\pm 0.5}$	57.75$_{\pm 0.4}$	60.74$_{\pm 0.6}$
Task-Specific (2014)	61.62$_{\pm 0.3}$	55.38$_{\pm 0.6}$	56.16$_{\pm 0.6}$	59.59$_{\pm 0.3}$
Task-Specific (Latest)	59.91$_{\pm 0.3}$	55.47$_{\pm 1.0}$	56.61$_{\pm 0.4}$	59.87$_{\pm 0.6}$
MTL	60.51$_{\pm 0.3}$	55.16$_{\pm 1.6}$	57.89$_{\pm 0.4}$	59.95$_{\pm 0.3}$
	Emoji Prediction			
RoBERTa-base	28.73$_{\pm 0.2}$	26.86$_{\pm 0.2}$	25.71$_{\pm 0.1}$	24.42$_{\pm 0.2}$
Sequential PT	32.69$_{\pm 0.2}$	30.55$_{\pm 0.3}$	29.30$_{\pm 0.1}$	27.69$_{\pm 0.1}$
ER	32.88$_{\pm 0.2}$	30.52$_{\pm 0.2}$	29.50$_{\pm 0.1}$	27.75$_{\pm 0.1}$
Adapter	32.15$_{\pm 0.2}$	29.85$_{\pm 0.0}$	28.72$_{\pm 0.0}$	26.80$_{\pm 0.3}$
Logit-KD	33.08$_{\pm 0.3}$	30.88$_{\pm 0.1}$	29.77$_{\pm 0.1}$	27.80$_{\pm 0.1}$
Rep-KD	32.71$_{\pm 0.2}$	30.51$_{\pm 0.2}$	29.45$_{\pm 0.1}$	27.27$_{\pm 0.2}$
Contrast-KD	32.90$_{\pm 0.1}$	31.01$_{\pm 0.1}$	29.48$_{\pm 0.2}$	27.72$_{\pm 0.3}$
SEED-KD	32.91$_{\pm 0.1}$	30.84$_{\pm 0.3}$	30.12$_{\pm 0.1}$	27.66$_{\pm 0.1}$
SEED-Logit-KD	33.28$_{\pm 0.1}$	31.17$_{\pm 0.1}$	29.98$_{\pm 0.1}$	27.84$_{\pm 0.2}$
Task-Specific (2014)	33.37$_{\pm 0.2}$	30.54$_{\pm 0.3}$	28.94$_{\pm 0.0}$	26.98$_{\pm 0.2}$
Task-Specific (Latest)	32.31$_{\pm 0.0}$	29.83$_{\pm 0.5}$	29.06$_{\pm 0.2}$	27.19$_{\pm 0.1}$
MTL	32.78$_{\pm 0.1}$	30.54$_{\pm 0.0}$	29.52$_{\pm 0.2}$	27.47$_{\pm 0.0}$

Table 5: Full performance on Twitter Hashtag prediction and Emoji prediction, fine-tuned from the pre-trained model in the final time step.

C Full Results over the Tweet Stream

Tables 5 and 6 summarize full results over the Tweet stream. Compared to the table 4 in the main text, we add downstream performance over data from years 2014 and 2016 (D_1, D_2), and temporal generalization from year 2014 to 2020 ($D_1 \rightarrow D_4$).

D Dataset Details

The research paper stream consists of full text of 6.6M, 12.1M, 7.8M, and 7.5M research papers from the S2ORC (Lo et al., 2020) dataset. We evaluate downstream fine-tuning performance on two in-domain datasets for each research area: Chemprot relation exaction dataset (Vindahl, 2016) and RCT abstract sentence role labeling dataset (Dernoncourt and Lee, 2017) for the bio-medical domain; ACL-ARC citation intent classification dataset (Jurgens et al., 2018) and SciERC relation extraction dataset (Luan et al., 2018) for the

Task	2014 → 2020	2016 → 2020	2018 → 2020
Crossyear Hashtag Prediction			
RoBERTa-base	$39.31_{\pm 2.7}$	$42.23_{\pm 2.7}$	$37.19_{\pm 2.1}$
Sequential PT	$44.00_{\pm 1.1}$	$49.87_{\pm 1.8}$	$46.63_{\pm 0.9}$
ER	$43.31_{\pm 0.2}$	$50.72_{\pm 0.6}$	$46.27_{\pm 0.4}$
Adapter	$42.61_{\pm 0.5}$	$48.00_{\pm 1.6}$	$42.63_{\pm 0.9}$
Logit-KD	$44.26_{\pm 0.9}$	$50.92_{\pm 0.8}$	$46.84_{\pm 1.0}$
Rep-KD	$42.48_{\pm 0.2}$	$50.38_{\pm 1.5}$	$42.23_{\pm 0.2}$
Contrast-KD	$45.22_{\pm 0.1}$	$52.14_{\pm 1.1}$	$47.47_{\pm 0.8}$
SEED-KD	$43.39_{\pm 0.4}$	$49.62_{\pm 1.0}$	$46.37_{\pm 0.8}$
SEED-Logit-KD	$45.35_{\pm 0.6}$	$51.56_{\pm 0.7}$	$47.74_{\pm 0.3}$
Task-Specific (2014)	$44.34_{\pm 0.6}$	$49.26_{\pm 0.7}$	$45.09_{\pm 0.7}$
Task-Specific (2020)	$43.44_{\pm 0.5}$	$49.41_{\pm 1.1}$	$44.34_{\pm 0.4}$
- 4x steps	$44.34_{\pm 0.6}$	$51.78_{\pm 0.7}$	$44.69_{\pm 0.7}$
MTL	$44.04_{\pm 0.3}$	$50.37_{\pm 0.3}$	$44.31_{\pm 0.0}$
Crossyear Emoji Prediction			
RoBERTa-base	$12.02_{\pm 0.4}$	$13.24_{\pm 0.2}$	$18.67_{\pm 0.1}$
Sequential PT	$14.20_{\pm 0.2}$	$16.08_{\pm 1.4}$	$21.06_{\pm 0.9}$
ER	$14.36_{\pm 0.4}$	$16.82_{\pm 0.3}$	$21.57_{\pm 0.1}$
Adapter	$13.53_{\pm 0.2}$	$15.68_{\pm 0.3}$	$20.64_{\pm 0.1}$
Logit-KD	$14.20_{\pm 0.3}$	$16.28_{\pm 1.1}$	$21.29_{\pm 1.0}$
Rep-KD	$13.89_{\pm 0.1}$	$16.03_{\pm 0.3}$	$20.86_{\pm 0.2}$
Contrast-KD	$14.42_{\pm 0.3}$	$17.52_{\pm 0.1}$	$21.43_{\pm 0.1}$
SEED-KD	$14.36_{\pm 0.1}$	$16.97_{\pm 0.4}$	$21.88_{\pm 0.3}$
SEED-Logit-KD	$14.36_{\pm 0.1}$	$16.97_{\pm 0.3}$	$21.62_{\pm 0.1}$
Task-Specific (2014)	$13.39_{\pm 0.2}$	$15.14_{\pm 0.2}$	$20.79_{\pm 0.3}$
Task-Specific (2020)	$13.00_{\pm 0.2}$	$14.48_{\pm 0.3}$	$19.30_{\pm 0.2}$
- 4x steps	$12.90_{\pm 0.4}$	$14.85_{\pm 0.3}$	$19.83_{\pm 0.2}$
MTL	$14.07_{\pm 0.2}$	$16.64_{\pm 0.2}$	$20.94_{\pm 0.7}$

Table 6: Temporal generalization performance on Twitter Hashtag prediction datasets fine-tuned from the final pretrained model. `Year 1`→`Year 2` indicates the hashtag prediction model is fine-tuned on data in year `Year 1`, and evaluated on test data in `Year 2`.

computer science domain; relation extraction over Synthesis procedures (Mysore et al., 2019) and named entity recognition over material science papers (MNER) (Olivetti et al., 2020) for material science domain; keyphrase classification and hyponym classification after filtering out physics papers for the physics domain (Augenstein et al., 2017). We report micro-averaged F1 on Chemprot, RCT, MNER datasets following the evaluation metrics in the original work, and report macro-averaged F1 on all other datasets. We use the official data splits for all datasets except for RCT, where we employ a low-resource training setup following Gururangan et al. (2020).

The pretraining corpora for the tweet stream consist of 25M tweets in each year. For downstream tasks, we use a separate set of 1M tweets from each year to construct multi-label hashtag prediction (Gong and Zhang, 2016) datasets and single-label emoji prediction datasets (Barbieri et al., 2018). We replace user names to special tokens. For Hashtag prediction, the label space consists of tweets containing 200 most frequent hashtags in each year. We independently sample 500 tweets per label (hashtag) as training, validation and test sets, which results $10k$ examples in each of the data splits. For emoji prediction, we construct 20-way single-label emoji prediction datasets for each year following Barbieri et al. (2018) with the 1M held out tweets. We sample 5,000 tweets per emoji in each split, resulting in balanced datasets of the same size as the hashtag prediction datasets.

E Details of Continual Learning Algorithms

E.1 Contrastive Distillation

During continual pretraining, in addition to the language model pretraining objective, we add an unsupervised contrastive learning objective, namely the SimCSE (Gao et al., 2021) objective, so that the similarity in the sentence representation better reflects the semantic similarity in the sentence. We use the l^2-normalized representation of the start-of-sequence token at the final layer as the sentence representation, noted as $\boldsymbol{h}$. Then, we distill the intra-batch representational similarity from the previous model f_{t-1} to the current model f_t. Given a mini-batch of N examples $\boldsymbol{x}$, we compute the representational dot-product similarity matrix between normalized sentence representations $\boldsymbol{h}$ between each pair of examples with f_{t-1} and f_t, noted as $\mathbf{B}^{t-1}$ and $\mathbf{B}^t$, where each element $\mathbf{B}_{ij}$ is,

$$\mathbf{B}_{ij} = \frac{\exp(\boldsymbol{h}_i \cdot \boldsymbol{h}_j/\tau)}{\sum_{k=1..N} \exp(\boldsymbol{h}_i \cdot \boldsymbol{h}_k/\tau)} \quad (1)$$

where τ is a temperature hyperparameter. We specify a temperature $\tau_t = 0.05$ for the teacher model f_{t-1} and a temperature τ_s for the student model $f_t = 0.01$. We compute the cross-entropy between $\mathbf{B}^{t-1}$ and $\mathbf{B}^t$ as the distillation loss,

$$\ell_{\text{distill}} = -\frac{1}{N}\sum_{i=1}^{N}\sum_{j=1}^{N} \mathbf{B}_{ij}^{t-1} \log \mathbf{B}_{ij}^{t} \quad (2)$$

E.2 SEED Distillation

SEED distillation proposed by (Fang et al., 2021) has a similar spirit as the contrastive distillation with differences in the examples used for computing similarity matrices computes. The algorithm distills representational similarity *between the batch and a large set of other examples*, maintained in an example queue Q. As the number of target examples K can be much larger than the batch size, it allows distillation of richer information by regularizing similarities. During pretraining, the method maintains a fixed-size queue

Q to cache examples from the current domain D_t. Given a mini-batch of training examples $\boldsymbol{x}$, it computes cosine similarity between each pair of examples within the batch $\boldsymbol{x}$ and Q with f_{t-1} and f_t, resulting in two similarity matrices $\mathbf{B}^{t-1}$, $\mathbf{P}^{y} \in \mathbb{R}^{|B|\times|Q|}$. Similar to the contrastive distillation, the distillation loss is the cross-entropy between two similarity matrices $\mathbf{B}^{t-1}$ and $\mathbf{B}^{t}$ computed in the same way as Eq. 2.

F Analysis and Controlled Experiments of Computational Costs

Computational cost is a crucial matter for online continual learning systems. In this section, we analyze the computational costs of continual learning algorithms and perform controlled experiments of computational costs.

We quantify computational costs with the total number of *forward (C_f) and backward (C_b)* computations ($C = C_f + C_b$) over the PTLMs, which is easy to control; in practice, we find the wall clock time of training was approximately linear to C. We summarize the number of forward and backward passes and the wall clock time of training in Table 7. In the visit of b batches from the training stream, Sequential PT performs b forward and backward passes respectively over the PTLM, resulting in $C = 2b$. Experience replay further replays 1 batch of examples every r steps over the training stream, which results in $C = (2 + 2/k)b$. In our main experiments, r is set to 10 (Sec. 3.3). Logit-Distill and Rep-Distill require one additional forward pass over a frozen PTLM to compute the target of distillation, resulting in $C = (3 + 3/k)b$. Distillation algorithms that perform contrastive learning with SimCSE (*i.e.* SEED-Distill and SEED-Logit-Distill) additionally require one forward and backward pass using the same batch of examples with different dropout masks. Therefore, for SEED-Logit-Distill, $C = (5 + 5/k)b$.

To control the number of forward and backward passes, we present approaches to compensate the lower computation costs compared to Distillation algorithms and one approach to shrink the computational cost of distillation algorithms: (1) for Sequential PT, we train the models for 1.2 times more steps so that $C = 2.4b$, noted as Sequential $\text{PT}_{b'=1.2b}$; (2) for ER, we increase the replay frequency k to 5 from the default setup 10, so that $C = 2.4b$. We also decrease the cost of Logit-KD and SEED-Logit-KD by reducing the frequency of distillation from every 1 batch to every $r' = 10$ steps, while still replaying and distilling knowledge over 1 batch of memory examples every 10 training steps. This results in $C_f = (1 + 2/k + 1/k')b$ and $C_b = (1 + 1/k)b$, where $C = 2.4b$ when both r and r' are 10. The approach is referred to as Sparse Logit-KD. Finally, for SEED-Logit-KD, we remove the SimCSE loss from training and perform sparse distillation similar to Sparse-Logit-KD, which also results in $C = 2.4b$.

The performance of the models is presented in Table 8. We notice that at the end of pretraining, increasing the number of training steps in Sequential PT by 1.2 times does not lead to performance boost on the latest domain (D_4), while the performance over tasks from earlier domains (Chemprot, ACL-ARC, SciERC) slightly dropped, possibly due to increased forgetting. For ER, we notice replaying only slightly more frequently ($\text{ER}_{k=5}$) than the default setup (k=10) greatly increased the perplexity of MLM, implying significantly increased overfitting to the memory; while the performance differences of downstream tasks compared to the default ER is mixed. When we decrease the replay frequency of distillation, the performance on Logit-KD and SEED-KD also decreased and does not outperform ER.

The results show additional computation costs can be necessary for continual learning algorithms such as Logit-KD and SEED-Logit-KD. However, the results also show that there is no simple trade-off between computational cost and performance. We have seen that it is not always beneficial to increase the number of training steps over the emerging data, as it increases forgetting in earlier domains. Similarly, increasing the frequency of replay may lead to significant overfitting to the replay memory. Investigating into more effective continual learning algorithms, despite increased computation costs, allows us to obtain performance improvement that cannot be simply traded with more computation with arbitrary continual learning algorithms. We leave more thorough studies into this topic as future work.

G Experiments with BERT on Tweet Stream After 2019

In this section, we present an additional set of experiments on BERT-base (Devlin et al., 2019) model, which is originally pretrained with Wikipedia articles before 2019, with Tweets only after 2019. The

Method	#. of Forward	#. of Backward	#. Total	#. Total (k=10)	Wall Time$_{4k}$
Main results					
Sequential PT	b	b	$2b$	$2b$	4.0×10^4 sec.
ER	$(1+1/k)b$	$(1+1/k)b$	$(2+2/k)b$	$2.2b$	4.2×10^4 sec.
Logit-Distill	$(2+2/k)b$	$(1+1/k)b$	$(3+3/k)b$	$3.3b$	6.9×10^4 sec.
SEED-Logit-Distill	$(3+3/k)b$	$(2+2/k)b$	$(5+5/k)b$	$5.5b$	9.7×10^4 sec.
Additional Controlled Experiments					
Sequential PT$_{b'=1.2b}$	$1.2b$	$1.2b$	$2.4b$	$2.4b$	4.4×10^4 sec.
ER$_{k=5}$	$1.2b$	$1.2b$	$2.4b$	$2.4b$	4.4×10^4 sec.
Sparse Logit-KD	$1.3b$	$1.1b$	$2.4b$	$2.4b$	4.4×10^4 sec.
Sparse SEED-Logit-KD$_{\setminus contrast}$	$1.3b$	$1.1b$	$2.4b$	$2.4b$	4.5×10^4 sec.

Table 7: Number of forward and backward passes over PTLMs and wall clock time of different approaches. The number of forward and backwards passes are computed over visits of b batches from the training data stream, where k is the frequency of replay. The wall clock time is calculated over $4k$ steps of training (which is the number of training steps of a single domain in the Research Paper stream) excluding the first domain, as no replay or distillation happens while learning the first domain. We use 2 Quadro RTX 8000 GPUs for training each model. In the additional controlled experiments (described in Appendix. F), we control the total number of forward and backward passes of different approaches. This also yields approximately the same wall clock time for approaches.

Task	D_1 - Biomedical			D_2 - Computer Science			D_3 - Materials Science			D_4 - Physics		
Dataset	Chemprot	RCT-Sample	MLM	ACL-ARC	SciERC	MLM	MNER	Synthesis	MLM	Keyphrase	Hyponym	MLM
Sequential Pretraining	$82.09_{\pm 0.5}$	$79.60_{\pm 0.5}$	1.654	$72.73_{\pm 2.9}$	$81.43_{\pm 0.8}$	1.807	$83.99_{\pm 0.3}$	$92.10_{\pm 1.0}$	1.590	$67.57_{\pm 1.0}$	$74.68_{\pm 4.4}$	1.381
Sequential Pretraining$_{b'=1.2b}$	$81.68_{\pm 0.5}$	$79.80_{\pm 0.4}$	1.656	$70.57_{\pm 3.0}$	$80.89_{\pm 1.2}$	1.793	$83.65_{\pm 0.3}$	$92.16_{\pm 0.7}$	1.578	$\mathbf{67.61}_{\pm 1.4}$	$75.03_{\pm 4.1}$	**1.379**
ER	$82.73_{\pm 0.3}$	$\mathbf{79.98}_{\pm 0.3}$	1.737	$72.50_{\pm 1.0}$	$81.64_{\pm 1.1}$	1.857	$83.99_{\pm 0.4}$	$\mathbf{92.65}_{\pm 0.4}$	1.621	$66.11_{\pm 1.1}$	$72.82_{\pm 4.3}$	1.391
ER$_{k=5}$	$\mathbf{83.00}_{\pm 0.1}$	$79.79_{\pm 0.4}$	1.913	$69.85_{\pm 2.6}$	$\mathbf{82.30}_{\pm 1.2}$	2.049	$\mathbf{84.03}_{\pm 0.2}$	$91.60_{\pm 0.6}$	1.721	$65.55_{\pm 0.4}$	$75.64_{\pm 3.2}$	1.418
Logit-KD-Sparse	$82.80_{\pm 0.4}$	$79.80_{\pm 0.5}$	1.476	$73.31_{\pm 2.0}$	$81.19_{\pm 0.8}$	1.744	$83.84_{\pm 0.4}$	$92.29_{\pm 0.7}$	**1.472**	$66.65_{\pm 0.7}$	$\mathbf{77.27}_{\pm 7.1}$	1.385
SEED-KD-Sparse	$82.51_{\pm 0.4}$	$79.52_{\pm 0.5}$	**1.474**	$\mathbf{73.70}_{\pm 3.4}$	$81.92_{\pm 0.8}$	**1.741**	$83.96_{\pm 0.3}$	$92.20_{\pm 1.0}$	1.480	$64.75_{\pm 1.1}$	$71.29_{\pm 3.6}$	1.381

Table 8: Performance of distillation algorithms in the setup of controlled computational costs.

Task	2019-1	2019-2	2020-1	2020-2
	Hashtag Prediction			
BERT-base	$46.38_{\pm 0.4}$	$48.05_{\pm 0.8}$	$41.67_{\pm 1.0}$	$69.00_{\pm 0.5}$
Sequential PT	$50.46_{\pm 0.1}$	$52.70_{\pm 0.7}$	$46.49_{\pm 1.0}$	$71.63_{\pm 0.7}$
ER	$49.90_{\pm 0.4}$	$52.33_{\pm 0.6}$	$46.84_{\pm 0.3}$	$71.67_{\pm 0.4}$
Logit-KD	$50.19_{\pm 0.9}$	$\mathbf{53.70}_{\pm 0.4}$	$\mathbf{47.64}_{\pm 0.4}$	$\mathbf{72.44}_{\pm 0.5}$
SEED-Logit-KD	$\mathbf{50.79}_{\pm 0.8}$	$52.84_{\pm 0.5}$	$46.04_{\pm 0.4}$	$72.24_{\pm 0.6}$

Table 9: Hashtag prediction performance of continually pretrained BERT models over tweets after 2019.

Task	2019-1→2019-2	2019-1→2020-1	2019-1→2020-2
	Hashtag Prediction		
BERT-base	$40.19_{\pm 0.3}$	$41.00_{\pm 0.6}$	$40.85_{\pm 0.8}$
Sequential PT	$43.30_{\pm 0.7}$	$\mathbf{48.60}_{\pm 2.1}$	$44.07_{\pm 0.8}$
ER	$42.96_{\pm 0.9}$	$46.07_{\pm 1.6}$	$44.26_{\pm 0.7}$
Logit-KD	$\mathbf{43.35}_{\pm 1.6}$	$46.91_{\pm 0.5}$	$\mathbf{45.03}_{\pm 0.2}$
SEED-Logit-KD	$43.56_{\pm 0.4}$	$45.77_{\pm 0.7}$	$43.76_{\pm 0.5}$

Table 10: Temporal generalization performance of Hashtag prediction models fine-tuned from continually pretrained BERT models over tweets after 2019.

training corpora $D_{1..4}$ consist of tweets from the first half of 2019, the second half of 2019, the first half of 2020, and the second half of 2020 respectively. We accordingly construct hashtag prediction and cross-year hashtag prediction datasets. The performance of downstream tasks fine-tuned from the final pretrained model is presented in Table 9. We see Sequential PT clearly outperforms BERT-base which is not continually pretrained, and that Logit-KD generally improves hashtag prediction performance compared to Sequential PT except on the first half of 2019. We hypothesize the small temporal gap between $D_{1..4}$ makes improvements less significant than our main experiment setup. We present temporal generalization performance in cross-year hashtag prediction tasks in Table 10. Similarly, Logit-KD improves over Sequential PT in two out of three cross-year hashtag prediction setups.

H Analysis of Data Streams

In this section, we provide further analysis about the created research paper stream and the tweet stream. We measure cosine distances d_v of vocabulary distributions between each pair of different domains ($D_{1..4}$) and summarize the results in Figure 7. The results indicate that the Tweet stream has a magnitude smaller vocabulary distribution gap between domains, which is in the scale of $1e^{-5}$, compared to the research paper stream, which is in the scale of $1e^{-2}$. On the Tweet stream, we see the differences of vocabulary distributions align with the temporal gap between domains. On the

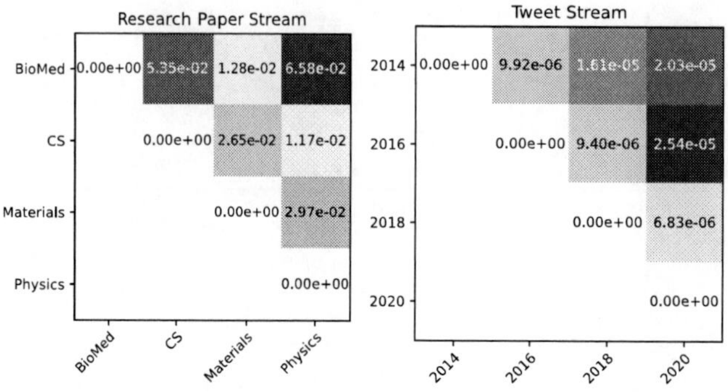

(a) Research Paper Stream

(b) Tweet Stream

Figure 7: Cosine distance of vocabulary distributions between each pair of datasets in two data streams.

research paper stream, we find some domains to be more similar than others. For example, Biomedical (D_1) and Material Science domains (D_3) have larger similarity in their vocabulary distributions, which explains general downstream performance increase on D_1 after the model is pretrained on D_3 (Fig. 4 (a,b)).

The differences in vocabulary distribution explain inconsistency in results between two data streams, specifically, whether lifelong pretraining improves downstream model performance on the latest domain, as we mentioned in Sec. 4.3. Other than this, our main findings, such as the effect of distillation-based CL algorithms on reducing forgetting, are consistent over two datasets with such significant differences in their changes of vocabulary distribution. We believe it implies the conclusions in this paper should be reliable in diverse data streams.

I Ethic Risks

We would like to note that, in practice, continually pretrained models over real-world data streams would require identification and removal of biased contents from pretraining corpora, which may affect the prediction of downstream models. As PTLMs are continuously updated, the bias in earlier pretraining may have a profound negative impact. In future works, it is preferable to develop algorithms to "forget" certain biased knowledge from language models. We further note that any data released in this paper, especially the tweet stream, should only be used for research purposes.

Using ASR-Generated Text for Spoken Language Modeling

Nicolas Hervé[1], Valentin Pelloin[2], Benoit Favre[3], Franck Dary[3]
Antoine Laurent[2], Sylvain Meignier[2], Laurent Besacier[4]
[1]Institut National de l'Audiovisuel (INA), France
[2]Laboratoire d'Informatique de l'Université du Mans (LIUM), France
[3]Aix Marseille Univ, Université de Toulon, CNRS, LIS, Marseille, France
[4]Naver Labs Europe (NLE), Meylan, France
nherve@ina.fr

Abstract

This papers aims at improving spoken language modeling (LM) using very large amount of automatically transcribed speech. We leverage the INA (French National Audiovisual Institute[1]) collection and obtain 19GB of text after applying ASR on 350,000 hours of diverse TV shows. From this, spoken language models are trained either by fine-tuning an existing LM (FlauBERT[2]) or through training a LM from scratch. The new models (FlauBERT-Oral) are shared with the community[3] and are evaluated not only in terms of word prediction accuracy but also for two downstream tasks: classification of TV shows and syntactic parsing of speech. Experimental results show that FlauBERT-Oral is better than its initial FlauBERT version demonstrating that, despite its inherent noisy nature, ASR-Generated text can be useful to improve spoken language modeling.

1 Introduction

Large language models are trained with massive texts which do not reflect well the specific aspects of spoken language. Hence, modeling spoken language is challenging as crawling 'oral-style' transcripts is a difficult task. To overcome this, our pilot study investigates the use of massive automatic speech recognition (ASR) generated text for spoken language modeling. We believe that this methodology could bring diversity (oral/spontaneous style, different topics) to the language modeling data. This might be also useful for languages with fewer text resources but potential high availability of speech recordings. We also see long-term benefits to using ASR generated text as speech recordings convey potentially useful metadata (ex: male/female speech) that could be leveraged for building LMs from more balanced data. Finally, as speech transcripts are naturally grounded with other modalities (if extracted from videos for instance), ASR could help building large scale multimodal language understanding corpora.

The contributions of this paper are the following:

- we build and share FlauBERT-Oral models from a massive amount (350,000 hours) of French TV shows,
- we evaluate them on word prediction (on both written and spoken corpora), automatic classification of TV shows and speech syntactic parsing,
- we demonstrate that ASR-Generated text can be useful for spoken LM.

2 Related Works

We mention here related works to better position our approach: learning LMs from spoken transcripts, multimodal models and using LMs to rescore ASR.

Learning LMs from spoken transcripts. Kumar et al. (2021) probes BERT based language models (BERT, RoBERTa) trained on spoken transcripts to investigate their ability to encode properties of spoken language. Their empirical results show that LM is surprisingly good at capturing conversational properties such as pause prediction and overtalk detection from lexical tokens. But their LMs evaluated are mostly trained on clean (non ASR) spoken transcripts except one called ASRoBERTa which is trained on 2000h of transcribed speech only (1k Librispeech + 1k proprietary dataset). As a comparison with this study, we train our models on 175x more ASR data.

Multimodal models. While our approach uses ASR to build text-based spoken language models, Chuang et al. (2019) proposed an audio-and-text jointly learned SpeechBERT model for spoken question answering task. They show their model

[1]https://www.ina.fr
[2]https://github.com/getalp/Flaubert
[3]https://huggingface.co/nherve

Proceedings of BigScience Episode #5 – Workshop on Challenges & Perspectives in Creating Large Language Models, pages 17 - 25
May 27, 2022 ©2022 Association for Computational Linguistics

is able to extract information out of audio data that is complementary to (noisy) ASR output text. The architecture proposed by Sundararaman et al. (2021) is different in the sense that it learns a joint language model with phoneme sequence and ASR transcript to learn phonetic-aware representations that are robust to ASR errors (not exactly a multimodal model). While speech or multimodal unsupervised representation learning is an interesting direction, this is out of the scope of this paper which focuses on language modeling from text transcripts only.

BERT for ASR re-ranking. We also mention here LMs to rescore ASR as this could be an interesting application of our proposed spoken language models. Chiu and Chen (2021) used BERT models for reranking of N-best hypotheses produced by automatic speech recognition (ASR). Their experiments on the AMI benchmark demonstrate the effectiveness of the approach in comparison to RNN-based re-ranking. A similar idea is introduced by Fohr and Illina (2021) where BERT features are added to the neural re-ranker used to rescore ASR hypotheses. Even more recently, Xu et al. (2022) showed how to train a BERT-based rescoring model to incorporate a discriminative loss into the fine-tuning step of deep bidirectional pretrained models for ASR.

3 From FlauBERT to FlauBERT-Oral

3.1 ASR system

The speech recognition system used to produce the text transcripts for this study was built using Kaldi (Povey et al., 2011). The acoustic model is based on the lattice-free MMI, so-called "chain" model (Povey et al., 2016). We used a time-delay neural network (Peddinti et al., 2015) and a discriminative training on the top of it using the state-level minimum Bayes risk (sMBR) criterion (Veselý et al., 2013).

For the acoustic model training, we used several TV and RADIO corpora (ESTER 1&2 (Galliano et al., 2009), REPERE (Giraudel et al., 2012) and VERA (Goryainova et al., 2014)). A regular back-off n-gram model was estimated using the speech transcripts augmented with several French newspapers (see section 4.2.3 in Deléglise et al. (2009)) using SRILM.

A 2-gram decoding is performed, followed by a 3-gram and a 4-gram rescoring step. The LM interpolation weights between the different data sources were optimized on the REPERE (Giraudel et al., 2012) development corpus. The vocabulary contains the 160k most frequents words in the manually transcribed train corpus. Automatic speech diarization of the INA collection was performed using the open source toolkit LIUMSpkDiarization (Meignier and Merlin, 2010).

Some results on different test corpora can be found in table 1.

Corpus	WER
REPERE test corpus	12.1
ESTER1 test corpus	8.8
ESTER2 test corpus	10.7

Table 1: ASR Performances on French TV or Radio corpora

3.2 Automatically transcribing 350,000 hours of the INA collection

The transcripts used in these experiments were taken from time slots corresponding to news programmes on French television and radio between 2013 and 2020. We transcribed the continuous news media between 6am and midnight each day (BFMTV, LCI, CNews, France 24, France Info and franceinfo). For radio, the morning news were used (Europe1, RMC, RTL, France Inter) and for generalist television channels we transcribed the evening news (TF1, France 2, France 3, M6). A total of 350,000 hours were automatically transcribed. The system we use provides us with raw text, without punctuation or capitalization. In order to have a pseudo sentence tokenization, we leverage the speaker diarization output to segment our transcriptions into "sentences". We end up with a total of 51M unique speech segments for a total of 3.5G words (19GB of data). The ASR generated text is strongly biased towards news content.

3.3 Fine-tuning or re-training FlauBERT-Oral

The initial French language model (**FBU**), trained in 2020 on natural text, is FlauBERT (Le et al., 2020). Models of different sizes were trained using masked language modeling (MLM) following a RoBERTa architecture (Liu et al., 2019) and using the CNRS Jean Zay supercomputer. They were shared on HuggingFace.[4] For comparison, these

[4] https://huggingface.co/flaubert

models were trained on 71GB of natural text.

Following the architecture of Le et al. (2020), we propose several learning configurations in order to observe the impact of different parameters on the performance of the models obtained. Since we only have lowercase transcripts, we consider the *flaubert-base-uncased* model as our reference.[5]

The first configuration, **FlauBERT-O-base_uncased (FT)**, consists in fine-tuning the public *flaubert-base-uncased* model for some epochs using our ASR transcripts.

The second configuration **FlauBERT-O-mixed (MIX)** is a full model re-trained using a mix of ASR text and written text, as training data. Written text comes from two main sources: the French wikipedia dump and press articles captured by the OTMedia research platform (Hervé, 2019) (online press and AFP agency for the same time period). Overall, this learning dataset is also strongly news-oriented. For the written text, we use the same sentence segmentation tool as the one used for FlauBERT. Our dataset is balanced between ASR and written text: we use 94M randomly selected written text sentences representing 13G of data to which we removed the punctuation and capitalization to make it consistent with our ASR data. For this mixed model, we also retrain the BPE tokenizer (50K sub-word units).

The third configuration, **FlauBERT-O-asr**, consists in re-training LMs from scratch using ASR data only. For the first model (**ORAL**), we use the tokenizer provided with the *flaubert-base-uncased* model and for the second one (**ORAL_NB**) we retrain a BPE tokenizer (50K sub-word units). Both tokenizers share 35088 (overlap) out of 67536 (FlauBERT initial) tokens, only 52% overlap.

These different configurations therefore provide us with 4 language models to evaluate. Training was done on a single server with 2 Xeon CPUs of 12 cores each, 256 GB of RAM and 8 Nvidia GeForce RTX 2080 Ti graphics cards with 11 GB of memory. With this hardware, it took us 15 days to train 50 epochs of each model in the flaubert-base configuration (137M parameters) using FlauBERT code.

4 Word Prediction Experiments

The first step in evaluating our models is to look at their behaviour for the word prediction task. In addition to the performance on the trained models, we also want to have an idea of the performance on texts of different nature (written style or oral style). We therefore assembled several datasets to measure the word prediction performance of the models we trained.

We make sure that these datasets are not included in the training data of the default FlauBERT model nor in our own. We have a first corpus (**afp2021**) of AFP dispatches from the year 2021, i.e. after the period of our training data collected from the online press. This will allow us to have a measure of performance on written text. Secondly, we want to evaluate our models on oral texts. We use the transcripts of the French National Assembly sessions.[6] We are using the 13th (under Sarkozy **parl_13**) and 15th (currently under Macron **parl_15**) mandates. These texts are a manual transcription of what is said in the hemicycle, which are prepared speeches with some degree of spontaneous style as well. A second corpus is constituted with, once again, the manual transcriptions made for educational videos[7] and interviews[8] that INA makes available via its web studio (**studio_manual**). These transcriptions are of very good quality. We also transcribed these videos from the studio with our ASR system (**studio_asr**) in order to be able to compare the performance on both types of data.

We report in the graphs the accuracy obtained on the different datasets for a word prediction task after a word has been masked. The masking parameters are the same as those used during training with MLM loss.

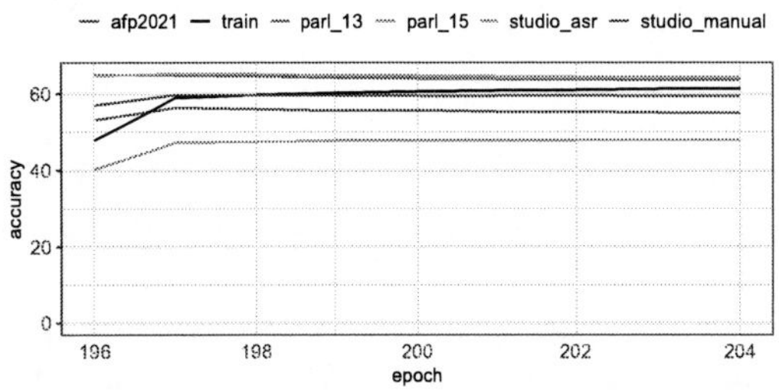

Figure 1: **FT** - Word prediction accuracy of *FlauBERT-O-base_uncased*

Figures 1 to 4 show the results assessed at each epoch. In table 2, we summarise the results for the last epoch and also for the default

[5]https://huggingface.co/flaubert/flaubert_base_uncased

[6]https://data.assemblee-nationale.fr/

[7]https://www.ina.fr/offres-et-services/fresques-numeriques

[8]https://entretiens.ina.fr/

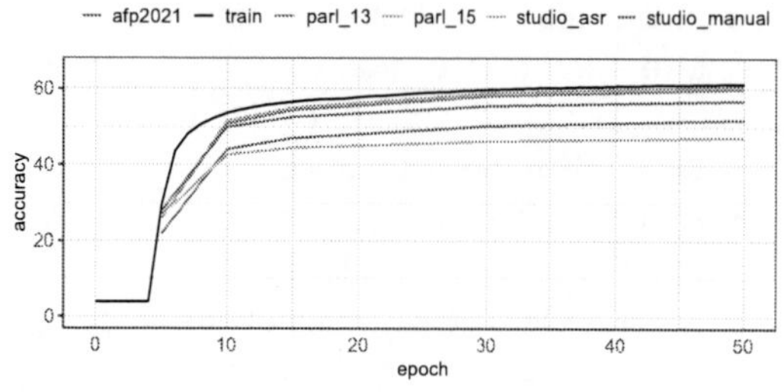

Figure 2: **ORAL** - Word prediction accuracy of *FlauBERT-O-asr*, using the initial *flaubert-base-uncased* BPE tokenizer

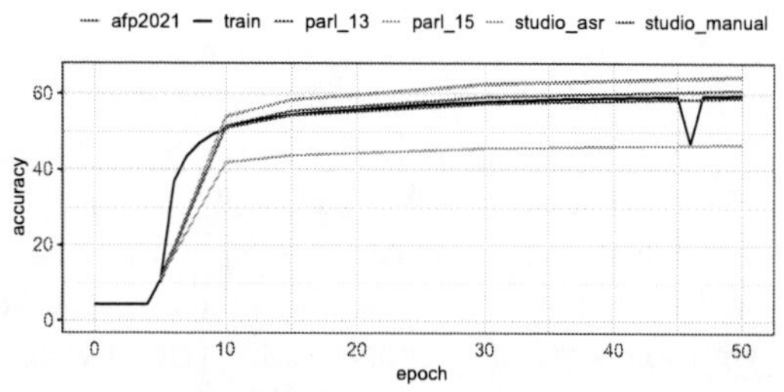

Figure 3: **MIX** - Word prediction accuracy of *FlauBERT-O-mixed*

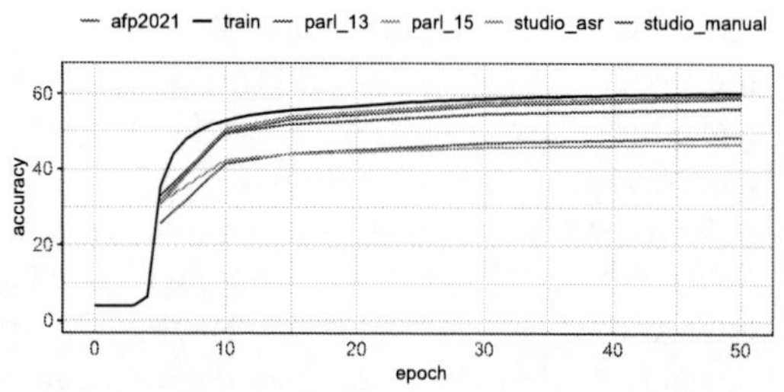

Figure 4: **ORAL_NB** - Word prediction accuracy of *FlauBERT-O-asr_newbpe*, using a new BPE tokenizer trained on ASR data

flaubert_base_uncased model (**FBU**). For the fine-tuned FlauBERT-O-base_uncased model, we notice a slight improvement in performance for afp and studio datasets, obtained from the first epoch, which means that adding ASR generated text improves word prediction task on these datasets. We observe that globally, whatever the model, the datasets of the parliamentary sessions are those for which the best performances are obtained on the word prediction task, even exceeding that of the training dataset for the FlauBERT-O-base_uncased and FlauBERT-O-mixed models. These models are trained on written and spoken texts and it is not surprising that the performance is good since the very nature of the parliamentary data is a mixture of prepared and spontaneous speech. There is no significant difference between parl_13 and parl_15. On these parlementary speeches, there is no significant performance difference between the 3 models that have seen written text during their training (FBU, FT and MIX). As we observed also that our FlauBERT-O models improve also on written text (afp2021), we explain this by the fact that those texts are strongly related to news events, so they are in a similar context to our ASR data which is focused on news slot transcripts. For the last corpus, from the INA web studio, we have educational videos or interviews of personalities which are more distant from news data. There is a great disparity in performance depending on whether we consider manual (studio_manual) or automatic (studio_asr) transcription. We believe that the different sentence segmentation algorithms have a very clear impact on this corpus. Finally, we notice that the ORAL_NB model performs slightly worse than the ORAL model. The BPE tokenizer obviously has an impact on the overall performance of the LMs and it seems, from this result, that using BPE units extracted from clean data (and not noisy ASR data) is beneficial even if the training material is itself ASR generated text.

Corpus	FBU	FT	MIX	ORAL_NB	ORAL
afp2021	53.1	55.1	**60.9**	48.6	51.9
parl_13	**64.9**	63.6	64.5	58.8	60.0
parl_15	**64.6**	64.3	64.3	59.7	60.7
studio_asr	40.2	**48.0**	46.6	46.8	47.2
studio_manual	57.0	**59.4**	58.9	56.3	56.9

Table 2: Word prediction task accuracies

5 Downstream Task 1: Automatic Classification of TV Shows

We evaluate our different models on a news classification task. For the main generalist channels, INA's documentalists finely segment the newscasts and annotate them in order to describe their content. This very rich metadata is used in particular to establish quantitative studies on the news in France. The InaStat barometer[9] has set up a stable method-

[9] http://www.inatheque.fr/publications-evenements/ina-stat/

ology over time to classify these news items into 14 categories (such as society, French politics, sport or environment). We use the news items of 4 channels (TF1, France 2, France 3 and M6) for the years 2017, 2018 and 2019, which gives us a total of 47 867 short TV shows. The average length of these shows is 92 seconds.

5.1 Standard Learning Setting

The objective is to assess to what extent it is possible to classify these topics into the 14 categories solely on the basis of what is pronounced, i.e. from the ASR transcripts. We establish a baseline using a simple SVM classifier (with a non-parametric triangular kernel) on TF-IDF vectors with two vocabulary sizes of 5K and 20K words. To test the FlauBERT models, we use the HuggingFace Transformers library and the *FlaubertForSequenceClassification* class, which adds a simple dense classification layer on top of our models. To obtain a vector representation of our texts before this classification layer, we use the 'mean' summary type. We do not make any model selection and report the results for all learning epochs. Since the 14 categories are not well-balanced, we use the weighted F1 measure to evaluate the performance. The experiments are systematically performed on 10 different random splits of the dataset, taking into account the cardinality of the 14 categories, so as to have 38K examples for the training set and 5K for the test set. We show the average results and the standard deviation in figure 5.

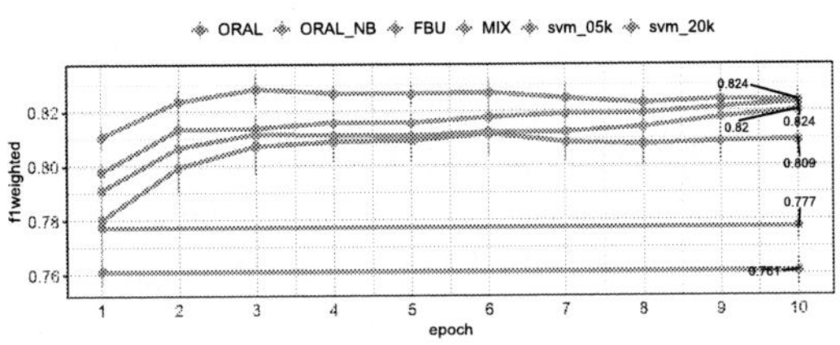

Figure 5: TV news classification - train 38K, test 5K

We can see in this configuration the contribution of the LMs compared to the SVMs along the training epochs of the classifier. If we look at the performance at the first epoch, we can see that the flaubert_base_uncased model has almost equivalent performance to the SVM (0.78). It is only after a few iterations of learning that the model fits the ASR data and reaches 0.81. On the other hand, the models that have already seen ASR data during their training have a better performance from the first epoch. The model trained only on ASR data is the best performing (ORAL). After 10 epochs, the 3 FlauBERT-Oral models converge and are equivalent for this task.

5.2 Few Shot Learning Setting

In order to test the LMs under more challenging conditions, we progressively reduce the number of training examples to get closer to few-shot learning conditions. We thus restart the classification with 5K training examples, then 500 and finally 200. Again, we take into account the cardinality of the 14 categories. For the last experiment with only 200 training examples, the vocabulary is too small and we can only test the SVM baseline with a vocabulary of 5K words, but not the version with 20K words. Moreover, we push to 30 epochs in this latter case.

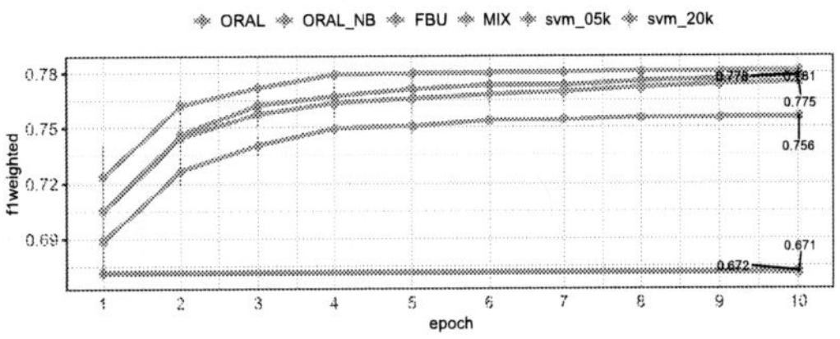

Figure 6: TV news classification - train 5K, test 38K

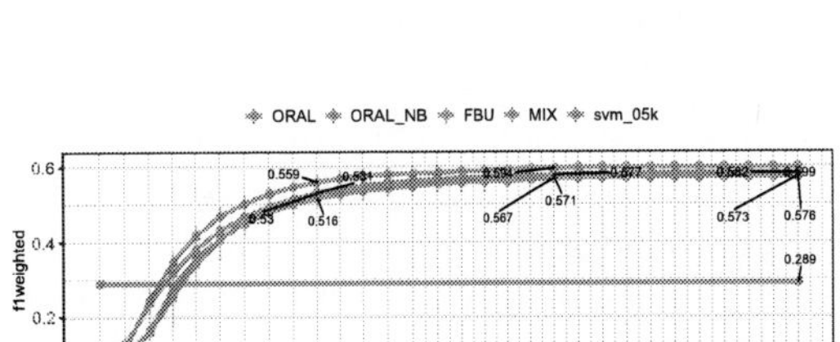

Figure 7: TV news classification - train 500, test 47K

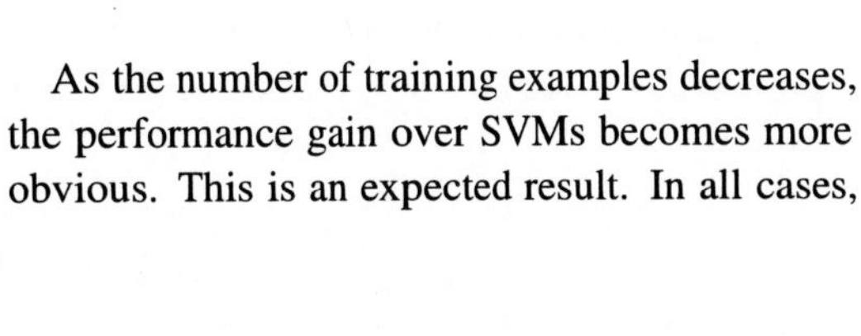

Figure 8: TV news classification - train 200, test 47K

As the number of training examples decreases, the performance gain over SVMs becomes more obvious. This is an expected result. In all cases,

ina-stat-sommaire.html

the models trained on ASR only text (ORAL) are the best of the FlauBERT-O models. Compared to the ORAL_NB model, only the tokenizer is different. This result may appear counter-intuitive in a first place, as one would expect a model entirely learned on ASR data to perform better on a classification task using only ASR data as input. However, this is probably counterbalanced by the fact that using BPE units extracted from clean data is important (as we have seen in the word prediction experiments). This invites us to further investigate the role of the tokenizer in spoken language modeling. As in the previous case, the Flaubert models converge almost with a 2 F1 point difference in favour of the FlauBERT-O models over the initial FlauBERT model.

6 Downstream Task 2: Syntactic Analysis of Spoken Conversations

This section is about the downstream task of jointly predicting part of speech tags (POS) and building a labelled dependency tree. The models performing these tasks typically rely on word representations, that are often pretrained, especially when the data is scarce. We will use our different spoken language models to obtain contextual word representations of a syntactically annotated and manually transcribed oral French corpus. For each of these representations, a model will be trained to perform the joint prediction of POS tags and labelled dependencies. We also use as baseline a model trained using non-contextual representations obtained with FastText,[10] and a model learning its own representations without any pretraining.

6.1 Data

We used the annotated subset of the speech corpus of the Orfeo project (Benzitoun et al., 2016; Nasr et al., 2020), gathered with the goal of reflecting the contemporary usage of the French language.

The audio extracts on which this corpus is based come from various origins and modalities: from one to multiple speakers, work meetings, family dinner conversations, narration, political meeting, interview, goal-oriented telephone conversations. Their duration varies from four minutes to an hour.

The reference audio transcripts have been obtained after correcting the output of an ASR system. The corpus is annotated in part of speech (POS) tags, lemmas, labeled dependency trees and sentences boundaries. There are 20 possible POS tags and 12 syntactic functions.

We randomly split the corpus into train/dev/test sets of respective sizes 134,716/27,937/29,529 words; we sampled from each source so that the various origins of the audios are equally represented in each split.

6.2 Parsing Model

The model is a transition based parser using the arc-eager transition system (Nivre, 2008), which has been extended for the joint prediction of POS tags and parsing transitions (Dary and Nasr, 2021).

It consists of a single classifier, taking as input a numeric representation of the current state of the analysis, called a configuration. The classifier predicts a probability distribution over the set of POS tagging actions or parsing actions, depending of the current state of the configuration. The analysis assume that the text is already tokenized and segmented into sentences; the words of each sentence are considered one by one, in the reading order; a POS action is predicted for the current word, then a sequence of arc-eager actions is predicted until the current word is either attached to a word on its left or shifted to a stack for future attachment to a word on its right. The predictions are greedy: it is always the top scoring action among the allowed ones. We do not use beam search for decoding.

The numeric representation of the current configuration is comprised of:

- The concatenation of the word embeddings, reduced from dimension 768 to dimension 64 by a linear layer, of the following context: the current word, the three preceding ones, the two following ones, the three topmost stack elements and the rightmost and leftmost dependents of the three topmost stack elements,
- The output of three different BiLSTM processing sequences of tags of the same nature. The first one is taking as input the sequence of POS tags and syntactic function of the current word, the three previous ones and the three topmost stack elements. The second one is taking the sequence of the last 10 actions that have been applied to this configuration. The last one is taking the sequence of distances (in number of words) between the current word and the three topmost stack elements. In each case,

[10] https://fasttext.cc

the sequence elements are encoded by learnable and randomly initialized embeddings of size 128, and the output of the BiLSTM is a vector of size 128,

- A learnable and randomly initialized embedding encoding the current state of the configuration (POS tagging or dependency parsing).

A dropout of 50% is applied to the resulting vector; then it passes through two hidden layers of respective sizes 3200 and 1600, both with a dropout of 40% and a ReLU activation. Finally, the network is ended by one of the two decision layers, depending on the current state, which is simply a linear layer of dimension the number of possible actions followed by a softmax.

Each model was trained for 40 epochs; after every epoch the model was evaluated on the dev set and was saved if it was an improvement. After the fourth epoch, the entire train set was decoded using the model that was being trained, in order to generate and integrate novel configurations in the dataset for the epochs to come. This technique allows the model to be more robust, exploring non-optimal configurations during its training. It is based on the dynamical oracle model of Goldberg and Nivre (2012).

6.3 Experiments

The first set of experiments compares input representations from the FlauBERT variants (FBU, MIX, ORAL) to uncontextual word embeddings (Fasttext) and randomly initialized embeddings. Except for random embeddings, token representations are frozen when the parsing system is trained.

As pre-processing, we deanonymize the transcripts by replacing masked proper name tokens with non-ambiguous names randomly chosen for each recording. In the fasttext setting, representations are computed for unknown words from their character n-gram factors. Contextual representations are computed at the whole recording level in chunks of 512 tokens without overlap. The parser is applied on the reference transcript and reference segmentation. We use mean pooling for words that are split in multiple tokens by BPE.

Parsing performance is evaluated with Labeled Attachment Score (LAS), the accuracy of predicting the governor of each word and its dependency label, Unlabeled Attachment Score (UAS), which ignores the dependency label, and Part-of-speech tagging accuracy (UPOS). The scoring script is from CoNLL campaigns.

Repr.	**LAS**	**UAS**	**UPOS**
No pretraining	84.92	88.48	94.51
Fasttext	85.36	88.76	95.12
FBU	85.55	89.02	93.36
MIX	86.33	89.79	94.43
ORAL	**87.65**	**90.92**	95.55
ORAL_NB	87.54	90.73	**95.63**

Table 3: Main result on syntax prediction. Metrics are Labeled Attachment Score (LAS), Unlabeled Attachment Score (UAS) and Part-of-speech tagging accuracy (UPOS). Higher is better, highest figure in bold.

Results presented in Table 3 show that pretraining is valuable for syntactic parsing in that setting and that pretraining on ASR (**MIX** and **ORAL**) leads to a substancial improvement in LAS over the text-only FlauBERT model (**FBU**) even though there is no domain overlap between the TV shows on which the earlier is trained and the data of the Orfeo corpus. There is no benefit from retraining BPE (**ORAL_NB**).

Repr.	**LAS**	**UAS**	**UPOS**
FBU	85.55	89.02	93.36
FBU w/ punct	87.48	90.69	95.03
ORAL	87.65	90.92	95.55

Table 4: Effect of repunctuating speech transcripts on syntactic parsing prior to extracting representations. Results from the ORAL representations are given for reference.

As noted earlier, speech recordings do not have punctuation and it is debated whether punctuation is suitable for spontaenous conversations. As punctuation is rather regular in text, it would make sense for LMs trained on text to over-rely on the cues it brings, and representations to be affected by a lack of punctuation. Table 4 shows syntactic parsing results on representations where a simple heuristic is applied to add a period at the end of each sentence prior to extracting representations. This punctuation is stripped before passing the tokens to the syntactic parser and only used at the encoding stage. Results show that most of the difference in performance between the **FBU** and **ORAL** models can be compensated by this use of virtual punctuation. Using accurately predicted punctuation with diverse symbols and intra-sentence marks is

Repr.	LAS			UAS			UPOS		
	Global	OOV	Δ	Global	OOV	Δ	Global	OOV	Δ
FBU	85.55	74.10	-11.45	89.02	82.20	-6.82	93.36	79.00	-14.36
MIX	86.33	74.40	-11.93	89.79	82.47	-7.33	94.43	80.35	-14.07
ORAL	87.65	73.68	-13.97	90.92	82.81	-8.11	95.55	79.00	-16.55

Table 5: Syntactic parsing performance on OOV words according to automatic transcription system. The Δ column contains the difference between the global accuracy and the accuracy on OOVs only.

left as future work, but we conjecture that it will marginally improve over this crude heuristic.

Gauging the impact of speech-to-text errors on representations from LMs trained on such data is difficult since there are no manual references available for large quantities of speech transcripts. Since the system used to transcribe the recordings is closed vocabulary, one way to look at this problem is to compute the accuracy of the syntactic parser on words that are out-of-vocabulary (OOV) for the LM training data. Due to BPE, those words are necesseraly tokenized in smaller units which are pooled prior to passing them to the parser, and might hamper the quality of the associated representations. Table 5 details the performance of the syntactic parser on OOVs. Due to their infrequent nature, OOVs are mainly swear words, proper names, and tokenization artifacts. They are difficult to handle for all models, and suffer from a large performance reduction compared to the global figure, even for the **FBU** model which has seen a much larger variety of texts. The system fed with representations of the model trained on ASR data only (**ORAL**) is the most affected despite its better global performance.

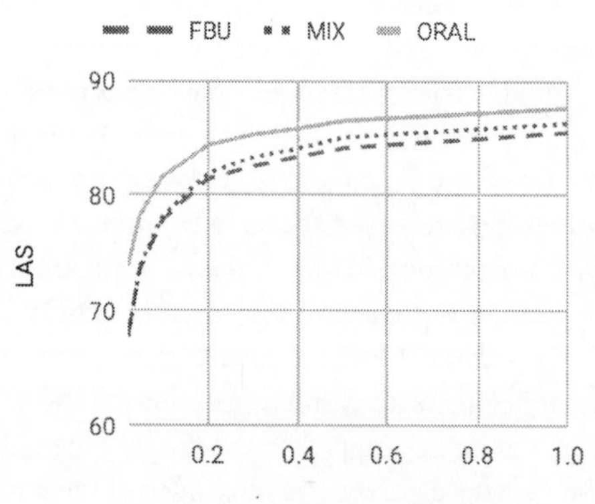

Figure 9: LAS learning curve for syntactic parser according to quantity of training data. Similar shape is obtained for UAS and UPOS.

Finally, Figure 9 shows the learning curve when reducing the training data available to the syntactic parser. For this, we randomly sampled 10 subsets of the training data at the recording level in order to fit a target ratio from 2.5% to 100%. The figure shows that LAS is always better for **ORAL** representations and that **MIX** is closer to **FBU** when less data is available.

6.4 Takeaways

It seems that exploiting ASR transcripts for learning LMs is beneficial for syntactic parsing of speech transcripts. Analyses presented show that punctuation plays an important role in representations. Our analysis of parsing performance on OOV words (according to the speech-to-text system) reveals that our FlauBERT-O-asr (**ORAL**) model is more affected than its initial FlauBERT baseline (**FBU**), despite overall better performance.

7 Conclusion and future work

We investigated spoken language modeling using ASR generated text (350,000 hours of diverse TV shows). The new models for French (FlauBERT-O) are shared with the community. Experimental results show that FlauBERT-O is generally better than its initial FlauBERT version for the downstream speech tasks we experimented with. However we should also check its performance on text downstream tasks (such as (Le et al., 2020)) and on more downstream speech tasks (SLU or ASR re-scoring).

In this work, all our texts were uncased as our ASR only generates lowercased transcripts. We believe that applying massively re-capitalisation (and restoring punctuation as well) might be beneficial to train stronger spoken LMs. We also plan to analyze more the specificities of our ASR-generated texts (do they contain more oral features such as word repetitions, more interjections?). Finally, some of the results obtained lead us to believe that it is important to further evaluate the impact of BPE units for spoken language modeling.

References

Christophe Benzitoun, Jeanne-Marie Debaisieux, and Henri-José Deulofeu. 2016. Le projet orféo: un corpus d'étude pour le français contemporain. *Corpus*, (15).

Shih-Hsuan Chiu and Berlin Chen. 2021. Innovative bert-based reranking language models for speech recognition. *2021 IEEE Spoken Language Technology Workshop (SLT)*.

Yung-Sung Chuang, Chi-Liang Liu, and Hung-yi Lee. 2019. Speechbert: Cross-modal pre-trained language model for end-to-end spoken question answering. *CoRR*, abs/1910.11559.

Franck Dary and Alexis Nasr. 2021. The reading machine: A versatile framework for studying incremental parsing strategies. In *Proceedings of the 17th International Conference on Parsing Technologies and the IWPT 2021 Shared Task on Parsing into Enhanced Universal Dependencies (IWPT 2021)*, pages 26–37, Online. Association for Computational Linguistics.

Paul Deléglise, Yannick Esteve, Sylvain Meignier, and Teva Merlin. 2009. Improvements to the lium french asr system based on cmu sphinx: what helps to significantly reduce the word error rate? In *Tenth Annual Conference of the International Speech Communication Association*.

Dominique Fohr and Irina Illina. 2021. BERT-based Semantic Model for Rescoring N-best Speech Recognition List. In *INTERSPEECH 2021*, Proceedings of INTERSPEECH 2021, Brno, Czech Republic.

Sylvain Galliano, Guillaume Gravier, and Laura Chaubard. 2009. The ester 2 evaluation campaign for the rich transcription of french radio broadcasts. In *Tenth Annual Conference of the International Speech Communication Association*.

Aude Giraudel, Matthieu Carré, Valérie Mapelli, Juliette Kahn, Olivier Galibert, and Ludovic Quintard. 2012. The repere corpus: a multimodal corpus for person recognition. In *LREC*, pages 1102–1107.

Yoav Goldberg and Joakim Nivre. 2012. A dynamic oracle for arc-eager dependency parsing. In *Proceedings of COLING 2012*, pages 959–976.

Maria Goryainova, Cyril Grouin, Sophie Rosset, and Ioana Vasilescu. 2014. Morpho-syntactic study of errors from speech recognition system. In *LREC*, volume 14, pages 3050–3056.

Nicolas Hervé. 2019. OTMedia, the TransMedia news observatory. In *FIAT/IFTA Media Management Seminar 2019*.

Ayush Kumar, Mukuntha Narayanan Sundararaman, and Jithendra Vepa. 2021. What BERT based language model learns in spoken transcripts: An empirical study. In *Proceedings of the Fourth BlackboxNLP Workshop on Analyzing and Interpreting Neural Networks for NLP*, pages 322–336, Punta Cana, Dominican Republic. Association for Computational Linguistics.

Hang Le, Loïc Vial, Jibril Frej, Vincent Segonne, Maximin Coavoux, Benjamin Lecouteux, Alexandre Allauzen, Benoit Crabbé, Laurent Besacier, and Didier Schwab. 2020. FlauBERT: Unsupervised language model pre-training for French. In *Proceedings of the 12th Language Resources and Evaluation Conference*, pages 2479–2490, Marseille, France. European Language Resources Association.

Yinhan Liu, Myle Ott, Naman Goyal, Jingfei Du, Mandar Joshi, Danqi Chen, Omer Levy, Mike Lewis, Luke Zettlemoyer, and Veselin Stoyanov. 2019. Roberta: A robustly optimized BERT pretraining approach. *CoRR*, abs/1907.11692.

Sylvain Meignier and Teva Merlin. 2010. Lium spkdiarization: an open source toolkit for diarization. In *CMU SPUD Workshop*.

Alexis Nasr, Franck Dary, Frédéric Bechet, and Benoît Fabre. 2020. Annotation syntaxique automatique de la partie orale du orféo. *Langages*, (3):87–102.

Joakim Nivre. 2008. Algorithms for deterministic incremental dependency parsing. *Computational Linguistics*, 34(4):513–553.

Vijayaditya Peddinti, Daniel Povey, and Sanjeev Khudanpur. 2015. A time delay neural network architecture for efficient modeling of long temporal contexts. In *Sixteenth Annual Conference of the International Speech Communication Association*.

Daniel Povey, Arnab Ghoshal, Gilles Boulianne, Lukas Burget, Ondrej Glembek, Nagendra Goel, Mirko Hannemann, Petr Motlicek, Yanmin Qian, Petr Schwarz, et al. 2011. The kaldi speech recognition toolkit. Technical report, IEEE Signal Processing Society.

Daniel Povey, Vijayaditya Peddinti, Daniel Galvez, Pegah Ghahremani, Vimal Manohar, Xingyu Na, Yiming Wang, and Sanjeev Khudanpur. 2016. Purely sequence-trained neural networks for asr based on lattice-free mmi. In *Interspeech*, pages 2751–2755.

Mukuntha Narayanan Sundararaman, Ayush Kumar, and Jithendra Vepa. 2021. Phoneme-bert: Joint language modelling of phoneme sequence and asr transcript.

Karel Veselỳ, Arnab Ghoshal, Lukás Burget, and Daniel Povey. 2013. Sequence-discriminative training of deep neural networks. In *Interspeech*, volume 2013, pages 2345–2349.

Liyan Xu, Yile Gu, Jari Kolehmainen, Haidar Khan, Ankur Gandhe, Ariya Rastrow, Andreas Stolcke, and Ivan Bulyko. 2022. Rescorebert: Discriminative speech recognition rescoring with bert.

You Reap What You Sow: On the Challenges of Bias Evaluation Under Multilingual Settings

Zeerak Talat[1], Aurélie Névéol[2], Stella Biderman[3,4], Miruna Clinciu[5,6,7], Manan Dey[8], Shayne Longpre[9], Alexandra Sasha Luccioni[10], Maraim Masoud[11], Margaret Mitchell[10], Dragomir Radev[12], Shanya Sharma[13], Arjun Subramonian[14,15], Jaesung Tae[10,12], Samson Tan[16,17], Deepak Tunuguntla[18], Oskar van der Wal[19]

[1]Digital Democracies Institute, Simon Fraser University [2]Université Paris-Saclay, CNRS, LISN [3]Booz Allen Hamilton [4]EleutherAI [5]Edinburgh Centre for Robotics [6]Heriot-Watt University [7]University of Edinburgh [8]SAP [9]MIT [10]Hugging Face [11]Adapt Centre, Trinity College Dublin [12]Yale University [13]Walmart Labs, India [14]University of California, Los Angeles [15]Queer-in-AI [16]AWS AI Research and Education [17]National University of Singapore [18]Independent Researcher [19]University of Amsterdam

Abstract

Evaluating bias, fairness, and social impact in monolingual language models is a difficult task. This challenge is further compounded when language modeling occurs in a multilingual context. Considering the implication of evaluation biases for large multilingual language models, we situate the discussion of bias evaluation within a wider context of social scientific research with computational work. We highlight three dimensions of developing multilingual bias evaluation frameworks: (1) increasing transparency through documentation, (2) expanding targets of bias beyond gender, and (3) addressing cultural differences that exist between languages. We further discuss the power dynamics and consequences of training large language models and recommend that researchers remain cognizant of the ramifications of developing such technologies.

1 Introduction

Machine learning (ML) systems, especially large language models (LLMs), are prone to (re)produce harmful outcomes and social biases (Bender et al., 2021; Raji et al., 2021; Blodgett et al., 2020; Aguera y Arcas et al., 2018). Despite recent advances in LLMs (Bender and Koller, 2020), they have shown to disproportionately produce harmful content when addressing certain topics (Gehman et al., 2020; Lin et al., 2021) and demographics (Sheng et al., 2019; Liang et al., 2021; Dev et al., 2021a)—in part due to the training data used (Dunn, 2020; Gao et al., 2020; Bender et al., 2021), and the design of modeling processes (Talat et al., 2021; Hovy and Prabhumoye, 2021). In response, previous work has explored ways in which such social biases can be measured and counteracted (Nangia et al., 2020; Gehman et al., 2020; Czarnowska et al., 2021). Typically, these issues have been addressed either by conceptualizing the underlying systemic discrimination as "bias" or by developing evaluation datasets that shed light on how LLMs produce harmful social outcomes. However, in the former case, as Blodgett et al. (2020) points out, these conceptualizations often lack clear descriptions, e.g., type of systemic discrimination and affected demographics. This results in a highly under-specified "bias", which could lead to a downstream issue in the validity of the technical approaches that are developed (Blodgett et al., 2021). Similarly, the ill-defined "bias" is further compounded by the specifics of many benchmarks. Often, benchmarks exhibit discrepancies between understandings of the unobservable theoretical constructs against which "bias" is being measured and their operationalization (Jacobs and Wallach, 2021; Friedler et al., 2021). Furthermore, many prior benchmark datasets were developed with specific modeling architectures in mind (Nangia et al., 2020). They are limited to English and are culturally Anglo-centric.[1]

In this position paper, we present an overview of the current state-of-the-art concerning challenges and measures taken to address bias in language models. Specifically, we document the challenges of evaluating language models, with a focus on the generation of harmful text. By engaging our challenges with the relevant social scientific literature, we propose (1) a more transparent evaluation of bias via scoping and documentation, (2) focusing on the diversity of stereotypes for increased inclusivity, (3) careful curation of culturally aware datasets, and (4) creation of general bias measures that are independent of model architecture but capture the context of the task.

We recognize that many of the challenges that we have encountered and described here are large open problems that will require joint work to address. Our goal is to analyze these challenges and provide scaffolding for future work.

2 Grounding Bias, Fairness and Social Impact across Disciplines

Considering biases in socio-technical systems as a purely technical construct is an insufficient consideration of the problem (Blodgett et al., 2020). In this section, we situate LLMs, and their applications, within the wider interdisciplinary literature on social harms and discrimination.

[1]For example, the BigScience biomedical working group has estimated that 82% of evaluation datasets in the biomedical and clinical field are for corpora in English (Datta et al., 2021).

Proceedings of BigScience Episode #5 – Workshop on Challenges & Perspectives in Creating Large Language Models, pages 26 - 41
May 27, 2022

2.1 Social Discrimination

Issues of socially discriminatory (human and technological) systems have long been the subject of study for scholars across disciplines, e.g. in Science and Technology Studies (Haraway, 1988), discard studies (Lepawsky, 2019), social anthropology (Douglas, 1978), philosophy of democracy (Fraser, 1990), gender and LGBTQIA+ studies (Spade, 2015; Rajunov and Duane, 2019; Keyes et al., 2021; D'Ignazio and Klein, 2020), media studies (Gitelman, 2013), archival studies (Agostinho et al., 2019), sociolinguistics (Labov, 1986; Cheshire, 2007), and critical race theory (Noble, 2018; Benjamin, 2019).[2]

Scholars argue that technical systems are embedded in social contexts (Lepawsky, 2019; Haraway, 1988) and are therefore necessarily evaluated as socio-technical systems interacting with complex social hierarchies (Winner, 1980; Benjamin, 2019; Costanza-Chock, 2018; Friedler et al., 2021). When technological systems prioritize majorities, there is a risk they oppress minorities at the personal, communal, and institutional levels (Costanza-Chock, 2018). Haraway (1988) argues that researchers default to a "view from nowhere", without reflecting on the context or use of their research. This default view often represents the interests of dominant majorities, disregarding knowledges from marginalized communities. Considering machine learning systems, Chun (2021) argues that the development of such technological systems relies on faulty assumptions (e.g., that past data collections can adequately and fairly predict future human behavior) which can lead to embedded social biases. Situating ourselves in the wider academic literature of social discrimination and marginalization, compels us to recognize that our technical systems must be considered in the social context in which they exist.

2.2 Machine-learned Systems in Social Context

On the topic of socially discriminatory systems within machine learning, Buolamwini and Gebru (2018) and Raji and Buolamwini (2019) show that there are significant disparities along gendered and racialized lines in commercially available facial recognition and analysis systems. Similar issues of discriminatory social biases in natural language processing (NLP) systems have resulted in emerging research dedicated to the identification, quantification (e.g. Rudinger et al., 2018; De-Arteaga et al., 2019; Czarnowska et al., 2021), and mitigation of bias (Bolukbasi et al., 2016; Sun et al., 2019; Garimella et al., 2021) in NLP systems.

However, these methods tend to obscure rather than remove social biases (Gonen and Goldberg, 2019), and are particularly brittle when applied to complex, contextual language representations (Dev et al., 2020).

Further, operationalization of under-specified "bias" has varied widely across studies, and in some cases has been internally inconsistent with their stated goals (Blodgett et al., 2020; Jacobs and Wallach, 2021). The recent surge of LLMs is no exception to such concerns. Hovy and Prabhumoye (2021); Talat et al. (2021), and Cao and Daumé III (2020) argue that socially discriminatory biases can be encoded in several stages of the LLM development process (Biderman and Scheirer, 2020), including data sampling, annotation, selection of input representations or model, research design, and how the models are situated with regards to the language communities that they are applied to. Language generation models, despite their inference-time flexibility, are particularly susceptible to reproducing hegemonic social biases and generating offensive language, even when not explicitly prompted to do so (Sheng et al., 2021; Wallace et al., 2019; Bender et al., 2021).

In efforts to address the expression of such social biases, a number of bias evaluation benchmarks have been proposed (Dev et al., 2021b; Zhao et al., 2018; Cao and Daumé III, 2020). However, common evaluation benchmarks are fraught with pitfalls in their conceptualization of bias, stereotypes, and harms, including meaningless or poorly formed stereotype constructions, non-intersectional examples, contexts that don't reflect downstream use, and reliance on specific model architectures (Blodgett et al., 2021; Jin et al., 2021). Furthermore, bias evaluation benchmarks often make strong assumptions about the validity, reliability, and existence of observable properties, e.g. pronouns, as signals for unobservable theoretical constructs such as gender (Jacobs and Wallach, 2021). This is particularly problematic when building benchmarks for biases against communities that resist categorization based on observable characteristics (e.g. LGBTQIA+ and racialized people) and leads to reliance on existing stereotypes (Tomasev et al., 2021; Dev et al., 2021a).

This rapid development of NLP resources and tools have further yielded a non-inclusive environment, skewed heavily towards English and Anglo-centric biases (Joshi et al., 2020). Sambasivan et al. (2021) and Chan et al. (2021) contend there remains a significant gap between the communities governing and governed by AI, and advocate for a redistribution of powers and responsibilities in developing responsible AI.

Considering gender bias, Stanczak and Augenstein (2021) show that existing methods (1) largely avoid ethical considerations or evaluations of gender bias, (2) focus primarily on binary gender treatment, in mostly Anglo-centric settings, and (3) employ limited or flawed evaluation methodologies. Such issues are in part exacerbated by the general poverty of documentation of datasets (Gebru et al., 2018; Bender and Friedman, 2018) and machine learning models (Mitchell et al., 2019). One way to mitigate these biases includes creating diverse teams with varied backgrounds and life experiences to assure the expression of diverse perspectives (Monteiro and Castillo, 2019; Nekoto et al., 2020).

[2]Many recent works on socially biased technological systems are interdisciplinary, e.g., 'Race After Technology: The New Jim Code' (Benjamin, 2019) spans critical race theory, science and technology, Black feminism, and media studies.

However, as critiqued by Talat et al. (2021); West et al. (2019), incorporating the diversity factor may be inadequate. Biases in language representations and task models can not only reflect, but also amplify bias present in the datasets (Barocas and Selbst, 2016; Wang et al., 2019). These biases have been investigated and attempts made at creating interpretable representations and providing post-hoc explanations of model predictions.

2.3 Bias, Fairness, and Explainability

Given the grave consequences that inherent or conceptualized biases in ML systems can inflict, *responsible AI* has received a growing amount of research attention (Amershi et al., 2020). Responsible AI refers to the creation of ethical principles for AI and the development of AI systems based on these principles (Dignum, 2017; Schiff, 2020). Colloquially, responsible AI encompasses distinct machine learning fields such as fairness, explainability, privacy, and interpretability. Concretely, how can responsible AI principles best contribute to the development of equitable systems?

Examining this question, Friedler et al. (2021) propose that building just ML systems requires an *a priori* definition of fairness. However, contemporary decision-making systems build on a so-called what-you-see-is-what-you-get (WYSIWYG) approach that implicitly imbibes multiple fairness definitions or world views, leading to a system based on the conflict between the underlying value systems. To tackle this issue, ML engineers should explicitly state the underlying systemic values, as systems will inevitably comprise certain assumptions (Birhane et al., 2021). Thus, implying that biases as inherent to these decision-making systems and should be clearly articulated (Bender et al., 2021) by explaining the whys and whats (explainability).

However, a more promising course of action for researchers would be to prioritize fairness in the entire life cycle of a language model. The tendency to consider and mitigate undesirable biases in models after training has completed leaves harmful residues that affect the communities we seek to protect (Dev et al., 2021a). Hence, a fruitful approach could be to reduce systemic unfairness by grounding the discussion on clear definitions of fairness based on input from the communities that could be harmed by the system (Liao and Muller, 2019), explaining the inherent biases, and, if possible, minimizing bias issues by employing the measures discussed in, both, the previous and the following sections.

3 Challenges of Bias

Evaluating the social impacts and harmful biases LLMs exhibit is an important development step. However, despite the increased interest in developing bias benchmarks, the field still faces various challenges in evaluating LLMs with *off-the-shelf* benchmarks. In this section, we provide examples of existing bias measures currently used in NLP. We then discuss the challenges that originate from these: (1) they rely on vague definitions of bias, (2) are restricted to particular model architectures, (3) have limited relevance for different cultural contexts, and (4) are difficult to validate and interpret.

3.1 Examples of Bias Measure Studies

Recently, researchers and practitioners have begun to pay more attention to bias measures in NLP systems (Blodgett et al., 2020; Dev et al., 2021b). One line of work has focused on identifying bias in word embeddings: The Word Embedding Association Test (WEAT, Caliskan et al., 2017) measures bias by comparing the relative distances of two sets of target words (e.g. occupation words: *nurse, doctor*) with respect to two sets of attribute words (e.g., gender attributes: *male, female*)—and has inspired other similar approaches (Kurita et al., 2019; May et al., 2019; Dev et al., 2020).

Although word embeddings may help identify biases in the context of LLMs, it is often difficult to access the learned contextual language representations of the model (Abid et al., 2021; Dev et al., 2020). Furthermore, such methods are developed to address static word embeddings rather than the dynamic contextual word embeddings LLMs rely on (Subramonian, 2021).

Another research direction is the use of causal inference for measuring biases in LLMs, for example to analyze if the generated text by an LLM is affected considerably by only changing the protected attributes or categories in the input (Huang et al., 2020; Madaan et al., 2021; Cheng et al., 2021). In line with this idea, Huang et al. (2020) used a sentiment classifier to quantify and reduce the sentiment bias existent in LLMs. Similarly, the CrowS-Pairs benchmark (Nangia et al., 2020) leverages the paradigm of minimal pairs to contrast sentences expressing stereotypes against social categories with the same sentences addressing different social categories. Crows-Pairs is designed such for language models to be probed for disparate behavior between the sentences pairs, with the hypothesis that systematic difference in the treatment reflecting the preference for stereotype indicates the presence of bias in the language models. Other examples of bias measures benchmarks include StereoSet (Nadeem et al., 2020), WinoMT (Stanovsky et al., 2019), BBQ (Parrish et al., 2021), BOLD (Dhamala et al., 2021), and Toxicity Comment Classification competition (Jigsaw, 2017).

3.2 Defining Bias

The term "bias" is overloaded in the ML and NLP communities, as it is used in the lay (a prejudice towards or against some entity) and the statistical sense (a systematic deviation from a distribution's mean) (Campolo et al., 2018). Moreover, researchers often refer to vague definitions of bias and gloss over the details, which results in methods that lack specificity (Blodgett et al., 2020). When discussing methods to address bias, it is critical to be precise about the bias being addressed.

Bias can, for instance, be made more specific by being defined along socially relevant dimensions. Nangia et al. (2020) consider the protected categories from the US Equal Employment Opportunities Commission and Queer in AI uses a similar list (*gender identity and expression, sexual orientation, disability, neurodivergence, skill set, physical appearance, body size, race, caste, age, nationality, citizenship status, colonial experience, religion*), yet other characteristics may be relevant elsewhere in the world (e.g. illness, migrant, and social status).[3] However, protected classes are only one dimension along which to define bias; researchers should also be mindful of political biases and biases resulting from the focus on prestigious, highly resourced language varieties, in additions to the intersections of multiple dimensions (Kearns et al., 2018; Buolamwini and Gebru, 2018; Crenshaw, 1991).

With respect to any of the aforementioned dimensions, a "bias" is a preferential disposition towards or against an entity. Colloquially, it is perceived negatively and considered to be unfair treatment. As pointed out by Barocas et al. (2017), biases in language models can manifest in the form of *quality-of-service* and *representation* disparities. As quality-of-service bias describes subpar performance of a language model when used by a particular group. For example, LLM-driven machine translation systems provide significantly better support for "prestigious", high-resource languages, and consequently deny quality performance to individuals who do not speak these languages (Nekoto et al., 2020). Furthermore, in fundamental NLP tasks such as coreference resolution, LLMs can fail for people who use neopronouns, and often capture meaningless representations for language associated with trans and non-binary individuals. (Cao and Daumé III, 2020; Dev et al., 2021a). Additionally, Blodgett et al. (2018) show that parsing systems trained primarily on White Mainstream American English exhibit disparate performance on African American English and Tan et al. (2020) show that English question answering and machine translation systems often fail on the morphological variation that is often present in non-prestige and Learner Englishes.

Representation biases consist of stereotypes and under-representation (or over-representation) of data or model outputs. Stereotyping is a cognitive process that manifests from often negative cultural norms about a characteristic; stereotyping permeates what people do, say, or write. A long line of work has shown that language models capture social stereotypes, for example, with respect to binary gender and occupations (Zhao et al., 2018; Bordia and Bowman, 2019; de Vassimon Manela et al., 2021). With regard to (under)representation, in MIMIC-III, a clinical notes dataset, only 1.9% of patients identify as Asian, in comparison to 71.5% who identify as white (Chen et al., 2020). Furthermore, blocklists in the Colossal Clean Crawled Corpus (C4) dataset disproportionately filter words related to queerness and language that is not White-aligned English (Dodge et al., 2021). Notably, quality-of-service and representation biases are not mutually exclusive; for instance, the brittle representations learned by a LLM for language associated with trans and non-binary individuals largely stems from the severe under-representation of this in training data (Dev et al., 2021a; Barocas and Selbst, 2016).

The breakdown of biases into quality-of-service and representation disparities is only one of many possible lenses. It is also critical to explicitly consider biases stemming from disparities in resources, broadly defined in terms of data availability, time to invest into dataset curation, access to compute resources, financial resources, and more (Bender et al., 2021).

3.3 Overreliance on Model Architectures

Current benchmarks often measure bias in specific downstream tasks (e.g. Machine Translation (Stanovsky et al., 2019), Question Answering (Parrish et al., 2021), or Text Generation (Dhamala et al., 2021)), while others focus on bias in LLMs more generally (e.g Kurita et al., 2019; Nadeem et al., 2020; Nangia et al., 2020). This has the advantage of being more widely applicable, as many NLP systems are based on LLMs, and it avoids the need for creating and validating a new benchmark for each possible downstream task. Yet, when the benchmarks heavily rely on the model architecture rather than the task specification, quantitative comparison between different models based on these benchmarks is no longer possible. In such cases, it also becomes more difficult to assess the validity of the bias measure in how it relates to other benchmarks (criterion validity) and the more abstract notion of fairness (construct validity).

Some researchers circumvent this problem by adapting the original bias metric, but care should be taken when doing so. For instance, bias metrics originally developed for masked language models have been adapted by using perplexity (e.g. Nadeem et al., 2020) or prompting (e.g. Gao et al., 2021; Sanh et al., 2021) instead. While these could still result in important insights, they also open new questions. Are the underlying assumptions of the bias measure still valid? Can you compare the bias metrics across different (future) types of models? Do the results of the initial validation of the benchmark still hold? And how does the kind of training data impact the evaluation that assumes a different training domain (e.g., legal texts vs. social media)?

While bias is ideally defined independently of the particular model architecture—not least because implementations change over time—we should not fall into a generalization trap either. As argued before, bias is inherent to systems and context-sensitive, and we should not strive for a panacea bias measure. Instead, the goal should be to develop methods that are task-specific yet independent of a given architecture, to the degree that

[3] Queer in AI (`http://queerinai.org/`) is a grassroots D&I organization that seeks to empower queer and trans researchers in AI and advance research at the intersections of AI and queerness. Their list of categories can be found here: `http://queerinai.org/code-of-conduct`.

this is possible. Researchers should keep this tension between task- and architecture-specific measures in mind when designing methods for measuring biases in LLMs.

3.4 Bias Measures are Anglo-centric

Despite the need for evaluating LLMs for a wide range of languages, bias benchmarks that cover non-English languages are rare (Zhou et al., 2019; Joshi et al., 2020). As a solution, simply translating existing English benchmarks is not ideal: manual translation is a labor-intensive and highly skilled task, while automated translations are prone to errors and could potentially introduce new algorithmic sources of bias. Moreover, translated benchmarks may only test for Anglo-centric biases, which do not necessarily hold in many non-Western cultural contexts. For instance, many gender bias evaluations focus on Western professions, which are grammatically gendered in some languages (Chen et al., 2021; Zhou et al., 2019) or may not cover other prevalent occupations outside the U.S. (Escudé Font and Costa-jussà, 2019). WinoMT (Stanovsky et al., 2019) is one of the few benchmarks that covers multiple languages, but it comes with its own downsides. The sentences are generated from templates that capture a limited range of actual language use; the samples are translated from English examples, which may not reflect how stereotypes would occur in other languages; and the scope is limited to machine translation systems, and therefore WinoMT may not be suitable for multilingual models that are not trained on this specific task. The tightly coupled nature of bias and cultural context should be emphasized when designing a multilingual bias benchmark.

3.5 Validity of Bias Measures

Towards making NLP systems more just, we must understand the flaws of common bias measures and develop better guidelines to address biases. According to Jacobs and Wallach (2021) and Blodgett et al. (2021), bias measures are measurement models which link observable properties, e.g., quality-of-service and representational biases, with unobservable theoretical constructs such as social discrimination, power dynamics, and systemic oppression. Consequently, bias measures are deeply political. Notably, a vast majority of bias measures themselves rely on other measurement models, such as the presence of gendered pronouns, to infer theoretical protected categories, e.g., gender. Moreover, bias measures may cause further epistemic violence onto the marginalized by creating a veneer of fairness, in spite of ongoing marginalization (Gonen and Goldberg, 2019; Talat et al., 2021; Jacobs and Wallach, 2021). In ensuring the reliability, validity, and correct interpretation of bias measures, it is critical to examine all components in a bias measurement method.

Upstream measurement models that infer protected categories can be unreliable or even non-existent. For instance, pronouns and gendered names are usually employed as proxies for binary gender, which is problematic (Dev et al., 2021a). Furthermore, characteristics like sexuality and disability are usually unobservable, which can lead to a reliance on hegemonic stereotypes and unnatural language in bias evaluation benchmarks (Tomasev et al., 2021; Hutchinson et al., 2020).

With regard to validity, Blodgett et al. (2021) reviews how bias measures often rely on operationalization of stereotypes that are invalid for reasons such as misalignment and conflation. Additionally, the mathematical formalization of most bias measures is based on notions of parity-based fairness and do not reflect other conceptualizations of fairness such as distributive justice (Jacobs and Wallach, 2021). Another source of invalidity of bias measures lies in the purported generality of associated benchmarks. Raji et al. (2021) argue that the "instantiation [of benchmarks] in particular data, metrics and practice" undermines the validity of their construction to have "general applicability." Moreover, measurement models for protected categories fallaciously assume that the identities being indirectly observed can be discretized. Hence, Dev et al. (2021b) advocate for documenting the limitations of bias measures and related data in terms of their validity. In this process, it is critical to describe the relationship between the context of the data, model usage, and bias measure at stake.

4 The Elephant in the Room: Power, Privilege, and Point of View

Throughout the paper, we have primarily discussed bias in language models as a mechanical phenomenon. However, it is important to situate these discussions within the context and power dynamics of the way that NLP is practiced — both in research and in application (Miceli et al., 2022). In this section, we discuss sociopolitical influences on AI ethics and bias research in NLP. We argue that contemporary developments of LLMs have been an exercise in financial, institutional, ecological, linguistic, and cultural privilege. They are the consequence of the political will to create totalizing technologies and evaluation of bias, fairness and social impact should be viewed as a countervailing power mechanism, although in some cases serve to obscure these.

4.1 Large Language Models are Expensive

The current dominant paradigm in natural language processing is driven by the creation of ever-larger pretrained transformer models (Brown et al., 2020). As the size of LLMs increases, so do the requirements for hardware, energy, and time. For example, GPT-NeoX 20B (Black et al., 2022) was trained for 1830 hours on 96 A100 GPUs, consuming 43.92 MWh of electricity and emitting 23 metric tons of CO_2. Based on the current price listing of the cloud provider the model was trained on, training such a model would cost between 250,000 and 500,000 USD.[4] While this is not on the scale of the

[4]The lower end of this range reflects the common practice of giving discounts of up to 50% for large purchases, while

largest research programs, it is a significant amount of money and beyond the funding of many institutions, or beyond their political will to spend.

While the development of such models can contribute towards improving the ability of people with less resources to pursue cutting edge *downstream* research, such pursuits have significant costs and barriers to entry for *upstream* research. This creates a stratification of research, wherein money is a barrier of entry for some forms of research but not for others.

4.2 Language is Multicultural, Language Models are Not

Although there are thousands of spoken languages in the world, the overwhelming majority of LLMs are monolingual and encode white respectability politics (Thylstrup and Talat, 2020; Kerrison et al., 2018) onto minoritized variants of English (Gehman et al., 2020). In this way, the cost of the developing LLMs extends from externalizing computational and infrastructural costs, to externalizing languages and language variants (Lau, 2021). Specifically, the vast majority of LLMs are trained to operate on an unspecified variant of "English" (Bender, 2019), and in some cases Chinese (see Table 1 for a detailed overview of the top 25 LLMs). The dominance of English, and to a lesser degree Chinese, reifies cultural hegemonies and precipitates technological imperialism. Even when researchers seek to include other languages, these purportedly multilingual models often underserve certain languages and communities (Kerrison et al., 2018; Virtanen et al., 2019; Kreutzer et al., 2022; Gururangan et al., 2022). We also note that few of these models have been assessed for bias or fairness (see table 1).

This act relies on two foundations. First, LLMs should only be used for languages that they have been developed for, with the cultural stereotypes that they have been trained on, thus limiting LLMs to be used within a small set of cultural contexts, or casting cultural contexts for which they are trained onto ones that they are not developed for. Second, should a multilingual LLM be trained, its primary data sources will still be in English, whereas the remaining languages will only be incidental to it. Such cultural imperialism is evident from the fact that only 2 of the 14 organizations involved in developing LLMs have teams in multiple countries (see table 1). Further, all multinational LLM efforts, except for one, draw their membership from the USA, UK, Germany, & Australia. GPT-NeoX 20B (Black et al., 2022) is an exception, as it also includes authors from India. A commonly-used resource for developing LLMs, CommonCrawl, relies on data that primarily stems from the US (Dodge et al., 2021) and is written in privileged dialects of English (Dunn, 2020). This prioritization is reflected by 16 teams being physically located in the U.S. Consequently, the current state of LLM development is a totalizing endeavor (Talat et al., 2021), which engages in externalization across a number of axes, as is apparent from the infrastructural and development practices and the efforts to evaluate and mitigate social harms that arise from such technologies.

4.3 Large Language Models Allow Powerful Actors to Control NLP Research

Due to the costs involved with training large language models and the small number of actors who have decided to train them, the overwhelming majority of research studying their properties is not carried out by people who train LLMs. When the actors that do possess the models choose to not publicly release them, model trainers are afforded control over the research that can be conducted with and by these models. Famously, OpenAI's initial announcement of GPT-3 asserted that access to the model would be heavily restricted while the company continued to research ethical interventions in their model. OpenAI is not alone in this; the idea that it is inherently dangerous to release models to the public has been put forth by several other actors in this space (Weidinger et al., 2021a; Askell et al., 2021).

It is essential to recognize that the decisions regarding access and the kind of research that can be conducted on large language models (or any ML models, for that matter) is an inherently political one (Leahy and Biderman, 2021). Regardless of the truth of the aforementioned claims, they are highly contentious political claims and should be treated as such rather than passively accepted.

Direct access to LLMs is important to perform independent research on their datasets, functions, and societal impact (Kandpal et al., 2022; Carlini et al., 2022). While language models produced by the academic research community are widely available for critical examination, commercial systems are often only available through APIs provided by the developers (see table 1 for an overview on access for the 25 largest pretrained language models. Such restrictions to access to the models and resources that they are developed for provide a significant barrier to a) principles of open science and b) research on how the datasets and language models themselves embed and amplify social biases.

5 Addressing Bias

Researchers have developed various strategies to address bias in large language models. As discussed in earlier sections, however, these strategies are insufficient to tackle multiple dimensions of bias. Below, we enumerate a few ways in which bias can be addressed by the research community to effectively engage with our aforementioned concerns: (1) moving towards a more transparent way of evaluating bias, (2) focusing on the diversity of stereotypes and increasing inclusivity, and (3) considering the impact of linguistic and cultural differences on the identification and mitigation of bias in designing culturally comparable datasets. We would like to highlight that these suggestions are not exhaustive. They will, however, guide the work in this area.

the upper end reflects the sticker price of the systems.

5.1 Transparency Through Documentation

Stereotypes and biases cover a broad definition and vary in conceptualization across geographical and cultural contexts. To ensure that the nuances are well communicated and that practitioners understand the applicability of the evaluation approach, we suggest documenting a thorough analysis of the scope. Below, we provide a starting point based on Mitchell et al. (2019); Gebru et al. (2018); Dev et al. (2021b); Blodgett et al. (2020).

Defining the scope of the approach Blodgett et al. (2020) found that works around bias "often fail to explain what kinds of system behaviors are harmful, in what ways, to whom, and why." It thus becomes imperative to question what underrepresented groups would benefit more from a given evaluation benchmark. We therefore urge researchers and practitioners to clearly specify the demographic a particular method is relevant for. Moreover, given how social hierarchies intertwine tightly with language and may present themselves through its peculiarities, we also encourage researchers to specify the limitations and scope of their approaches.

As an example, we consider the gender bias evaluation in English (Zhao et al., 2018; Stanovsky et al., 2019; Levy et al., 2021; Sharma et al., 2021), where the bias might present itself through strong associations between grammatical constructs like pronouns. The same does not hold true for genderless languages, despite the existence of the bias (Zmigrod et al., 2019). Thus, evaluation benchmarks and approaches do not always transfer well to other languages. Additionally, while such benchmarks use gender associations to professions for their evaluation, this method covers only one aspect of the social hierarchy, and does not address gender bias in language in its entirety. By being binary in nature and tightly coupled to Anglo-centric contexts (see §3) benchmarks are limited in their scope and relevance. While most recent works do include ethical considerations, the limitations and scope are only vaguely specified. We advocate for such limitations to be highlighted and pointed out for the community to have a clearer picture about the steps that need to be taken towards greater inclusivity.

Documenting the demographics Previous work has highlighted the importance of engaging with individuals on the receiving end of the bias (Bender et al., 2021). It thus becomes important to understand the demographics of those involved in the creation of the benchmarks. As previously shown (Al Kuwatly et al., 2020) there exists a relation between annotators' identities and toxicity/bias in dataset. On this basis, we urge the researchers to collect and document the demographic information and annotator attitude scores (Sap et al., 2021). Building upon the same, we encourage the collection and reporting of this information about the researchers involved.

5.2 Diversity Beyond Gender Bias

The majority of previous work on bias has focused particularly on gender bias (Zhao et al., 2018; Stanovsky et al., 2019; Levy et al., 2021; Sharma et al., 2021) and the very few works (Nadeem et al., 2020; Nangia et al., 2020) that take other dimensions of biases into account, have their own shortcomings, as discussed in Section 3. It thus becomes important to diversify the range of bias and stereotypes that are being investigated by research, and covered by a certain evaluation technique. In extending the coverage to more dimensions, context stands as an important aspect of bias. The contextual aspects of bias as represented in language, culture, and history hold a significant role in forming and assessing the bias itself. Hence, as a practice, we encourage researchers to consider these three aspects when constructing bias measures and datasets.

In discussing bias, it is important to note that discrimination does not occur in a vacuum. An act of discrimination against a person may be directed towards several intersecting identities. Considering bias using a single-axis framework makes it impossible to engage with and evaluate the harms extended to the social groups that lie at the intersection of multiple identities (Crenshaw, 1991). In an Indian context, for example, even those who identify as belonging to the "same" caste (Malik et al., 2021), can have varied lived experiences based on class, gender, and other identities. More precisely, it is impossible to disentangle which specific identity a discriminatory act is directed against. Previous works have highlighted the importance of studying intersectional bias (Bender et al., 2021; Buolamwini and Gebru, 2018; Field et al., 2021; Guo et al., 2019; Crenshaw, 1991) but little research has been conducted around addressing such biases (Magee et al., 2021; Guo and Caliskan, 2021). We thus encourage researchers to develop measures and benchmarks which are grounded in intersectional understanding of bias and adequately address the lived experiences of various social groups, towards increased inclusivity and fairness.

Not only can the dimensions and context influence our definitions and approaches to bias, but the categories (values) assigned to each dimension (e.g., age) can also limit our understanding and solution of bias. For instance, the majority of gender-bias evaluation datasets solely deal with binary gender, i.e., male and female, with just a handful covering non-binary genders with only minimal representation (Dev et al., 2021a; Cao and Daumé III, 2020). As a result, category inclusiveness is critical in the development of a high-quality bias evaluation dataset. A set of categories that can act as a starting point are provided by Queer in AI in Section 3.2.

5.3 Acknowledging Differences

Stereotype and bias formation is influenced by culture. As a result, what might be a stereotype in a given culture might not stand relevant in another. For instance, the characterization that `parental leave is for mothers` is considered stereotypical in the United States, but not in Sweden, where parental leave is split between both parents.

	Organization	Author Location	Language	Parameters	Model Access	Bias Eval
MT-NLG	Microsoft, NVIDIA	USA	English	530 B	Closed	Smith et al. (2022)
Gopher	DeepMind	USA	English	280 B	Closed	Weidinger et al. (2021b)
ERNIE 3.0	Baidu	China	English, Chinese	260 B	Closed	—
Yuan 1.0	Inspur AI	China	Chinese	245 B	Closed	—
HyperCLOVA	NAVER	Korea	Korean	204 B	Closed	—
PanGu-α	Huawei	China	Chinese	200 B	Closed	—
Jurassic-1	AI21 Labs	Israel	English	178 B	Commercial	—
GPT-3	OpenAI	USA	English	175 B	Commercial	Brown et al. (2020)
LaMDA	Google	USA	English	137 B	Closed	Thoppilan et al. (2022)
Anthropic LM	Anthropic	USA	English	52 B	Closed	Askell et al. (2021)
GPT-NeoX-20B	EleutherAI	Multinational	English	20 B	Open	(Gao et al., 2020; Biderman et al., 2022)
Turing NLG	Microsoft	USA	English	17 B	Closed	—
FairSeq Dense	Meta AI	Multinational	English	13 B	Open	—
mT5	Google	USA	Multilingual	13 B	Open	—
ByT5	Google	USA	English	13 B	Open	—
T5	Google	USA	English	11 B	Open	—
CPM 2.1	Tsinghua University	China	Chinese	11 B	Open	—
Megatron 11B	NVIDIA	USA	English	11 B	Open	—
WuDao-GLM-XXL	Beijing Academy of AI	China	Chinese	10 B	Open	—
WuDao-GLM-XXL	Beijing Academy of AI	China	English	10 B	Open	—
BlenderBot	Meta AI	USA	English	9 B	Open	—
Megatron-LM	NVIDIA	USA	English	8 B	Closed	—
XGLM	Meta AI	Multinational	Multilingual	7 B	Open	—
GPT-J-6B	EleutherAI	Multinational	English	6 B	Open	(Gao et al., 2020; Biderman et al., 2022)

Table 1: The 25 largest pretrained dense language models, ranging from 6 billion parameters to 530 billion. Models are overwhelmingly trained by teams located in the US and on English text. Less than half of the language models were evaluated for bias by their creators.

Previous sections have criticized the Anglo-centricity in the research of NLP bias and the influence on languages other than English. In particular, the lack of culturally-aware datasets limits the degree to which future NLP algorithms can be evaluated for biases. More crucially, these unspecified languages and cultures are on the receiving end of unmanaged effects. As a result, researchers are encouraged to develop bias datasets and benchmarks for non Anglo-centric cultures and languages (Bender et al., 2021). Involving experts in related areas, especially participants with lived experiences of language-related harms, might aid decisions at all parts of this process, e.g. deciding what groups and content to include in research or dataset design (Liao and Muller, 2019; Dev et al., 2021a; McMillan-Major et al., 2022). Overall, having culturally diverse and comparable datasets for a diverse set of languages (ideally covering all languages) is critical for evaluating multilingual models. Moreover, the applicability of bias measures across various languages suggests the necessity for cross-linguistic metrics or measurements that can be extended to different languages or cultures (Zhou et al., 2019; Escudé Font and Costa-jussà, 2019; Malik et al., 2021).

6 Conclusion

Recent improvements in LLMs to mimic human text have led to a surge in research that seeks to identify and address the harms arising from their training and deployment. However, the considerations on social harms that arise has been limited to narrow, Anglo-centric, contradictory, and often underspecified definitions of fairness and bias. Furthermore, the development of contemporary methods has conflated task-specific and architecture-specific designations. Compounded with the structural inequalities around resources, language, and identity, this has yielded an overreliance on prestige forms of English for developing LLMs and interrogating and addressing the social biases that they harbor. Situating these methods within such Englishes has had the consequence of over-emphasizing Western-centric social categories. Moreover, datasets for evaluating social biases in LLMs have traditionally failed to denote and specify the context within which biases are situated. Such concerns have been the cause for questions around the validity of the developed measures, and in particular for multilingual LLMs.

To address such challenges, we propose that developing methods for multilingual LLMs requires researchers to provide thorough documentation of their approaches, including documenting the scope, demographics of speakers, and potential annotators. Additionally, we also recommend that researchers situate their bias evaluation methods within the specific context of the languages that the model operates on. In doing so, bias evaluation methods can be made to specifically address biases under the conditions and contexts that they occur in each of the model's languages. Furthermore, we recommend that researchers examine diversity issues beyond gender bias, with a particular focus on intersectional issues (Guo and Caliskan, 2021).

Finally, we recommend that researchers are cognizant of the social and environmental harms that developing LLMs have. For instance, developing ever-larger language models that achieve marginal improvements for English may bring a smaller benefit than developing a LLM for other languages. Thus, in a consideration of developing a new language model, we implore researchers to consider ways in which harms can be limited, or the benefits can come to compensate for their costs.

References

Abubakar Abid, Maheen Farooqi, and James Zou. 2021. Persistent Anti-Muslim Bias in Large Language Models. In *AIES 2021 - Proceedings of the 2021 AAAI/ACM Conference on AI, Ethics, and Society*.

Daniela Agostinho, Catherine D'Ignazio, Annie Ring, Nanna Bonde Thylstrup, and Kristin Veel. 2019. Uncertain Archives: Approaching the Unknowns, Errors, and Vulnerabilities of Big Data through Cultural Theories of the Archive. *Surveillance & Society*, 17(3/4):422–441.

Blaise Aguera y Arcas, Alexander Todorov, and Margaret Mitchell. 2018. Do algorithms reveal sexual orientation or just expose our stereotypes?

Hala Al Kuwatly, Maximilian Wich, and Georg Groh. 2020. Identifying and measuring annotator bias based on annotators' demographic characteristics. In *Proceedings of the Fourth Workshop on Online Abuse and Harms*, pages 184–190, Online. Association for Computational Linguistics.

Liz Allen, Alison O'Connell, and Veronique Kiermer. 2019. How can we ensure visibility and diversity in research contributions? How the Contributor Role Taxonomy (CRediT) is helping the shift from authorship to contributorship. *Learned Publishing*, 32(1):71–74.

Saleema Amershi, Ece Kamar, Kristin Lauter, Jenn Wortman Vaughan, and Hanna Wallach. 2020. Research Supporting Responsible AI.

Amanda Askell, Yuntao Bai, Anna Chen, Dawn Drain, Deep Ganguli, Tom Henighan, Andy Jones, Nicholas Joseph, Ben Mann, Nova DasSarma, Nelson Elhage, Zac Hatfield-Dodds, Danny Hernandez, Jackson Kernion, Kamal Ndousse, Catherine Olsson, Dario Amodei, Tom Brown, Jack Clark, Sam McCandlish, Chris Olah, and Jared Kaplan. 2021. A general language assistant as a laboratory for alignment.

Solon Barocas, Kate Crawford, Aaron Shapiro, and Hanna Wallach. 2017. The problem with bias: from allocative to representational harms in machine learning. special interest group for computing. *Information and Society (SIGCIS)*, 2.

Solon Barocas and Andrew D. Selbst. 2016. Big Data's Disparate Impact. *California Law Review*, 104(3).

Emily Bender. 2019. The #BenderRule: On Naming the Languages We Study and Why It Matters.

Emily M. Bender and Batya Friedman. 2018. Data Statements for Natural Language Processing: Toward Mitigating System Bias and Enabling Better Science. *Transactions of the Association for Computational Linguistics*, 6:587–604.

Emily M. Bender, Timnit Gebru, Angelina McMillan-Major, and Shmargaret Shmitchell. 2021. On the dangers of stochastic parrots: Can language models be too big? . In *Proceedings of the 2021 ACM Conference on Fairness, Accountability, and Transparency*, FAccT '21, page 610–623, New York, NY, USA. Association for Computing Machinery.

Emily M. Bender and Alexander Koller. 2020. Climbing towards NLU: On Meaning, Form, and Understanding in the Age of Data. In *Proceedings of the 58th Annual Meeting of the Association for Computational Linguistics*, pages 5185–5198, Online. Association for Computational Linguistics.

Ruha Benjamin. 2019. *Race after technology: abolitionist tools for the new Jim code*. Polity, Medford, MA.

Stella Biderman, Kieran Bicheno, and Leo Gao. 2022. Datasheet for the Pile. *arXiv:2201.07311 [cs]*. ArXiv: 2201.07311.

Stella Biderman and Walter Scheirer. 2020. Pitfalls in machine learning research: Reexamining the development cycle. In *"I Can't Believe It's Not Better!" NeurIPS 2020 workshop*.

Abeba Birhane, Pratyusha Kalluri, Dallas Card, William Agnew, Ravit Dotan, and Michelle Bao. 2021. The Values Encoded in Machine Learning Research. *arXiv:2106.15590 [cs]*. ArXiv: 2106.15590.

Sid Black, Stella Biderman, Eric Hallahan, Quentin Anthony, Leo Gao, Laurence Golding, Horace He, Connor Leahy, Kyle McDonell, Jason Phang, Michael Pieler, USVSN Sai Prashanth, Shivanshu Purohit, Laria Reynolds, Jonathan Tow, Ben Wang, and Samuel Weinbach. 2022. GPT-NeoX-20B: An Open-Source Autoregressive Language Model.

Su Lin Blodgett, Solon Barocas, Hal Daumé III, and Hanna Wallach. 2020. Language (Technology) is Power: A Critical Survey of "Bias" in NLP. In *Proceedings of the 58th Annual Meeting of the Association for Computational Linguistics*, pages 5454–5476, Online. Association for Computational Linguistics.

Su Lin Blodgett, Gilsinia Lopez, Alexandra Olteanu, Robert Sim, and Hanna Wallach. 2021. Stereotyping Norwegian Salmon: An Inventory of Pitfalls in Fairness Benchmark Datasets. In *Proceedings of the 59th Annual Meeting of the Association for Computational Linguistics and the 11th International Joint Conference on Natural Language Processing (Volume 1: Long Papers)*, pages 1004–1015, Online. Association for Computational Linguistics.

Su Lin Blodgett, Johnny Wei, and Brendan O'Connor. 2018. Twitter Universal Dependency parsing for African-American and mainstream American English. In *Proceedings of the 56th Annual Meeting of the Association for Computational Linguistics (Volume 1: Long Papers)*, pages 1415–1425, Melbourne, Australia. Association for Computational Linguistics.

Tolga Bolukbasi, Kai-Wei Chang, James Y Zou, Venkatesh Saligrama, and Adam T Kalai. 2016. Man is to computer programmer as woman is to homemaker? debiasing word embeddings. In *Advances in Neural Information Processing Systems*, volume 29. Curran Associates, Inc.

Shikha Bordia and Samuel R. Bowman. 2019. Identifying and Reducing Gender Bias in Word-Level Language Models. In *Proceedings of the 2019 Conference of the North*, pages 7–15, Minneapolis, Minnesota. Association for Computational Linguistics.

Tom Brown, Benjamin Mann, Nick Ryder, Melanie Subbiah, Jared D. Kaplan, Prafulla Dhariwal, Arvind Neelakantan, Pranav Shyam, Girish Sastry, Amanda Askell, Sandhini Agarwal, Ariel Herbert-Voss, Gretchen Krueger, Tom Henighan, Rewon Child, Aditya Ramesh, Daniel Ziegler, Jeffrey Wu, Clemens Winter, Chris Hesse, Mark Chen, Eric Sigler, Mateusz Litwin, Scott Gray, Benjamin Chess, Jack Clark, Christopher Berner, Sam McCandlish, Alec Radford, Ilya Sutskever, and Dario Amodei. 2020. Language Models are Few-Shot Learners. In *Advances in Neural Information Processing Systems*, volume 33, pages 1877–1901. Curran Associates, Inc.

Joy Buolamwini and Timnit Gebru. 2018. Gender Shades: Intersectional Accuracy Disparities in Commercial Gender Classification. In *Proceedings of the 1st Conference on Fairness, Accountability and Transparency*, volume 81 of *Proceedings of Machine Learning Research*, pages 77–91, New York, NY, USA. PMLR.

Aylin Caliskan, Joanna J. Bryson, and Arvind Narayanan. 2017. Semantics derived automatically from language corpora contain human-like biases. *Science*, 356(6334).

Alex Campolo, Madelyn Sanfilippo, Meredith Whittaker, and Kate Crawford. 2018. AI now 2017 report. In *AI now 2017 symposium and workshop*. AI Now Institute at New York University. Edition: AI Now 2017 Symposium and Workshop.

Yang Trista Cao and Hal Daumé III. 2020. Toward Gender-Inclusive Coreference Resolution. In *Proceedings of the 58th Annual Meeting of the Association for Computational Linguistics*, pages 4568–4595, Online. Association for Computational Linguistics.

Nicholas Carlini, Daphne Ippolito, Matthew Jagielski, Katherine Lee, Florian Tramer, and Chiyuan Zhang. 2022. Quantifying memorization across neural language models. *arXiv preprint arXiv:2202.07646*.

Alan Chan, Chinasa T. Okolo, Zachary Terner, and Angelina Wang. 2021. The Limits of Global Inclusion in AI Development. *arXiv:2102.01265 [cs]*. ArXiv: 2102.01265.

John Chen, Ian Berlot-Attwell, Xindi Wang, Safwan Hossain, and Frank Rudzicz. 2020. Exploring text specific and blackbox fairness algorithms in multimodal clinical NLP. In *Proceedings of the 3rd Clinical Natural Language Processing Workshop*, pages 301–312, Online. Association for Computational Linguistics.

Yan Chen, Christopher Mahoney, Isabella Grasso, Esma Wali, Abigail Matthews, Thomas Middleton, Mariama Njie, and Jeanna Matthews. 2021. Gender Bias and Under-Representation in Natural Language Processing Across Human Languages. In *Proceedings of the 2021 AAAI/ACM Conference on AI, Ethics, and Society*, pages 24–34, Virtual Event USA. ACM.

Lu Cheng, Ahmadreza Mosallanezhad, Paras Sheth, and Huan Liu. 2021. Causal Learning for Socially Responsible AI. In *Proceedings of the Thirtieth International Joint Conference on Artificial Intelligence*.

Jenny Cheshire. 2007. An untitled review of "style and sociolinguistic variation". *Language*, 83(2):432–435.

Wendy Hui Kyong Chun. 2021. *Discriminating data: correlation, neighborhoods, and the new politics of recognition*. The MIT Press, Cambridge, Massachusetts.

Sasha Costanza-Chock. 2018. Design Justice, A.I., and Escape from the Matrix of Domination. *Journal of Design and Science*.

Kimberle Crenshaw. 1991. Mapping the margins: Intersectionality, identity politics, and violence against women of color. *Stanford Law Review*, 43(6):1241–1299.

Paula Czarnowska, Yogarshi Vyas, and Kashif Shah. 2021. Quantifying Social Biases in NLP: A Generalization and Empirical Comparison of Extrinsic Fairness Metrics. *Transactions of the Association for Computational Linguistics*, 9:1249–1267.

Debajyoti Datta, Jason A. Fries, Michael McKenna, Aurélie Névéol, Vassilina Nikoulina, and Maya Varma. 2021. Challenges in language modelling for biomedicine.

Maria De-Arteaga, Alexey Romanov, Hanna Wallach, Jennifer Chayes, Christian Borgs, Alexandra Chouldechova, Sahin Geyik, Krishnaram Kenthapadi, and Adam Tauman Kalai. 2019. Bias in Bios: A Case Study of Semantic Representation Bias in a High-Stakes Setting. In *Proceedings of the Conference on Fairness, Accountability, and Transparency*, pages 120–128, Atlanta GA USA. ACM.

Daniel de Vassimon Manela, David Errington, Thomas Fisher, Boris van Breugel, and Pasquale Minervini. 2021. Stereotype and Skew: Quantifying Gender Bias in Pre-trained and Fine-tuned Language Models. In *Proceedings of the 16th Conference of the European Chapter of the Association for Computational Linguistics: Main Volume*, pages 2232–2242, Online. Association for Computational Linguistics.

Sunipa Dev, Tao Li, Jeff M. Phillips, and Vivek Srikumar. 2020. On measuring and mitigating biased inferences of word embeddings. *Proceedings of the AAAI Conference on Artificial Intelligence*, 34(05):7659–7666.

Sunipa Dev, Masoud Monajatipoor, Anaelia Ovalle, Arjun Subramonian, Jeff Phillips, and Kai-Wei Chang. 2021a. Harms of gender exclusivity and challenges in non-binary representation in language technologies. In *Proceedings of the 2021 Conference on Empirical Methods in Natural Language Processing*, pages 1968–1994, Online and Punta Cana, Dominican Republic. Association for Computational Linguistics.

Sunipa Dev, Emily Sheng, Jieyu Zhao, Jiao Sun, Yu Hou, Mattie Sanseverino, Jiin Kim, Nanyun Peng, and Kai-Wei Chang. 2021b. What do bias measures measure?

Jwala Dhamala, Tony Sun, Varun Kumar, Satyapriya Krishna, Yada Pruksachatkun, Kai-Wei Chang, and Rahul Gupta. 2021. BOLD: Dataset and Metrics for Measuring Biases in Open-Ended Language Generation. In *Proceedings of the 2021 ACM Conference on Fairness, Accountability, and Transparency*, pages 862–872, Virtual Event Canada. ACM.

Catherine D'Ignazio and Lauren F. Klein. 2020. *Data feminism*. Strong ideas series. The MIT Press, Cambridge, Massachusetts.

Virginia Dignum. 2017. Responsible artificial intelligence: Designing ai for human values. *ICT Discoveries*.

Jesse Dodge, Maarten Sap, Ana Marasović, William Agnew, Gabriel Ilharco, Dirk Groeneveld, Margaret Mitchell, and Matt Gardner. 2021. Documenting large webtext corpora: A case study on the colossal clean crawled corpus. In *Proceedings of the 2021 Conference on Empirical Methods in Natural Language Processing*, pages 1286–1305, Online and Punta Cana, Dominican Republic. Association for Computational Linguistics.

Mary Douglas. 1978. *Purity and danger: an analysis of the concepts of pollution and taboo*, repr edition. Routledge, London. OCLC: 248038797.

Jonathan Dunn. 2020. Mapping languages: the Corpus of Global Language Use. *Language Resources and Evaluation*, 54(4):999–1018.

Joel Escudé Font and Marta R. Costa-jussà. 2019. Equalizing gender bias in neural machine translation with word embeddings techniques. In *Proceedings of the First Workshop on Gender Bias in Natural Language Processing*, pages 147–154, Florence, Italy. Association for Computational Linguistics.

Anjalie Field, Su Lin Blodgett, Zeerak Waseem, and Yulia Tsvetkov. 2021. A Survey of Race, Racism, and Anti-Racism in NLP. In *Proceedings of the 59th Annual Meeting of the Association for Computational Linguistics and the 11th International Joint Conference on Natural Language Processing (Volume 1: Long Papers)*, pages 1905–1925, Online. Association for Computational Linguistics.

Nancy Fraser. 1990. Rethinking the Public Sphere: A Contribution to the Critique of Actually Existing Democracy. *Social Text*, (25/26):56.

Sorelle A. Friedler, Carlos Scheidegger, and Suresh Venkatasubramanian. 2021. The (Im)possibility of fairness: different value systems require different mechanisms for fair decision making. *Communications of the ACM*, 64(4):136–143.

Leo Gao, Stella Biderman, Sid Black, Laurence Golding, Travis Hoppe, Charles Foster, Jason Phang, Horace He, Anish Thite, Noa Nabeshima, Shawn Presser, and Connor Leahy. 2020. The Pile: An 800GB Dataset of Diverse Text for Language Modeling. *arXiv:2101.00027 [cs]*. ArXiv: 2101.00027.

Tianyu Gao, Adam Fisch, and Danqi Chen. 2021. Making pre-trained language models better few-shot learners. In *Proceedings of the 59th Annual Meeting of the Association for Computational Linguistics and the 11th International Joint Conference on Natural Language Processing (Volume 1: Long Papers)*, pages 3816–3830, Online. Association for Computational Linguistics.

Aparna Garimella, Akhash Amarnath, Kiran Kumar, Akash Pramod Yalla, Anandhavelu N, Niyati Chhaya, and Balaji Vasan Srinivasan. 2021. He is very intelligent, she is very beautiful? On Mitigating Social Biases in Language Modelling and Generation. In *Findings of the Association for Computational Linguistics: ACL-IJCNLP 2021*, pages 4534–4545, Online. Association for Computational Linguistics.

Timnit Gebru, Jamie Morgenstern, Briana Vecchione, Jennifer Wortman Vaughan, Hanna Wallach, Hal Daumé III, and Kate Crawford. 2018. Datasheets for Datasets. *arXiv:1803.09010 [cs]*. ArXiv: 1803.09010.

Samuel Gehman, Suchin Gururangan, Maarten Sap, Yejin Choi, and Noah A. Smith. 2020. RealToxicityPrompts: Evaluating Neural Toxic Degeneration in Language Models. In *Findings of the Association for Computational Linguistics: EMNLP 2020*, pages 3356–3369, Online. Association for Computational Linguistics.

Lisa Gitelman. 2013. *Raw data is an oxymoron*. MIT press.

Hila Gonen and Yoav Goldberg. 2019. Lipstick on a Pig: Debiasing Methods Cover up Systematic Gender Biases in Word Embeddings But do not Remove Them. In *Proceedings of the 2019 Conference of the North*, pages 609–614, Minneapolis, Minnesota. Association for Computational Linguistics.

Anhong Guo, Ece Kamar, Jennifer Wortman Vaughan, Hanna Wallach, and Meredith Ringel Morris. 2019. Toward fairness in ai for people with disabilities: A research roadmap.

Wei Guo and Aylin Caliskan. 2021. Detecting Emergent Intersectional Biases: Contextualized Word Embeddings Contain a Distribution of Human-like Biases. In *Proceedings of the 2021 AAAI/ACM Conference on AI, Ethics, and Society*, pages 122–133, Virtual Event USA. ACM.

Suchin Gururangan, Dallas Card, Sarah K. Dreier, Emily K. Gade, Leroy Z. Wang, Zeyu Wang, Luke Zettlemoyer, and Noah A. Smith. 2022. Whose Language Counts as High Quality? Measuring Language Ideologies in Text Data Selection. *arXiv:2201.10474 [cs]*. ArXiv: 2201.10474.

Donna Haraway. 1988. Situated Knowledges: The Science Question in Feminism and the Privilege of Partial Perspective. *Feminist Studies*, 14(3):575–599.

Dirk Hovy and Shrimai Prabhumoye. 2021. Five sources of bias in natural language processing. *Language and Linguistics Compass*, 15(8):e12432.

Po Sen Huang, Huan Zhang, Ray Jiang, Robert Stanforth, Johannes Welbl, Jack W. Rae, Vishal Maini, Dani Yogatama, and Pushmeet Kohli. 2020. Reducing sentiment bias in language models via counterfactual evaluation. In *Findings of the Association for Computational Linguistics Findings of ACL: EMNLP 2020*.

Ben Hutchinson, Vinodkumar Prabhakaran, Emily Denton, Kellie Webster, Yu Zhong, and Stephen Denuyl. 2020. Social biases in NLP models as barriers for persons with disabilities. In *Proceedings of the 58th Annual Meeting of the Association for Computational Linguistics*, pages 5491–5501, Online. Association for Computational Linguistics.

Abigail Z. Jacobs and Hanna Wallach. 2021. Measurement and Fairness. In *Proceedings of the 2021 ACM Conference on Fairness, Accountability, and Transparency*, pages 375–385, Virtual Event Canada. ACM.

Jigsaw. 2017. Kaggle's Toxicity Comment Classification competition.

Xisen Jin, Francesco Barbieri, Brendan Kennedy, Aida Mostafazadeh Davani, Leonardo Neves, and Xiang Ren. 2021. On transferability of bias mitigation effects in language model fine-tuning. In *Proceedings of the 2021 Conference of the North American Chapter of the Association for Computational Linguistics: Human Language Technologies*, pages 3770–3783, Online. Association for Computational Linguistics.

Pratik Joshi, Sebastin Santy, Amar Budhiraja, Kalika Bali, and Monojit Choudhury. 2020. The state and fate of linguistic diversity and inclusion in the NLP world. In *Proceedings of the 58th Annual Meeting of the Association for Computational Linguistics*, pages 6282–6293, Online. Association for Computational Linguistics.

Nikhil Kandpal, Eric Wallace, and Colin Raffel. 2022. Deduplicating Training Data Mitigates Privacy Risks in Language Models. *arXiv:2202.06539 [cs]*. ArXiv: 2202.06539.

Michael Kearns, Seth Neel, Aaron Roth, and Zhiwei Steven Wu. 2018. Preventing fairness gerrymandering: Auditing and learning for subgroup fairness. In *Proceedings of the 35th International Conference on Machine Learning*, volume 80 of *Proceedings of Machine Learning Research*, pages 2564–2572. PMLR.

Erin M. Kerrison, Jennifer Cobbina, and Kimberly Bender. 2018. "Your Pants Won't Save You": Why Black Youth Challenge Race-Based Police Surveillance and the Demands of Black Respectability Politics. *Race and Justice*, 8(1):7–26.

Os Keyes, Chandler May, and Annabelle Carrell. 2021. You keep using that word: Ways of thinking about gender in computing research. *Proc. ACM Hum.-Comput. Interact.*, 5(CSCW1).

Julia Kreutzer, Isaac Caswell, Lisa Wang, Ahsan Wahab, Daan van Esch, Nasanbayar Ulzii-Orshikh, Allahsera Tapo, Nishant Subramani, Artem Sokolov, Claytone Sikasote, Monang Setyawan, Supheakmungkol Sarin, Sokhar Samb, Benoît Sagot, Clara Rivera, Annette Rios, Isabel Papadimitriou, Salomey Osei, Pedro Ortiz Suarez, Iroro Orife, Kelechi Ogueji, Andre Niyongabo Rubungo, Toan Q. Nguyen, Mathias Müller, André Müller, Shamsuddeen Hassan Muhammad, Nanda Muhammad, Ayanda Mnyakeni, Jamshidbek Mirzakhalov, Tapiwanashe Matangira, Colin Leong, Nze Lawson, Sneha Kudugunta, Yacine Jernite, Mathias Jenny, Orhan Firat, Bonaventure F. P. Dossou, Sakhile Dlamini, Nisansa de Silva, Sakine Çabuk Ballı, Stella Biderman, Alessia Battisti, Ahmed Baruwa, Ankur Bapna, Pallavi Baljekar, Israel Abebe Azime, Ayodele Awokoya, Duygu Ataman, Orevaoghene Ahia, Oghenefego Ahia, Sweta Agrawal, and Mofetoluwa Adeyemi. 2022. Quality at a Glance: An Audit of Web-Crawled Multilingual Datasets. *Transactions of the Association for Computational Linguistics*, 10:50–72.

Keita Kurita, Nidhi Vyas, Ayush Pareek, Alan W Black, and Yulia Tsvetkov. 2019. Measuring Bias in Contextualized Word Representations. In *Proceedings of the First Workshop on Gender Bias in Natural Language Processing*, pages 166–172, Florence, Italy. Association for Computational Linguistics.

William Labov. 1986. The social stratification of (r) in new york city department stores. In Harold B. Allen and Michael D. Linn, editors, *Dialect and Language Variation*, pages 304–329. Academic Press, Boston.

Mandy Lau. 2021. Artificial intelligence language models and the false fantasy of participatory language policies. *Working papers in Applied Linguistics and Linguistics at York*, 1:4–15.

Connor Leahy and Stella Biderman. 2021. The hard problem of aligning AI to human values. In *The State of AI Ethics Report (Volume 4)*. The Montreal AI Ethics Institute.

Josh Lepawsky. 2019. No insides on the outsides. *Discard Studies*, 0(0).

Shahar Levy, Koren Lazar, and Gabriel Stanovsky. 2021. Collecting a large-scale gender bias dataset for coreference resolution and machine translation.

Paul Pu Liang, Chiyu Wu, Louis-Philippe Morency, and Ruslan Salakhutdinov. 2021. Towards Understanding and Mitigating Social Biases in Language Models. In *Proceedings of the 38th International Conference on Machine Learning*, volume 139 of *Proceedings of Machine Learning Research*, pages 6565–6576. PMLR.

Q. Vera Liao and Michael Muller. 2019. Enabling value sensitive ai systems through participatory design fictions.

Stephanie Lin, Jacob Hilton, and Owain Evans. 2021. TruthfulQA: Measuring How Models Mimic Human Falsehoods. *arXiv:2109.07958 [cs]*. ArXiv: 2109.07958.

Nishtha Madaan, Inkit Padhi, Naveen Panwar, and Diptikalyan Saha. 2021. Generate your counterfactuals: Towards controlled counterfactual generation for text. *Proceedings of the AAAI Conference on Artificial Intelligence*, 35(15):13516–13524.

Liam Magee, Lida Ghahremanlou, Karen Soldatic, and Shanthi Robertson. 2021. Intersectional Bias in Causal Language Models. *arXiv:2107.07691 [cs]*. ArXiv: 2107.07691.

Vijit Malik, Sunipa Dev, Akihiro Nishi, Nanyun Peng, and Kai-Wei Chang. 2021. Socially aware bias measurements for hindi language representations.

Chandler May, Alex Wang, Shikha Bordia, Samuel R. Bowman, and Rachel Rudinger. 2019. On measuring social biases in sentence encoders. In *Proceedings of the 2019 Conference of the North American Chapter of the Association for Computational Linguistics: Human Language Technologies, Volume 1 (Long and Short Papers)*, pages 622–628, Minneapolis, Minnesota. Association for Computational Linguistics.

Angelina McMillan-Major, Zaid Alyafeai, Stella Biderman, Kimbo Chen, Francesco De Toni, Gérard Dupont, Hady Elsahar, Chris Emezue, Alham Fikri Aji, Suzana Ilić, Nurulaqilla Khamis, Colin Leong, Maraim Masoud, Aitor Soroa, Pedro Ortiz Suarez, Zeerak Talat, Daniel van Strien, and Yacine Jernite. 2022. Documenting Geographically and Contextually Diverse Data Sources: The BigScience Catalogue of Language Data and Resources. *arXiv:2201.10066 [cs]*. ArXiv: 2201.10066.

Milagros Miceli, Julian Posada, and Tianling Yang. 2022. Studying Up Machine Learning Data: Why Talk About Bias When We Mean Power? *Proceedings of the ACM on Human-Computer Interaction*, 6(GROUP):1–14.

Margaret Mitchell, Simone Wu, Andrew Zaldivar, Parker Barnes, Lucy Vasserman, Ben Hutchinson, Elena Spitzer, Inioluwa Deborah Raji, and Timnit Gebru. 2019. Model Cards for Model Reporting. In *Proceedings of the Conference on Fairness, Accountability, and Transparency*, FAT* '19, pages 220–229, Atlanta, GA, USA. Association for Computing Machinery.

Mike Monteiro and Vivianne Castillo. 2019. *Ruined by design: how designers destroyed the world, and what we can do to fix it*. Mule Design, Fresno.

Moin Nadeem, Anna Bethke, and Siva Reddy. 2020. Stereoset: Measuring stereotypical bias in pretrained language models.

Nikita Nangia, Clara Vania, Rasika Bhalerao, and Samuel R. Bowman. 2020. CrowS-pairs: A challenge dataset for measuring social biases in masked language models. In *Proceedings of the 2020 Conference on Empirical Methods in Natural Language Processing (EMNLP)*, pages 1953–1967, Online. Association for Computational Linguistics.

Wilhelmina Nekoto, Vukosi Marivate, Tshinondiwa Matsila, Timi Fasubaa, Taiwo Fagbohungbe, Solomon Oluwole Akinola, Shamsuddeen Muhammad, Salomon Kabongo Kabenamualu, Salomey Osei, Freshia Sackey, Rubungo Andre Niyongabo, Ricky Macharm, Perez Ogayo, Orevaoghene Ahia, Musie Meressa Berhe, Mofetoluwa Adeyemi, Masabata Mokgesi-Selinga, Lawrence Okegbemi, Laura Martinus, Kolawole Tajudeen, Kevin Degila, Kelechi Ogueji, Kathleen Siminyu, Julia Kreutzer, Jason Webster, Jamiil Toure Ali, Jade Abbott, Iroro Orife, Ignatius Ezeani, Idris Abdulkadir Dangana, Herman Kamper, Hady Elsahar, Goodness Duru, Ghollah Kioko, Murhabazi Espoir, Elan van Biljon, Daniel Whitenack, Christopher Onyefuluchi, Chris Chinenye Emezue, Bonaventure F. P. Dossou, Blessing Sibanda, Blessing Bassey, Ayodele Olabiyi, Arshath Ramkilowan, Alp Öktem, Adewale Akinfaderin, and Abdallah Bashir. 2020. Participatory research for low-resourced machine translation: A case study in African languages. In *Findings of the Association for Computational Linguistics: EMNLP 2020*, pages 2144–2160, Online. Association for Computational Linguistics.

Safiya Umoja Noble. 2018. *Algorithms of oppression: how search engines reinforce racism*. New York University Press, New York.

Alicia Parrish, Angelica Chen, Nikita Nangia, Vishakh Padmakumar, Jason Phang, Jana Thompson, Phu Mon Htut, and Samuel R. Bowman. 2021. Bbq: A hand-built bias benchmark for question answering.

Inioluwa Deborah Raji, Emily M. Bender, Amandalynne Paullada, Emily Denton, and Alex Hanna. 2021. AI and the Everything in the Whole Wide World Benchmark. *arXiv:2111.15366 [cs]*. ArXiv: 2111.15366.

Inioluwa Deborah Raji and Joy Buolamwini. 2019. Actionable Auditing: Investigating the Impact of Publicly Naming Biased Performance Results of Commercial AI Products. In *Proceedings of the 2019 AAAI/ACM Conference on AI, Ethics, and Society*, pages 429–435, Honolulu HI USA. ACM.

Micah Rajunov and Scott Duane. 2019. *Nonbinary: Memoirs of Gender and Identity*. Columbia University Press.

Rachel Rudinger, Jason Naradowsky, Brian Leonard, and Benjamin Van Durme. 2018. Gender bias in coreference resolution. In *Proceedings of the 2018 Conference of the North American Chapter of the Association for Computational Linguistics: Human Language Technologies, Volume 2 (Short Papers)*, pages 8–14, New Orleans, Louisiana. Association for Computational Linguistics.

Nithya Sambasivan, Erin Arnesen, Ben Hutchinson, Tulsee Doshi, and Vinodkumar Prabhakaran. 2021. Re-imagining Algorithmic Fairness in India and Beyond. In *Proceedings of the 2021 ACM Conference on Fairness, Accountability, and Transparency*, pages 315–328, Virtual Event Canada. ACM.

Victor Sanh, Albert Webson, Colin Raffel, Stephen H. Bach, Lintang Sutawika, Zaid Alyafeai, Antoine Chaffin, Arnaud Stiegler, Teven Le Scao, Arun Raja, Manan Dey, M. Saiful Bari, Canwen Xu, Urmish Thakker, Shanya Sharma Sharma, Eliza Szczechla, Taewoon Kim, Gunjan Chhablani, Nihal Nayak, Debajyoti Datta, Jonathan Chang, Mike Tian-Jian Jiang, Han Wang, Matteo Manica, Sheng Shen, Zheng Xin Yong, Harshit Pandey, Rachel Bawden, Thomas Wang, Trishala Neeraj, Jos Rozen, Abheesht Sharma, Andrea Santilli, Thibault Fevry, Jason Alan Fries, Ryan Teehan, Stella Biderman, Leo Gao, Tali Bers, Thomas Wolf, and Alexander M. Rush. 2021. Multitask Prompted Training Enables Zero-Shot Task Generalization. *arXiv:2110.08207 [cs]*. ArXiv: 2110.08207.

Maarten Sap, Swabha Swayamdipta, Laura Vianna, Xuhui Zhou, Yejin Choi, and Noah A. Smith. 2021. Annotators with Attitudes: How Annotator Beliefs And Identities Bias Toxic Language Detection. *arXiv:2111.07997 [cs]*. ArXiv: 2111.07997.

Daniel Schiff. 2020. Principles to Practices for Responsible AI: Closing the Gap. *2020 European Conference on AI Workshop on Advancing Towards the SDGs*.

Shanya Sharma, Manan Dey, and Koustuv Sinha. 2021. Evaluating gender bias in natural language inference.

Emily Sheng, Kai-Wei Chang, Prem Natarajan, and Nanyun Peng. 2021. Societal Biases in Language Generation: Progress and Challenges. In *Proceedings of the 59th Annual Meeting of the Association for Computational Linguistics and the 11th International Joint Conference on Natural Language Processing (Volume 1: Long Papers)*, pages 4275–4293, Online. Association for Computational Linguistics.

Emily Sheng, Kai-Wei Chang, Premkumar Natarajan, and Nanyun Peng. 2019. The Woman Worked as a Babysitter: On Biases in Language Generation. In *Proceedings of the 2019 Conference on Empirical Methods in Natural Language Processing and the 9th International Joint Conference on Natural Language Processing (EMNLP-IJCNLP)*, pages 3405–3410, Hong Kong, China. Association for Computational Linguistics.

Shaden Smith, Mostofa Patwary, Brandon Norick, Patrick LeGresley, Samyam Rajbhandari, Jared Casper, Zhun Liu, Shrimai Prabhumoye, George Zerveas, Vijay Korthikanti, Elton Zhang, Rewon Child, Reza Yazdani Aminabadi, Julie Bernauer, Xia Song, Mohammad Shoeybi, Yuxiong He, Michael Houston, Saurabh Tiwary, and Bryan Catanzaro. 2022. Using DeepSpeed and Megatron to Train Megatron-Turing NLG 530B, A Large-Scale Generative Language Model. *arXiv:2201.11990 [cs]*. ArXiv: 2201.11990.

Dean Spade. 2015. *Normal Life: Administrative Violence, Critical Trans Politics, and the Limits of Law*. Duke University Press.

Karolina Stanczak and Isabelle Augenstein. 2021. A Survey on Gender Bias in Natural Language Processing. *arXiv:2112.14168 [cs]*. ArXiv: 2112.14168.

Gabriel Stanovsky, Noah A. Smith, and Luke Zettlemoyer. 2019. Evaluating gender bias in machine translation. In *Proceedings of the 57th Annual Meeting of the Association for Computational Linguistics*, pages 1679–1684, Florence, Italy. Association for Computational Linguistics.

Arjun Subramonian. 2021. Allennlp: Fairness and bias mitigation.

Tony Sun, Andrew Gaut, Shirlyn Tang, Yuxin Huang, Mai ElSherief, Jieyu Zhao, Diba Mirza, Elizabeth Belding, Kai-Wei Chang, and William Yang Wang. 2019. Mitigating Gender Bias in Natural Language Processing: Literature Review. In *Proceedings of the 57th Annual Meeting of the Association for Computational Linguistics*, pages 1630–1640, Florence, Italy. Association for Computational Linguistics.

Zeerak Talat, Smarika Lulz, Joachim Bingel, and Isabelle Augenstein. 2021. Disembodied Machine Learning: On the Illusion of Objectivity in NLP. ArXiv: 2101.11974.

Samson Tan, Shafiq Joty, Min-Yen Kan, and Richard Socher. 2020. It's morphin' time! Combating linguistic discrimination with inflectional perturbations. In *Proceedings of the 58th Annual Meeting of the Association for Computational Linguistics*, pages 2920–2935, Online. Association for Computational Linguistics.

Romal Thoppilan, Daniel De Freitas, Jamie Hall, Noam Shazeer, Apoorv Kulshreshtha, Heng-Tze Cheng, Alicia Jin, Taylor Bos, Leslie Baker, Yu Du, YaGuang Li, Hongrae Lee, Huaixiu Steven Zheng, Amin Ghafouri, Marcelo Menegali, Yanping Huang, Maxim Krikun, Dmitry Lepikhin, James Qin, Dehao Chen, Yuanzhong Xu, Zhifeng Chen, Adam Roberts, Maarten Bosma, Vincent Zhao, Yanqi Zhou, Chung-Ching Chang, Igor Krivokon, Will Rusch, Marc Pickett, Pranesh Srinivasan, Laichee Man, Kathleen Meier-Hellstern, Meredith Ringel Morris, Tulsee Doshi, Renelito Delos Santos, Toju Duke, Johnny Soraker, Ben Zevenbergen, Vinodkumar Prabhakaran,

Mark Diaz, Ben Hutchinson, Kristen Olson, Alejandra Molina, Erin Hoffman-John, Josh Lee, Lora Aroyo, Ravi Rajakumar, Alena Butryna, Matthew Lamm, Viktoriya Kuzmina, Joe Fenton, Aaron Cohen, Rachel Bernstein, Ray Kurzweil, Blaise Aguera-Arcas, Claire Cui, Marian Croak, Ed Chi, and Quoc Le. 2022. LaMDA: Language Models for Dialog Applications. *arXiv:2201.08239 [cs]*. ArXiv: 2201.08239.

Nanna Thylstrup and Zeerak Talat. 2020. Detecting 'Dirt' and 'Toxicity': Rethinking Content Moderation as Pollution Behaviour. *SSRN Electronic Journal*.

Nenad Tomasev, Kevin R. McKee, Jackie Kay, and Shakir Mohamed. 2021. *Fairness for Unobserved Characteristics: Insights from Technological Impacts on Queer Communities*, page 254–265. Association for Computing Machinery, New York, NY, USA.

Antti Virtanen, Jenna Kanerva, Rami Ilo, Jouni Luoma, Juhani Luotolahti, Tapio Salakoski, Filip Ginter, and Sampo Pyysalo. 2019. Multilingual is not enough: BERT for Finnish. *arXiv:1912.07076 [cs]*. ArXiv: 1912.07076.

Eric Wallace, Shi Feng, Nikhil Kandpal, Matt Gardner, and Sameer Singh. 2019. Universal adversarial triggers for attacking and analyzing NLP. In *Proceedings of the 2019 Conference on Empirical Methods in Natural Language Processing and the 9th International Joint Conference on Natural Language Processing (EMNLP-IJCNLP)*, pages 2153–2162, Hong Kong, China. Association for Computational Linguistics.

Tianlu Wang, Jieyu Zhao, Mark Yatskar, Kai-Wei Chang, and Vicente Ordonez. 2019. Balanced Datasets Are Not Enough: Estimating and Mitigating Gender Bias in Deep Image Representations. In *2019 IEEE/CVF International Conference on Computer Vision (ICCV)*, pages 5309–5318, Seoul, Korea (South). IEEE.

Laura Weidinger, John Mellor, Maribeth Rauh, Conor Griffin, Jonathan Uesato, Po-Sen Huang, Myra Cheng, Mia Glaese, Borja Balle, Atoosa Kasirzadeh, Zac Kenton, Sasha Brown, Will Hawkins, Tom Stepleton, Courtney Biles, Abeba Birhane, Julia Haas, Laura Rimell, Lisa Anne Hendricks, William Isaac, Sean Legassick, Geoffrey Irving, and Iason Gabriel. 2021a. Ethical and social risks of harm from Language Models. *arXiv:2112.04359 [cs]*. ArXiv: 2112.04359.

Laura Weidinger, John Mellor, Maribeth Rauh, Conor Griffin, Jonathan Uesato, Po-Sen Huang, Myra Cheng, Mia Glaese, Borja Balle, Atoosa Kasirzadeh, et al. 2021b. Ethical and social risks of harm from language models. *arXiv preprint arXiv:2112.04359*.

Sarah West, Meredith Whittaker, and Kate Crawford. 2019. Discriminating Systems: Gender, Race, and Power in AI. Technical report, AI Now Institute, New York.

Langdon Winner. 1980. Do artifacts have politics? *Daedalus*, pages 121–136.

Jieyu Zhao, Tianlu Wang, Mark Yatskar, Vicente Ordonez, and Kai-Wei Chang. 2018. Gender bias in coreference resolution: Evaluation and debiasing methods. In *Proceedings of the 2018 Conference of the North American Chapter of the Association for Computational Linguistics: Human Language Technologies, Volume 2 (Short Papers)*, pages 15–20, New Orleans, Louisiana. Association for Computational Linguistics.

Pei Zhou, Weijia Shi, Jieyu Zhao, Kuan-Hao Huang, Muhao Chen, Ryan Cotterell, and Kai-Wei Chang. 2019. Examining Gender Bias in Languages with Grammatical Gender. In *Proceedings of the 2019 Conference on Empirical Methods in Natural Language Processing and the 9th International Joint Conference on Natural Language Processing (EMNLP-IJCNLP)*, pages 5275–5283, Hong Kong, China. Association for Computational Linguistics.

Ran Zmigrod, Sabrina Mielke, Hanna Wallach, and Ryan Cotterell. 2019. Counterfactual Data Augmentation for Mitigating Gender Stereotypes in Languages with Rich Morphology. In *Proceedings of the 57th Annual Meeting of the Association for Computational Linguistics*, pages 1651–1661, Florence, Italy. Association for Computational Linguistics.

A Acknowledgments

The work presented in this paper is the outcome of the discussions and work within the BigScience initiative. Notably, we would like to acknowledge Ioana Baldini and Xudong Sheng, who contributed significantly to an earlier iteration and whose work served as a foundation for the specific contributions and arguments of this paper.

B Credit Author Statement

We follow the recommendations and taxonomy provided by Allen et al. (2019) to determine and outline author contributions.

Stella Biderman: Writing — Original Draft (Section 4), Writing — Review & Editing.

Miruna Clinciu: Conceptualization, Writing — Original Draft (Section 3), Writing — Review & Editing (Section 3.5).

Manan Dey: Writing — Original draft preparation (Section 5), Writing — Review and Editing.

Shayne Longpre: Writing — Original draft preparation (Section 1–2), Writing — Review & Editing (Section 3).

Alexandra Sasha Luccioni: Writing — Original Draft (Section 4), Writing — Review & Editing.

Maraim Masoud: Conceptualization, Writing — Original draft preparation (Section 4), Writing — Review & Editing (Section 4).

Margaret Mitchell: Writing — Original draft & Review & Editing.

Aurélie Névéol: Supervision, Writing — Original draft preparation (Abstract, Section 3), Writing — Review & Editing.

Dragomir Radev: Writing — Original draft & Review & Editing.

Shanya Sharma: Writing — Original draft preparation (Section 5), Writing — Review and Editing (Sections 3 & 5).

Arjun Subramonian: Writing — Original draft preparation (Sections 2, 3, & 5), Writing — Review & Editing.

Jaesung Tae: Writing — Original draft preparation (Section 1), Writing — Review & Editing.

Zeerak Talat: Supervision, Conceptualization, Writing — Original draft preparation (Abstract, Section 1–2,4,6), Writing — Review & Editing.

Samson Tan: Supervision, Conceptualization, Writing — Original draft preparation (Sections 3.2 & 4.2), Writing — Review & Editing.

Deepak Tunuguntla: Conceptualization, Writing — Original draft preparation (Section 1-2), Writing — Review & Editing.

Oskar van der Wal: Conceptualization, Writing — Original Draft (Section 3), Writing — Review & Editing (Section 3).

C Determination of Author Order

Contributors are listed alphabetically, except for Zeerak Talat and Aurelié Nevéol, who managed paper writing and chaired the working group, respectively. All authors contributed to the conceptualizing and writing of the document.

Diverse Lottery Tickets Boost Ensemble from a Single Pretrained Model

Sosuke Kobayashi[1,2] **Shun Kiyono**[3,1] **Jun Suzuki**[1,3] **Kentaro Inui**[1,3]
Tohoku University[1] Preferred Networks, Inc.[2] RIKEN[3]
sosk@preferred.jp shun.kiyono@riken.jp
jun.suzuki@tohoku.ac.jp inui@tohoku.ac.jp

Abstract

Ensembling is a popular method used to improve performance as a last resort. However, ensembling multiple models finetuned from a single pretrained model has been not very effective; this could be due to the lack of diversity among ensemble members. This paper proposes *Multi-Ticket Ensemble*, which finetunes different subnetworks of a single pretrained model and ensembles them. We empirically demonstrated that winning-ticket subnetworks produced more diverse predictions than dense networks, and their ensemble outperformed the standard ensemble on some tasks.

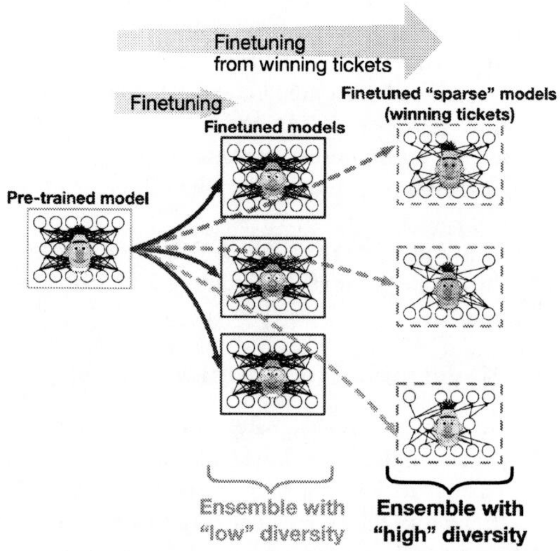

Figure 1: When finetuning from a single pretrained model (left), the models are less diverse (center). If we finetune different sparse subnetworks, they become more diverse and make the ensemble effective (right).

1 Introduction

Ensembling (Levin et al., 1989; Domingos, 1997) has long been an easy and effective approach to improve model performance by averaging the outputs of multiple comparable but independent models. Allen-Zhu and Li (2020) explain that different models obtain different views for judgments, and the ensemble uses complementary views to make more robust decisions. A good ensemble requires diverse member models. However, how to encourage diversity without sacrificing the accuracy of each model is non-trivial (Liu and Yao, 1999; Kirillov et al., 2016; Rame and Cord, 2021).

The *pretrain-then-finetune* paradigm has become another best practice for achieving state-of-the-art performance on NLP tasks (Devlin et al., 2019). The cost of large-scale pretraining, however, is enormously high (Sharir et al., 2020); This often makes it difficult to independently pretrain multiple models. Therefore, most researchers and practitioners only use a *single* pretrained model, which is distributed by resource-rich organizations.

This situation brings up a novel question to ensemble learning: Can we make an effective ensemble from only *a single pre-trained model*? Although ensembles can be combined with the pretrain-then-finetune paradigm, an ensemble of models finetuned from *a single pretrained model* is much less effective than that using *different pretrained models from scratch* in many tasks (Raffel et al., 2020). Naïve ensemble offers limited improvements, possibly due to the lack of diversity of finetuning from the same initial parameters.

In this paper, we propose a simple yet effective method called *Multi-Ticket Ensemble*, ensembling finetuned *winning-ticket subnetworks* (Frankle and Carbin, 2019) in a single pretrained model. We empirically demonstrate that pruning a single pretrained model can make diverse models, and their ensemble can outperform the naïve dense ensemble if winning-ticket subnetworks are found.

2 Diversity in a Single Pretrained Model

In this paper, we discuss the most standard way of ensemble, which averages the outputs of multiple neural networks; each has the same architecture but different parameters. That is, let $f(\boldsymbol{x};\boldsymbol{\theta})$ be the

Proceedings of BigScience Episode #5 – Workshop on Challenges & Perspectives in Creating Large Language Models, pages 42 - 50
May 27, 2022 ©2022 Association for Computational Linguistics

output of a model with the parameter vector $\boldsymbol{\theta}$ given the input $\boldsymbol{x}$, the output of an ensemble is $f_{\mathcal{M}}(\boldsymbol{x}) = \sum_{\boldsymbol{\theta} \in \mathcal{M}} f(\boldsymbol{x}; \boldsymbol{\theta})/|\mathcal{M}|$, where $\mathcal{M} = \{\boldsymbol{\theta}_1, ..., \boldsymbol{\theta}_{|\mathcal{M}|}\}$ is the member parameters.

2.1 Diversity from Finetuning

As discussed, when constructing an ensemble $f_{\mathcal{M}}$ by finetuning from a single pretrained model multiple times with different random seeds $\{s_1, ..., s_{|\mathcal{M}|}\}$, the boost in performance tends to be only marginal. In the case of BERT (Devlin et al., 2019) and its variants, three sources of diversities can be considered: random initialization of the task-specific layer, dataset shuffling for stochastic gradient descent (SGD), and dropout. However, empirically, such finetuned parameters tend not to be largely different from the initial parameters, and they do not lead to diverse models (Radiya-Dixit and Wang, 2020). Of course, if one adds significant noise to the parameters, it leads to diversity; however, it would also hurt accuracy.

2.2 Diversity from Pruning

To make models ensuring both accuracy and diversity, we focus on subnetworks in the pretrained model. Different subnetworks employ different subspaces of the pre-trained knowledge (Radiya-Dixit and Wang, 2020; Zhao et al., 2020; Cao et al., 2021); this would help the subnetworks to acquire different views, which can be a source of desired diversity[1]. Also, in terms of accuracy, recent studies on the *lottery ticket hypothesis* (Frankle and Carbin, 2019) suggest that a dense network at initialization contains a subnetwork, called the *winning ticket*, whose accuracy becomes comparable to that of the dense one after the same training. Interestingly, the pretrained BERT also has a winning ticket for finetuning on downstream tasks (Chen et al., 2020). Thus, if we can find *diverse winning tickets*, they can be good ensemble members with the two desirable properties: diversity and accuracy.

3 Subnetwork Exploration

We propose a simple yet effective method, *multi-ticket ensemble*, which finetunes different subnetworks instead of dense networks. Because it could be a key how to find subnetworks, we explore three variants based on iterative magnitude pruning.

[1]Some concurrent and recent studies also investigate subnetworks for effective ensemble (Durasov et al., 2021; Havasi et al., 2021) for training-from-scratch settings of image recognition.

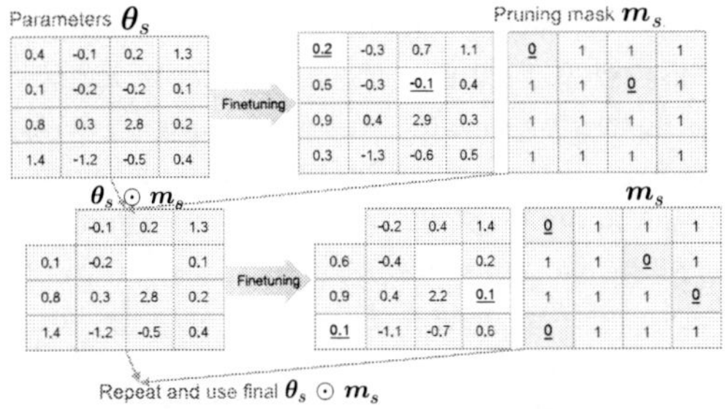

Figure 2: Overview of iterative magnitude pruning (Section 3.1). We can also use regularizers during finetuning to diversify pruning (Section 3.2).

3.1 Iterative Magnitude Pruning

We employ iterative magnitude pruning (Frankle and Carbin, 2019) to find winning tickets for simplicity. Other sophisticated options are left for future work. Here, we explain the algorithm (refer to the paper for details). The algorithm explores a good pruning mask via rehearsals of finetuning. First, it completes a finetuning procedure of an initialized dense network and identifies the parameters with the 10% lowest magnitudes as the targets of pruning. Then, it makes the pruned subnetwork and resets its parameters to the originally-initialized (sub-)parameters. This finetune-prune-reset process is repeated until reaching the desired pruning ratio. We used 30% as pruning ratio.

3.2 Pruning with Regularizer

We discussed that finetuning with different random seeds did not lead to diverse parameters in Section 2.1. Therefore, iterative magnitude pruning with different seeds could also produce less diverse subnetworks. Thus, we also explore means of diversifying pruning patterns by enforcing different parameters to have lower magnitudes. Motivated by this, we experiment with a simple approach, applying an L_1 regularizer (i.e., magnitude decay) to different parameters selectively depending on the random seeds. Specifically, we explore two policies to determine which parameters are decayed and how strongly they are, i.e., the element-wise coefficients of the L_1 regularizer, $\boldsymbol{l}_s \in \mathbb{R}_{\geq 0}{}^{|\theta|}$. During finetuning (for pruning), we add a regularization term $\tau||\boldsymbol{\theta}_s \odot \boldsymbol{l}_s||_1$ with a positive scalar coefficient τ into the loss of the task (e.g., cross entropy for classification), where $\odot$ is element-wise product. This softly enforces various parameters to have a lower magnitude among a set of random seeds and could lead various parameters to be pruned.

Active Masking To maximize the diversity of the surviving parameters of member models, it is necessary to prune the surviving parameters of the random seed s_1 when building a model with the next random seed s_2. Thus, during finetuning with seed s_2, we apply the L_1 regularizer on the first surviving parameters. Likewise, with the following seeds $s_3, s_4, ..., s_i, ..., s_{|\mathcal{M}|}$, we cumulatively use the average of the surviving masks as the regularizer coefficient mask. Let $\boldsymbol{m}_{s_j} \in \{0,1\}^{|\boldsymbol{\theta}|}$ be the pruning mask indicating surviving parameters from seed s_j, the coefficient mask with seed s_i is $\boldsymbol{l}_{s_i} = \sum_{j<i} \boldsymbol{m}_{s_j}/(i-1)$. We call this affirmative policy as *active masking*.

Random Masking In active masking, each coefficient mask has a sequential dependence on the preceding random seeds. Thus, the training of ensemble members cannot be parallelized. Therefore, we also experiment with a simpler and parallelizable variant, *random masking*, where a mask is independently and randomly generated from a random seed. With a random seed s_i, we generate the seed-dependent random binary mask, i.e., $\boldsymbol{l}_s = \boldsymbol{m}^{\text{rand}}_{s_i} \in \{0,1\}^{|\boldsymbol{\theta}|}$, where each element is sampled from Bernoulli distribution and 0's probability equals to the target pruning ratio.

4 Experiments

We evaluate the performance of ensembles using four finetuning schemes: (1) finetuning without pruning (BASELINE), (2) finetuning of lottery-ticket subnetworks found with the naïve iterative magnitude pruning (BASE-LT), and (3) with L_1 regularizer by the active masking (ACTIVE-LT) or (4) random masking (RANDOM-LT). We also compare with (5) BAGGING-based ensemble, which trains dense models on different random 90% training subsets. We use the GLUE benchmark (Wang et al., 2018) as tasks. The implementation and settings follow Chen et al. (2020)[2] using the Transformers library (Wolf et al., 2020) and its bert-base-uncased pretrained model. We report the average performance using twenty different random seeds. Ensembles are evaluated using exhaustive combinations of five members. We also perform Student's t-test for validating statistical significance[3]. Note that, while the experiments focus on using BERT, we believe that the insights would be helpful to other pretrain-then-finetune settings in general[4].

	MRPC			STS-B		
	single	ens.	diff.	single	ens.	diff.
BASELINE	83.48	84.34	+0.86	88.35	89.04	+0.69
(BAGGING)	82.87	84.19	+1.32	88.17	88.84	+0.68
BASE-LT	83.84	*84.98*	*+1.14*	88.37	*89.16*	*+0.79*
ACTIVE-LT	83.22	*84.60*	***+1.38***	88.39	***89.32***	***+0.94***
RANDOM-LT	83.53	*85.05*	***+1.52***	88.49	***89.35***	***+0.86***

Table 1: The performances (single, ens.) and the improvements by ensembling (diff.). *Italic* indicates that the value is significantly larger than that of BASELINE. ***Bold-italic*** indicates significantly larger than that of both BASELINE and BASE-LT. Underline indicates the best.

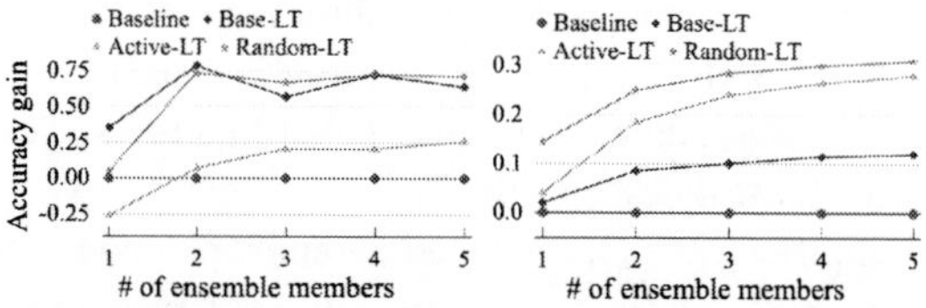

Figure 3: Comparison of the performances and the number of ensemble members on MRPC (left) and STS-B (right). They are represented as the relative gain compared with BASELINE's accuracy.

4.1 Accuracy

We show the results on MRPC (Dolan and Brockett, 2005) and STS-B (Cer et al., 2017) in Table 1. Multi-ticket ensembles (*-LT) outperform BASELINE and BAGGING significantly ($p < 0.001$). This result supports the effectiveness of multi-ticket ensemble. Note that the improvements of *-LT are attributable to ensembling (diff.) rather than to any performance gains of the individual models (single). We also plot the improvements (ens. values relative to BASELINE) as a function of the number of ensemble members on MRPC and STS-B in Figure 3. This also clearly shows that while the single models of *-LT have accuracy similar to BASELINE, the gains appear when ensembling them. While multi-ticket ensemble works well even with the naive pruning method (BASE-LT), RANDOM-LT and ACTIVE-LT achieve the better ensembling effect on average; this suggests the effectiveness of regularizers. Interestingly, RANDOM-LT is simpler but more effective than ACTIVE-LT.

[2] We found a bug in Chen et al. (2020)'s implementation on GitHub, so we fixed it and experimented with the correct version.

[3] Note that not all evaluation samples satisfy independence assumption.

[4] Raffel et al. (2020) reported that the same problem happened on almost all tasks (GLUE (Wang et al., 2018), SuperGLUE (Wang et al., 2019), SQuAD (Rajpurkar et al., 2016), summarization, and machine translation) using the T5 model.

When Winning Tickets are Less Accurate Does multi-ticket ensemble work well on any tasks? The answer is no. To enjoy the benefit from multi-ticket ensemble, we have to find diverse winning-ticket subnetworks sufficiently comparable to their dense network. When winning tickets are less accurate than the baseline, their ensembles often fail to outperform the baseline's ensemble. It happened to CoLA (Warstadt et al., 2019), QNLI (Rajpurkar et al., 2016), SST-2 (Socher et al., 2013), MNLI (Williams et al., 2018); the naive iterative magnitude pruning did not find comparable winning-ticket subnetworks (with or sometimes even without regularizers)[5,6,7]. Note that, even in such a case, RANDOM-LT often yielded a higher effect of ensembling (diff.), while the degradation of single models canceled out the effect in total, and BAGGING also failed to improve. More sophisticated pruning methods (Blalock et al., 2020; Sanh et al., 2020) or tuning will find better winning-ticket subnetworks and maximize the opportunities for multi-ticket ensemble in future work.

4.2 Diversity of Predictions

As an auxiliary analysis of behaviors, we show that each subnetwork produces diverse predictions. Because any existing diversity scores do not completely explain or justify the ensemble performance[8], we discuss only rough trends in five popular metrics of classification diversity; Q statistic (Yule, 1900), ratio errors (Aksela, 2003), negative double fault (Giacinto and Roli, 2001), disagreement measure (Skalak, 1996), and correlation coefficient (Kuncheva and Whitaker, 2003). See Kuncheva and Whitaker (2003); Cruz et al. (2020) for their summarized definitions. As shown in Table 2, in all the metrics, winning-ticket subnetworks (*-LT) produced more diverse predictions than the baseline using the dense networks (BASELINE).

	Q↓	R↑	ND↑	D↑	C↓
BASELINE	0.96	0.72	-0.12	0.09	0.69
BASE-LT	0.93	1.00	-0.11	0.10	0.62
ACTIVE-LT	0.94	0.94	-0.11	0.11	0.62
RANDOM-LT	0.94	0.94	-0.11	0.10	0.63

Table 2: Diversity metrics on MRPC. The signs, ↓ and ↑, indicate that the metric gets lower and higher when the predictions are diverse. Q = Q statistic, R = ratio errors, ND = negative double fault, D = disagreement measure, C = correlation coefficient.

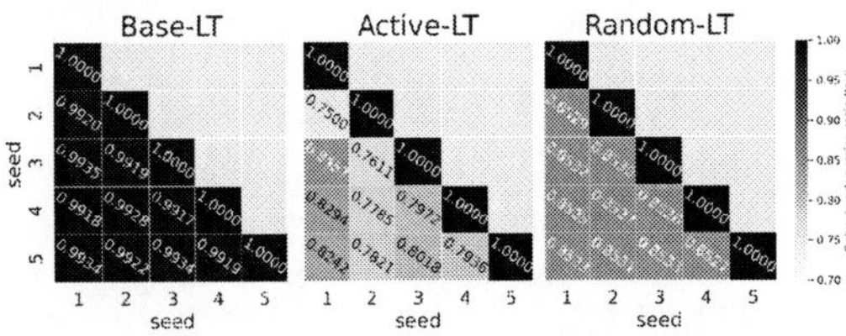

Figure 4: Overlap ratio of pruning masks m_{s_i} between different seeds on MRPC. The lower (yellower) the value is, the more dissimilar the two masks are.

4.3 Diversity of Subnetwork Structures

We finally revealed the diversity of the subnetwork structures on MRPC. We calculated the overlap ratio of two pruning masks, which is defined as intersection over union, IoU $= \frac{|m_i \cap m_j|}{|m_i \cup m_j|}$ (Chen et al., 2020). In Figure 4, we show the overlap ratio between the pruning masks for the five random seeds, i.e., $\{m_{s_1}, ..., m_{s_5}\}$. At first, we can see that ACTIVE-LT and RANDOM-LT using the regularizers resulted in diverse pruning. This higher diversity could lead to the best improvements by ensembling, as discussed in Section 4.1. Secondly, BASE-LT produced surprisingly similar (99%) pruning masks with different random seeds. However, recall that even BASE-LT using the naïve iterative magnitude pruning performed better than BASELINE. This result shows that even seemingly small changes in structure can improve the diversity of predictions and the performance of the ensemble.

5 Conclusion

We raised a question on difficulty of ensembling large-scale pretrained models. As an efficient remedy, we explored methods to use subnetworks in a single model. We empirically demonstrated that ensembling winning-ticket subnetworks could outperform the dense ensembles via diversification and indicated a limitation too.

[5]Although some studies (Prasanna et al., 2020; Chen et al., 2020; Liang et al., 2021) reported that they found winning-ticket subnetworks on these tasks, our finding did not contradict it. Their subnetworks were often actually a little worse than their dense networks, as well as we found. Chen et al. (2020) defined winning tickets as subnetworks with performances within one standard deviation from the dense networks. Prasanna et al. (2020) considered subnetworks with even 90% performance as winning tickets.

[6]For example, comparing BASELINE with RANDOM-LT of pruning ratio 20%, their average values of single/ensemble/difference are 91.38/91.93/+0.55 vs. 91.09/91.90/+0.81 on SST-2.

[7]This also happens to experiments with roberta-base while multi-ticket ensemble still works well on MRPC.

[8]Finding such a convenient diversity metric itself is still a challenge in the research community (Wu et al., 2021).

Acknowledgments

We appreciate the helpful comments from the anonymous reviewers. This work was supported by JSPS KAKENHI Grant Number JP19H04162.

References

Matti Aksela. 2003. Comparison of classifier selection methods for improving committee performance. In *Proceedings of the 4th International Conference on Multiple Classifier Systems*, MCS'03, page 84–93, Berlin, Heidelberg. Springer-Verlag.

Zeyuan Allen-Zhu and Yuanzhi Li. 2020. Towards understanding ensemble, knowledge distillation and self-distillation in deep learning. *CoRR*, abs/2012.09816.

Davis Blalock, Jose Javier Gonzalez Ortiz, Jonathan Frankle, and John Guttag. 2020. What is the state of neural network pruning? In *Proceedings of Second Machine Learning and Systems (MLSys 2020)*, pages 129–146.

Steven Cao, Victor Sanh, and Alexander M. Rush. 2021. Low-complexity probing via finding subnetworks. In *Proceedings of the 2021 Conference of the North American Chapter of the Association for Computational Linguistics: Human Language Technologies (NAACL-HLT 2021)*. Association for Computational Linguistics.

Daniel Cer, Mona Diab, Eneko Agirre, Iñigo Lopez-Gazpio, and Lucia Specia. 2017. SemEval-2017 task 1: Semantic textual similarity multilingual and crosslingual focused evaluation. In *Proceedings of the 11th International Workshop on Semantic Evaluation (SemEval 2017)*, pages 1–14, Vancouver, Canada. Association for Computational Linguistics.

Tianlong Chen, Jonathan Frankle, Shiyu Chang, Sijia Liu, Yang Zhang, Zhangyang Wang, and Michael Carbin. 2020. The lottery ticket hypothesis for pre-trained bert networks. In *Advances in Neural Information Processing Systems 33 (NeurIPS 2020)*, pages 15834–15846. Curran Associates, Inc.

Rafael M. O. Cruz, Luiz G. Hafemann, Robert Sabourin, and George D. C. Cavalcanti. 2020. Deslib: A dynamic ensemble selection library in python. *Journal of Machine Learning Research*, 21(8):1–5.

Jacob Devlin, Ming-Wei Chang, Kenton Lee, and Kristina Toutanova. 2019. BERT: Pre-training of deep bidirectional transformers for language understanding. In *Proceedings of the 2019 Conference of the North American Chapter of the Association for Computational Linguistics: Human Language Technologies (NAACL-HLT 2019)*, pages 4171–4186, Minneapolis, Minnesota. Association for Computational Linguistics.

William B. Dolan and Chris Brockett. 2005. Automatically constructing a corpus of sentential paraphrases. In *Proceedings of the Third International Workshop on Paraphrasing (IWP 2005)*.

Pedro Domingos. 1997. Why does bagging work? a bayesian account and its implications. In *Proceedings of the Third International Conference on Knowledge Discovery and Data Mining (KDD 1997)*, page 155–158. AAAI Press.

Nikita Durasov, Timur Bagautdinov, Pierre Baque, and Pascal Fua. 2021. Masksembles for uncertainty estimation. In *Proceedings of the IEEE/CVF Conference on Computer Vision and Pattern Recognition (CVPR)*, pages 13539–13548.

Jonathan Frankle and Michael Carbin. 2019. The lottery ticket hypothesis: Finding sparse, trainable neural networks. In *Proceedings of the 7th International Conference on Learning Representations (ICLR 2019)*.

Yarin Gal and Zoubin Ghahramani. 2016. Dropout as a bayesian approximation: Representing model uncertainty in deep learning. In *Proceedings of The 33rd International Conference on Machine Learning*, volume 48 of *Proceedings of Machine Learning Research*, pages 1050–1059, New York, New York, USA. PMLR.

Giorgio Giacinto and Fabio Roli. 2001. Design of effective neural network ensembles for image classification purposes. *Image and Vision Computing*, 19(9):699–707.

Marton Havasi, Rodolphe Jenatton, Stanislav Fort, Jeremiah Zhe Liu, Jasper Snoek, Balaji Lakshminarayanan, Andrew Mingbo Dai, and Dustin Tran. 2021. Training independent subnetworks for robust prediction. In *International Conference on Learning Representations*.

Alexander Kirillov, Bogdan Savchynskyy, Carsten Rother, Stefan Lee, and Dhruv Batra. 2016. CVPR tutorial: Diversity meets deep networks - inference, ensemble learning, and applications.

Ludmila I. Kuncheva and Christopher J. Whitaker. 2003. Measures of diversity in classifier ensembles and their relationship with the ensemble accuracy. *Machine Learning*, 51(2):181–207.

Esther Levin, Naftali Tishby, and Sara A. Solla. 1989. A statistical approach to learning and generalization in layered neural networks. In *Proceedings of the Second Annual Workshop on Computational Learning Theory (COLT 1989)*, page 245–260, San Francisco, CA, USA. Morgan Kaufmann Publishers Inc.

Chen Liang, Simiao Zuo, Minshuo Chen, Haoming Jiang, Xiaodong Liu, Pengcheng He, Tuo Zhao, and Weizhu Chen. 2021. Super tickets in pre-trained language models: From model compression to improving generalization. In *Proceedings of the 59th Annual Meeting of the Association for Computational*

Linguistics and the 11th International Joint Conference on Natural Language Processing (Volume 1: Long Papers), pages 6524–6538, Online. Association for Computational Linguistics.

Y. Liu and X. Yao. 1999. Ensemble learning via negative correlation. *Neural Networks*, 12(10):1399–1404.

Yinhan Liu, Myle Ott, Naman Goyal, Jingfei Du, Mandar Joshi, Danqi Chen, Omer Levy, Mike Lewis, Luke Zettlemoyer, and Veselin Stoyanov. 2019. RoBERTa: A robustly optimized BERT pretraining approach. *CoRR*, abs/1907.11692.

Tianyu Pang, Kun Xu, Chao Du, Ning Chen, and Jun Zhu. 2019. Improving adversarial robustness via promoting ensemble diversity. In *Proceedings of the 36th International Conference on Machine Learning*, volume 97 of *Proceedings of Machine Learning Research*, pages 4970–4979. PMLR.

Sai Prasanna, Anna Rogers, and Anna Rumshisky. 2020. When BERT Plays the Lottery, All Tickets Are Winning. In *Proceedings of the 2020 Conference on Empirical Methods in Natural Language Processing (EMNLP 2020)*, pages 3208–3229, Online. Association for Computational Linguistics.

Evani Radiya-Dixit and Xin Wang. 2020. How fine can fine-tuning be? learning efficient language models. In *Proceedings of the Twenty Third International Conference on Artificial Intelligence and Statistics (ICML 2020)*, volume 108 of *Proceedings of Machine Learning Research*, pages 2435–2443. PMLR.

Colin Raffel, Noam Shazeer, Adam Roberts, Katherine Lee, Sharan Narang, Michael Matena, Yanqi Zhou, Wei Li, and Peter J. Liu. 2020. Exploring the limits of transfer learning with a unified text-to-text transformer. *Journal of Machine Learning Research*, 21(140):1–67.

Pranav Rajpurkar, Jian Zhang, Konstantin Lopyrev, and Percy Liang. 2016. SQuAD: 100,000+ questions for machine comprehension of text. In *Proceedings of the 2016 Conference on Empirical Methods in Natural Language Processing (EMNLP 2016)*, pages 2383–2392, Austin, Texas. Association for Computational Linguistics.

Alexandre Rame and Matthieu Cord. 2021. {DICE}: Diversity in deep ensembles via conditional redundancy adversarial estimation. In *Proceedings of the 9th International Conference on Learning Representations (ICLR 2021)*.

Victor Sanh, Thomas Wolf, and Alexander Rush. 2020. Movement pruning: Adaptive sparsity by fine-tuning. In *Advances in Neural Information Processing Systems*, volume 33, pages 20378–20389. Curran Associates, Inc.

Thibault Sellam, Steve Yadlowsky, Ian Tenney, Jason Wei, Naomi Saphra, Alexander D'Amour, Tal Linzen, Jasmijn Bastings, Iulia Raluca Turc, Jacob Eisenstein, Dipanjan Das, and Ellie Pavlick. 2022. The multiBERTs: BERT reproductions for robustness analysis. In *International Conference on Learning Representations (ICLR 2022)*.

Or Sharir, Barak Peleg, and Yoav Shoham. 2020. The cost of training NLP models: A concise overview. *CoRR*, abs/2004.08900.

David B. Skalak. 1996. The sources of increased accuracy for two proposed boosting algorithms. In *In Proc. American Association for Arti Intelligence, AAAI-96, Integrating Multiple Learned Models Workshop*, pages 120–125.

Richard Socher, Alex Perelygin, Jean Wu, Jason Chuang, Christopher D. Manning, Andrew Ng, and Christopher Potts. 2013. Recursive deep models for semantic compositionality over a sentiment treebank. In *Proceedings of the 2013 Conference on Empirical Methods in Natural Language Processing (EMNLP 2013)*, pages 1631–1642, Seattle, Washington, USA. Association for Computational Linguistics.

Yi Tay, Mostafa Dehghani, Jinfeng Rao, William Fedus, Samira Abnar, Hyung Won Chung, Sharan Narang, Dani Yogatama, Ashish Vaswani, and Donald Metzler. 2022. Scale efficiently: Insights from pretraining and finetuning transformers. In *International Conference on Learning Representations*.

Alex Wang, Yada Pruksachatkun, Nikita Nangia, Amanpreet Singh, Julian Michael, Felix Hill, Omer Levy, and Samuel Bowman. 2019. SuperGLUE: A stickier benchmark for general-purpose language understanding systems. In *Advances in Neural Information Processing Systems 32 (NeurIPS 2019)*. Curran Associates, Inc.

Alex Wang, Amanpreet Singh, Julian Michael, Felix Hill, Omer Levy, and Samuel Bowman. 2018. GLUE: A multi-task benchmark and analysis platform for natural language understanding. In *Proceedings of the 2018 EMNLP Workshop BlackboxNLP: Analyzing and Interpreting Neural Networks for NLP*, pages 353–355, Brussels, Belgium. Association for Computational Linguistics.

Alex Warstadt, Amanpreet Singh, and Samuel R. Bowman. 2019. Neural network acceptability judgments. *Transactions of the Association for Computational Linguistics*, 7:625–641.

Adina Williams, Nikita Nangia, and Samuel Bowman. 2018. A broad-coverage challenge corpus for sentence understanding through inference. In *Proceedings of the 2018 Conference of the North American Chapter of the Association for Computational Linguistics: Human Language Technologies, Volume 1 (Long Papers)*, pages 1112–1122, New Orleans, Louisiana. Association for Computational Linguistics.

Thomas Wolf, Lysandre Debut, Victor Sanh, Julien Chaumond, Clement Delangue, Anthony Moi, Pierric Cistac, Tim Rault, Rémi Louf, Morgan Funtowicz,

Joe Davison, Sam Shleifer, Patrick von Platen, Clara Ma, Yacine Jernite, Julien Plu, Canwen Xu, Teven Le Scao, Sylvain Gugger, Mariama Drame, Quentin Lhoest, and Alexander M. Rush. 2020. Transformers: State-of-the-art natural language processing. In *Proceedings of the 2020 Conference on Empirical Methods in Natural Language Processing: System Demonstrations (EMNLP 2020)*, pages 38–45, Online. Association for Computational Linguistics.

Yanzhao Wu, Ling Liu, Zhongwei Xie, Ka-Ho Chow, and Wenqi Wei. 2021. Boosting ensemble accuracy by revisiting ensemble diversity metrics. In *Proceedings of the IEEE/CVF Conference on Computer Vision and Pattern Recognition (CVPR)*, pages 16469–16477.

G. Udny Yule. 1900. On the association of attributes in statistics: With illustrations from the material of the childhood society, &c. *Philosophical Transactions of the Royal Society of London*, 194:257–319.

Zhilu Zhang, Vianne R. Gao, and Mert R. Sabuncu. 2021. Ex uno plures: Splitting one model into an ensemble of subnetworks.

Mengjie Zhao, Tao Lin, Fei Mi, Martin Jaggi, and Hinrich Schütze. 2020. Masking as an efficient alternative to finetuning for pretrained language models. In *Proceedings of the 2020 Conference on Empirical Methods in Natural Language Processing (EMNLP 2020)*, pages 2226–2241, Online. Association for Computational Linguistics.

A The Setting of Fine-tuning

We follow the setting of Chen et al. (2020)'s implementation; epoch: 3, initial learning rate: 2e-5 with linear decay, maximum sequence length: 128, batch size: 32, dropout probability: 0.1. This is one of the most-used settings for finetuning a BERT; e.g., the example of finetuning in the Transformers library (Wolf et al., 2020) uses the setting[9].

We did not prune the embedding layer, following Chen et al. (2020); Prasanna et al. (2020). The coefficient of L_1 regularizer, τ, is decayed using the same scheduler as the learning rate. We tuned it on MRPC and used it for other tasks.

B The Learning Rate Scheduler of Chen et al. (2020)

Our implementation used in the experiments are derived from Chen et al. (2020)'s implementation[10]. However, we found a bug in Chen et al. (2020)'s implementation on GitHub. Thus, we fixed it and experimented with the correct version. In their implementation, the learning rate schedule did not follow the common setting and the description mentioned in the paper; *'We use standard implementations and hyperparameters [49]. Learning rate decays linearly from initial value to zero'*. Specifically, the learning rate with linear decay did not reach zero but was at significant levels even at the end of the finetuning. Our implementation corrected it so that it did reach zero as specified in their paper and in the common setting.

C The Combinations of Ensembles

In the experiments, we first prepared twenty random seeds and split them into two groups, each of which trained ten models. For stabilizing the measurement of the result, we exhaustively evaluated all the possible combinations of ensembles (i.e., depending on the number of members, ${}_{10}C_2$, ${}_{10}C_3$, ${}_{10}C_4$, ${}_{10}C_5$ patterns, respectively) among the ten models for each group, and averaged the results with the two groups. The performance of the members is also averaged over all the seeds.

[9]https://github.com/huggingface/transformers/blob/7e406f4a65727baf8e22ae922f410224cde99ed6/examples/pytorch/text-classification/README.md#glue-tasks

[10]https://github.com/VITA-Group/BERT-Tickets

	MRPC			STS-B		
	single	ens.	diff.	single	ens.	diff.
BASELINE	87.77	88.47	+0.70	89.52	90.00	+0.48
(BAGGING)	87.64	88.12	+0.49	89.34	89.91	+0.54
BASE-LT	87.72	88.25	+0.53	89.71	90.07	+0.36
ACTIVE-LT	87.39	88.51	+1.12	88.46	89.50	+1.04
RANDOM-LT	87.86	89.26	+1.40	88.41	89.39	+0.98

Table 3: The performances (single, ens.) and the improvements by ensembling (diff.) of RoBERTa-base models.

D The Results with RoBERTa

We simply conducted supplementary experiments with RoBERTa (Liu et al., 2019) (robeta-base model), although optimal hyperparameters were not searched well. The results were similar to the cases of base-base-uncased. The patterns can be categorized into the three. First, multi-ticket ensembles worked well with roberta on MRPC, as shown in Table 3. Secondly, accurate winning-ticket subnetworks were not found on CoLA and QNLI. Although the effect of ensembleing was improved after pruning, each single model got worse and the final ensemble accuracy did not outperform the dense baseline. Thirdly, although accurate winning-ticket subnetworks were found on STS-B and SST-2, regularizations worsened single-model performances. While this case also improved the effect of ensembling, the final accuracy did not outperform the baseline. These experiments further emphasized the importance of development of more sophisticated pruning methods without sacrifice of model performances in the context of the lottery ticket hypothesis.

E Related Work

Some concurrent studies also investigate the usage of subnetworks for ensembles. Gal and Ghahramani (2016) is a pioneer to use subnetwork ensemble. A trained neural network with dropout can infer with many different subnetworks, and their ensemble can be used for uncertainty estimation, which is called MC-dropout. Durasov et al. (2021) improved the efficiency of MC-dropout by exploring subnetworks. Zhang et al. (2021) (unpublished) experimented with an ensemble of subnetworks of different structures and initialization when trained from scratch, while the improvements possibly could be due to regularization of each single model. Havasi et al. (2021) is a similar but more elegant approach, which does not explicitly identify subnetworks. Instead, it trains a single dense model with training using multi-input multi-output inference; the optimization can implicitly find multiple disentangled subnetworks in the dense model during optimization from random initialization. These studies support our assumption that different subnetworks can improve ensemble by diversity.

Some other directions for introducing diversity exist, while most are unstable. Promising directions are to use entropy (Pang et al., 2019) or adversarial training (Rame and Cord, 2021). Although they required complex optimization processes, they improved the robustness or ensemble performance on small image recognition datasets.

Recently, concurrent work (Sellam et al., 2022; Tay et al., 2022) provide multiple BERT or T5 models pretrained from different seeds or configurations for investigation of seed or configuration dependency using large-scale computational resources. Further research with the models and such computational resources will be helpful for more solid comparison and analysis.

Note that no prior work tackled the problem of ensembles from a pre-trained model. Framing the problem is one of the contributions of this paper. Secondly, our multi-ticket ensemble based on random masking enables an independently parallelizable training while existing methods require a sequential processing or a grouped training procedure. Finally, multi-ticket ensemble can be combined with other methods, which can improve the total performance together.

UNIREX: A Unified Learning Framework for Language Model Rationale Extraction

Aaron Chan[1*], Maziar Sanjabi[2], Lambert Mathias[2], Liang Tan[2], Shaoliang Nie[2], Xiaochang Peng[2], Xiang Ren[1], Hamed Firooz[2]

[1]University of Southern California, [2]Meta AI

{chanaaro,xiangren}@usc.edu,

{maziars,mathiasl,liangtan,snie,xiaochang,mhfirooz}@fb.com

Abstract

An extractive rationale explains a language model's (LM's) prediction on a given task instance by highlighting the text inputs that most influenced the prediction. Ideally, rationale extraction should be *faithful* (reflective of LM's actual behavior) and *plausible* (convincing to humans), without compromising the LM's (*i.e.,* task model's) *task performance*. Although attribution algorithms and select-predict pipelines are commonly used in rationale extraction, they both rely on certain heuristics that hinder them from satisfying all three desiderata. In light of this, we propose UNIREX, a flexible learning framework which generalizes rationale extractor optimization as follows: (1) specify architecture for a learned rationale extractor; (2) select explainability objectives (*i.e.,* faithfulness and plausibility criteria); and (3) jointly train the task model and rationale extractor on the task using selected objectives. UNIREX enables replacing prior works' heuristic design choices with a generic learned rationale extractor in (1) and optimizing it for all three desiderata in (2)-(3). To facilitate comparison between methods w.r.t. multiple desiderata, we introduce the Normalized Relative Gain (NRG) metric. Across five English text classification datasets, our best UNIREX configuration outperforms the strongest baselines by an average of 32.9% NRG. Plus, we find that UNIREX-trained rationale extractors' faithfulness can even generalize to unseen datasets and tasks.

1 Introduction

Large neural language models (LMs) have yielded state-of-the-art performance on various natural language processing (NLP) tasks (Devlin et al., 2018; Liu et al., 2019). However, LMs' complex reasoning processes are notoriously opaque (Rudin, 2019), posing concerns about the societal implications of using LMs for high-stakes decision-making (Bender et al., 2021). Thus, explaining LMs' behavior is crucial for promoting trust, ethics, and safety in NLP systems (Doshi-Velez and Kim, 2017; Lipton, 2018). Given a LM's (*i.e.,* task model's) predicted label on a text classification instance, an *extractive rationale* is a type of explanation that highlights the tokens that most influenced the model to predict that label (Luo et al., 2021). Ideally, rationale extraction should be *faithful* (Ismail et al., 2021; Jain et al., 2020) and *plausible* (DeYoung et al., 2019), without hurting the LM's *task performance* (DeYoung et al., 2019) (Fig. 1).

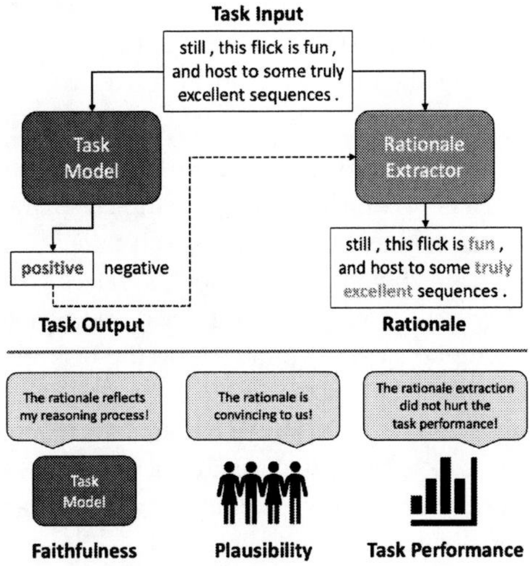

Figure 1: **Desiderata of Rationale Extraction.** Unlike prior works, UNIREX enables optimizing for all three desiderata.

Configuring the rationale extractor and its training can greatly impact these desiderata, yet prior works have commonly adopted two suboptimal heuristics. First, many works rely in some way on *attribution algorithms* (AAs), which extract rationales via handcrafted functions (Sundararajan et al., 2017; Ismail et al., 2021; Situ et al., 2021). AAs cannot be directly trained and tend to be compute-intensive (Bastings and Filippova, 2020). Also, AAs can be a bottleneck for plausibility, as producing human-like rationales is a complex objec-

*Work done while AC was a research intern at Meta AI.

Proceedings of BigScience Episode #5 – Workshop on Challenges & Perspectives in Creating Large Language Models, pages 51 - 67
May 27, 2022 ©2022 Association for Computational Linguistics

tive requiring high capacity rationale extractors (Narang et al., 2020; DeYoung et al., 2019). Second, many works use a specialized *select-predict pipeline* (SPP), where a predictor module is trained to solve the task using only tokens chosen by a selector module (Jain et al., 2020; Yu et al., 2021; Paranjape et al., 2020). Instead of faithfulness optimization, SPPs heuristically aim for "faithfulness by construction" by treating the selected tokens as a rationale for the predictor's output (which depends only on those tokens). Still, SPPs typically have worse task performance than vanilla LMs since SPPs hide the full input from the predictor.

To tackle this challenge, we propose the **UNI**fied Learning Framework for **R**ationale **EX**traction (**UNIREX**), which generalizes rationale extractor optimization as follows: (1) specify architecture for a learned rationale extractor; (2) select explainability objectives (*i.e.,* faithfulness and plausibility criteria); and (3) jointly train the task model and rationale extractor on the task using selected objectives (Sec. 3). UNIREX enables replacing prior works' heuristic design choices in (1) with a generic learned rationale extractor and optimizing it for all three desiderata in (2)-(3).

UNIREX provides significant flexibility in performing (1)-(3). For (1), any model architecture is applicable, but we study Transformer LM based rationale extractors in this work (Zaheer et al., 2020; DeYoung et al., 2019). We focus on two architectures: (A) Dual LM, where task model and rationale extractor are separate and (B) Shared LM, where task model and rationale extractor share parameters. For (2), any faithfulness and plausibility criteria can be used. Following DeYoung et al. (2019), we focus on comprehensiveness and sufficiency as faithfulness criteria, while using similarity to gold rationales as plausibility criteria. For (3), trade-offs between the three desiderata can be easily managed during rationale extractor optimization by setting arbitrary loss weights for the faithfulness and plausibility objectives. Plus, though computing the faithfulness criteria involves discrete (non-differentiable) token selection, using Shared LM can approximate end-to-end training and enable both task model and rationale extractor to be optimized w.r.t. all three desiderata (Sec. 3.3).

To evaluate all three desiderata in aggregate, we introduce the Normalized Relative Gain (NRG) metric. Across five English text classification datasets – SST, Movies, CoS-E, MultiRC, and e-SNLI (Carton et al., 2020; DeYoung et al., 2019) – our best UNIREX configuration outperforms the strongest baselines by an average of 32.9% NRG (Sec. 4.2), showing that UNIREX can optimize rationale extractors for all three desiderata. In addition, we verify our UNIREX design choices via extensive ablation studies (Sec. 4.3). Furthermore, UNIREX-trained extractors have high generalization power, yielding high plausiblity with minimal gold rationale supervision (Sec. 4.4) and high faithfulness on unseen datasets and tasks (Sec. 4.5). Finally, our user study shows that humans judge UNIREX rationales as more plausible than rationales extracted using other methods (Sec. 4.6).

2 Problem Formulation

Rationale Extraction Let $\mathcal{F}_{\text{task}} = f_{\text{task}}(f_{\text{enc}}(\cdot))$ be a task model for M-class text classification (Sec. A.1), where f_{enc} is the text encoder and f_{task} is the task output head. Typically, $\mathcal{F}_{\text{task}}$ has a BERT-style architecture (Devlin et al., 2018), in which f_{enc} is a Transformer (Vaswani et al., 2017) while f_{task} is a linear layer with softmax classifier. Let $\mathbf{x}_i = [x_i^t]_{t=1}^n$ be the n-token input sequence (*e.g.,* a sentence) for task instance i, and $\mathcal{F}_{\text{task}}(\mathbf{x}_i) \in \mathbb{R}^M$ be the logit vector for the output of the task model. Let $\hat{y}_i = \arg\max_j \mathcal{F}_{\text{task}}(\mathbf{x}_i)_j$ be the class predicted by $\mathcal{F}_{\text{task}}$. Given $\mathcal{F}_{\text{task}}$, $\mathbf{x}_i$, and $\hat{y}_i$, the goal of rationale extraction is to output vector $\mathbf{s}_i = [s_i^t]_{t=1}^n \in \mathbb{R}^n$, such that each $s_i^t \in \mathbb{R}$ is an *importance score* indicating how much token x_i^t influenced $\mathcal{F}_{\text{task}}$ to predict class $\hat{y}_i$. Let $\mathcal{F}_{\text{ext}}$ be a rationale extractor, such that $\mathbf{s}_i = \mathcal{F}_{\text{ext}}(\mathcal{F}_{\text{task}}, \mathbf{x}_i, \hat{y}_i)$. $\mathcal{F}_{\text{ext}}$ can be a learned or heuristic function. In practice, the final rationale is often obtained by binarizing $\mathbf{s}_i$ as $\mathbf{r}_i \in \{0,1\}^n$, via the top-$k$% strategy: $r_i^t = 1$ if s_i^t is one of the top-k% scores in $\mathbf{s}_i$; otherwise, $r_i^t = 0$ (DeYoung et al., 2019; Jain et al., 2020; Pruthi et al., 2020; Chan et al., 2021). For top-k%, let $\mathbf{r}_i^{(k)}$ be the "important" (*i.e.,* ones) tokens in $\mathbf{r}_i$, when using $0 \leq k \leq 100$.

Faithfulness means how well a rationale reflects $\mathcal{F}_{\text{task}}$'s true reasoning process for predicting $\hat{y}_i$ (Jacovi and Goldberg, 2020). Hence, faithfulness metrics measure how much the $\mathbf{r}_i^{(k)}$ tokens impact $p_{\hat{y}_i}(\mathbf{x}_i)$, which denotes $\mathcal{F}_{\text{task}}$'s confidence probability for $\hat{y}_i$ when using $\mathbf{x}_i$ as input (DeYoung et al., 2019; Shrikumar et al., 2017; Hooker et al., 2018; Pruthi et al., 2020). Recently, comprehensiveness and sufficiency have emerged as popular faithfulness metrics (DeYoung et al.,

2019). ***Comprehensiveness*** (comp) measures the change in $p_{\hat{y}_i}$ when $\mathbf{r}_i^{(k)}$ is *removed* from the input: $\text{comp} = p_{\hat{y}_i}(\mathbf{x}_i) - p_{\hat{y}_i}(\mathbf{x}_i \backslash \mathbf{r}_i^{(k)})$. ***Sufficiency*** (suff) measures the change in $p_{\hat{y}_i}$ when only $\mathbf{r}_i^{(k)}$ is *kept* in the input: $\text{suff} = p_{\hat{y}_i}(\mathbf{x}_i) - p_{\hat{y}_i}(\mathbf{r}_i^{(k)})$. High faithfulness is signaled by high comp and low suff.

Plausibility means how convincing a rationale is to humans (Jacovi and Goldberg, 2020). This can be measured by automatically computing the similarity between $\mathcal{F}_{\text{ext}}$'s rationales (either $\mathbf{s}_i$ or $\mathbf{r}_i$) and human-annotated gold rationales (DeYoung et al., 2019), or by asking human annotators to rate whether $\mathcal{F}_{\text{ext}}$'s rationales make sense for predicting $\hat{y}_i$ (Strout et al., 2019; Doshi-Velez and Kim, 2017). Typically, a gold rationale is a binary vector $\mathbf{r}_i^* \in \{0,1\}^n$, where ones/zeros indicate important/unimportant tokens (Lei et al., 2016).

Task Performance, w.r.t. rationale extraction, concerns how much $\mathcal{F}_{\text{task}}$'s task performance (on test set) drops when $\mathcal{F}_{\text{task}}$ is trained with explainability objectives (*i.e.,* faithfulness, plausibility) for $\mathcal{F}_{\text{ext}}$. As long as $\mathcal{F}_{\text{task}}$ is trained with non-task losses, $\mathcal{F}_{\text{task}}$'s task performance can be affected.

3 UNIREX

Given task model $\mathcal{F}_{\text{task}}$, UNIREX generalizes rationale extractor optimization as follows: (1) choose architecture for a learned rationale extractor $\mathcal{F}_{\text{ext}}$; (2) select explainability objectives (*i.e.,* faithfulness loss $\mathcal{L}_{\text{faith}}$ and plausibility loss $\mathcal{L}_{\text{plaus}}$); and (3) jointly train $\mathcal{F}_{\text{task}}$ and $\mathcal{F}_{\text{ext}}$ using $\mathcal{L}_{\text{task}}$ (task loss), $\mathcal{L}_{\text{faith}}$, and $\mathcal{L}_{\text{plaus}}$. UNIREX training consists of two backpropagation paths (Fig. 2). The first path is used to update $\mathcal{F}_{\text{task}}$ w.r.t. $\mathcal{L}_{\text{task}}$ and $\mathcal{L}_{\text{faith}}$. Whereas $\mathcal{L}_{\text{task}}$ is computed w.r.t. the task target y_i, $\mathcal{L}_{\text{faith}}$ is computed only using the task input $\mathbf{x}_i$ and the top-$k\%$ important tokens $\mathbf{r}_i^{(k)}$ (obtained via $\mathcal{F}_{\text{ext}}$), based on some combination of comp and suff (Sec. 2). The second path is used to update $\mathcal{F}_{\text{ext}}$ w.r.t. $\mathcal{L}_{\text{plaus}}$, which encourages importance scores $\mathbf{s}_i$ to approximate gold rationale $\mathbf{r}_i^*$. Thus, UNIREX frames rationale extraction as the following optimization problem:

$$\begin{aligned} \min_{\mathcal{F}_{\text{task}}, \mathcal{F}_{\text{ext}}} \; & \mathcal{L}_{\text{task}}(\mathbf{x}_i, y_i; \mathcal{F}_{\text{task}}) \\ & + \alpha_f \mathcal{L}_{\text{faith}}(\mathbf{x}_i, \mathbf{r}_i^{(k)}; \mathcal{F}_{\text{task}}) \\ & + \alpha_p \mathcal{L}_{\text{plaus}}(\mathbf{x}_i, \mathbf{r}_i^*; \mathcal{F}_{\text{ext}}), \end{aligned} \tag{1}$$

where α_f and α_p are loss weights. If $\mathcal{F}_{\text{task}}$ and $\mathcal{F}_{\text{ext}}$ share parameters, then the shared parameters will be optimized w.r.t. all losses. During inference, for task input $\mathbf{x}_i$, we first use $\mathcal{F}_{\text{task}}$ to predict y_i, then use $\mathcal{F}_{\text{ext}}$ to output a rationale $\mathbf{r}_i$ for $\mathcal{F}_{\text{task}}$'s prediction $\hat{y}_i$. Below, we discuss options for the rationale extractor and explainability objectives.

3.1 Rationale Extractor

In UNIREX, $\mathcal{F}_{\text{ext}}$ is a learned function by default. Learned $\mathcal{F}_{\text{ext}}$ can be any model that transforms x_i^t into s_i^t. Given their success in NLP explainability (DeYoung et al., 2019), we focus on pre-trained Transformer LMs and highlight two architectures: Dual LM (DLM) and Shared LM (SLM) (Fig. 3). For DLM, $\mathcal{F}_{\text{task}}$ and $\mathcal{F}_{\text{ext}}$ are two separate Transformer LMs. DLM provides more dedicated capacity for $\mathcal{F}_{\text{ext}}$, which can help $\mathcal{F}_{\text{ext}}$ output plausible rationales. For SLM, $\mathcal{F}_{\text{task}}$ and $\mathcal{F}_{\text{ext}}$ are two Transformer LMs sharing encoder f_{enc}, while $\mathcal{F}_{\text{ext}}$ has its own output head f_{ext}. SLM leverages multitask learning between $\mathcal{F}_{\text{task}}$ and $\mathcal{F}_{\text{ext}}$, which can improve faithfulness since $\mathcal{F}_{\text{ext}}$ gets more information about $\mathcal{F}_{\text{task}}$'s reasoning process. Unlike heuristic $\mathcal{F}_{\text{ext}}$ (Sec. A.2), learned $\mathcal{F}_{\text{ext}}$ can be optimized for faithfulness/plausibility, but cannot be used out of the box without training. Learned $\mathcal{F}_{\text{ext}}$ is preferred if: (A) optimizing for both faithfulness and plausibility, and (B) gold rationales are available for plausibility optimization (Sec. A.3).

3.2 Explainability Objectives

After selecting $\mathcal{F}_{\text{ext}}$, we specify the explainability objectives, which can be any combination of faithfulness and plausibility criteria. In prior approaches (*e.g.,* AA, SPPs), the rationale extractor is not optimized for both faithfulness and plausibility, but UNIREX makes this possible. For any choice of learned $\mathcal{F}_{\text{ext}}$, UNIREX lets us easily "plug and play" different criteria and loss weights, based on our needs and domain knowledge, to find those that best balance the rationale extraction desiderata.

Faithfulness Evaluating rationale faithfulness is still an open problem with many existing metrics, and UNIREX is not tailored for any specific metric. Still, given the prevalence of comp/suff (Sec. 2), we focus on comp/suff based objectives.

Recall that comp measures the importance of tokens in $\mathbf{r}_i^{(k)}$ as how $p_{\hat{y}_i}(\hat{\mathbf{x}}_i)$, $\mathcal{F}_{\text{task}}$'s predicted probability for class $\hat{y}_i$, changes when those tokens are removed from $\mathbf{x}_i$. Intuitively, we want $p_{\hat{y}_i}(\hat{\mathbf{x}}_i)$ to be higher than $p_{\hat{y}_i}(\mathbf{x}_i \backslash \mathbf{r}_i^{(k)})$, so higher comp is better. Since comp is defined for a single class' probability rather than the label distribution, we can define the comp loss $\mathcal{L}_{\text{comp}}$ via cross-entropy loss $\mathcal{L}_{\text{CE}}$, as in

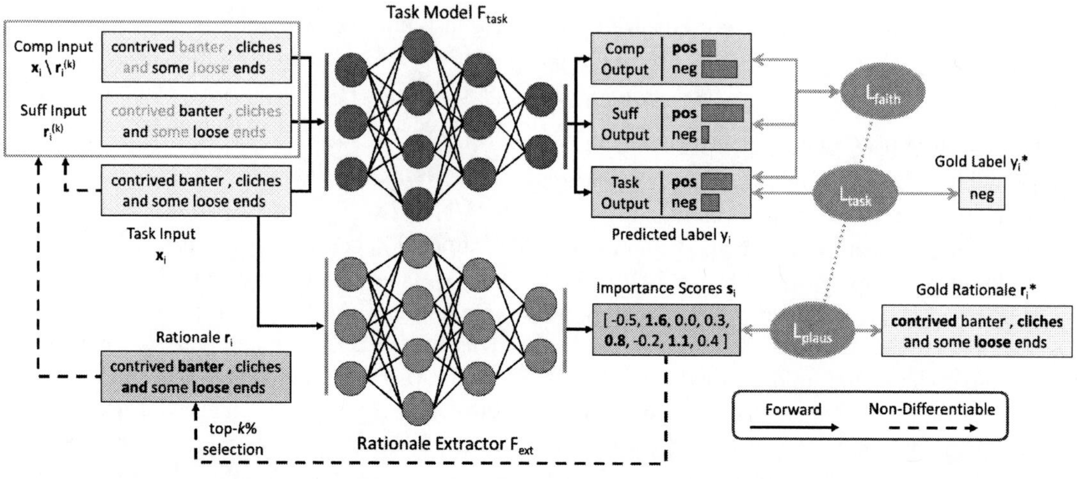

Figure 2: **UNIREX Framework.** UNIREX enables jointly optimizing the task model ($\mathcal{F}_{\text{task}}$) and rationale extractor ($\mathcal{F}_{\text{ext}}$), w.r.t. faithfulness ($\mathcal{L}_{\text{faith}}$), plausibility ($\mathcal{L}_{\text{plaus}}$), and task performance ($\mathcal{L}_{\text{task}}$).

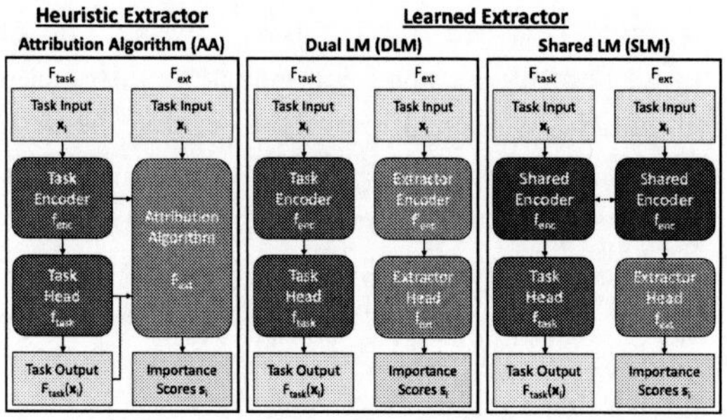

Figure 3: **Rationale Extractor Types.**

the following *difference criterion* for $\mathcal{L}_{\text{comp}}$:

$$\begin{aligned}\mathcal{L}_{\text{comp-diff}} = &\ \mathcal{L}_{\text{CE}}(\mathcal{F}_{\text{task}}(\mathbf{x}_i), y_i) \\ &- \mathcal{L}_{\text{CE}}(\mathcal{F}_{\text{task}}(\mathbf{x}_i \backslash \mathbf{r}_i^{(k)}), y_i))\end{aligned} \tag{2}$$

$$\mathcal{L}_{\text{CE}}(\mathcal{F}_{\text{task}}(\mathbf{x}_i), y_i) = -y_i \log(\mathcal{F}_{\text{task}}(\mathbf{x}_i)) \tag{3}$$

For training stability, we compute comp loss for target class y_i here instead of $\mathcal{F}_{\text{task}}$'s predicted class $\hat{y}_i$, since $\hat{y}_i$ is a moving target during training. Using $\mathcal{L}_{\text{comp-diff}}$, it is possible for $\mathcal{L}_{\text{CE}}(\mathcal{F}_{\text{task}}(\mathbf{x}_i \backslash \mathbf{r}_i^{(k)}), y_i))$ to become much larger than $\mathcal{L}_{\text{CE}}(\mathcal{F}_{\text{task}}(\mathbf{x}_i), y_i)$, leading to arbitrarily negative losses. To avoid this, we can add margin m_c to the loss function, giving the *margin criterion*:

$$\begin{aligned}\mathcal{L}_{\text{comp-margin}} = &\max(-m_c, \mathcal{L}_{\text{CE}}(\mathcal{F}_{\text{task}}(\mathbf{x}_i), y_i) \\ &- \mathcal{L}_{\text{CE}}(\mathcal{F}_{\text{task}}(\mathbf{x}_i \backslash \mathbf{r}_i^{(k)}), y_i)) + m_c\end{aligned} \tag{4}$$

Recall that suff measures the importance of tokens in $\mathbf{r}_i^{(k)}$ as how $p_{\hat{y}_i}(\hat{\mathbf{x}}_i)$, $\mathcal{F}_{\text{task}}$'s predicted probability for class $\hat{y}_i$, changes when they are the only tokens kept in $\mathbf{x}_i$. Based on suff's definition, we want $p_{\hat{y}_i}(\mathbf{r}_i^{(k)})$ to be higher than $p_{\hat{y}_i}(\hat{\mathbf{x}}_i)$, so lower suff is better. For suff loss $\mathcal{L}_{\text{suff}}$, we define the difference and margin criteria analogously with margin m_s but the opposite sign (since lower suff is better):

$$\begin{aligned}\mathcal{L}_{\text{suff-diff}} = &\ \mathcal{L}_{\text{CE}}(\mathcal{F}_{\text{task}}(\mathbf{r}_i^{(k)}), y_i) \\ &- \mathcal{L}_{\text{CE}}(\mathcal{F}_{\text{task}}(\mathbf{x}_i), y_i)\end{aligned} \tag{5}$$

$$\begin{aligned}\mathcal{L}_{\text{suff-margin}} = &\max(-m_s, \mathcal{L}_{\text{CE}}(\mathcal{F}_{\text{task}}(\mathbf{r}_i^{(k)}), y_i) \\ &- \mathcal{L}_{\text{CE}}(\mathcal{F}_{\text{task}}(\mathbf{x}_i), y_i)) + m_s\end{aligned} \tag{6}$$

In our experiments, we find that the margin-based comp/suff criteria are effective (Sec. 4.3), though others (*e.g.,* KL Div, MAE) can be used too (Sec. A.4.1). Note that $\mathbf{r}_i^{(k)}$ is computed via top-$k\%$ thresholding (Sec. 2), so we also need to specify a set K of threshold values. We separately compute the comp/suff losses for each $k \in K$, then obtain the final comp/suff losses by averaging over all k values via area-over-precision-curve (AOPC) (DeYoung et al., 2019). To reflect this, we denote the comp and suff losses as $\mathcal{L}_{\text{comp},K}$ and $\mathcal{L}_{\text{suff},K}$, respectively. Let $\alpha_f \mathcal{L}_{\text{faith}} = \alpha_c \mathcal{L}_{\text{comp},K} + \alpha_s \mathcal{L}_{\text{suff},K}$, where α_c and α_s are loss weights.

Plausibility Plausibility is defined as how convincing a rationale is to humans (Jacovi and Goldberg, 2020), *i.e.,* whether humans would agree the rationale supports the model's prediction. While optimizing for plausibility should ideally involve human-in-the-loop feedback, this is prohibitive. Instead, many works consider gold rationales as a cheaper form of plausibility annotation (DeYoung et al., 2019; Narang et al., 2020; Jain et al., 2020). Thus, if gold rationale supervision is available, then we can optimize for plausibility. With gold rationale $\mathbf{r}_i^*$ for input $\mathbf{x}_i$, plausibility optimization entails training $\mathcal{F}_{\text{ext}}$ to predict binary importance label $\mathbf{r}_i^{*,t}$ for each token x_i^t. This is essentially token classification, so one natural choice for $\mathcal{L}_{\text{plaus}}$ is the token-level binary cross-entropy (BCE) criterion:

$$\mathcal{L}_{\text{plaus-BCE}} = -\sum_t \mathbf{r}_i^{*,t} \log(\mathcal{F}_{\text{ext}}(x_i^t)) \tag{7}$$

Besides BCE loss, we can also consider other criteria like sequence-level KL divergence and L1 loss. See Sec. A.4.2 for discussion of these and other plausibility criteria.

3.3 Training and Inference

After setting $\mathcal{F}_{\text{ext}}$, $\mathcal{L}_{\text{faith}}$, and $\mathcal{L}_{\text{plaus}}$, we can move on to training $\mathcal{F}_{\text{task}}$ and $\mathcal{F}_{\text{ext}}$. Since top-$k\%$ rationale binarization (Sec. 3.2) is not differentiable, by default, we cannot backpropagate $\mathcal{L}_{\text{faith}}$ through all of $\mathcal{F}_{\text{ext}}$'s parameters. Thus, $\mathcal{F}_{\text{task}}$ is trained via $\mathcal{L}_{\text{task}}$ and $\mathcal{L}_{\text{faith}}$, while $\mathcal{F}_{\text{ext}}$ is only trained via $\mathcal{L}_{\text{plaus}}$. This means $\mathcal{F}_{\text{ext}}$'s rationales $\mathbf{r}_i$ are indirectly optimized for faithfulness by regularizing $\mathcal{F}_{\text{task}}$ such that its behavior aligns with $\mathbf{r}_i$. The exception is if we are using the SLM variant, where encoder f_{enc} is shared by $\mathcal{F}_{\text{task}}$ and $\mathcal{F}_{\text{ext}}$. In this case, f_{enc} is optimized w.r.t. all losses, f_{task} is optimized w.r.t. $\mathcal{L}_{\text{task}}$ and $\mathcal{L}_{\text{faith}}$, and f_{ext} is optimized w.r.t. $\mathcal{L}_{\text{plaus}}$. SLM is a simple way to approximate end-to-end training of $\mathcal{F}_{\text{task}}$ and $\mathcal{F}_{\text{ext}}$. In contrast, past SPPs have used more complex methods like reinforcement learning (Lei et al., 2016) and the reparameterization trick (Bastings et al., 2019), whose training instability can hurt task performance (Jain et al., 2020).

Now, we summarize the full learning objective. Given that cross-entropy loss $\mathcal{L}_{\text{task}} = \mathcal{L}_{\text{CE}}(\mathcal{F}_{\text{task}}(\mathbf{x}_i), y_i)$ is used to train $\mathcal{F}_{\text{task}}$ to predict y_i, the full learning objective is:

$$\begin{aligned}\mathcal{L} &= \mathcal{L}_{\text{task}} + \alpha_f \mathcal{L}_{\text{faith}} + \alpha_p \mathcal{L}_{\text{plaus}} \\ &= \mathcal{L}_{\text{task}} + \alpha_c \mathcal{L}_{\text{comp},K} + \alpha_s \mathcal{L}_{\text{suff},K} + \alpha_p \mathcal{L}_{\text{plaus}}.\end{aligned} \tag{8}$$

During inference, we use $\mathcal{F}_{\text{task}}$ to predict y_i, then use $\mathcal{F}_{\text{ext}}$ to output $\mathbf{r}_i$ for $\mathcal{F}_{\text{task}}$'s predicted label $\hat{y}_i$.

4 Experiments

We present empirical results demonstrating UNIREX's effectiveness in managing trade-offs between faithfulness, plausibility, and task performance during rationale extractor optimization. First, our main experiments compare methods w.r.t. faithfulness, plausibility, and task performance (Sec. 4.2). Second, we perform various ablation studies to verify our design choices for UNIREX (Sec. 4.3). Third, we present experiments highlighting UNIREX's generalization ability, both in terms of limited gold rationale supervision (Sec. 4.4) and zero-shot transfer (Sec. 4.5). Fourth, we conduct a user study to further evaluate UNIREX rationales' plausibility, relative to those generated by other methods (Sec. 4.6). See Sec. A.5 for implementation details (LM architecture, AA settings, training).

4.1 Experiment Setup

Datasets We primarily use SST (Socher et al., 2013; Carton et al., 2020), Movies (Zaidan and Eisner, 2008), CoS-E (Rajani et al., 2019), MultiRC (Khashabi et al., 2018), and e-SNLI (Camburu et al., 2018), all of which have gold rationale annotations. The latter four datasets were taken from the ERASER benchmark (DeYoung et al., 2019).

Metrics We use the metrics from the ERASER explainability benchmark (DeYoung et al., 2019). For faithfulness, we use comprehensiveness (Comp) and sufficiency (Suff), for $k = [1, 5, 10, 20, 50]$ (DeYoung et al., 2019). For plausibility, we use area under precision-recall curve (AUPRC) and token F1 (TF1) to measure similarity to gold rationales (DeYoung et al., 2019; Narang et al., 2020). For task performance, we follow (DeYoung et al., 2019) and (Carton et al., 2020) in using accuracy (SST, CoS-E) and macro F1 (Movies, MultiRC, e-SNLI).

To aggregately evaluate multiple desiderata, we introduce the Normalized Relative Gain (NRG) metric, which is based on the ARG metric from Ye et al. (2021). NRG normalizes raw metrics (*e.g.*, F1, sufficiency) to scores between 0 and 1 (higher is better). Given a set of raw metric scores $Z = \{z_1, z_2, ...\}$ (each from a different method), $\text{NRG}(z_i)$ captures z_i's value relative to $\min(Z)$ and $\max(Z)$. If higher values are better for the given metric (*e.g.*, F1), then we have: $\text{NRG}(z_i) = \frac{z_i - \min(Z)}{\max(Z) - \min(Z)}$. If lower values are better (*e.g.*, sufficiency), then we have: $\text{NRG}(z_i) = \frac{\max(Z) - z_i}{\max(Z) - \min(Z)}$. After computing NRG for multiple raw metrics, we can aggregate them w.r.t. desiderata via averaging. Let FNRG, PNRG, and TNRG be the NRG values for faithfulness, plausibility, and task performance, respectively. Finally, we compute the composite NRG as: $\text{CNRG} = \frac{\text{FNRG}+\text{PNRG}+\text{TNRG}}{3}$.

Results Reporting For all results, we report average over three seeds and the five k values. We

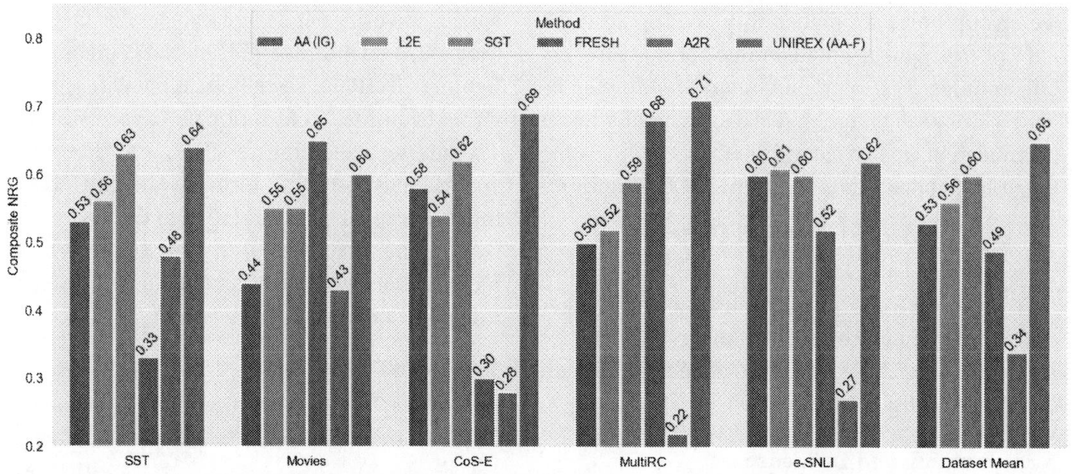

Figure 4: **Composite NRG Comparison (w/o Plausibility Optimization).** Composite NRG (CNRG) is the mean of the three desiderata NRG scores. For each dataset, we use CNRG to compare methods that *do not* optimize for plausibility.

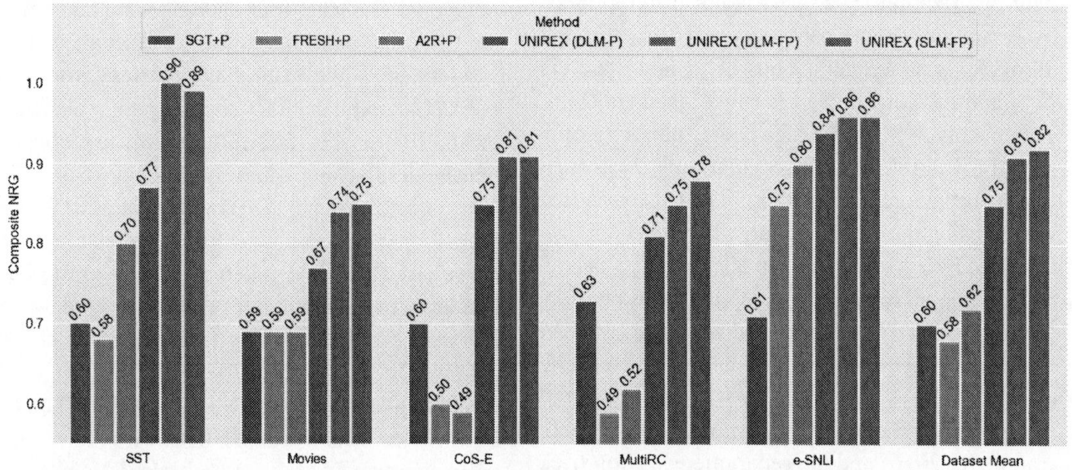

Figure 5: **Composite NRG Comparison (w/ Plausibility Optimization).** Composite NRG (CNRG) is the mean of the three desiderata NRG scores. For each dataset, we use CNRG to compare methods that *do* optimize for plausibility.

denote each UNIREX configuration with "([*rationale extractor*]-[*explainability objectives*])". F, P, and FP denote faithfulness, plausibility, and faithfulness+plausibility, respectively.

Baselines The first category is AAs, which are not trained: AA (Grad) (Simonyan et al., 2013), AA (Input*Grad) (Denil et al., 2014), AA (DeepLIFT) (Lundberg and Lee, 2017), AA (IG) (Sundararajan et al., 2017). We also experiment with IG for L2E (Situ et al., 2021), which distills knowledge from an AA to an LM. The second category is SPPs: FRESH (Jain et al., 2020) and A2R (Yu et al., 2021). For FRESH, we use a strong variant where IG rationales are directly given to the predictor, rather than output by a trained selector. A2R aims to improve SPP task performance by regularizing the predictor with an attention-based predictor that uses the full input. In addition, we introduce FRESH+P and A2R+P, which augment FRESH and A2R, respectively, with plausibility optimization. The third category is AA-based regularization: SGT (Ismail et al., 2021), which uses a sufficiency-based criterion to optimize for faithfulness. We also consider SGT+P, which augments SGT with plausibility optimization.

4.2 Main Results

Fig. 4-6 display the main results. In Fig. 4/5, we compare the CNRG for all methods and datasets, without/with gold rationales. In both plots, we see that UNIREX variants achieve the best CNRG across all datasets, indicating that they are effective in balancing the three desiderata. In particular, UNIREX (DLM-FP) and UNIREX (SLM-

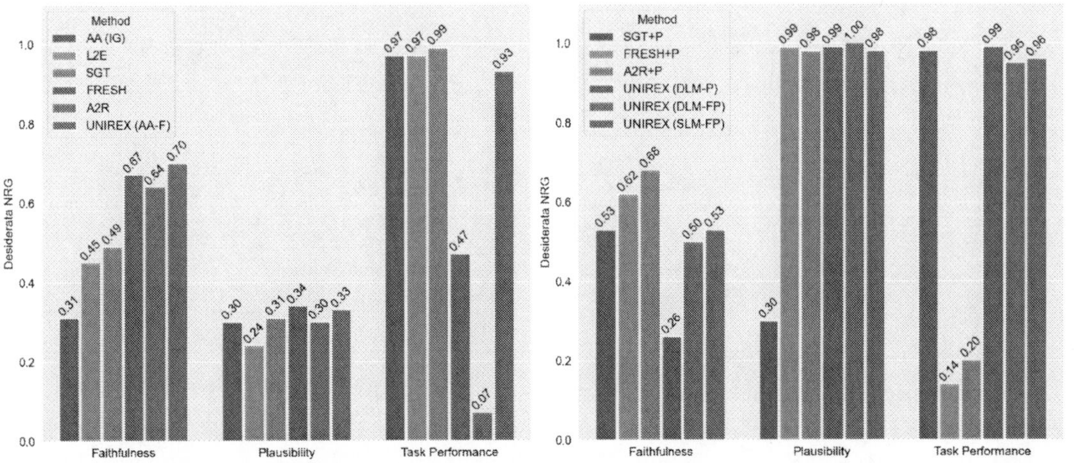

Figure 6: **NRG Comparison by Desiderata.** We show FNRG, PNRG, and TNRG for all methods, averaged over all datasets.

FP) have very high CNRG scores, both yielding more than 30% improvement over the strongest baselines. Fig. 6 compares methods w.r.t. desiderata NRG (*i.e.*, FNRG, PNRG, TNRG). Here, the left/right plots show methods without/with gold rationales. Again, we see that UNIREX variants achieve a good NRG balance of faithfulness, plausibility, and task performance. Meanwhile, many baselines (*e.g.*, AA (IG), A2R, SGT+P) do well on some desiderata but very poorly on others.

4.3 Ablation Studies

We present five ablation studies to validate the effectiveness of our UNIREX design choices. The ablation results are displayed in Table 1. In this table, each of the five sections shows results for a different ablation. Thus, all numbers within the same section and column are comparable.

Extractor Type In the Ext Type (F) section, we compare four heuristic rationale extractors, using AA-F. Rand uses random importance scores, Gold directly uses the gold rationales, Inv uses the inverse of the gold rationales, and IG uses IG. All heuristics yield similar task performance, but IG dominates on all faithfulness metrics. This makes sense because IG is computed using $\mathcal{F}_{\text{task}}$'s inputs/parameters/outputs, while the others do not have this information. For plausibility, Gold is the best, Inv is the worst, and Rand and IG are about the same, as none of the heuristics are optimized for plausibility. In the Ext Type (FP) section, we compare four learned rationale extractors. By default, attribution algorithms' dimension scores are pooled into token scores via sum pooling. AA-FP (Sum) uses IG with sum pooling, while AA-FP

Ablation	UNIREX Config	Faithfulness		Plausibility	Performance
		Comp (↑)	Suff (↓)	AUPRC (↑)	Acc (↑)
Ext Type (F)	AA-F (Rand)	0.171 (±0.040)	0.327 (±0.050)	44.92 (±0.00)	**94.05** (±0.35)
	AA-F (Gold)	0.232 (±0.088)	0.249 (±0.021)	**100.00** (±0.00)	93.81 (±0.54)
	AA-F (Inv)	0.242 (±0.010)	0.357 (±0.019)	20.49 (±0.00)	93.47 (±1.81)
	AA-F (IG)	**0.292** (±0.051)	**0.171** (±0.038)	48.13 (±1.14)	92.97 (±0.44)
Ext Type (FP)	AA-FP (Sum)	0.296 (±0.067)	0.185 (±0.048)	47.60 (±2.44)	93.25 (±0.45)
	AA-FP (MLP)	0.285 (±0.051)	0.197 (±0.100)	54.82 (±1.97)	93.23 (±0.92)
	DLM-FP	**0.319** (±0.090)	0.167 (±0.036)	**85.80** (±0.74)	**93.81** (±0.18)
	SLM-FP	0.302 (±0.039)	**0.113** (±0.013)	82.55 (±0.84)	93.68 (±0.67)
Comp/Suff Loss	SLM-FP (Comp)	**0.350** (±0.048)	0.310 (±0.049)	82.79 (±0.62)	93.59 (±0.11)
	SLM-FP (Suff)	0.166 (±0.003)	0.152 (±0.012)	**83.74** (±0.84)	**94.16** (±0.39)
	SLM-FP (Comp+Suff)	0.302 (±0.039)	**0.113** (±0.013)	82.55 (±0.84)	93.68 (±0.67)
Suff Criterion	SLM-FP (KL Div)	**0.306** (±0.098)	0.131 (±0.005)	82.62 (±0.88)	93.06 (±0.25)
	SLM-FP (MAE)	0.278 (±0.058)	0.143 (±0.008)	**82.66** (±0.61)	**93.78** (±0.13)
	SLM-FP (Margin)	0.302 (±0.039)	**0.113** (±0.013)	82.55 (±0.84)	93.68 (±0.67)
SLM Ext Head	SLM-FP (Linear)	0.302 (±0.039)	**0.113** (±0.013)	82.55 (±0.84)	**93.68** (±0.67)
	SLM-FP (MLP-2048-2)	**0.323** (±0.071)	0.144 (±0.012)	83.82 (±0.77)	93.67 (±0.18)
	SLM-FP (MLP-4096-3)	0.295 (±0.057)	0.154 (±0.027)	**84.53** (±0.61)	93.19 (±0.79)

Table 1: **UNIREX Ablation Studies on SST.**

(MLP) replaces the sum pooler with a MLP-based pooler to increase capacity for plausibility optimization. Task performance for all four methods is similar, AA-FP (Sum) dominates on faithfulness, and DLM-FP and SLM-FP dominate on plausibility. AA-FP (MLP) does not perform as well on faithfulness but slightly improves on plausibility compared to AA-FP (Sum).

Comp/Suff Losses The Comp/Suff Loss section compares different combinations of Comp and Suff losses, using SLM-FP. Note that SLM-FP (Comp+Suff) is equivalent to SLM-FP shown in other tables/sections. As expected, SLM-FP (Comp) does best on Comp, but SLM-FP (Comp+Suff) actually does best on Suff. Meanwhile, SLM-FP, (Suff) does second-best on Suff but is much worse on Comp. This shows that Comp and Suff are complementary for optimization.

Suff Criterion The Suff Criterion section compares different Suff criteria, using SLM-FP. SLM-FP (KLDiv) uses the KL divergence criterion, SLM-FP (MAE) uses the MAE criterion, and SLM-FP (Margin) uses the margin criterion. SLM-FP (Margin) is equivalent to SLM-FP in other ta-

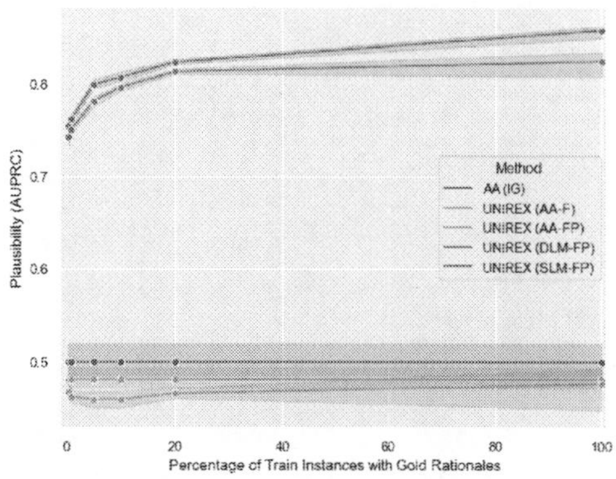

Figure 7: **Gold Rationale Data Efficiency on SST.**

Task	Dataset	Method	Faithfulness		Task Performance
			Comp (↑)	Suff (↓)	Perf (↑)
SA	SST	AA (IG)	0.119 (±0.009)	0.258 (±0.031)	**93.81** (±0.55)
		UNIREX (AA-F)	0.292 (±0.051)	0.171 (±0.038)	92.97 (±0.44)
		UNIREX (DLM-FP)	**0.319** (±0.090)	**0.167** (±0.036)	**93.81** (±0.54)
	Yelp	AA (IG)	0.069 (±0.004)	0.219 (±0.028)	**92.50** (±2.07)
		UNIREX (AA-F)	0.138 (±0.078)	0.126 (±0.059)	83.93 (±13.20)
		UNIREX (DLM-FP)	**0.265** (±0.094)	**0.097** (±0.033)	92.37 (±0.46)
	Amazon	AA (IG)	0.076 (±0.010)	0.224 (±0.037)	**91.13** (±0.28)
		UNIREX (AA-F)	0.130 (±0.077)	**0.073** (±0.039)	77.90 (±13.12)
		UNIREX (DLM-FP)	**0.232** (±0.072)	0.098 (±0.033)	89.35 (±2.22)
HSD	Stormfront	AA (IG)	0.135 (±0.010)	0.245 (±0.059)	**10.48** (±1.66)
		UNIREX (AA-F)	**0.219** (±0.009)	**0.092** (±0.025)	10.36 (±1.94)
		UNIREX (DLM-FP)	0.167 (±0.084)	0.115 (±0.059)	10.37 (±2.66)
OSD	OffenseEval	AA (IG)	0.097 (±0.009)	0.244 (±0.052)	33.51 (±0.99)
		UNIREX (AA-F)	0.074 (±0.040)	0.102 (±0.024)	32.62 (±4.85)
		UNIREX (DLM-FP)	**0.140** (±0.049)	**0.087** (±0.045)	**35.52** (±1.26)
ID	SemEval2018	AA (IG)	0.128 (±0.014)	0.248 (±0.064)	29.63 (±4.72)
		UNIREX (AA-F)	0.069 (±0.041)	**0.096** (±0.011)	**49.95** (±8.31)
		UNIREX (DLM-FP)	**0.149** (±0.052)	0.102 (±0.053)	31.97 (±2.80)

Table 2: **Zero-Shot Faithfulness Transfer from SST.**

bles/sections. All criteria yield similar performance and plausibility, while Margin is slightly better on faithfulness.

SLM Extractor Head The SLM Ext Head section compares different extractor heads, using SLM-FP. Linear is the default choice and uses a linear layer. MLP-2048-2 uses a MLP with two 2048-dim hidden layers. MLP-4096-3 uses a MLP with three 4096-dim hidden layers. All three output head types yield similar performance, but decreasing head capacity yields better faithfulness, while increasing head capacity heads yields better plausibility. This trades off faithfulness and plausibility, although larger heads will be more compute-intensive.

4.4 Gold Rationale Data Efficiency

UNIREX supports arbitrary amounts of gold rationale supervision and allows us to account for data efficiency. In Fig. 7, we compare plausibility (in AUPRC) for $\gamma = [0.5, 1, 5, 10, 20, 100]$ (*i.e.*, % of train instances with gold rationales). We compare AA (IG) and four UNIREX variants (AA-F, AA-FP, DLM-FP, SLM-FP). AA (IG) and AA-F do not use gold rationales and thus have the same AUPRC for all γ. Standard deviation is shown by the error bands. UNIREX (DLM-FP) and UNIREX (SLM-FP) dominate across all γ values, with AUPRC slowly decreasing as γ decreases. Even at $\gamma = 0.5$, they can still achieve high AUPRC. This suggests that UNIREX's gold rationale batching procedure (Sec. A.3) is effective for learning from minimal gold rationale supervision and demonstrates how UNIREX enables us to manage this trade-off. See Sec. A.6 for similar results on CoS-E.

4.5 Zero-Shot Faithfulness Transfer

In Table 2, we investigate if $\mathcal{F}_{\text{ext}}$'s faithfulness, via UNIREX training on some source dataset, can generalize to unseen target datasets/tasks in a zero-shot setting (*i.e.*, no fine-tuning on target datasets). Plausibility is not evaluated here, since these unseen datasets do not have gold rationales. As the source model, we compare various SST-trained models: AA (IG) and UNIREX (AA-F, DLM-FP). First, we evaluate on unseen datasets for a seen task (sentiment analysis (SA)): Yelp (Zhang et al., 2015) and Amazon (McAuley and Leskovec, 2013). Second, we evaluate on unseen datasets for unseen tasks: Stormfront (hate speech detection (HSD), binary F1) (de Gibert et al., 2018), OffenseEval (offensive speech detection (OSD), macro F1) (Zampieri et al., 2019), and SemEval2018 (irony detection (ID), binary F1) (Van Hee et al., 2018).

We want to show that, even if $\mathcal{F}_{\text{task}}$ yields poor task performance on unseen datasets, $\mathcal{F}_{\text{ext}}$'s rationales can still be faithful. As expected, all methods achieve much lower task performance in the third setting than in the first two settings. However, faithfulness does not appear to be strongly correlated with task performance, as unseen tasks' comp/suff scores are similar to seen tasks'. Across all datasets, DLM-FP has the best faithfulness and is the only method whose comp is always higher than suff. AA-F is not as consistently strong as DLM-FP, but almost always beats AA (IG) on comp and suff. Meanwhile, AA (IG) has the worst comp and suff overall. Ultimately, these results suggest that UNIREX-trained models' faithfulness (*i.e.*, alignment between $\mathcal{F}_{\text{task}}$'s and $\mathcal{F}_{\text{ext}}$'s outputs) is a dataset/task agnostic property (*i.e.*, can generalize across datasets/tasks), further establishing UNIREX's utility in low-resource settings.

Method	Forward Simulation		Subjective Rating
	Accuracy (%)	Confidence (1-4)	Alignment (1-5)
No Rationale	92.00 (±3.35)	3.02 (±0.39)	-
SGT+P	80.80 (±9.73)	2.34 (±0.31)	3.64 (±0.28)
A2R+P	41.20 (±4.71)	**2.83** (±0.28)	2.97 (±0.12)
UNIREX (AA-FP)	72.00 (±7.78)	2.00 (±0.31)	3.26 (±0.31)
UNIREX (DLM-FP)	**83.60** (±5.41)	2.77 (±0.28)	**3.96** (±0.22)
Gold	81.20 (±3.03)	2.88 (±0.30)	4.00 (±0.20)

Table 3: **Plausibility User Study on SST.**

4.6 User Study on Plausibility

Gold rationale based plausibility evaluation is noisy because gold rationales are for the target label, not a model's predicted label. Thus, we conduct two five-annotator user studies (Table 3) to get a better plausibility measurement. Given 50 random test instances from SST, we get the rationales for SGT+P, A2R+P, UNIREX (AA-FP), and UNIREX (DLM-FP), plus the gold rationales. For each instance, we threshold all rationales to have the same number of positive tokens as the gold rationale. The first user study is forward simulation (Hase and Bansal, 2020; Jain et al., 2020). Here, the annotator is given an input and a rationale for some model's prediction, then asked what (binary) sentiment label the model most likely predicted. For forward simulation, we also consider a No Rationale baseline, where no tokens are highlighted. For No Rationale and Gold, the target label is the correct choice. Annotators are also asked to rate their confidence (4-point Likert scale) in their answer to this question. The second user study involves giving a subjective rating of how plausible the rationale is (Hase and Bansal, 2020). Here, the annotator is given the input, rationale, and model's predicted label, then asked to rate (5-point Likert scale) how aligned the rationale is with the prediction.

In both forward simulation and subjective rating, we find that DLM-FP performs best among all non-oracle methods and even beats Gold on accuracy, further supporting that DLM-FP rationales are plausible. As expected, the fact that Gold does not achieve near-100% accuracy shows the discrepancy between evaluating plausibility based on the target label (*i.e.,* gold rationale similarity) and $\mathcal{F}_{\text{task}}$'s predicted label (forward simulation). Meanwhile, SGT+P and AA-FP, which had lower AUPRC/TF1 in our automatic evaluation, also do worse in accuracy/alignment. Also, users found SGT+P and AA-FP rationales harder to understand, as shown by their lower confidence scores. Meanwhile, A2R+P had high AUPRC/TF1, but gets very low accuracy/alignment because A2R+P's predicted label often not the target label, leading to misalignment with its gold-like rationale. A2R+P is a great example of how automatic plausibility evaluation can be misleading. For the accuracy, confidence, and alignment questions, we achieved Fleiss' Kappa (Fleiss, 1971) inter-annotator agreement scores of 0.2456 (fair), 0.1282 (slight), and, 0.1561 (slight), respectively. This lack of agreement shows the difficulty of measuring plausibility.

5 Related Work

Faithfulness Many prior works have tried to improve the faithfulness of extractive rationales through the use of AAs (Bastings and Filippova, 2020). Typically, this involves designing gradient-based (Sundararajan et al., 2017; Denil et al., 2014; Lundberg and Lee, 2017; Li et al., 2015) or perturbation-based (Li et al., 2016; Poerner et al., 2018; Kádár et al., 2017) AAs. However, attribution algorithms cannot be optimized and tend to be compute-intensive (often requiring multiple LM forward/backward passes). Recently, Ismail et al. (2021) addressed the optimization issue by regularizing the task model to yield faithful rationales via the AA, while other works (Situ et al., 2021; Schwarzenberg et al., 2021) addressed the compute cost issue by training an LM (requiring only one forward pass) to mimic an AA's behavior. Another line of work aims to produce faithful rationales by construction, via SPPs (Jain et al., 2020; Yu et al., 2021; Paranjape et al., 2020; Bastings et al., 2019; Yu et al., 2019; Lei et al., 2016). Still, SPPs' faithfulness can only guarantee sufficiency – not comprehensiveness (DeYoung et al., 2019). Also, SPPs generally perform worse than vanilla LMs because they hide much of the original text input from the predictor and are hard to train end-to-end.

Plausibility Existing approaches for improving extractive rationale plausibility typically involve supervising LM-based extractors (Bhat et al., 2021) or SPPs (Jain et al., 2020; Paranjape et al., 2020; DeYoung et al., 2019) with gold rationales. However, existing LM-based extractors have not been trained for faithfulness, while SPPs' faithfulness by construction comes at the great cost of task performance. Meanwhile, more existing works focus on improving the plausibility of free-text rationales (Narang et al., 2020; Lakhotia et al., 2020; Camburu et al., 2018), often with task-specific pipelines (Rajani et al., 2019; Kumar and Talukdar, 2020).

Connection to UNIREX Unlike prior works,

UNIREX enables both the task model and rationale extractor to be jointly optimized for faithfulness, plausibility, and task performance. As a result, UNIREX-trained rationale extractors achieve a better balance of faithfulness and plausibility, without compromising the task model's performance. Also, by using a learned rationale extractor, which generally only requires one model forward pass, UNIREX does not have the computational expenses that limit many AAs.

References

Jasmijn Bastings, Wilker Aziz, and Ivan Titov. 2019. Interpretable neural predictions with differentiable binary variables. *arXiv preprint arXiv:1905.08160.*

Jasmijn Bastings and Katja Filippova. 2020. The elephant in the interpretability room: Why use attention as explanation when we have saliency methods? *arXiv preprint arXiv:2010.05607.*

Emily M Bender, Timnit Gebru, Angelina McMillan-Major, and Shmargaret Shmitchell. 2021. On the dangers of stochastic parrots: Can language models be too big?. In *Proceedings of the 2021 ACM Conference on Fairness, Accountability, and Transparency*, pages 610–623.

Meghana Moorthy Bhat, Alessandro Sordoni, and Subhabrata Mukherjee. 2021. Self-training with few-shot rationalization: Teacher explanations aid student in few-shot nlu. *arXiv preprint arXiv:2109.08259.*

Oana-Maria Camburu, Tim Rocktäschel, Thomas Lukasiewicz, and Phil Blunsom. 2018. e-snli: Natural language inference with natural language explanations. *arXiv preprint arXiv:1812.01193.*

Samuel Carton, Anirudh Rathore, and Chenhao Tan. 2020. Evaluating and characterizing human rationales. *arXiv preprint arXiv:2010.04736.*

Aaron Chan, Jiashu Xu, Boyuan Long, Soumya Sanyal, Tanishq Gupta, and Xiang Ren. 2021. Salkg: Learning from knowledge graph explanations for commonsense reasoning. *Advances in Neural Information Processing Systems*, 34.

Ona de Gibert, Naiara Perez, Aitor García-Pablos, and Montse Cuadros. 2018. Hate speech dataset from a white supremacy forum. *arXiv preprint arXiv:1809.04444.*

Misha Denil, Alban Demiraj, and Nando De Freitas. 2014. Extraction of salient sentences from labelled documents. *arXiv preprint arXiv:1412.6815.*

Jacob Devlin, Ming-Wei Chang, Kenton Lee, and Kristina Toutanova. 2018. Bert: Pre-training of deep bidirectional transformers for language understanding. *arXiv preprint arXiv:1810.04805.*

Jay DeYoung, Sarthak Jain, Nazneen Fatema Rajani, Eric Lehman, Caiming Xiong, Richard Socher, and Byron C Wallace. 2019. Eraser: A benchmark to evaluate rationalized nlp models. *arXiv preprint arXiv:1911.03429.*

Finale Doshi-Velez and Been Kim. 2017. Towards a rigorous science of interpretable machine learning. *arXiv preprint arXiv:1702.08608.*

William Falcon and The PyTorch Lightning team. 2019. PyTorch Lightning.

Joseph L Fleiss. 1971. Measuring nominal scale agreement among many raters. *Psychological bulletin*, 76(5):378.

Peter Hase and Mohit Bansal. 2020. Evaluating explainable ai: Which algorithmic explanations help users predict model behavior? *arXiv preprint arXiv:2005.01831.*

Sara Hooker, Dumitru Erhan, Pieter-Jan Kindermans, and Been Kim. 2018. A benchmark for interpretability methods in deep neural networks. *arXiv preprint arXiv:1806.10758.*

Aya Abdelsalam Ismail, Hector Corrada Bravo, and Soheil Feizi. 2021. Improving deep learning interpretability by saliency guided training. *Advances in Neural Information Processing Systems*, 34.

Alon Jacovi and Yoav Goldberg. 2020. Towards faithfully interpretable nlp systems: How should we define and evaluate faithfulness? *arXiv preprint arXiv:2004.03685.*

Sarthak Jain, Sarah Wiegreffe, Yuval Pinter, and Byron C Wallace. 2020. Learning to faithfully rationalize by construction. *arXiv preprint arXiv:2005.00115.*

Akos Kádár, Grzegorz Chrupała, and Afra Alishahi. 2017. Representation of linguistic form and function in recurrent neural networks. *Computational Linguistics*, 43(4):761–780.

Daniel Khashabi, Snigdha Chaturvedi, Michael Roth, Shyam Upadhyay, and Dan Roth. 2018. Looking beyond the surface: A challenge set for reading comprehension over multiple sentences. In *Proceedings of the 2018 Conference of the North American Chapter of the Association for Computational Linguistics: Human Language Technologies, Volume 1 (Long Papers)*, pages 252–262.

Sawan Kumar and Partha Talukdar. 2020. Nile: Natural language inference with faithful natural language explanations. *arXiv preprint arXiv:2005.12116.*

Kushal Lakhotia, Bhargavi Paranjape, Asish Ghoshal, Wen-tau Yih, Yashar Mehdad, and Srinivasan Iyer. 2020. Fid-ex: Improving sequence-to-sequence models for extractive rationale generation. *arXiv preprint arXiv:2012.15482.*

Tao Lei, Regina Barzilay, and Tommi Jaakkola. 2016. Rationalizing neural predictions. *arXiv preprint arXiv:1606.04155.*

Jiwei Li, Xinlei Chen, Eduard Hovy, and Dan Jurafsky. 2015. Visualizing and understanding neural models in nlp. *arXiv preprint arXiv:1506.01066.*

Jiwei Li, Will Monroe, and Dan Jurafsky. 2016. Understanding neural networks through representation erasure. *arXiv preprint arXiv:1612.08220.*

Zachary C Lipton. 2018. The mythos of model interpretability: In machine learning, the concept of interpretability is both important and slippery. *Queue*, 16(3):31–57.

Yinhan Liu, Myle Ott, Naman Goyal, Jingfei Du, Mandar Joshi, Danqi Chen, Omer Levy, Mike Lewis, Luke Zettlemoyer, and Veselin Stoyanov. 2019. Roberta: A robustly optimized bert pretraining approach. *arXiv preprint arXiv:1907.11692.*

Scott M Lundberg and Su-In Lee. 2017. A unified approach to interpreting model predictions. In *Proceedings of the 31st international conference on neural information processing systems*, pages 4768–4777.

Siwen Luo, Hamish Ivison, Caren Han, and Josiah Poon. 2021. Local interpretations for explainable natural language processing: A survey. *arXiv preprint arXiv:2103.11072.*

Julian McAuley and Jure Leskovec. 2013. Hidden factors and hidden topics: understanding rating dimensions with review text. In *Proceedings of the 7th ACM conference on Recommender systems*, pages 165–172.

Shervin Minaee, Nal Kalchbrenner, Erik Cambria, Narjes Nikzad, Meysam Chenaghlu, and Jianfeng Gao. 2021. Deep learning–based text classification: A comprehensive review. *ACM Computing Surveys (CSUR)*, 54(3):1–40.

Sharan Narang, Colin Raffel, Katherine Lee, Adam Roberts, Noah Fiedel, and Karishma Malkan. 2020. Wt5?! training text-to-text models to explain their predictions. *arXiv preprint arXiv:2004.14546.*

Bhargavi Paranjape, Mandar Joshi, John Thickstun, Hannaneh Hajishirzi, and Luke Zettlemoyer. 2020. An information bottleneck approach for controlling conciseness in rationale extraction. *arXiv preprint arXiv:2005.00652.*

Adam Paszke, Sam Gross, Francisco Massa, Adam Lerer, James Bradbury, Gregory Chanan, Trevor Killeen, Zeming Lin, Natalia Gimelshein, Luca Antiga, et al. 2019. Pytorch: An imperative style, high-performance deep learning library. *Advances in neural information processing systems*, 32:8026–8037.

Nina Poerner, Benjamin Roth, and Hinrich Schütze. 2018. Evaluating neural network explanation methods using hybrid documents and morphological agreement. *arXiv preprint arXiv:1801.06422.*

Danish Pruthi, Bhuwan Dhingra, Livio Baldini Soares, Michael Collins, Zachary C Lipton, Graham Neubig, and William W Cohen. 2020. Evaluating explanations: How much do explanations from the teacher aid students? *arXiv preprint arXiv:2012.00893.*

Nazneen Fatema Rajani, Bryan McCann, Caiming Xiong, and Richard Socher. 2019. Explain yourself! leveraging language models for commonsense reasoning. *arXiv preprint arXiv:1906.02361.*

Cynthia Rudin. 2019. Stop explaining black box machine learning models for high stakes decisions and use interpretable models instead. *Nature Machine Intelligence*, 1(5):206–215.

Robert Schwarzenberg, Nils Feldhus, and Sebastian Möller. 2021. Efficient explanations from empirical explainers. *arXiv preprint arXiv:2103.15429.*

Avanti Shrikumar, Peyton Greenside, and Anshul Kundaje. 2017. Learning important features through propagating activation differences. In *International Conference on Machine Learning*, pages 3145–3153. PMLR.

Karen Simonyan, Andrea Vedaldi, and Andrew Zisserman. 2013. Deep inside convolutional networks: Visualising image classification models and saliency maps. *arXiv preprint arXiv:1312.6034.*

Xuelin Situ, Ingrid Zukerman, Cecile Paris, Sameen Maruf, and Gholamreza Haffari. 2021. Learning to explain: Generating stable explanations fast. In *Proceedings of the 59th Annual Meeting of the Association for Computational Linguistics and the 11th International Joint Conference on Natural Language Processing (Volume 1: Long Papers)*, pages 5340–5355.

Richard Socher, Alex Perelygin, Jean Wu, Jason Chuang, Christopher D Manning, Andrew Y Ng, and Christopher Potts. 2013. Recursive deep models for semantic compositionality over a sentiment treebank. In *Proceedings of the 2013 conference on empirical methods in natural language processing*, pages 1631–1642.

Julia Strout, Ye Zhang, and Raymond J Mooney. 2019. Do human rationales improve machine explanations? *arXiv preprint arXiv:1905.13714.*

Mukund Sundararajan, Ankur Taly, and Qiqi Yan. 2017. Axiomatic attribution for deep networks. In *International Conference on Machine Learning*, pages 3319–3328. PMLR.

Alon Talmor, Jonathan Herzig, Nicholas Lourie, and Jonathan Berant. 2018. Commonsenseqa: A question answering challenge targeting commonsense knowledge. *arXiv preprint arXiv:1811.00937.*

Cynthia Van Hee, Els Lefever, and Véronique Hoste. 2018. Semeval-2018 task 3: Irony detection in english tweets. In *Proceedings of The 12th International Workshop on Semantic Evaluation*, pages 39–50.

Ashish Vaswani, Noam Shazeer, Niki Parmar, Jakob Uszkoreit, Llion Jones, Aidan N Gomez, Łukasz Kaiser, and Illia Polosukhin. 2017. Attention is all you need. In *Advances in neural information processing systems*, pages 5998–6008.

Thomas Wolf, Lysandre Debut, Victor Sanh, Julien Chaumond, Clement Delangue, Anthony Moi, Pierric Cistac, Tim Rault, Rémi Louf, Morgan Funtowicz, et al. 2019. Huggingface's transformers: State-of-the-art natural language processing. *arXiv preprint arXiv:1910.03771*.

Qinyuan Ye, Bill Yuchen Lin, and Xiang Ren. 2021. Crossfit: A few-shot learning challenge for cross-task generalization in nlp. *arXiv preprint arXiv:2104.08835*.

Mo Yu, Shiyu Chang, Yang Zhang, and Tommi S Jaakkola. 2019. Rethinking cooperative rationalization: Introspective extraction and complement control. *arXiv preprint arXiv:1910.13294*.

Mo Yu, Yang Zhang, Shiyu Chang, and Tommi Jaakkola. 2021. Understanding interlocking dynamics of cooperative rationalization. *Advances in Neural Information Processing Systems*, 34.

Manzil Zaheer, Guru Guruganesh, Kumar Avinava Dubey, Joshua Ainslie, Chris Alberti, Santiago Ontanon, Philip Pham, Anirudh Ravula, Qifan Wang, Li Yang, et al. 2020. Big bird: Transformers for longer sequences. In *NeurIPS*.

Omar Zaidan and Jason Eisner. 2008. Modeling annotators: A generative approach to learning from annotator rationales. In *Proceedings of the 2008 conference on Empirical methods in natural language processing*, pages 31–40.

Marcos Zampieri, Shervin Malmasi, Preslav Nakov, Sara Rosenthal, Noura Farra, and Ritesh Kumar. 2019. Semeval-2019 task 6: Identifying and categorizing offensive language in social media (offenseval). *arXiv preprint arXiv:1903.08983*.

Xiang Zhang, Junbo Zhao, and Yann LeCun. 2015. Character-level Convolutional Networks for Text Classification. *arXiv:1509.01626 [cs]*.

A Appendix

A.1 Text Classification

Here, we formalize the text classification problem in more detail. Let $\mathcal{D} = \{\mathcal{X}, \mathcal{Y}\}_{i=1}^N$ be a dataset, where $\mathcal{X} = \{\mathbf{x}_i\}_{i=1}^N$ are the text inputs, $\mathcal{Y} = \{y_i^*\}_{i=1}^N$ are the labels, and N is the number of instances $(\mathbf{x}_i, y_i^*)$ in $\mathcal{D}$. We also assume $\mathcal{D}$ can be partitioned into train set $\mathcal{D}_{\text{train}}$, dev set $\mathcal{D}_{\text{dev}}$, and test set $\mathcal{D}_{\text{test}}$. Let $\mathcal{F}_{\text{task}} = f_{\text{task}}(f_{\text{enc}}(\cdot))$ be a task LM, where f_{enc} is the text encoder, and f_{task} is the task output head. Typically, $\mathcal{F}_{\text{task}}$ has a BERT-style architecture (Devlin et al., 2018), in which f_{enc} is a Transformer (Vaswani et al., 2017) while f_{task} is a linear layer. Below, we define the sequence classification (SST, Movies, MultiRC, e-SNLI) and multi-choice QA (CoS-E) tasks, which are different types of text classification.

Sequence Classification In sequence classification, $\mathbf{x}_i$ is a token sequence (*e.g.,* a single sentence, a pair of sentences), while y_i^* is the target class for $\mathbf{x}_i$. Here, we assume a fixed label space $Y = \{1, ..., M\}$ of size M, where $y_i^* \in Y$ for all i. Thus, f_{task} outputs a vector of size M, such that $\mathcal{F}_{\text{task}}(\mathbf{x}_i) = f_{\text{task}}(f_{\text{enc}}(\mathbf{x}_i)) = \hat{\mathbf{y}}_i \in \mathbb{R}^M$ is the logit vector used to classify $\mathbf{x}_i$. Given $\hat{\mathbf{y}}_i = [\hat{y}_{i,j}]_{j=1}^M$, let $y_i = \arg\max_j \hat{y}_{i,j}$ be the class predicted by $\mathcal{F}_{\text{task}}$. The goal of sequence classification is to learn $\mathcal{F}_{\text{task}}$ such that $y_i^* = y_i$, for all $(\mathbf{x}_i, y_i^*)$ (Minaee et al., 2021).

Multi-Choice QA Instead of a fixed label space, multi-choice QA has a different (but fixed-size) set of answer choices per instance. For instance i, let q_i be the question (*e.g., "A friend is greeting me, what would they say?"*) and $A_i = \{a_{i,j}\}_{j=1}^M$ be the corresponding answer choices (*e.g.,* {*"say hello", "greet", "associate", "socialize", "smile"*}), where M is now the number of answer choices. Define $\mathbf{x}_{i,j} = q_i \oplus a_{i,j}$, where $\oplus$ denotes concatenation. In multi-choice QA, we have $\mathbf{x}_i = \{\mathbf{x}_{i,j}\}_{j=1}^M$, while $y_i^* \in A_i$ is the correct answer for $\mathbf{x}_i$. Thus, f_{task} outputs a scalar, such that $\mathcal{F}_{\text{task}}(\mathbf{x}_{i,j}) = f_{\text{task}}(f_{\text{enc}}(\mathbf{x}_{i,j})) = \hat{y}_{i,j} \in \mathbb{R}$ is the logit for $\mathbf{x}_{i,j}$. Given $\hat{\mathbf{y}}_i = [\hat{y}_{i,j}]_{j=1}^M$, let $j' = \arg\max_j \hat{y}_{i,j}$, where $y_i = a_{i,j'}$ is the answer predicted by $\mathcal{F}_{\text{task}}$. The goal of multi-choice QA is to learn $\mathcal{F}_{\text{task}}$ such that $y_i^* = y_i$, for all $(\mathbf{x}_i, y_i^*)$ (Talmor et al., 2018).

A.2 Heuristic Rationale Extractors

A heuristic $\mathcal{F}_{\text{task}}$ is an AA, which can be any handcrafted function that calculates an importance score s_i^t for each input token x_i^t (Bastings and Filippova, 2020). AAs are typically gradient-based (Sundararajan et al., 2017; Denil et al., 2014; Lundberg and Lee, 2017; Li et al., 2015) or perturbation-based (Li et al., 2016; Poerner et al., 2018; Kádár et al., 2017) methods. Gradient-based methods compute s_i^t via the gradient of $\mathcal{F}_{\text{task}}$'s output $\hat{\mathbf{y}}_i$ w.r.t. x_i^t, via one or more $\mathcal{F}_{\text{task}}$ backward passes. Perturbation-based methods measure s_i^t as $\hat{\mathbf{y}}_i$'s change when perturbing (*e.g.*, removing) x_i^t, via multiple $\mathcal{F}_{\text{task}}$ forward passes.

AAs can be used out of the box without training and are designed to satisfy certain faithfulness-related axiomatic properties (Sundararajan et al., 2017; Lundberg and Lee, 2017). However, AAs' lack of learnable parameters means they cannot be optimized for faithfulness/plausibility. Thus, if $\mathcal{F}_{\text{task}}$ is trained for explainability using AA-based rationales, then only $\mathcal{F}_{\text{task}}$ is optimized. Also, faithful AAs tend to be compute-intensive, requiring many $\mathcal{F}_{\text{task}}$ backward/forward passes per instance (Sundararajan et al., 2017; Lundberg and Lee, 2017; Li et al., 2016).

A.3 Gold Rationale Supervision

If a learned rationale extractor is chosen, UNIREX enables users to specify how much gold rationale supervision to use. Ideally, each train instance would be annotated with a gold rationale. In this case, we could directly minimize the plausibility loss for each train instance. However, since gold rationales can be expensive to annotate, UNIREX provides a special batching procedure for training with limited gold rationale supervision.

Given $N_{\text{train}} = |\mathcal{D}_{\text{train}}|$ train instances, let $0 < \gamma < 100$ be the percentage of train instances with gold rationales, $N_{\text{gold}} = \lceil \frac{\gamma}{100} N_{\text{train}} \rceil \geq 1$ be the number of train instances with gold rationales, b be the desired train batch size, and $\beta > 1$ be a scaling factor. Define $\mathcal{D}_{\text{gold}} \subseteq \mathcal{D}_{\text{train}}$ as the set of train instances with gold rationales, where $|\mathcal{D}_{\text{gold}}| = N_{\text{gold}}$. Note that, if all train instances have gold rationales, then $\mathcal{D}_{\text{gold}} = \mathcal{D}_{\text{train}}$ and $\gamma = 100$.

Each batch is constructed as follows: (1) randomly sample $b_{\text{gold}} = \max(1, \frac{b}{\beta})$ instances from $\mathcal{D}_{\text{gold}}$ without replacement, then (2) randomly sample $b - b_{\text{gold}}$ instances from $\mathcal{D}_{\text{train}} \backslash \mathcal{D}_{\text{gold}}$ without replacement. This results in a batch with b total train instances, b_{gold} with gold rationales and the rest without. Since N_{gold} is generally small, we only sample from $\mathcal{D}_{\text{gold}}$ without replacement for a given batch, but not a given epoch. Thus, instances from $\mathcal{D}_{\text{gold}}$ may appear more than once in the same epoch. However, we do sample from $\mathcal{D}_{\text{train}} \backslash \mathcal{D}_{\text{gold}}$ without replacement for each batch and epoch, so every instance in $\mathcal{D}_{\text{train}} \backslash \mathcal{D}_{\text{gold}}$ appears exactly once per epoch.

After constructing the batch, we compute the plausibility loss for the batch as follows: $\sum_{i=1}^{b} \mathbb{1}_{(\mathbf{x}_i, y_i^*) \in \mathcal{D}_{\text{gold}}} \; \mathcal{L}_{\text{plaus}}(\mathcal{F}_{\text{ext}}(\mathbf{x}_i), \mathbf{r}_i^*)$, where $\mathcal{L}_{\text{plaus}}$ is the plausibility loss for train instance $(\mathbf{x}_i, y_i^*)$. This function zeroes out the plausibility loss for instances without gold rationales, so that plausibility is only being optimized with respect to instances with gold rationales. However, in Sec. ??, we show that it is possible to achieve high plausibility via rationale extractors trained on minimal gold rationale supervision.

A.4 Explainability Objectives

A.4.1 Faithfulness

Sufficiency In addition, to the criteria presented in Sec. 3.2, we consider two other sufficiency loss functions. The first is the *KL divergence criterion* used in (Ismail et al., 2021), which considers the entire label distribution and is defined as $\mathcal{L}_{\text{suff-KL}} = \text{KL}(\mathcal{F}_{\text{task}}(\mathbf{r}_i^{(k)})) \mid\mid \mathcal{F}_{\text{task}}(\mathbf{x}_i))$. The second is the *mean absolute error (MAE) criterion*, which is defined as $\mathcal{L}_{\text{suff-MAE}} = |\mathcal{L}_{\text{CE}}(\mathcal{F}_{\text{task}}(\mathbf{r}_i^{(k)})), y_i^*) - \mathcal{L}_{\text{CE}}(\mathcal{F}_{\text{task}}(\mathbf{x}_i), y_i^*)|$. Unlike the difference criterion $\mathcal{L}_{\text{suff-diff}}$ and margin criterion $\mathcal{L}_{\text{suff-margin}}$ (Sec. 3.2), the MAE criterion assumes that using $\mathbf{r}_i^{(k)}$ as input should not yield better task performance than using $\mathbf{x}_i$ as input. In our experiments, we find that $\mathcal{L}_{\text{suff-margin}}$ is effective, though others (*e.g.*, KL divergence, MAE) can be used too.

A.4.2 Plausibility

Similar to faithfulness, UNIREX places no restrictions on the choice of plausibility objective. As described in Sec. 3.2, given gold rationale $\mathbf{r}_i^*$ for input $\mathbf{x}_i$, plausibility optimization entails training $\mathcal{F}_{\text{ext}}$ to predict binary importance label $\mathbf{r}_i^{*,t}$ for each token x_i^t. This is essentially binary token classification, so one natural choice for $\mathcal{L}_{\text{plaus}}$ is the token-level binary cross-entropy (BCE) criterion: $\mathcal{L}_{\text{plaus-BCE}} = -\sum_t \mathbf{r}_i^{*,t} \log(\mathcal{F}_{\text{ext}}(x_i^t))$ (Sec. 3.2). Another option is the sequence-level *KL divergence criterion*, which is defined as: $\mathcal{L}_{\text{plaus-KL}} =$

$\mathrm{KL}(\mathcal{F}_{\text{ext}}(\mathbf{x}_i) \mid\mid \mathbf{r}_i^*)$.

Additionally, we can directly penalize $\mathcal{F}_{\text{ext}}(\mathbf{x}_i)$ in the logit space via a *linear loss*, defined as: $\mathcal{L}_{\text{plaus-linear}} = \Phi(\mathbf{r}_i^*)\ \mathcal{F}_{\text{ext}}(\mathbf{x}_i)$, where $\Phi(u) = -2u + 1$ maps positive and negative tokens to -1 and $+1$, respectively. The linear loss directly pushes the logits corresponding to positive/negative tokens to be higher/lower and increase the margin between them. To prevent linear loss values from becoming arbitrarily negative, we can also lower bound the loss with a margin m_p, yielding: $\mathcal{L}_{\text{plaus-linear-margin}} = \max(-m_p, \mathcal{L}_{\text{plaus-linear}}) + m_p$.

A.5 Implementation Details

LM Architecture While many prior works use BERT (Devlin et al., 2018) Transformer LMs, BERT is limited to having sequences with up to 512 tokens, which is problematic since many datasets (*e.g.,* Movies) contain much longer sequences. Meanwhile, BigBird (Zaheer et al., 2020) is a state-of-the-art Transformer LM designed to handle long input sequences with up to 4096 tokens. Thus, we use BigBird-Base, which is initialized with RoBERTa-Base (Liu et al., 2019), in all of our experiments (*i.e.,* both baselines and UNIREX). We obtain the pre-trained BigBird-Base model from the Hugging Face Transformers library (Wolf et al., 2019). Note that UNIREX is agnostic to the choice of LM architecture, so RNNs, CNNs, and other Transformer LMs are also supported by UNIREX. However, we leave exploration of other LM architectures for future work.

Training Building upon Sec. **??**, we discuss additional training details here. We find that $\alpha_c = 0.5$ and $\alpha_s = 0.5$ are usually best. For the batching factor β (Sec. A.3), we use 2. For model selection, we choose the model with the best dev performance averaged over three seeds. We can also perform model selection based on dev explainability metrics, but we leave this extended tuning for future work. All experiments are implemented using PyTorch-Lightning (Paszke et al., 2019; Falcon and The PyTorch Lightning team, 2019).

A.6 Gold Rationale Data Efficiency

Fig. **??** shows the gold rationale data efficiency results for CoS-E, using the same setup as Sec. **??**. Overall, we see that the CoS-E results are quite similar to the SST results. Again, UNIREX (DLM-FP) and UNIREX (SLM-FP) dominate across all γ values, with AUPRC slowly decreasing as γ decreases. Interestingly, UNIREX (AA-FP) yields a noticeable dip in AUPRC for lower γ values. Since AA-FP has limited capacity (via the task model) for plausibility optimization, it is possible that this fluctuation is due to random noise. We leave further analysis of this for future work.

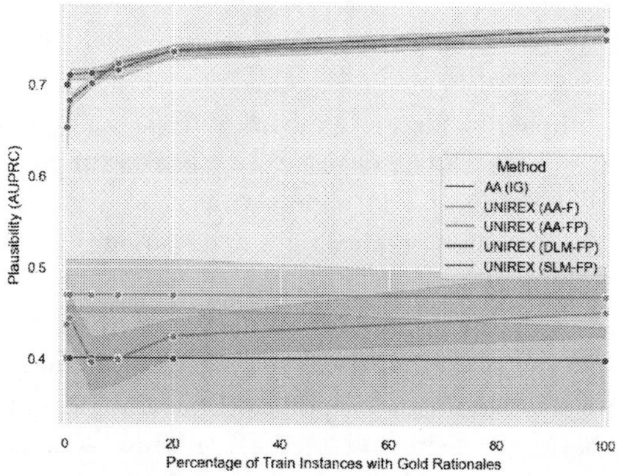

Figure 8: **Gold Rationale Data Efficiency on CoS-E.**

A.7 Additional Empirical Results

In this subsection, we present additional results from our experiments. Besides the aggregated results shown in Sec. 4 of the main text, Tables 4-10 contain more detailed results, using both raw and NRG metrics. Specifically, Tables 4-8 show all raw/NRG results for each dataset, Table 9 shows the ablation results for all raw metrics, and Table 10 includes the zero-shot explainability transfer results for UNIREX (SLM-FP). Generally, the computation of NRG should involve globally aggregating the raw metrics for all available methods, as done in the main results. However, for a number of more focused experiments (Tables 9-10), only a subset of the available methods are considered. Thus, to make the faithfulness results in Tables 9-10 easier to digest, we introduce a metric called Comp-Suff Difference (CSD), which locally aggregates comp and suff as: CSD $=$ comp $-$ suff. Therefore, since higher/lower comp/suff signal higher faithfulness, then higher CSD signals higher faithfulness.

Method	Composite	Faithfulness			Plausibility			Performance	
	NRG (↑)	NRG (↑)	Comp (↑)	Suff (↓)	NRG (↑)	AUPRC (↑)	TF1 (↑)	NRG (↑)	Acc (↑)
AA (Grad)	0.488	0.337	0.142 (±0.010)	0.256 (±0.006)	0.192	58.86 (±3.65)	27.40 (±0.00)	0.935	93.81 (±0.55)
AA (Input*Grad)	0.420	0.107	0.078 (±0.013)	0.342 (±0.014)	0.218	44.16 (±1.43)	45.02 (±0.39)	0.935	93.81 (±0.55)
AA (DeepLIFT)	0.453	0.122	0.085 (±0.006)	0.340 (±0.018)	0.302	46.50 (±1.32)	50.18 (±0.32)	0.935	93.81 (±0.55)
AA (IG)	0.526	0.297	0.119 (±0.009)	0.258 (±0.031)	0.347	49.94 (±1.77)	50.75 (±0.54)	0.935	93.81 (±0.55)
L2E	0.557	0.487	0.012 (±0.004)	0.009 (±0.024)	0.250	44.84 (±0.32)	47.24 (±0.87)	0.935	93.81 (±0.55)
SGT	0.632	0.555	0.147 (±0.024)	0.113 (±0.031)	0.371	51.38 (±2.47)	51.35 (±1.64)	0.971	94.40 (±0.57)
FRESH	0.330	0.837	0.219 (±0.057)	0.000 (±0.000)	0.152	42.06 (±8.84)	41.19 (±4.01)	0.000	78.78 (±6.48)
A2R	0.479	0.941	0.283 (±0.104)	0.000 (±0.000)	0.457	63.36 (±6.01)	46.74 (±6.65)	0.038	79.39 (±11.67)
UNIREX (AA-F)	0.639	0.706	0.292 (±0.051)	0.171 (±0.038)	0.329	48.13 (±1.14)	50.96 (±0.93)	0.882	92.97 (±0.44)
SGT+P	0.596	0.507	0.139 (±0.032)	0.137 (±0.026)	0.355	50.38 (±1.45)	50.98 (±0.46)	0.928	93.70 (±0.88)
FRESH+P	0.426	0.765	0.175 (±0.043)	0.000 (±0.000)	0.503	60.87 (±9.83)	53.55 (±8.27)	0.011	78.95 (±5.18)
A2R+P	0.695	0.953	0.290 (±0.016)	0.000 (±0.000)	0.978	85.56 (±1.01)	70.97 (±1.03)	0.154	81.26 (±0.52)
UNIREX (DLM-P)	0.770	0.339	0.142 (±0.008)	0.255 (±0.007)	0.970	84.35 (±0.87)	71.54 (±0.53)	1.000	94.86 (±0.41)
UNIREX (AA-FP)	0.636	0.339	0.296 (±0.067)	0.185 (±0.048)	0.315	47.60 (±2.44)	50.23 (±2.26)	0.900	93.25 (±0.45)
UNIREX (DLM-FP)	0.897	0.756	0.319 (±0.090)	0.167 (±0.036)	1.000	85.80 (±0.74)	72.76 (±0.19)	0.935	93.81 (±0.54)
UNIREX (SLM-FP)	0.891	0.807	0.302 (±0.039)	0.113 (±0.013)	0.940	82.55 (±0.84)	70.65 (±0.44)	0.927	93.68 (±0.67)

Table 4: **Main Results on SST.**

Method	Composite	Faithfulness			Plausibility			Performance	
	NRG (↑)	NRG (↑)	Comp (↑)	Suff (↓)	NRG (↑)	AUPRC (↑)	TF1 (↑)	NRG (↑)	F1 (↑)
AA (Grad)	0.481	0.457	0.184 (±0.023)	0.107 (±0.017)	0.028	13.31 (±0.91)	5.02 (±0.00)	0.957	95.33 (±0.65)
AA (Input*Grad)	0.503	0.359	0.148 (±0.031)	0.137 (±0.019)	0.194	8.68 (±0.37)	37.58 (±0.55)	0.957	95.33 (±0.65)
AA (DeepLIFT)	0.468	0.259	0.122 (±0.029)	0.172 (±0.022)	0.187	9.00 (±0.16)	36.15 (±1.45)	0.957	95.33 (±0.65)
AA (IG)	0.439	0.173	0.134 (±0.016)	0.219 (±0.044)	0.188	8.88 (±0.21)	36.39 (±1.29)	0.957	95.33 (±0.65)
L2E	0.550	0.445	0.000 (±0.007)	0.026 (±0.015)	0.248	16.68 (±10.20)	38.92 (±4.07)	0.957	95.33 (±0.65)
SGT	0.553	0.474	0.124 (±0.053)	0.071 (±0.064)	0.184	10.05 (±1.23)	34.64 (±1.67)	1.000	96.33 (±0.76)
FRESH	0.645	0.732	0.234 (±0.034)	0.000 (±0.000)	0.305	17.02 (±6.22)	48.26 (±5.87)	0.899	94.00 (±1.44)
A2R	0.431	0.764	0.267 (±0.050)	0.000 (±0.000)	0.244	35.44 (±21.69)	19.78 (±25.56)	0.284	79.78 (±7.14)
UNIREX (AA-F)	0.601	0.744	0.505 (±0.134)	0.122 (±0.100)	0.189	9.14 (±2.51)	36.28 (±1.84)	0.870	93.33 (±1.61)
SGT+P	0.586	0.604	0.152 (±0.013)	0.022 (±0.004)	0.183	9.16 (±1.59)	35.33 (±0.41)	0.971	95.66 (±1.16)
FRESH+P	0.491	0.691	0.193 (±0.062)	0.000 (±0.000)	0.710	65.78 (±11.16)	68.70 (±15.78)	0.070	74.84 (±12.22)
A2R+P	0.585	0.764	0.267 (±0.076)	0.000 (±0.000)	0.991	93.53 (±0.93)	88.77 (±1.22)	0.000	73.22 (±0.75)
UNIREX (DLM-P)	0.667	0.024	0.024 (±0.003)	0.238 (±0.004)	1.000	94.32 (±0.12)	89.53 (±1.63)	0.978	95.83 (±0.29)
UNIREX (AA-FP)	0.543	0.514	0.428 (±0.174)	0.195 (±0.105)	0.193	8.53 (±0.46)	37.71 (±3.12)	0.921	94.50 (±1.00)
UNIREX (DLM-FP)	0.744	0.326	0.283 (±0.217)	0.216 (±0.005)	0.991	93.65 (±0.36)	88.68 (±2.29)	0.913	94.33 (±1.61)
UNIREX (SLM-FP)	0.754	0.362	0.313 (±0.059)	0.213 (±0.014)	0.965	91.70 (±1.84)	86.17 (±1.20)	0.935	94.83 (±0.76)

Table 5: **Main Results on Movies.**

Method	Composite	Faithfulness			Plausibility			Performance	
	NRG (↑)	NRG (↑)	Comp (↑)	Suff (↓)	NRG (↑)	AUPRC (↑)	TF1 (↑)	NRG (↑)	Acc (↑)
AA (Grad)	0.537	0.504	0.331 (±0.012)	0.352 (±0.007)	0.130	37.33 (±0.62)	22.65 (±0.00)	0.977	63.56 (±1.27)
AA (Input*Grad)	0.573	0.361	0.249 (±0.018)	0.385 (±0.008)	0.383	39.56 (±0.54)	44.43 (±0.40)	0.977	63.56 (±1.27)
AA (DeepLIFT)	0.605	0.346	0.254 (±0.035)	0.403 (±0.042)	0.491	42.82 (±1.83)	51.72 (±1.26)	0.977	63.56 (±1.27)
AA (IG)	0.578	0.327	0.216 (±0.007)	0.378 (±0.010)	0.429	40.07 (±5.47)	48.34 (±3.16)	0.977	63.56 (±1.27)
L2E	0.544	0.493	0.005 (±0.003)	0.010 (±0.008)	0.161	23.56 (±1.09)	37.80 (±1.10)	0.977	63.56 (±1.27)
SGT	0.618	0.367	0.197 (±0.040)	0.324 (±0.015)	0.491	43.68 (±4.68)	51.00 (±3.05)	0.995	64.35 (±0.46)
FRESH	0.302	0.546	0.037 (±0.036)	0.000 (±0.000)	0.261	32.35 (±7.66)	39.37 (±0.70)	0.101	24.81 (±3.46)
A2R	0.277	0.516	0.014 (±0.021)	0.000 (±0.000)	0.282	41.61 (±3.85)	33.12 (±9.06)	0.032	21.77 (±1.31)
UNIREX (AA-F)	0.690	0.538	0.297 (±0.141)	0.286 (±0.084)	0.554	46.97 (±3.41)	53.99 (±1.66)	0.978	63.58 (±0.61)
SGT+P	0.601	0.367	0.201 (±0.032)	0.328 (±0.022)	0.436	41.30 (±6.70)	47.95 (±1.65)	1.000	64.57 (±0.33)
FRESH+P	0.374	0.515	0.013 (±0.021)	0.013 (±0.021)	0.606	53.40 (±12.87)	53.17 (±7.83)	0.000	20.36 (±0.66)
A2R+P	0.488	0.500	0.001 (±0.001)	0.000 (±0.000)	0.951	73.59 (±0.81)	67.63 (±1.54)	0.012	20.91 (±0.48)
UNIREX (DLM-P)	0.751	0.267	0.180 (±0.016)	0.390 (±0.035)	0.997	76.07 (±1.63)	69.76 (±0.27)	0.990	64.13 (±0.46)
UNIREX (AA-FP)	0.685	0.551	0.395 (±0.109)	0.381 (±0.101)	0.537	45.21 (±4.46)	53.91 (±3.23)	0.968	63.14 (±0.33)
UNIREX (DLM-FP)	0.814	0.492	0.293 (±0.043)	0.321 (±0.070)	0.997	76.38 (±0.57)	69.52 (±0.24)	0.953	62.50 (±1.34)
UNIREX (SLM-FP)	0.807	0.494	0.390 (±0.087)	0.424 (±0.110)	0.983	75.12 (±0.41)	69.25 (±0.41)	0.944	62.09 (±2.12)

Table 6: **Main Results on CoS-E.**

Method	Composite	Faithfulness			Plausibility			Performance	
	NRG (↑)	NRG (↑)	Comp (↑)	Suff (↓)	NRG (↑)	AUPRC (↑)	TF1 (↑)	NRG (↑)	F1 (↑)
AA (Grad)	0.498	0.462	0.222 (±0.028)	0.120 (±0.018)	0.035	22.27 (±0.17)	13.81 (±0.00)	0.997	69.80 (±0.60)
AA (Input*Grad)	0.506	0.289	0.225 (±0.048)	0.260 (±0.059)	0.231	18.51 (±0.23)	43.45 (±0.05)	0.997	69.80 (±0.60)
AA (DeepLIFT)	0.493	0.249	0.225 (±0.012)	0.292 (±0.014)	0.234	18.80 (±0.19)	43.51 (±0.04)	0.997	69.80 (±0.60)
AA (IG)	0.499	0.280	0.162 (±0.086)	0.222 (±0.086)	0.220	18.71 (±0.40)	41.79 (±1.33)	0.997	69.80 (±0.60)
L2E	0.522	0.366	0.007 (±0.006)	0.042 (±0.024)	0.205	24.48 (±2.71)	32.63 (±6.12)	0.997	69.80 (±0.60)
SGT	0.594	0.564	0.214 (±0.105)	0.033 (±0.077)	0.224	18.60 (±0.42)	42.42 (±0.51)	0.995	69.73 (±0.13)
FRESH	0.675	0.571	0.176 (±0.029)	0.000 (±0.000)	0.617	24.68 (±7.98)	48.02 (±3.04)	0.838	64.47 (±3.41)
A2R	0.217	0.404	-0.010 (±0.029)	0.000 (±0.000)	0.249	18.72 (±0.67)	45.45 (±0.02)	0.000	36.39 (±0.00)
UNIREX (AA-F)	0.711	0.956	0.505 (±0.050)	-0.071 (±0.020)	0.236	18.82 (±0.40)	43.68 (±0.38)	0.939	66.17 (±4.58)
SGT+P	0.630	0.665	0.280 (±0.029)	0.283 (±0.039)	0.226	18.63 (±0.52)	42.71 (±0.39)	1.000	69.91 (±0.81)
FRESH+P	0.404	0.413	0.000 (±0.013)	0.000 (±0.000)	0.739	55.87 (±10.13)	63.70 (±9.58)	0.060	38.41 (±5.34)
A2R+P	0.516	0.422	0.011 (±0.024)	0.000 (±0.000)	0.977	70.86 (±1.30)	76.21 (±1.68)	0.150	41.42 (±8.73)
UNIREX (DLM-P)	0.708	0.123	0.127 (±0.010)	0.322 (±0.017)	0.999	71.80 (±0.27)	77.94 (±0.57)	1.000	69.91 (±0.76)
UNIREX (AA-FP)	0.706	1.000	0.545 (±0.045)	-0.077 (±0.099)	0.231	19.13 (±0.71)	42.66 (±1.18)	0.888	66.17 (±4.58)
UNIREX (DLM-FP)	0.751	0.327	0.135 (±0.072)	0.165 (±0.029)	0.998	71.89 (±0.41)	77.63 (±0.62)	0.929	67.53 (±1.06)
UNIREX (SLM-FP)	0.784	0.377	0.198 (±0.038)	0.171 (±0.027)	0.997	71.69 (±0.21)	77.79 (±0.09)	0.979	69.20 (±1.58)

Table 7: **Main Results on MultiRC.**

Method	Composite	Faithfulness			Plausibility			Performance	
	NRG (↑)	NRG (↑)	Comp (↑)	Suff (↓)	NRG (↑)	AUPRC (↑)	TF1 (↑)	NRG (↑)	F1 (↑)
AA (Grad)	0.587	0.518	0.313 (±0.009)	0.380 (±0.025)	0.244	59.80 (±1.32)	15.27 (±0.00)	0.999	90.78 (±0.27)
AA (Input*Grad)	0.503	0.287	0.205 (±0.005)	0.446 (±0.020)	0.223	32.98 (±1.37)	43.13 (±0.86)	0.999	90.78 (±0.27)
AA (DeepLIFT)	0.508	0.270	0.195 (±0.012)	0.448 (±0.014)	0.254	33.47 (±1.31)	46.44 (±0.04)	0.999	90.78 (±0.27)
AA (IG)	0.596	0.473	0.308 (±0.011)	0.414 (±0.020)	0.317	47.83 (±1.04)	37.87 (±1.39)	0.999	90.78 (±0.27)
L2E	0.606	0.460	0.009 (±0.015)	0.036 (±0.022)	0.358	58.11 (±0.97)	31.35 (±0.27)	0.999	90.78 (±0.27)
SGT	0.595	0.503	0.288 (±0.025)	0.361 (±0.038)	0.298	42.46 (±3.03)	41.70 (±1.78)	0.985	90.23 (±0.16)
FRESH	0.518	0.661	0.120 (±0.075)	0.000 (±0.000)	0.361	38.77 (±6.82)	53.71 (±3.30)	0.530	72.92 (±8.71)
A2R	0.273	0.564	0.053 (±0.048)	0.000 (±0.000)	0.256	48.48 (±11.14)	29.54 (±24.72)	0.000	52.72 (±14.08)
UNIREX (AA-F)	0.622	0.539	0.330 (±0.018)	0.383 (±0.055)	0.340	45.29 (±3.02)	43.69 (±1.98)	0.987	90.31 (±0.19)
SGT+P	0.608	0.524	0.286 (±0.034)	0.339 (±0.032)	0.311	43.03 (±1.69)	42.59 (±1.63)	0.988	90.36 (±0.08)
FRESH+P	0.614	0.695	0.143 (±0.072)	0.000 (±0.000)	0.603	56.21 (±10.47)	64.09 (±5.59)	0.544	73.44 (±12.88)
A2R+P	0.800	0.751	0.182 (±0.097)	0.000 (±0.000)	0.992	87.30 (±0.44)	77.31 (±0.72)	0.656	77.31 (±0.72)
UNIREX (DLM-P)	0.842	0.525	0.311 (±0.011)	0.371 (±0.032)	1.000	87.85 (±0.13)	77.63 (±0.35)	1.000	90.80 (±0.33)
UNIREX (AA-FP)	0.626	0.529	0.341 (±0.008)	0.406 (±0.046)	0.363	44.79 (±0.81)	47.18 (±0.83)	0.985	90.21 (±0.08)
UNIREX (DLM-FP)	0.857	0.588	0.335 (±0.018)	0.346 (±0.023)	0.991	86.99 (±0.40)	77.53 (±0.15)	0.992	90.51 (±0.12)
UNIREX (SLM-FP)	0.864	0.603	0.353 (±0.017)	0.356 (±0.015)	0.994	87.58 (±0.14)	77.22 (±0.28)	0.994	90.59 (±0.09)

Table 8: **Main Results on e-SNLI.**

Ablation	Method	Performance	Faithfulness			Plausibility	
		Acc (↑)	CSD (↑)	Comp (↑)	Suff (↓)	AUPRC (↑)	TF1 (↑)
Ext Type (F)	UNIREX (AA-F, Rand)	94.05 (±0.35)	-0.156 (±-0.156)	0.171 (±0.040)	0.327 (±0.050)	44.92 (±0.00)	46.15 (±0.00)
	UNIREX (AA-F, Gold)	93.81 (±0.54)	-0.017 (±0.070)	0.232 (±0.088)	0.249 (±0.021)	100.00 (±0.00)	100.00 (±0.00)
	UNIREX (AA-F, Inv)	93.47 (±1.81)	-0.115 (±0.018)	0.242 (±0.010)	0.357 (±0.019)	20.49 (±0.00)	0.00 (±0.00)
	UNIREX (AA-F, IG)	93.81 (±0.55)	-0.138 (±0.040)	0.119 (±0.009)	0.258 (±0.031)	49.94 (±1.77)	50.75 (±0.54)
Ext Type (FP)	UNIREX (AA-FP, Sum)	93.81 (±0.55)	-0.138 (±0.040)	0.119 (±0.009)	0.258 (±0.031)	49.94 (±1.77)	50.75 (±0.54)
	UNIREX (AA-FP, MLP)	93.23 (±0.92)	0.087 (±0.134)	0.285 (±0.051)	0.197 (±0.100)	54.82 (±1.97)	49.62 (±0.65)
	UNIREX (DLM-FP)	93.81 (±0.18)	0.151 (±0.056)	0.319 (±0.090)	0.167 (±0.036)	85.80 (±0.74)	72.76 (±0.19)
	UNIREX (SLM-FP)	93.68 (±0.67)	0.189 (±0.030)	0.302 (±0.039)	0.113 (±0.013)	82.55 (±0.84)	70.65 (±0.44)
Comp/Suff Loss	UNIREX (SLM-FP, Comp)	93.59 (±0.11)	0.040 (±0.096)	0.350 (±0.048)	0.310 (±0.049)	82.79 (±0.62)	70.74 (±0.81)
	UNIREX (SLM-FP, Suff)	94.16 (±0.39)	0.014 (±0.010)	0.166 (±0.003)	0.152 (±0.012)	83.74 (±0.84)	70.94 (±0.86)
	UNIREX (SLM-FP, Comp+Suff)	93.68 (±0.67)	0.189 (±0.030)	0.302 (±0.039)	0.113 (±0.013)	82.55 (±0.84)	70.65 (±0.44)
Suff Criterion	UNIREX (SLM-FP, KL Div)	93.06 (±0.25)	0.174 (±0.100)	0.306 (±0.098)	0.131 (±0.005)	82.62 (±0.88)	70.43 (±0.65)
	UNIREX (SLM-FP, MAE)	93.78 (±0.13)	0.135 (±0.053)	0.278 (±0.058)	0.143 (±0.008)	82.66 (±0.61)	70.25 (±0.45)
	UNIREX (SLM-FP, Margin)	93.68 (±0.67)	0.189 (±0.030)	0.302 (±0.039)	0.113 (±0.013)	82.55 (±0.84)	70.65 (±0.44)
SLM Ext Head	UNIREX (SLM-FP, Linear)	93.68 (±0.67)	0.189 (±0.030)	0.302 (±0.039)	0.113 (±0.013)	82.55 (±0.84)	70.65 (±0.44)
	UNIREX (SLM-FP, MLP-2048-2)	93.67 (±0.18)	0.179 (±0.060)	0.323 (±0.071)	0.144 (±0.012)	83.82 (±0.77)	70.93 (±0.87)
	UNIREX (SLM-FP, MLP-4096-3)	93.19 (±0.79)	0.141 (±0.030)	0.295 (±0.057)	0.154 (±0.027)	84.53 (±0.61)	71.41 (±0.91)

Table 9: **UNIREX Ablation Studies on SST.**

Task	Dataset	Method	Performance	Faithfulness		
			Perf (↑)	CSD (↑)	Comp (↑)	Suff (↓)
Sentiment Analysis	SST	Vanilla	93.81 (±0.74)	-0.070 (±0.061)	0.145 (±0.023)	0.215 (±0.038)
		UNIREX (AA-F)	93.19 (±0.40)	0.360 (±0.055)	0.405 (±0.031)	0.045 (±0.024)
		UNIREX (DLM-FP)	93.81 (±0.18)	0.151 (±0.056)	0.319 (±0.090)	0.167 (±0.036)
		UNIREX (SLM-FP)	93.68 (±0.67)	0.189 (±0.030)	0.302 (±0.039)	0.113 (±0.013)
	Yelp	Vanilla	92.50 (±2.07)	-0.156 (±0.028)	0.067 (±0.004)	0.222 (±0.031)
		UNIREX (AA-F)	90.75 (±1.30)	-0.138 (±0.120)	0.096 (±0.026)	0.233 (±0.096)
		UNIREX (DLM-FP)	92.37 (±0.46)	0.169 (±0.060)	0.265 (±0.094)	0.097 (±0.033)
		UNIREX (SLM-FP)	86.60 (±1.57)	0.114 (±0.056)	0.175 (±0.055)	0.060 (±0.001)
	Amazon	Vanilla	91.13 (±0.28)	-0.120 (±0.038)	0.096 (±0.008)	0.217 (±0.033)
		UNIREX (AA-F)	86.60 (±0.95)	-0.111 (±0.161)	0.100 (±0.042)	0.210 (±0.122)
		UNIREX (DLM-FP)	89.35 (±2.22)	0.133 (±0.039)	0.232 (±0.072)	0.098 (±0.033)
		UNIREX (SLM-FP)	81.82 (±7.62)	0.097 (±0.027)	0.147 (±0.012)	0.050 (±0.017)
Hate Speech Detection	Stormfront	Vanilla	10.48 (±1.66)	-0.066 (±0.072)	0.153 (±0.002)	0.219 (±0.071)
		UNIREX (AA-F)	9.43 (±1.45)	0.329 (±0.104)	0.337 (±0.073)	0.008 (±0.031)
		UNIREX (DLM-FP)	10.37 (±2.66)	0.052 (±0.027)	0.167 (±0.084)	0.115 (±0.059)
		UNIREX (SLM-FP)	4.51 (±1.87)	0.049 (±0.041)	0.110 (±0.039)	0.062 (±0.043)
Offensive Speech Detection	OffenseEval	Vanilla	33.51 (±0.99)	-0.125 (±0.068)	0.104 (±0.007)	0.229 (±0.064)
		UNIREX (AA-F)	35.69 (±2.30)	-0.028 (±0.084)	0.076 (±0.008)	0.104 (±0.076)
		UNIREX (DLM-FP)	35.52 (±1.26)	0.053 (±0.012)	0.140 (±0.049)	0.087 (±0.045)
		UNIREX (SLM-FP)	38.17 (±0.96)	0.039 (±0.031)	0.087 (±0.016)	0.048 (±0.024)
Irony Detection	SemEval2018-Irony	Vanilla	29.63 (±4.72)	-0.058 (±0.075)	0.154 (±0.001)	0.212 (±0.074)
		UNIREX (AA-F)	47.99 (±6.33)	0.026 (±0.080)	0.087 (±0.022)	0.061 (±0.071)
		UNIREX (DLM-FP)	31.97 (±2.80)	0.047 (±0.017)	0.149 (±0.052)	0.102 (±0.053)
		UNIREX (SLM-FP)	17.42 (±4.04)	0.027 (±0.047)	0.091 (±0.027)	0.064 (±0.033)

Table 10: **Zero-Shot Explainability Transfer from SST to Unseen Datasets/Tasks.**

Pipelines for Social Bias Testing of Large Language Models

Debora Nozza, Federico Bianchi, Dirk Hovy
Bocconi University
Via Sarfatti 25
Milan, Italy
{debora.nozza,f.bianchi,dirk.hovy}@unibocconi.it

Abstract

The maturity level of language models is now at a stage in which many companies rely on them to solve various tasks. However, while research has shown how biased and harmful these models are, systematic ways of integrating social bias tests into development pipelines are still lacking. This short paper suggests how to use these verification techniques in development pipelines. We take inspiration from software testing and suggest addressing social bias evaluation as software testing. We hope to open a discussion on the best methodologies to handle social bias testing in language models.

1 Introduction

Current language models are now primarily deployed on large infrastructures (e.g., HuggingFace repository[1]) and used by many practitioners and researchers with few lines of code. This releasing mechanism has brought tremendous value to the community as researchers everywhere can access models, download them on their laptops, and run experiments. However, these models are quickly adopted without complete understanding their possible limitations (Bianchi and Hovy, 2021).

Recent literature is now rich of papers that demonstrate how social bias is embedded in large language models and propose many different verification and validation datasets (e.g., May et al., 2019; Nozza et al., 2021; Nadeem et al., 2021, *inter alia*). Researchers and practitioners can use all these contributions to understand if a model is safe to use or not. We will refer to these works and the datasets used as verification as social bias tests from this point on.

This literature often misses the long-term goal. What is the point of having so many social bias tests that effectively capture different aspects of the problem if we do not find a systematic way of using them? Indeed, this work is also inspired by the recent approaches and methodologies defined to provide more comprehensive evaluations of models (Ribeiro et al., 2020; Chia et al., 2022).

Indeed, other computer science fields have developed insights into how to handle testing. Software development has long been wrestling with the need for good evaluation practices for source code. For example, Continuous Integration and Continuous Deployment (CI/CD) is a general methodology in software development. It assumes frequent testing to ensure that the product under development passes specific qualitative tests that guarantee it is working. In this direction, frequent testing of language models can be part of the solution.

The main contribution of this short paper is first to identify the main recurring themes and the primary methodologies of social bias literature. We then suggest a more practical and developmental direction: all these methods can be used the same way as tests in software testing pipelines. Unstable/unsafe software should not go into production, which is also true for language models.

We are aware that a single social bias test cannot provide a complete picture of the problems and that we cannot treat a model that *passes* the tests as entirely safe. Nonetheless, we believe that some frequent tests are better than no tests. As a community, we need to come together and work closely to stress test these models even during the development phase.

Contributions Our contribution is twofold: we first give an overview of the literature on social bias tests and explore the main themes and methods. We then suggest that this literature can be used in practical contexts to frequently evaluate language models to understand better how the tools we use can be harmful. With this work, we hope to start a discussion on the best methodologies to handle social bias testing in language models as we believe this is a fundamental step to sustain the future and correct usage of these technologies.

[1] https://huggingface.co/

Proceedings of BigScience Episode #5 – Workshop on Challenges & Perspectives in Creating Large Language Models, pages 68 - 74
May 27, 2022

2 Existing Social Bias tests

An overview of bias in NLP has been presented in several work (Blodgett et al., 2020; Shah et al., 2020; Hovy and Prabhumoye, 2021; Sheng et al., 2021; Stanczak and Augenstein, 2021). Here, we focus on the approaches proposed for contextual embeddings. We illustrate the main themes that have driven the developed of social bias tests. The categories we are going to describe are not mutually exclusive, however they showcase in a coherent manner what has been done in the literature.

2.1 Word List-based

Several studies have been conducted to analyse and determine the level of bias in static word embeddings in binary and multi-class scenarios (Bolukbasi et al., 2016; Caliskan et al., 2017; Garg et al., 2018; Swinger et al., 2019; Manzini et al., 2019; Lauscher and Glavaš, 2019; Gonen and Goldberg, 2019). Several works applied these bias evaluations to contextualized models by extracting static word embeddings for them (Basta et al., 2019; Lauscher et al., 2021; Wolfe and Caliskan, 2021).

Inspired by gender bias metrics for word embeddings, May et al. (2019) proposed the Sentence Encoder Association Test (SEAT), a template-based test founded on the Word Embedding Association Test (WEAT) (Caliskan et al., 2017). Afterward, Liang et al. (2020) used SEAT for measuring bias, also considering the religious dimension.

2.2 Template-based

Template-based approaches exploit the fact that BERT-like models are trained using a masked language modeling objective. I.e., given a sentence with omitted tokens indicated as [MASK], they predict the masked tokens. The predictions for these [MASK] tokens may provide us with some insight into the bias embedded in the actual representations. We can generate templates in two different ways. First, by accounting for certain targets (e.g., gendered words) and attributes (e.g. career-related words) (Kurita et al., 2019; Zhang et al., 2020; Dev et al., 2020). This enable, for example, to compute the association between the target *male* gender and the attribute *programmer*, by feeding "[MASK] is a programmer" to BERT, and compute the probability assigned to the sentence "he is a programmer". Another option is to create templates coupling protected group targets with neutral predicates (e.g., *"works as"*, *"is known for"*). For example, we can ask BERT to complete "the woman is known for [MASK]" or "the girl worked as [MASK]." Then, it is possible to exploit lexicons (Nozza et al., 2021, 2022), or hate speech (Ousidhoum et al., 2021; Sheng et al., 2019) and sentiment classifiers Hutchinson et al. (2020); Huang et al. (2020) to obtain a social bias score from the template-based generated text. Ideally, using a classifier lets us test the data more easily and accurately than lexicons.

The same approach can be applied to natural language generation models (Sheng et al., 2019; Huang et al., 2020). The models are not fed with a masked token but are asked to complete the template. So, instead of a single word, they return a set of words.

An interesting case has been proposed by Choenni et al.. They look into what kinds of stereotyped information are collected by LLMs exploiting a dataset comprising stereotypical attributes for various social groups. The dataset was created by feeding search engines queries that already imply a stereotype about a specific social group (e.g., '*Why are Asian parents so*'). Then, the authors count how many of the stereotypes found by the search engines are also encoded in the LLMs through masked language modeling.

2.3 Crowdsourced-based

Few works have collected datasets to compute bias scores. Nadeem et al. (2021) presented StereoSet, a crowdsourced English dataset to measure stereotypical biases in four domains: gender, profession, race, and religion. Nangia et al. (2020) introduced CrowS-Pairs, a crowdsourced benchmark comprising 1508 examples that cover stereotypes dealing with nine types of bias. Both Nadeem et al. (2021); Nangia et al. (2020) proposed a metric to measure for how many examples the model prefers stereotyped sentences over less stereotyped sentences.

2.4 Social Media-based

Barikeri et al. (2021) propose a bias evaluation framework for conversational LLMs using REDDITBIAS, an English conversational data set grounded in real-world human conversations from Reddit. The authors propose a perplexity-based bias measure meant to quantify the amount of bias in generative language models along several bias dimensions. Gehman et al. (2020) focus on collecting prompts from the OpenWebText Corpus (Gokaslan and Cohen, 2019) and annotating them with the Perspective API to evaluate the toxicity of the messages.

These messages are then split in half (a prompt and a continuation) and are used to study, for example, whether a model generates toxic continuations from a non-toxic prompt.

2.5 Discussion

While many social bias tests have been provided in the literature, they differ in methodology, covered languages, and protected groups. Most works are on English. Only (Nozza et al., 2021; Ousidhoum et al., 2021) considered languages beyond English. The majority of work focused on gender bias, and only a few investigated an extensive range of targets (Nangia et al., 2020; Nadeem et al., 2021; Ousidhoum et al., 2021; Barikeri et al., 2021). We also found that Hutchinson et al. (2020); Huang et al. (2020) did not provide data or code publicly. Blodgett et al. (2021) presented a critical review of some social bias tests and found significant issues with noise, unnaturalness, and reliability of the some work (Nangia et al., 2020; Nadeem et al., 2021). Finally, it is important to highlight that social biases are different depending on the cultural and historical context of application of the language model.

This brief analysis demonstrates that no existing social bias test is universal. While we may fill this research gap in the future, for now, we suggest using more than one test has to be used to measure bias.

3 Integration

We describe the different modalities that can be used to integrate social bias tests into development pipelines.

3.1 Continuous Social Bias Verification

Software testing is at the heart of software development. Without good evaluation, software easily breaks in production, causing economic damage to companies.

Most of the checks currently run to test language models are structural. For example, does it produce outputs correctly? Once fine-tuned, are the results we get in a sensible range? We suggest that tests should cover social biases.

We take inspiration from software testing and suggest testing methodologies for language models. In a CI/CD (continuous integration and continuous development) setting, code is continuously pushed into the repository and tested to ensure the model is stable. Software is deployed if and only if tests are correctly passed. We believe that we should replicate this pipeline in the development of language models. Every time a new model is released, we can run tests to verify if and how the model is hurtful.

Note that this is indeed a real problem. Many pipelines are now based on HuggingFace APIs that directly download the model from the HuggingFace Hub. Users might not know what happens on the backend: what happens when a model is updated, and the user downloads it thinking it is the same as the older version? We are not sure how many users keep track of commits and changelogs, and this might create a misunderstanding about which model is being used and with which training setup.

3.2 Badge System

Publishers may help maintain the fairness of the research ecosystem by establishing a badging mechanism. This approach would increase the likelihood that an LLM will be tested in advance for social biases and that end-users will pay attention to this issue.

Here, we propose a badging system based on the ACM one[2] and the one proposed for the NAACL 2022 reproducibility track[3]. We identified three possible badges: Social Bias Evaluated, Social Bias Available, and Results Validated.

Social Bias Evaluated This badge is given to LLMs who have successfully run the social bias tests. This badge does not require the scores to be made publicly available.

Social Bias Available This badge is given to LLMs that made the results of social bias tests retrievable. We propose to design one badge for each implemented social bias test and to show it along with the associated score. We discourage using badges as binary (i.e., test passed or test failed) for these particular cases. Considering the problem as binary might imply that a passing model is entirely free of bias, even if this is not the case.

Results Validated This badge is given to LLMs in which the social bias test results were successfully attained by a person or team other than the author.

[2] `https://www.acm.org/publications/policies/artifact-review-and-badging-current`

[3] `https://2022.naacl.org/blog/reproducibility-track/`

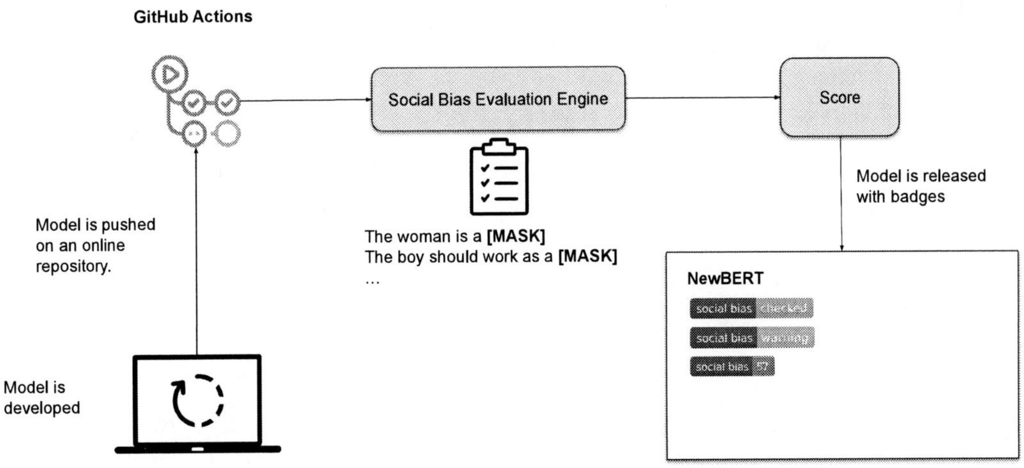

Figure 1: The figure shows an example of the possible integration of Social Bias tests into a development pipeline. A model can be developed and trained on a server and pushed online. Then we can use an automation tool (e.g., Github Actions) to start an evaluation engine that will eventually generate the predictions for the models. Once scored, the model can be released online with badges identifying possible issues that one might encounter with the model.

Badging is also a standard and straightforward system to showcase software validity in an online repository. These badges are often used to show information about the number of downloads, the test coverage, the quality of the documentation and allow users to understand the quality of what they are using with a quick look.

Figure 1 shows a possible integration of testing for harms in development pipelines. We can develop the models on a local server and push this model online after training is finished (with Git LSF, for example). Pushing should automatically start an evaluation pipeline (something close to Github Actions) that starts an evaluation engine: this engine should load the models and run the social bias tests. Once the results are collected, and the metrics have been scored, the model can finally appear on online repositories with badges that identify if and how the test have been run with the respective scores.

3.3 Limits of this Integration

An open question is if the test should be available to the developer of the models. On the one hand, releasing the tests makes it easier for everyone to evaluate their models internally before release. On the other hand, this makes it easier to "train on test" and hack the system to obtain better scores.

Hiding the test sets from the developer is closer to standard Quality And Assurance developers in companies that are meant to test the interfaces and the code that the developer has built. This approach is also in line with challenges that do not share test data and in which models are submitted using docker containers that are then internally evaluated and scored. As Goodhart's law states, "When a measure becomes a target, it ceases to be a good measure". Thus we should be aware that social bias tests cannot be the panacea for language models problems. We cannot rely only on a test to assess the validity of a model.[4]

Another point in discussion is that the pipelines we have designed are meant to evaluate *intrinsic* bias in language models. Unfortunately, this does not consider the verification of bias in downstream application: this *extrinsic* bias has been found to be poorly correlated with the original bias of language models (Goldfarb-Tarrant et al., 2021). However, we want to point out the an additional set of application-specific tests could be used to evaluate the models adapted for these tasks: for example, researchers could use hate speech check tests (Dixon et al., 2018; Nozza et al., 2019; Röttger et al., 2021) to verify social biases in hate speech detection models.

[4] Albeit, this comment is true for any measure we use in the field.

4 Conclusion

This paper proposes to use social bias tests in model development pipelines. We believe that our work can be helpful to make the development of these models fairer and easier to sustain from an ethical point of view. Future work is needed to answer several questions about this system. For example, who creates the tests and how can we make sure that these tests can be trusted? It becomes critical to involve marginalized communities to develop more sustainable and effective social bias tests.

Acknowledgements

This project has partially received funding from the European Research Council (ERC) under the European Union's Horizon 2020 research and innovation program (grant agreement No. 949944, INTEGRATOR), and by Fondazione Cariplo (grant No. 2020-4288, MONICA). Debora Nozza, Federico Bianchi, and Dirk Hovy are members of the MilaNLP group, and the Data and Marketing Insights Unit of the Bocconi Institute for Data Science and Analysis.

Ethical Statements

We understand that providing social bias tests as a quantifiable indicator for bias carries a significant risk. A low score on a social bias test might be used to assert that a model is fully devoid of bias. As Nangia et al. (2020), we strongly advise against this. Tests can be an indication of issues. Conversely,the absence of a high score does not necessarily entail the absence of bias. Neither do replace a thorough investigation of the data.

References

Soumya Barikeri, Anne Lauscher, Ivan Vulić, and Goran Glavaš. 2021. RedditBias: A real-world resource for bias evaluation and debiasing of conversational language models. In *Proceedings of the 59th Annual Meeting of the Association for Computational Linguistics and the 11th International Joint Conference on Natural Language Processing (Volume 1: Long Papers)*, pages 1941–1955, Online. Association for Computational Linguistics.

Christine Basta, Marta R. Costa-jussà, and Noe Casas. 2019. Evaluating the underlying gender bias in contextualized word embeddings. In *Proceedings of the First Workshop on Gender Bias in Natural Language Processing*, pages 33–39, Florence, Italy. Association for Computational Linguistics.

Federico Bianchi and Dirk Hovy. 2021. On the gap between adoption and understanding in NLP. In *Findings of the Association for Computational Linguistics: ACL-IJCNLP 2021*, pages 3895–3901, Online. Association for Computational Linguistics.

Su Lin Blodgett, Solon Barocas, Hal Daumé III, and Hanna Wallach. 2020. Language (technology) is power: A critical survey of "bias" in NLP. In *Proceedings of the 58th Annual Meeting of the Association for Computational Linguistics*, pages 5454–5476, Online. Association for Computational Linguistics.

Su Lin Blodgett, Gilsinia Lopez, Alexandra Olteanu, Robert Sim, and Hanna Wallach. 2021. Stereotyping Norwegian salmon: An inventory of pitfalls in fairness benchmark datasets. In *Proceedings of the 59th Annual Meeting of the Association for Computational Linguistics and the 11th International Joint Conference on Natural Language Processing (Volume 1: Long Papers)*, pages 1004–1015, Online. Association for Computational Linguistics.

Tolga Bolukbasi, Kai-Wei Chang, James Y. Zou, Venkatesh Saligrama, and Adam Tauman Kalai. 2016. Man is to computer programmer as woman is to homemaker? debiasing word embeddings. In *Advances in Neural Information Processing Systems 29: Annual Conference on Neural Information Processing Systems 2016, December 5-10, 2016, Barcelona, Spain*, pages 4349–4357.

Aylin Caliskan, Joanna J. Bryson, and Arvind Narayanan. 2017. Semantics derived automatically from language corpora contain human-like biases. *Science*, 356(6334):183–186.

Patrick John Chia, Jacopo Tagliabue, Federico Bianchi, Chloe He, and Brian Ko. 2022. Beyond ndcg: behavioral testing of recommender systems with reclist. In *Companion Proceedings of the Web Conference*.

Rochelle Choenni, Ekaterina Shutova, and Robert van Rooij. 2021. Stepmothers are mean and academics are pretentious: What do pretrained language models learn about you? In *Proceedings of the 2021 Conference on Empirical Methods in Natural Language Processing*, pages 1477–1491, Online and Punta Cana, Dominican Republic. Association for Computational Linguistics.

Sunipa Dev, Tao Li, Jeff M. Phillips, and Vivek Srikumar. 2020. On measuring and mitigating biased inferences of word embeddings. In *The Thirty-Fourth AAAI Conference on Artificial Intelligence, AAAI 2020, The Thirty-Second Innovative Applications of Artificial Intelligence Conference, IAAI 2020*, pages 7659–7666. AAAI Press.

Lucas Dixon, John Li, Jeffrey Sorensen, Nithum Thain, and Lucy Vasserman. 2018. Measuring and mitigating unintended bias in text classification. In *Proceedings of the 2018 AAAI/ACM Conference on AI, Ethics, and Society*, AIES '18, page 67–73, New York, NY, USA. Association for Computing Machinery.

Nikhil Garg, Londa Schiebinger, Dan Jurafsky, and James Zou. 2018. Word embeddings quantify 100 years of gender and ethnic stereotypes. *Proceedings of the National Academy of Sciences*, 115(16):E3635–E3644.

Samuel Gehman, Suchin Gururangan, Maarten Sap, Yejin Choi, and Noah A. Smith. 2020. RealToxicityPrompts: Evaluating neural toxic degeneration in language models. In *Findings of the Association for Computational Linguistics: EMNLP 2020*, pages 3356–3369, Online. Association for Computational Linguistics.

Aaron Gokaslan and Vanya Cohen. 2019. Openwebtext corpus. `http://Skylion007.github.io/OpenWebTextCorpus`.

Seraphina Goldfarb-Tarrant, Rebecca Marchant, Ricardo Muñoz Sánchez, Mugdha Pandya, and Adam Lopez. 2021. Intrinsic bias metrics do not correlate with application bias. In *Proceedings of the 59th Annual Meeting of the Association for Computational Linguistics and the 11th International Joint Conference on Natural Language Processing (Volume 1: Long Papers)*, pages 1926–1940, Online. Association for Computational Linguistics.

Hila Gonen and Yoav Goldberg. 2019. Lipstick on a pig: Debiasing methods cover up systematic gender biases in word embeddings but do not remove them. In *Proceedings of the 2019 Conference of the North American Chapter of the Association for Computational Linguistics: Human Language Technologies, Volume 1 (Long and Short Papers)*, pages 609–614, Minneapolis, Minnesota. Association for Computational Linguistics.

Dirk Hovy and Shrimai Prabhumoye. 2021. Five sources of bias in natural language processing. *Language and Linguistics Compass*, 15(8):e12432.

Po-Sen Huang, Huan Zhang, Ray Jiang, Robert Stanforth, Johannes Welbl, Jack Rae, Vishal Maini, Dani Yogatama, and Pushmeet Kohli. 2020. Reducing sentiment bias in language models via counterfactual evaluation. In *Findings of the Association for Computational Linguistics: EMNLP 2020*, pages 65–83, Online. Association for Computational Linguistics.

Ben Hutchinson, Vinodkumar Prabhakaran, Emily Denton, Kellie Webster, Yu Zhong, and Stephen Denuyl. 2020. Social biases in NLP models as barriers for persons with disabilities. In *Proceedings of the 58th Annual Meeting of the Association for Computational Linguistics*, pages 5491–5501, Online. Association for Computational Linguistics.

Keita Kurita, Nidhi Vyas, Ayush Pareek, Alan W Black, and Yulia Tsvetkov. 2019. Measuring bias in contextualized word representations. In *Proceedings of the First Workshop on Gender Bias in Natural Language Processing*, pages 166–172, Florence, Italy. Association for Computational Linguistics.

Anne Lauscher and Goran Glavaš. 2019. Are we consistently biased? multidimensional analysis of biases in distributional word vectors. In *Proceedings of the Eighth Joint Conference on Lexical and Computational Semantics (*SEM 2019)*, pages 85–91, Minneapolis, Minnesota. Association for Computational Linguistics.

Anne Lauscher, Tobias Lueken, and Goran Glavaš. 2021. Sustainable modular debiasing of language models. In *Findings of the Association for Computational Linguistics: EMNLP 2021*, pages 4782–4797, Punta Cana, Dominican Republic. Association for Computational Linguistics.

Paul Pu Liang, Irene Mengze Li, Emily Zheng, Yao Chong Lim, Ruslan Salakhutdinov, and Louis-Philippe Morency. 2020. Towards debiasing sentence representations. In *Proceedings of the 58th Annual Meeting of the Association for Computational Linguistics*, pages 5502–5515, Online. Association for Computational Linguistics.

Thomas Manzini, Lim Yao Chong, Alan W Black, and Yulia Tsvetkov. 2019. Black is to criminal as caucasian is to police: Detecting and removing multiclass bias in word embeddings. In *Proceedings of the 2019 Conference of the North American Chapter of the Association for Computational Linguistics: Human Language Technologies, Volume 1 (Long and Short Papers)*, pages 615–621, Minneapolis, Minnesota. Association for Computational Linguistics.

Chandler May, Alex Wang, Shikha Bordia, Samuel R. Bowman, and Rachel Rudinger. 2019. On measuring social biases in sentence encoders. In *Proceedings of the 2019 Conference of the North American Chapter of the Association for Computational Linguistics: Human Language Technologies, Volume 1 (Long and Short Papers)*, pages 622–628, Minneapolis, Minnesota. Association for Computational Linguistics.

Moin Nadeem, Anna Bethke, and Siva Reddy. 2021. StereoSet: Measuring stereotypical bias in pretrained language models. In *Proceedings of the 59th Annual Meeting of the Association for Computational Linguistics and the 11th International Joint Conference on Natural Language Processing (Volume 1: Long Papers)*, pages 5356–5371, Online. Association for Computational Linguistics.

Nikita Nangia, Clara Vania, Rasika Bhalerao, and Samuel R. Bowman. 2020. CrowS-pairs: A challenge dataset for measuring social biases in masked language models. In *Proceedings of the 2020 Conference on Empirical Methods in Natural Language Processing (EMNLP)*, pages 1953–1967, Online. Association for Computational Linguistics.

Debora Nozza, Federico Bianchi, and Dirk Hovy. 2021. HONEST: Measuring hurtful sentence completion in language models. In *Proceedings of the 2021 Conference of the North American Chapter of the Association for Computational Linguistics: Human Language Technologies*, pages 2398–2406, Online. Association for Computational Linguistics.

Debora Nozza, Federico Bianchi, Anne Lauscher, and Dirk Hovy. 2022. Measuring Harmful Sentence Completion in Language Models for LGBTQIA+ Individuals. In *Proceedings of the Second Workshop on Language Technology for Equality, Diversity and Inclusion*. Association for Computational Linguistics.

Debora Nozza, Claudia Volpetti, and Elisabetta Fersini. 2019. Unintended bias in misogyny detection. WI '19, page 149–155, New York, NY, USA. Association for Computing Machinery.

Nedjma Ousidhoum, Xinran Zhao, Tianqing Fang, Yangqiu Song, and Dit-Yan Yeung. 2021. Probing toxic content in large pre-trained language models. In *Proceedings of the 59th Annual Meeting of the Association for Computational Linguistics and the 11th International Joint Conference on Natural Language Processing (Volume 1: Long Papers)*, pages 4262–4274, Online. Association for Computational Linguistics.

Marco Tulio Ribeiro, Tongshuang Wu, Carlos Guestrin, and Sameer Singh. 2020. Beyond accuracy: Behavioral testing of NLP models with CheckList. In *Proceedings of the 58th Annual Meeting of the Association for Computational Linguistics*, pages 4902–4912, Online. Association for Computational Linguistics.

Paul Röttger, Bertie Vidgen, Dong Nguyen, Zeerak Waseem, Helen Margetts, and Janet Pierrehumbert. 2021. HateCheck: Functional tests for hate speech detection models. In *Proceedings of the 59th Annual Meeting of the Association for Computational Linguistics and the 11th International Joint Conference on Natural Language Processing (Volume 1: Long Papers)*, pages 41–58, Online. Association for Computational Linguistics.

Deven Santosh Shah, H. Andrew Schwartz, and Dirk Hovy. 2020. Predictive biases in natural language processing models: A conceptual framework and overview. In *Proceedings of the 58th Annual Meeting of the Association for Computational Linguistics*, pages 5248–5264, Online. Association for Computational Linguistics.

Emily Sheng, Kai-Wei Chang, Prem Natarajan, and Nanyun Peng. 2021. Societal biases in language generation: Progress and challenges. In *Proceedings of the 59th Annual Meeting of the Association for Computational Linguistics and the 11th International Joint Conference on Natural Language Processing (Volume 1: Long Papers)*, pages 4275–4293, Online. Association for Computational Linguistics.

Emily Sheng, Kai-Wei Chang, Premkumar Natarajan, and Nanyun Peng. 2019. The woman worked as a babysitter: On biases in language generation. In *Proceedings of the 2019 Conference on Empirical Methods in Natural Language Processing and the 9th International Joint Conference on Natural Language Processing (EMNLP-IJCNLP)*, pages 3407–3412, Hong Kong, China. Association for Computational Linguistics.

Karolina Stanczak and Isabelle Augenstein. 2021. A survey on gender bias in natural language processing. *arXiv preprint arXiv:2112.14168*.

Nathaniel Swinger, Maria De-Arteaga, Neil Thomas Heffernan IV, Mark DM Leiserson, and Adam Tauman Kalai. 2019. What are the biases in my word embedding? In *Proceedings of the 2019 AAAI/ACM Conference on AI, Ethics, and Society*, AIES '19, page 305–311, New York, NY, USA. Association for Computing Machinery.

Robert Wolfe and Aylin Caliskan. 2021. Low frequency names exhibit bias and overfitting in contextualizing language models. In *Proceedings of the 2021 Conference on Empirical Methods in Natural Language Processing*, pages 518–532, Online and Punta Cana, Dominican Republic. Association for Computational Linguistics.

Haoran Zhang, Amy X. Lu, Mohamed Abdalla, Matthew McDermott, and Marzyeh Ghassemi. 2020. Hurtful words: Quantifying biases in clinical contextual word embeddings. In *Proceedings of the ACM Conference on Health, Inference, and Learning*, CHIL '20, page 110–120, New York, NY, USA. Association for Computing Machinery.

Entities, Dates, and Languages: Zero-Shot on Historical Texts with T0

Francesco De Toni
The University of Western Australia,
Perth, Australia
francesco.detoni@uwa.edu.au

Christopher Akiki
Leipzig University,
Leipzig, Germany

Javier de la Rosa
National Library of Norway,
Oslo, Norway

Clémentine Fourrier
Inria,
Paris, France

Enrique Manjavacas
Leiden University,
Leiden, The Netherlands

Stefan Schweter
Bayerische Staatsbibliothek,
München, Germany

Daniel van Strien
British Library,
London, United Kingdom

Abstract

In this work, we explore whether the recently demonstrated zero-shot abilities of the T0 model extend to Named Entity Recognition for out-of-distribution languages and time periods. Using a historical newspaper corpus in 3 languages as test-bed, we use prompts to extract possible named entities. Our results show that a naive approach for prompt-based zero-shot multilingual Named Entity Recognition is error-prone, but highlights the potential of such an approach for historical languages lacking labeled datasets. Moreover, we also find that T0-like models can be probed to predict the publication date and language of a document, which could be very relevant for the study of historical texts*.

1 Introduction

This paper lies at the focal point of three orthogonal advances. First, the recent surge in GLAM[1]-led digitisation efforts (Terras, 2011), open citizen science (Haklay et al., 2021) and the expansive commodification of data (Hey and Trefethen, 2003), have enabled a new mode of historical inquiry that capitalises on the 'big data of the past' (Kaplan and Di Lenardo, 2017). Second, the 2017 breakthrough that was the transformer architecture (Vaswani et al., 2017) has led to the so-called ImageNet moment of Natural Language Processing (Ruder, 2018) and brought about unprecedented progress in transfer-learning (Raffel et al., 2020), few-shot learning (Schick and Schütze, 2021), zero-shot learning (Sanh et al., 2021), and prompt-based learning (Le Scao and Rush, 2021) for natural language. Third, the growing popularity of prompt-based methods (Liu et al., 2021) has resulted in a new paradigm for training and fine-tuning Large Language Models (LLM) as well as novel applications in Named Entity Recognition (NER) (Liu et al., 2022).

NER for historical texts has been the focus of a growing body of research, most recently surveyed by Ehrmann et al. (2021). Both NER and the related task of Entity Linking can enhance our ability to search and navigate digitised historical materials (Neudecker et al., 2014; Kim and Cassidy, 2015). However, applying NER to historical texts poses a number of challenges, including those due to errors in Optical Character Recognition (OCR) (Ehrmann et al., 2021; Hamdi et al., 2019; Boros et al., 2020) and domain transfer (Baptiste et al., 2021). To advance research in this area, an increasing number of datasets have been created to support the development and evaluation of NER approaches in historical text (Neudecker, 2016; Ehrmann et al., 2020, 2022)

In this paper, we examine the zero-shot abilities of T0—a prompt-based LLM developed as part of the BigScience project for open research (Sanh et al., 2021)—on the challenging task of historical NER[2]. This endeavour had two main hurdles: (1) the model was neither trained to recognize entities, nor was it ever tested on that task; (2) our

*Authorship attribution (alphabetical): §1: Akiki, De Toni, van Strien; §2.1: Fourrier; §2.2: Manjavacas; §2.3 and experiment execution: Fourrier, de la Rosa, De Toni, Schweter; §3: De Toni, Manjavacas; §4: Akiki, van Strien; §5: all the authors; Impacts Statement: Akiki, Fourrier, de la Rosa.

[1]Galleries, libraries, archives, and museums.

[2]https://github.com/bigscience-workshop/historical_texts

Proceedings of BigScience Episode #5 – Workshop on Challenges & Perspectives in Creating Large Language Models, pages 75 - 83
May 27, 2022 ©2022 Association for Computational Linguistics

evaluation dataset was out-of-distribution, containing both multilingual and historical data. To better contextualize the results of our experiments, we also run zero-shot prompt-based probing (Zhong et al., 2021) to assess T0's broader ability of extracting factual knowledge about two key factors in our experiment, that is, language variation and historical variation in the dataset.

2 Experimental setup

2.1 Data description

Our data comes from version 1.4 of the CLEF-HIPE[3] 2020 open-access dataset[4]: an OCR'ed newspaper corpus annotated for NER (Ehrmann et al., 2020). It contains Swiss and Luxembourgish newspapers from 1790 to 2010, in English, German and French. For our experiment, we use only entities of coarse type, according to their literal sense. Coarse entity types in the CLEF-HIPE 2020 dataset are persons, locations, organizations, dates and products (which includes media and doctrines).

We mix the original training and validation sets to constitute our test set[5], and we split this new set by language and date (using 20 years time intervals,[6] see Table 1). Each language dataset is relatively balanced between 1810 and 1910, with English containing between 2,202 and 4,697 tokens per split with the exception of one split (1850-1870 English) for which there are no tokens. German contains between 6,735 and 12,829 tokens, and French contains between 8,550 and 16,874 tokens. The end periods contain on average more tokens for German and French. Overall, the dataset contains 3.8% of named entities (from 1.9 to 5.6%, depending on time periods and datasets). The most balanced dataset across time periods is the French one (between 3.8 and 4.6% named entities).

2.2 Model description

In our experiments, we use the T0++ variant of the T0 language model (Sanh et al., 2021), based on the LM-adapted T5 model (Lester et al., 2021), itself a variant of the T5 model (Raffel et al., 2020), which further pretrains the original encoder-decoder architecture of T5 with an autoregressive language modeling objective.[7] Crucially, this pretraining is done using a prompt-based training setup, in which training examples are transformed into prompts using a variety of crowd-sourced prompt templates. This setup allows T0 to perform few-shot and zero-shot learning when presented with new prompts for a previously unseen task.

2.3 Experiments

Our goal in this paper is to see if and how state-of-the-art language models can be used for historical NLP tasks, with minimal modifications and fine-tuning.[8] As such, we choose to use a 'naive' approach, by directly asking the model which named entities a given sentence contains. To do so, we first design prompts for each named entity type (see Table 2). For each sentence in the dataset, we then 1) use all the generation prompts to determine if the sentence contains named entities of each entity type [9]; 2) filter the model's answer to keep only tokens that are actually in the input sentence, keeping the entity covering the longer span in case of nested entities; and 3) ask a disambiguation question if needed (if a token was assigned to multiple entities by the model). Results are stored at each step.

We then evaluate the results and conduct two additional experiments to better understand the impact of the dataset language and time period on the performance of the LM.

3 Results

3.1 Limitations

Results reveal limitations in our proposed approach. First, T0 exhibits a clear tendency to produce non-empty outputs regardless of the presence or absence of named entities in the input: none of the prompts generates an empty answer. This is especially visible for the entity PROD, for which T0 answers over 55% of the queries with the name of the entity itself (e.g. either *media* or *doctrine*) rather than with any other token from the input sentence. Second, adequately matching T0's output with tokens in the input sentence proved difficult. Even when T0 generates an answer semantically very close

[3]Conference and Labs of the Evaluation Forum - Identifying Historical People, Places and other Entities.

[4]`https://github.com/impresso/CLEF-HIPE-2020`

[5]For English, we use only the validation set, as the training set is absent

[6]We chose 20-year spans as the smallest time range producing somewhat balanced splits.

[7]The added specific pretraining of T0 uses a set of 11 varied tasks represented by a total of 55 datasets.

[8]Ecological concerns and funding inequalities raise considerations on how to best use already existing models for lower-resourced tasks, and with spending as little further computing power in fine-tuning as possible (Bender et al., 2021).

[9]For PROD entities, the generation prompt explicitly mentioned *media* and *doctrines*, as we regarded the word *product* as too generic to return an accurate answer from T0.

Time period	English			German			French		
	#Documents	#Tokens	NE%	#Documents	#Tokens	NE%	#Documents	#Tokens	NE%
1790-1810	10	4143	3.1	13	6735	4.6	14	8550	4.4
1810-1830	15	4697	3.4	13	8049	2.6	10	12 440	5.0
1830-1850	9	3974	4.0	19	15 601	2.8	10	11 659	3.9
1850-1870	0	0	-	21	16 021	3.8	9	10 321	3.9
1870-1890	7	2202	1.9	16	17 181	3.7	15	16 272	4.2
1890-1910	12	4509	2.9	12	12 829	4.3	19	16 874	4.6
1910-1930	13	5499	3.1	13	18 134	3.3	30	30 403	3.8
1930-1950	3	520	4.2	29	24 566	5.7	32	35 962	4.2
Total	69	25 544	3.2	136	119 116	4.0	139	142 481	4.2

Table 1: Data description: splits by date and language of the CLEF-HIPE 2020 dataset.

Entity	Step (1) Generation prompt
PERS	Input: `<sentence>\n` In input, what are the names of person? Separate answers with commas.
LOC	Input: `<sentence>\n` In input, what are the names of location? Separate answers with commas.
PROD	Input: `<sentence>\n` In input, what are the names of media or doctrine? Separate answers with commas.
Entities	**Step (3) Disambiguation prompt**
PERS, LOC	Input: `<sentence>\n` In input, is `<entity>` a person or a location? Give only one answer.
Fact	**Factual probing prompts**
Language	`<sentence>\n` Q:Name the language of the previous sentence.`\n`A:
Date	In which year is the following text likely to have been published: text: `<text>`

Table 2: Example prompts for generation and disambiguation (Sec. 2.3), as well as factual probing (Sec. 4).

to the correct token in the sentence, differences in spelling prevent the algorithm from correctly associating T0's answer with said token in the input sentence. This problem is inherent to the nature of our dataset: frequent OCR errors generate unpredictable variations in 'gold' word spelling (including spacing between words and letters or diacritics variation), which are automatically corrected by T0 during its predictions,[10] which negatively affects our ability to automatically match its answers with corresponding tokens in the sentence. In other instances, the model translated words from French and German into English. Further experiments might need to mitigate language variety by adding input text to the prompt, to help the model correctly assess the language in which it must answer. As all answers predicted are considered strictly incorrect, the algorithm never enters its disambiguation phase. We therefore analyse non disambiguated results.

3.2 Evaluation

To evaluate proximity between predictions and gold, we compare 'gold' tokens with predicted tokens using normalized Levenshtein distance,[11] using this metric as a proxy to identify best predictions for each entity query in each sentence. For a given example, we define (1) the true positive as the prediction with the shortest Levenshtein distance from the gold; (2) false positives as predictions of entities that are not actually present in the input sentence; and (3) false negatives as predictions that have longer Levenshtein distance to the gold tokens (i.e. predictions that would have failed to identify entity tokens in the sentence). Precision and F1-score are relatively low, especially for PROD entities, which were the most difficult to define in terms of text prompts. Higher values for recall are due to the fact that increasing the Levenshtein threshold makes it more likely to find an acceptable answer among those generated by T0. Unsurprisingly, the highest increase is found in TIME entities (dates have fixed formats, which makes it more likely to find an acceptable distance between predictions and correct tokens). Precision scores for each entity type are shown in Figure 1 (see Fig. 3 in Appendix for recall and F1-score). The results of our experiment suggest that, although T0 struggles to return

[10]E.g. Respelling words that were garbled due to noisy OCR.

[11]Normalization was done with regard to the length of the longest token (predicted or correct), and results were kept below a threshold. We tried 0.0, 0.1, 0.2, 0.3, 0.4 and 0.5.

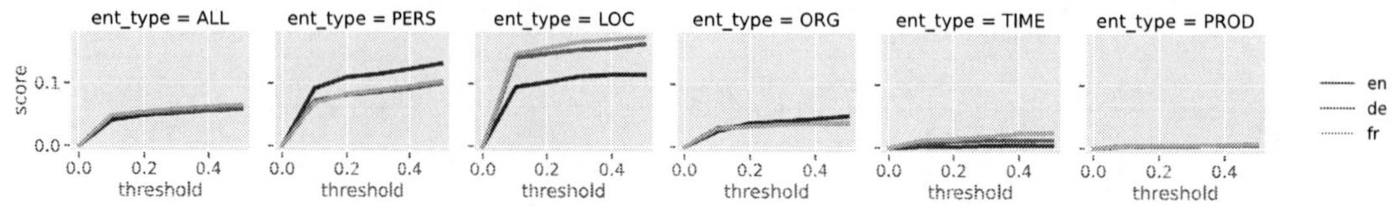

Figure 1: Precision for the different languages at different Levenshtein distance thresholds. Languages are distinguished by the line color.

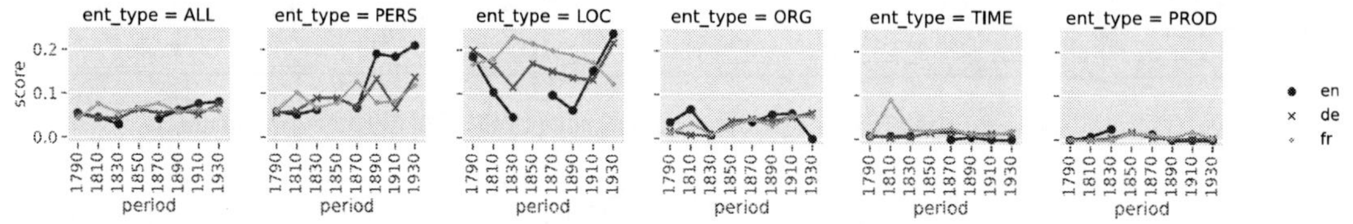

Figure 2: Precision for the different languages at Levenshtein threshold 0.4 across periods. Languages are distinguished by both the line color and the type of dot.

exact matches of the entities in the input sentence, it is still capable of generating answers that are semantically close to the correct tokens.

After manually inspecting the dataset and its numerous OCR artifacts, we choose 0.4 as a reasonable heuristic of close semantic similarity between T0's output and gold tokens. We find that using a threshold of 0.4 prevents the apparition of false positives, and therefore we use it to analyze differences between languages and between historical periods within the dataset. With respect to variations across languages, we observe that the precision of predictions in English does not have a clear edge over precision in French and German (Fig. 2; see also Fig. 4 in Appendix). This is unexpected, as T0 should display considerable bias towards English, which constitutes most of its training data. With respect to variations across periods, we observe an improvement in precision (and F1-score) for PERS and LOC entities in English texts from 1850s onwards (Fig. 3; for recall and F1-score, see Fig. 5 in Appendix), when for other entities and languages, precision and F1-score are either stable or show a downward trend (e.g. LOC in German)[12]. Variations in recall cannot be reduced to clear trends, but they are particularly erratic in English texts. A possible explanation could be that T0 is more sensitive to English text inputs, and therefore outputs a higher or lower number of irrelevant answers based on the specific content of each input sentence.

Baseline comparison with the results of the HIPE 2020 evaluation campaign[13] confirms that our implementation of zero-shot NER with T0 is below SOTA performance. As baselines, we considered the micro precision, recall and F1-score of coarse NER (literal sense) with fuzzy boundary matching from HIPE 2020 (see Table 3).

Languages	Precision	Recall	F1-score
English	0.794	0.817	0.806
German	0.870	0.886	0.878
French	0.912	0.931	0.921

Table 3: HIPE 2020's best results for coarse NER (literal) with fuzzy boundary.

All the scores from our experiments with T0 are below the best results from HIPE 2020. We note that the results from HIPE 2020 are based on experiments conducted on the HIPE test sets in each language (these are different from the test sets we used in our experiments, for which we combined the original HIPE training and validation sets; see Sec. 2.1). For this reason, we re-run our experiments on the original HIPE test sets, keeping the threshold for Levenshtein distance at 0.4. We observe no significant improvement in precision and F1-score compared to the results of our experiments on the combined training and validation sets. We observe some improvements in recall, especially for English and for TIME, with recall reaching 1.0 for some combinations of language, entity and time period. However, we believe that

[12]The absence of documents in the 1850-1870 English split explains the missing values for English in that period.

[13]https://github.com/impresso/CLEF-HIPE-2020/blob/master/evaluation-results/ranking_summary_final.md

this improvement is not significant and it is due to our choice of the Levenshtein threshold, as already explained above.

4 Prompt-based factual probing

In addition to our main experiment on NER, we run two further experiments to assess T0's ability to do inference in a multilingual setting and to identify historical variation in textual corpora.

Probing for language To gauge T0's ability to reason in a multilingual setting, we test the model's language identification ability. To that end, we use a trilingual[14] subset of the WiLI-2018 - Wikipedia Language Identification dataset (Thoma, 2018) and prompt the model on language (Table 2). We find that the model is able to correctly classify 83% of French sentences, 74.1% of German sentences, but only 35.4% of English sentences. The previously mentioned potential sensitivity of the model to its own mother tongue might explain this result.

Probing for publication date To assess T0's treatment of historical text, we study how well it predicts the likely date of publication for a piece of text from our test dataset by prompting on publication date (Table 2).

	Absolute errors	
Languages	Mean	Median
English	40.48	30.0
German	40.11	32.0
French	55.25	48.0

Table 4: Date prediction results.

Table 4 shows the prediction errors. Subtle language change can occur in a measurable way in as short a period as a decade (Juola, 2003), and therefore a median absolute error of 30 suggests that T0 is good in predicting publication dates. We notice some variation in performance between different languages, with French performing slightly worse on both metrics (possibly because it belongs to a different language family from English, contrary to German).

5 Conclusion

We have presented our experiment to evaluate T0 for zero-shot historical NER, as well as on the prediction of language and publication date of historical texts. Our results show that historical texts present additional challenges for zero-shot NER (especially because historical datasets often include noisy OCR), but that T0 can however be used as is for language and date prediction. Next steps will be experimenting on different prompts and matching methods, as well as testing few-shot NER.

Acknowledgements

This work took place under the umbrella of the "Language Models for Historical Texts" working group of the BigScience "Summer of Language Models 21" workshop[15]. We are thankful to the organizers of this workshop for providing a forum conducive to collaborative and open scientific inquiry. We are especially grateful to Suzana Ilić for her help setting up and organising the working group.

Broader Impacts Statement

In this paper, we take exploratory first steps toward instrumentalising the T0 large language model on the task of historical NER. We deem it appropriate to briefly discuss the ethical considerations that are implied by such a usage. First, if a model can be used in a context for which it was not explicitly intended for, it stands to reason that it can be misused in that same context: while recognizing entities in historical texts might at first glance seem innocuous, numerous studies focused on BIPOC representation in history have shown that this is not the case, as some marginalized groups tend to suffer from history erasure (Kellow, 1999; Ram, 2020; Stanley, 2021). Second, the automation and scaling of historical inquiry could potentially lead to unreflected (mis)interpretations of the past (Gibbs and Owens, 2013; Gibbs, 2016). Third, the experimental nature of prompt-based inference could lead to a considerable carbon footprint, owing to the trial-and-error nature of manual prompt calibration, though this cost would still be lower than training a new model from scratch or fine-tuning an existing LLM (see footnote 8).

References

Blouin Baptiste, Benoit Favre, Jeremy Auguste, and Christian Henriot. 2021. Transferring Modern Named Entity Recognition to the Historical Domain:

[14]French, German, and English; 1000 sentences each.

[15]https://bigscience.huggingface.co/

How to Take the Step? In *Workshop on Natural Language Processing for Digital Humanities (NLP4DH)*, Silchar (Online), India.

Emily M. Bender, Timnit Gebru, Angelina McMillan-Major, and Shmargaret Shmitchell. 2021. On the dangers of stochastic parrots: Can language models be too big? In *Proceedings of the 2021 ACM Conference on Fairness, Accountability, and Transparency*, FAccT '21, pages 610–623, New York, NY, USA. Association for Computing Machinery.

Emanuela Boros, Ahmed Hamdi, Elvys Linhares Pontes, Luis Adrián Cabrera-Diego, Jose G. Moreno, Nicolas Sidere, and Antoine Doucet. 2020. Alleviating digitization errors in named entity recognition for historical documents. In *Proceedings of the 24th Conference on Computational Natural Language Learning*, pages 431–441, Online. Association for Computational Linguistics.

Maud Ehrmann, Ahmed Hamdi, Elvys Linhares Pontes, Matteo Romanello, and Antoine Doucet. 2021. Named entity recognition and classification on historical documents: A survey. *CoRR*, abs/2109.11406.

Maud Ehrmann, Matteo Romanello, Antoine Doucet, and Simon Clematide. 2022. HIPE-2022 shared task named entity datasets.

Maud Ehrmann, Matteo Romanello, Alex Flückiger, and Simon Clematide. 2020. Extended Overview of CLEF HIPE 2020: Named entity processing on historical newspapers. In *CLEF 2020 Working Notes. Working Notes of CLEF 2020 - Conference and Labs of the Evaluation Forum*, volume 2696, page 38, Thessaloniki, Greece. CEUR-WS.

Fred Gibbs and Trevor Owens. 2013. The hermeneutics of data and historical writing. In Kristen Nawrotzki and Jack Dougherty, editors, *Writing History in the Digital Age*, pages 159–172. University of Michigan Press.

Frederick W Gibbs. 2016. New forms of history: Critiquing data and its representations. *The American Historian*, 7:31–36.

Muki Haklay, Dilek Fraisl, Bastian Tzovaras, Susanne Hecker, Margaret Gold, Gerid Hager, Luigi Ceccaroni, Barbara Kieslinger, Uta Wehn, Sasha Woods, Christian Nold, Bálint Balázs, Marzia Mazzonetto, Simone Ruefenacht, Lea Shanley, Katherin Wagenknecht, Alice Motion, Andrea Sforzi, Dorte Riemenschneider, and Katrin Vohland. 2021. Contours of citizen science: a vignette study. *Royal Society Open Science*, 8:202108.

Ahmed Hamdi, Axel Jean-Caurant, Nicolas Sidère, Mickaël Coustaty, and Antoine Doucet. 2019. An analysis of the performance of named entity recognition over ocred documents. *2019 ACM/IEEE Joint Conference on Digital Libraries (JCDL)*, pages 333–334.

Tony Hey and Anne Trefethen. 2003. *The Data Deluge: An e-Science Perspective*, chapter 36. John Wiley & Sons, Ltd.

Patrick Juola. 2003. The time course of language change. *Computers and the Humanities*, 37(1):77–96.

Frédéric Kaplan and Isabella Di Lenardo. 2017. Big data of the past. *Frontiers Digit. Humanit.*, 4:12.

Margaret MR Kellow. 1999. Erasing slavery: Memory, history, and race in new england. *Reviews in American History*, 27(4):526–533.

Sunghwan Mac Kim and Steve Cassidy. 2015. Finding names in Trove: Named entity recognition for Australian historical newspapers. In *Proceedings of the Australasian Language Technology Association Workshop 2015*, pages 57–65, Parramatta, Australia.

Teven Le Scao and Alexander Rush. 2021. How many data points is a prompt worth? In *Proceedings of the 2021 Conference of the North American Chapter of the Association for Computational Linguistics: Human Language Technologies*, pages 2627–2636, Online. Association for Computational Linguistics.

Brian Lester, Rami Al-Rfou, and Noah Constant. 2021. The power of scale for parameter-efficient prompt tuning. In *Proceedings of the 2021 Conference on Empirical Methods in Natural Language Processing*, pages 3045–3059, Online and Punta Cana, Dominican Republic. Association for Computational Linguistics.

Andy T. Liu, Wei Xiao, Henghui Zhu, Dejiao Zhang, Shang-Wen Li, and Andrew Arnold. 2022. QaNER: Prompting question answering models for few-shot named entity recognition.

Pengfei Liu, Weizhe Yuan, Jinlan Fu, Zhengbao Jiang, Hiroaki Hayashi, and Graham Neubig. 2021. Pre-train, prompt, and predict: A systematic survey of prompting methods in natural language processing.

Clemens Neudecker. 2016. An open corpus for named entity recognition in historic newspapers. In *Proceedings of the Tenth International Conference on Language Resources and Evaluation (LREC'16)*, pages 4348–4352, Portorož, Slovenia. European Language Resources Association (ELRA).

Clemens Neudecker, Lotte Wilms, Willem Jan Faber, and Theo van Veen. 2014. Large-scale refinement of digital historic newspapers with named entity recognition. In *IFLA Congress 2014 – Digital Transformation and the Changing Role of News Media in the 21st Century*.

Colin Raffel, Noam Shazeer, Adam Roberts, Katherine Lee, Sharan Narang, Michael Matena, Yanqi Zhou, Wei Li, and Peter J. Liu. 2020. Exploring the limits of transfer learning with a unified text-to-text transformer. *Journal of Machine Learning Research*, 21(140):1–67.

Christelle Ram. 2020. *Black historical erasure: A critical comparative analysis in Rosewood and Ocoee*. Ph.D. thesis, Rollins College.

Sebastian Ruder. 2018. NLP's ImageNet moment has arrived. `https://ruder.io/nlp-imagenet/`.

Victor Sanh, Albert Webson, Colin Raffel, Stephen H. Bach, Lintang Sutawika, Zaid Alyafeai, Antoine Chaffin, Arnaud Stiegler, Teven Le Scao, Arun Raja, Manan Dey, M. Saiful Bari, Canwen Xu, Urmish Thakker, Shanya Sharma, Eliza Szczechla, Taewoon Kim, Gunjan Chhablani, Nihal V. Nayak, Debajyoti Datta, Jonathan Chang, Mike Tian-Jian Jiang, Han Wang, Matteo Manica, Sheng Shen, Zheng Xin Yong, Harshit Pandey, Rachel Bawden, Thomas Wang, Trishala Neeraj, Jos Rozen, Abheesht Sharma, Andrea Santilli, Thibault Févry, Jason Alan Fries, Ryan Teehan, Stella Biderman, Leo Gao, Tali Bers, Thomas Wolf, and Alexander M. Rush. 2021. Multitask prompted training enables zero-shot task generalization. *CoRR*, abs/2110.08207.

Timo Schick and Hinrich Schütze. 2021. It's not just size that matters: Small language models are also few-shot learners. In *Proceedings of the 2021 Conference of the North American Chapter of the Association for Computational Linguistics: Human Language Technologies*, pages 2339–2352, Online. Association for Computational Linguistics.

Michelle A Stanley. 2021. *Beyond erasure: Indigenous genocide denial and settler colonialism*. Routledge.

Melissa M. Terras. 2011. The rise of digitization. In Ruth Rikowski, editor, *Digitisation Perspectives*, pages 3–20. Sense Publishers, Rotterdam.

Martin Thoma. 2018. WiLI-2018 - Wikipedia Language Identification database.

Ashish Vaswani, Noam Shazeer, Niki Parmar, Jakob Uszkoreit, Llion Jones, Aidan N. Gomez, Lukasz Kaiser, and Illia Polosukhin. 2017. Attention is all you need. In *Advances in Neural Information Processing Systems 30: Annual Conference on Neural Information Processing Systems 2017, December 4-9, 2017, Long Beach, CA, USA*, pages 5998–6008.

Zexuan Zhong, Dan Friedman, and Danqi Chen. 2021. Factual probing is [MASK]: Learning vs. learning to recall. In *Proceedings of the 2021 Conference of the North American Chapter of the Association for Computational Linguistics: Human Language Technologies*, pages 5017–5033, Online. Association for Computational Linguistics.

Appendix: Full scores of Levenshtein distance

The figures below and in the next page provide full results of evaluation on Levenshtein distance, including precision, recall and F1-score at different thresholds, at threshold 0.4, and across different time periods in the CLEF-HIPE 2020 dataset.

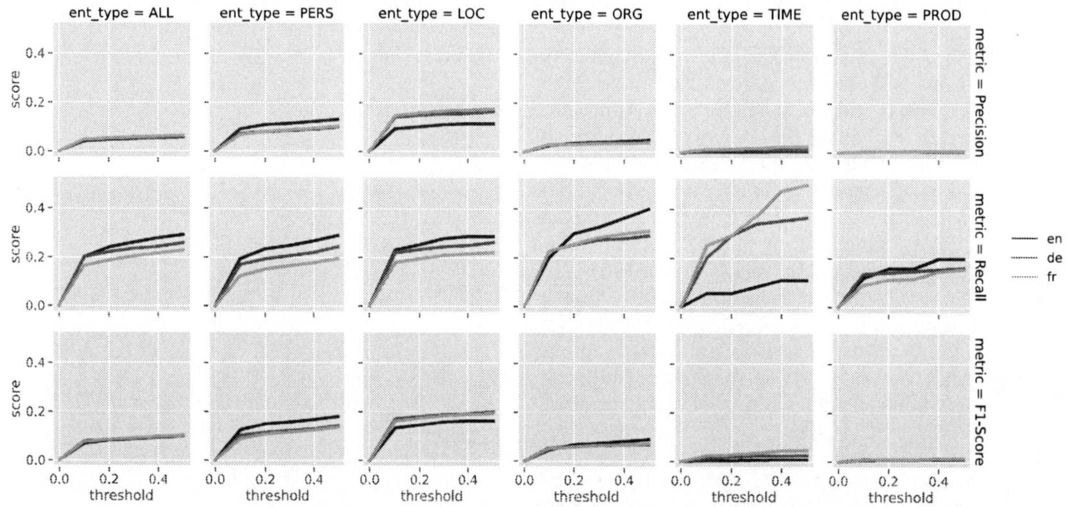

Figure 3: Precision, recall and F1-score (resp. first, second and third rows) at different Levenshtein distance thresholds and for different languages. Languages are distinguished by line color.

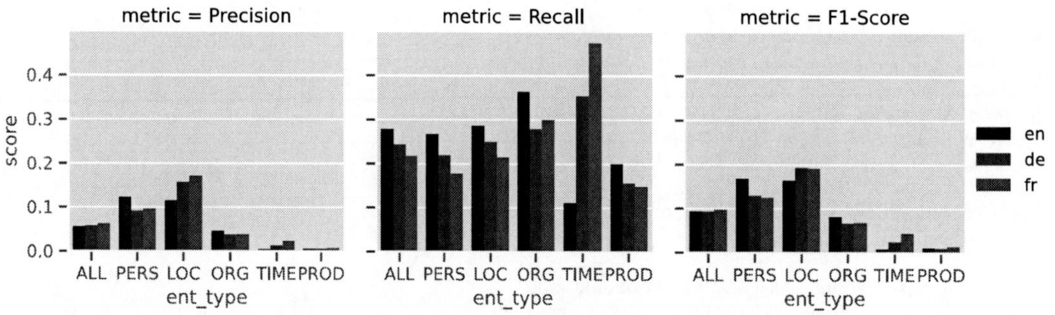

Figure 4: Precision, recall and F1-score (resp. first, second and third columns) by entity type at Levenshtein distance threshold 0.4 for different languages.

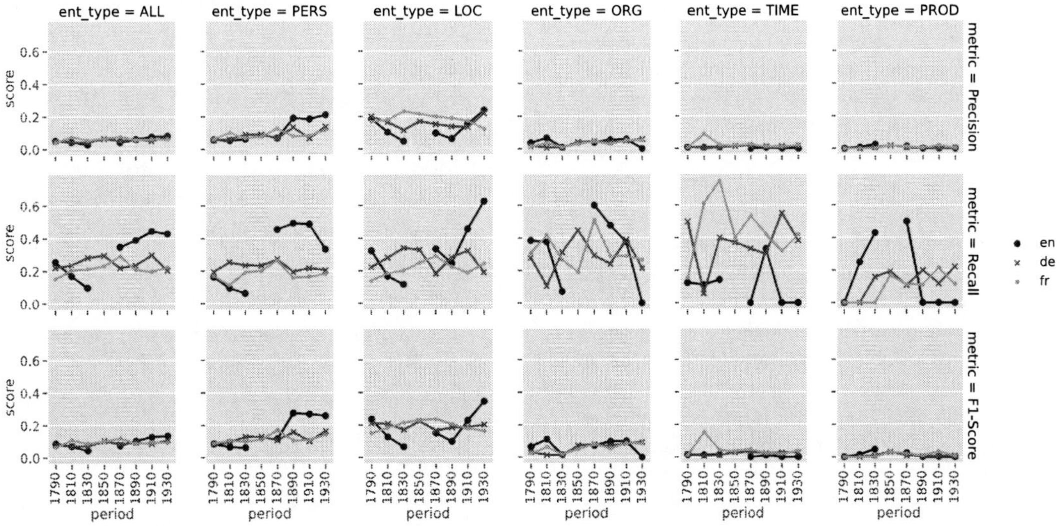

Figure 5: Precision, recall and F1-score (resp. first, second and third rows) at Levenshtein threshold 0.4 across periods for different languages. Languages are distinguished by both the line color and the type of dot.

A Holistic Assessment of the Carbon Footprint of Noor, a Very Large Arabic Language Model

Imad Lakim
TII, Abu Dhabi
imad.lakim@tii.ae

Ebtesam Almazrouei
TII, Abu Dhabi
ebtesam.almazrouei@tii.ae

Ibrahim Abu Alhaol
TII, Abu Dhabi
ibrahim.abualhaol@tii.ae

Merouane Debbah
TII, Abu Dhabi
merouane.debbah@tii.ae

Julien Launay
LightOn, Paris
julien@lighton.io

Abstract

As ever larger language models grow more ubiquitous, it is crucial to consider their environmental impact. Characterised by extreme size and resource use, recent generations of models have been criticised for their voracious appetite for compute, and thus significant carbon footprint. Although reporting of carbon impact has grown more common in machine learning papers, this reporting is usually limited to compute resources used strictly for training. In this work, we propose a holistic assessment of the footprint of an extreme-scale language model, Noor. Noor is an ongoing project aiming to develop the largest multi-task Arabic language models–with up to 13B parameters–leveraging zero-shot generalisation to enable a wide range of downstream tasks via natural language instructions. We assess the total carbon bill of the entire project: starting with data collection and storage costs, including research and development budgets, pretraining costs, future serving estimates, and other exogenous costs necessary for this international cooperation. Notably, we find that inference costs and exogenous factors can have a significant impact on total budget. Finally, we discuss pathways to reduce the carbon footprint of extreme-scale models.

1 Introduction

Recent progress in natural language processing (NLP) has been driven by the emergence of so-called foundation models (Bommasani et al., 2021). This paradigm shift is characterised by a homogenisation of modelling methods– crystallising around the Transformer architecture (Vaswani et al., 2017)– and by emergent capabilities (e.g. zero-shot generalisation) predominantly arising from sheer scale alone (Brown et al., 2020). NLP models are now experiencing a 3-4 months doubling time in size, as outlined by Figure 1. Most recent large language models such as MT-NLG 530B (Smith et al., 2022), Gopher 280B (Rae et al., 2021), or Jurassic-1 178B (Lieber et al., 2021), all report training budgets in the thousands of PF-days[1] range. Because AI accelerators performance per watt has plateaued compared to deep learning budgets (Reuther et al., 2021; Sevilla et al., 2022), practitioners have had to scale-out training over an increasingly large number of accelerators (Narayanan et al., 2021). Accordingly, the energy cost of training state-of-the-art models has grown significantly: increase in compute is no longer fuelled by improvements in hardware efficiency, but in hardware scale.

Although this increase in size and compute budget is backed by empirical scaling laws drawing a clear link between compute spent and model performance (Kaplan et al., 2020), the societal benefits of larger models have been questioned (Tomašev et al., 2020; Bender et al., 2021). Specifically to environmental concerns, in a time of climate crisis when carbon emissions must be drastically cut (Masson-Delmotte et al., 2018), one may question whether these large compute budgets are justified. A crucial step towards answering this question is an in-depth evaluation of the footprint of large models.

Existing assessments of the environmental impacts of large models are usually focused on hyperparameter tuning and pretraining costs (Strubell et al., 2019; Patterson et al., 2021). This trend is reflected by the growing number of tools available to help practitioners quantify the impact of machine learning computations (Bannour et al., 2021). If some studies have also endeavoured to quantify select aspects of the machine learning pipeline (e.g. conference attendance (Skiles et al., 2021), hardware lifecycle (Gupta et al., 2021), etc.), end-to-end evaluations of machine learning projects life cycle emissions remain rare (Wu et al., 2022).

[1] A PF-day is 1 PFLOPs (10 A100) sustained for a day.

Proceedings of BigScience Episode #5 – Workshop on Challenges & Perspectives in Creating Large Language Models, pages 84 - 94
May 27, 2022

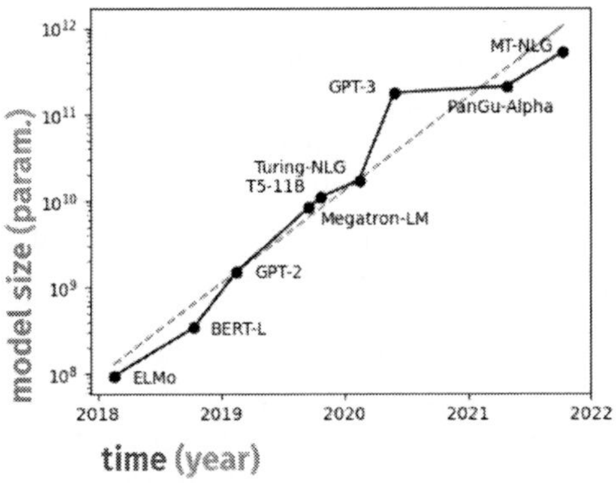

Figure 1: **Over the last four years, the size of state-of-the-art language models has doubled every 3-4 months.** Note that this trend has been slowing down, due to scale-out limitations.

To fill this gap, we produce an end-to-end assessment of the carbon footprint of Noor, a project seeking to train a very large Arabic language model. Our contributions are the following:

Holistic assessment. We evaluate the total carbon bill of the entire project: starting with data collection, curation, and storage, including research and development and hyper-parameters tuning budgets, pretraining costs, future serving estimates, and other exogenous impacts sparked by this international cooperation (e.g. flights, personnel, etc.)

Beyond pretraining. We identify pretraining compute as driving more than half of the emissions of the project. However, all combined, other R&D, storage, and personnel counts still amount for 35% of the carbon footprint. We also identify downstream use in the wild as potentially significant. This leads us to recommend for the end-to-end footprint to be systematically assessed on a per-project basis. Notably, in scenarios with a low-impact training electric mix, costs beyond pretraining may become the main sources of emissions.

Pathways to lower footprints. Finally, we discuss ways to reduce the environmental footprints of projects involving large models, and put in perspective the footprint of similar projects.

2 Related work

In light of ever increasing computational budgets (Sevilla et al., 2022) and of the need to cut on emissions to abate global warming (Masson-Delmotte et al., 2018), the environmental impact of deep learning has drawn significant interest.

Strubell et al., 2019 notably highlighted the potential high environmental costs of deep learning. However, its headline figures were produced in the specific context of neural architecture search, a relatively rare practice for extreme-scale models nowadays. Lacoste et al., 2019; Lottick et al., 2019; Schwartz et al., 2020 subsequently called for AI research to be more aware of its environmental cost. An increasing number of tools, such as `codecarbon` (Schmidt et al., 2021), have been developed to help with tracking the impact of deep learning experiments (Bannour et al., 2021). All of these lines of research share similar recommendations: the carbon footprint of deep learning is a direct consequence of the electricity mix and efficiency of the data center, suggesting that picking an appropriate provider is the most straightforward way to reduce environmental impact.

Specifically to extreme-scale models, Patterson et al., 2021 estimated the energy consumption of five large NLP models, including GPT-3. They identified that a judicious choice of neural architecture, datacenter and accelerator can help reduce considerably carbon budgets. Thompson et al., 2020 identified a clear relationship between large models performance and their carbon impact, building upon work on neural scaling laws (Kaplan et al., 2020). Taddeo et al., 2021 estimated the cost of training GPT-3 in different data centers across the worldwide, highlighting again the high dependency on the local energy mix and specific infrastructure.

Two recent studies have provided insights into the end-to-end carbon footprint of deployed models in the industry. Wu et al., 2022 studied the impact of the increasingly large recommender systems leveraged at Meta, while Patterson et al., 2022 provided an assessment of the costs (including inference) of large models at Google. They expect the carbon footprint of training to plateau in coming years, and then to shrink–owing to more efficient high performance computing platforms. They also assert that current studies are overestimating the real environmental costs of large models, in light of the wide availability of "clean" compute platforms.

In the field of astrophysics, Aujoux et al., 2021 did an extensive study to estimate the carbon footprint of the Giant Array for Neutrino Detection (GRAND) project, a multi-decade worldwide experiment. Inspired by their holistic methodology, we seek to establish the first end-to-end assessment of an extreme-scale NLP project.

3 The Noor Project

The current state-of-the-art generative language model in Modern Standard Arabic is AraGPT (Antoun et al., 2021), a 1.5B parameters model. The Noor project seeks to expand upon this model, introducing a 1.5B, 2.7B, 6.7B, and 13B Arabic models, trained a custom curated dataset of 150B tokens, inspired by The Pile (Gao et al., 2020). These larger scales are expected to make the model able to tackle novel tasks through zero-shot generalization, as exhibited by GPT-3 (Brown et al., 2020) or GPT-J (Wang and Komatsuzaki, 2021).

Noor is an on-going international cooperation between the Technology Innovation Institute in the United Arab Emirates and LightOn in France. The Noor project can be split in four parts:

- **Data curation.** A custom curated dataset of 150B tokens has been assembled for Noor. This dataset has been scrapped from diversified sources, and also includes data from Common Crawl. We filter this data with an LM-based quality-scoring system inspired by CCNet (Wenzek et al., 2019).
- **R&D experiments.** To validate tokenization, dataset, architecture, and establish scaling laws, we trained a number of R&D models (100M-1.5B parameters on 10-30B tokens).
- **Main training.** We train a suite of four models of 1.5B, 2.7B, 6.7B, and 13B parameters.
- **Model use.** Prospectively, we include some estimations of the future inference cost of these models as they are put in use.

4 Factors influencing the carbon footprint of large models

Before beginning our assessment, we propose to identify some of the key influencing factors on the potential carbon footprint of large models, focusing first on factors directly related to the models themselves and not to the project producing them.

Model size. The number of floating operations per forward pass is directly proportional to the size of the network. A common approximation for the total compute budget C required for training a Transformer model with N parameters on D tokens is $C = 6ND$ (Kaplan et al., 2020). As the optimal dataset size only grows sublinearly with model size for autoregressive modelling (Henighan et al., 2020), compute budget will scale more or less linearly with model size. The larger the number of operations, the more energy is needed to train the model. For inference, the cost for each token is reduced to a third compared to training, and environmental impact will be driven by the total number of words/tokens processed.

Hardware characteristics. The throughput (in FLOPs) that can be tackled by the hardware will drive the total time required to perform the task. More efficient hardware will have more throughput per Watt. We note however that most available chips suitable for large model training (e.g., NVIDIA GPUs, Google TPUs, etc.) exhibit similar efficiency characteristics (Reuther et al., 2021).

Modelling decisions. We identified above two key factors: number of tokens processed (for training or inference), and hardware throughput. We note that both of these are also strongly impacted by modelling decisions. A more fertile tokenizer will use less tokens for the same text, leading to faster processing. Similarly, small changes in model architecture (e.g., choosing hidden sizes in accordance with wave/tile quantization) and in implementation (e.g., 3D parallelism) can drastically increase throughput, and reduce total training time.

Data center efficiency. The energy consumed does not serve only to power up the servers, but also to cool down the data center itself and to respond to other electrical needs. The Power Usage Effectiveness (PUE) is used to assess the overall efficiency of a data center. It measures the quotient of the total energy requirement and the final energy used by the servers. The PUE will be influenced by the data center architecture. Worldwide average is around 1.8, but Google for instance reports an average PUE of 1.11. Waste heat in data centers can also be reused for collective water heating, driving down the PUE, as in the Jean Zay HPC.

Electricity mix. The breakdown of the energy sources powering a data center is a crucial factor, and depends primarily on the region. The electricity mix determines the carbon emissions per kWh of electricity. Today, the world average of carbon emission by kwh of electricity generated is 475 gCO2e/kWh, and an increasing number of data centers from cloud providers are using 100% renewable or nuclear energy to power their hardware. Taking Google Cloud as an example again, their

Montreal facility reports 27gCO2e/kWH, twenty times lower than the world average.

Beyond factors related to the models themselves, we seek in this study to take into account a number of other costs: storage, preprocessing, and transfer costs for the dataset, personnel costs such as travel and individual laptops, etc. We note however one limitation from our study: we do not take into account the lifecycle of the hardware used. Unfortunately, numbers are scarcely available, and not made public by the main manufacturers.

5 Carbon footprint of the Noor project

5.1 Electricity consumption

We begin by accounting for the electricity consumption of all aspects of the project. The impact of this consumption will be highly dependent on the carbon intensity of the electricity mix used. Non-electric sources (e.g., international flights) will be added to the carbon budget in a second phase.

5.1.1 Data storage and transfers

The energy consumption of data depends on both the energy required for powering the disks to store the data, and the energy consumed when moving the data from one server to another. We average storage costs over the 6 months of the project.

Storage. Although disk wattage is generally reported on per-disk level, Posani et al., 2019 estimates the power per TB of data using aggregated technical specifications. The paper reports that the average peak consumption of cloud storage is around 11.3W/TB. It means an energy consumption of 99 kWh/TB a year. This estimation considers a PUE of 1.6 and a redundancy factor of 2 since managed services will also have a back-up.

The breakdown of our data storage is as follows:

- **Curated data.** Including both raw and processed data, we have accumulated around 2TB of curated data. This is stored for the 6 months of the project, resulting in 99kWh used.

- **Bulk data.** We use Common Crawl (CC) for acquiring large amounts of web data. Each CC dump is on average around 10TB, and we discard it immediately after processing it. On average, it takes 24 hours to fully process a dump: we used 21 dumps from CC, meaning we stored 210TB of data for 24hours, equivalent to 57 kWh of energy consumption. After processing the dumps, we got on average 1.2TB of data per dump, thus 25TB in total. Considering that this data will be stored for 6 months, we end up with 1.3 MWh of energy consumption for the bulk data. Note that we keep the processed data in all languages (not just Modern Standard Arabic).

- **Models.** The weights of the Noor models (1.3B, 2.7B, 6.7B and 13B) are respectively 2.6GB, 5.4G, 13.4GB, and 26GB in half-precision. This corresponds to training checkpoints (including the full-precision optimizer) of 20.8GB, 43.2GB, 107.2GB, and 208GB. We save such checkpoints every 10B tokens. In total, we end-up with 5.7TB of model weights and intermediary checkpoints for future analysis and interpretability work, consuming 0.3MWh in total.

Transfers. Posani et al., 2019 provided an estimate of 23.9 kJ per GB (6.38 kWh per TB) transferred, using the formula of Baliga et al., 2011 and the same hypothesis as Aslan et al., 2017 (800km average distance between core nodes). The 210TB of CC data are downloaded on the preprocessing servers once; the 25TB of processed data are moved once to our archival machines, and another time to the HPC used for training; the curated data is downloaded once, moved to the archival machines, and then moved to the HPC; the 5.7TB of models are moved once from our HPC, and then to our inference servers for final models or to workstations for intermediary checkpoints. Consequently, we estimate the transfer energy bill at 1.8 MWh.

Total. Thus, the total energy consumption of data is estimated to be about 3.5 MWh, dominated by the multilingual Common Crawl data. We note that as ideal dataset size increases sublinearly with model size (Kaplan et al., 2020), we expect checkpoints and model transfers to eventually dominate the costs of storage and transfer for larger models.

Note that we neglect costs linked to a potential public release of the models, as it is difficult to predict traffic. As a rough estimation, 10,000 downloads of the 13B model would represent 260TB of traffic, and 1.66MWh consumed.

5.1.2 Data processing

We take all text data through a pipeline inspired by CCNet (Wenzek et al., 2019) for preprocessing. This pipeline takes care of deduplication, language identification, and finally quality filtering with a

Table 1: **Training compute budget and energy used for training the Noor models.** Assuming a pretraining dataset of 150B tokens and a throughput of 100 TFLOPs per A100.

Model	**Budget** [PF-days]	**Budget** [A100-hours]	**HPC**	**Consumption** [MWh]
1.3B	13.5	3300	MeluXina	2.1
2.7B	28.1	6800	Noor-HPC	4.8
6.7B	69.8	17000	Noor-HPC	11.8
13B	135	33000	Noor-HPC	22.9

reference language model trained on Wikipedia. Processing with our pipeline occurs on a CPU cluster with 768 cores, split over 16 nodes.

Using average high-performance CPUs TDP figures, we estimate the average power consumption of each node at 350W; hence, the power of the cluster is 5.6kW. We processed 21 dumps of CommonCrawl, plus our curated data, for a total of 381 wall-clock hours. Accordingly, assuming a PUE of 1.1 as reported by Google, the total energy consumed by data preprocessing is 2.35MWh.

Note that for CommonCrawl data, this results in data processed for every language supported (176 for identification, 48 for quality filtering). Accordingly, this cost could be amortised over future projects. For high-resource languages, this also results in very large amounts of data: processing more dumps would not be necessary, even to train a 1 trillion parameters model.

5.1.3 Research and development

We carried experiments to validate tokenization methods, dataset composition, tune hyperparameters, and establish scaling laws. This early research and development work was performed on MeluXina, a high-performance super-computer located in Luxembourg. We used a total of 16,800 A100-hours in this phase. Each node used in MeluXina has 4 A100 SXM 40GB with a TDP of 400W, and two AMD EPYC 7763 CPUs with a TDP of 280W. They report a PUE of 1.35. Thus, we estimate the consumption of this R&D phase to be of 10.7MWh.

We expect the budget of this phase to roughly scale with model size. Indeed, debugging potential issues (e.g., numerical instabilities (Kim et al., 2021), etc.) for the final larger model will cost significantly more.

5.1.4 Main training

Using the $C = 6ND$ approximation, it is possible to calculate in advance the training budget required for a specific model. We observe an effective throughput with our Megatron+DeepSpeed codebase of around 100 TFLOPs[2] across models, in line with the state-of-the-art. We train four main models (1.5B, 2.7B, 6.7B, 13B) on 150B tokens.

We train the smaller model on MeluXina, but the other three on our own HPC cluster. Each node contains 8 A100 80GB and 2 AMD EPYC 7763 CPUs. The PUE of our data center is 1.5, 20% more efficient than the world average.

Table 1 outlines the costs of the main training. The total electric energy consumed to train the Noor suite of models is thus 41.6 MWh, 55% of it spent on the largest 13B model.

5.1.5 Inference

As the models of Noor have yet to be deployed, this is only a prospective estimate. Inference costs in general are difficult to estimate in advance, even more so for open source models which will be deployed to platforms with varying characteristics. We provide an estimate of the energy consumption during inference per generated token.

We thereafter denote as *processed tokens* the tokens in the original prompt sent to the model, and as *generated tokens* the tokens generated by the model using the prompt. To simplify calculations, we make the following assumptions from our experience with another large-scale API: (1) an A100 is used, which is sufficient for Noor-13B, but could be reduced to a more efficient T4 for Noor-1.5B/2.7B; (2) inference time per generated token is constant, whichever the number of processed tokens (per our benchmarks, thanks to caching, this is true up to 512 processed tokens roughly); (3) batch size is assumed to be 1, as batching is more challenging and less consistent for inference workloads.

Under these hypothesises, an A100 can generate up to 72,000 tokens per hour. Accordingly, we estimate that 26 Joules are required per token generated (400W

[2] These are effective FLOPs for training the model, not hardware FLOPs. Hardware FLOPs are closer to 150 TFLOPs.

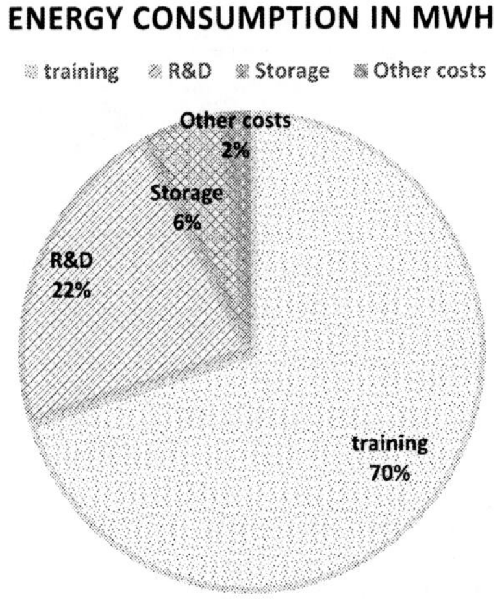

Figure 2: **Breakdown of the electricity consumption (total 59.14 MWh) of the Noor project.** Data preprocessing is included in R&D, amounting for 20% of it. We also note that R&D and dataset costs could be amortised through other projects or larger models.

for the GPU, 70W for the CPU, and 1.1 PUE on Google Cloud imply 517Wh of energy consumption for 72,000 tokens. Converted to Joule, it results in 26 Joules per token.) Accordingly, 3 billion tokens would have to be generated for inference costs to catch up with training costs. At some point during its beta, GPT-3 was reported to generate 4.5 billion words per day (Pilipiszyn, 2021).

5.1.6 Additional costs

Beyond costs related to data, R&D, training, and inference, one may wonder if direct electricity use from scientists involved in the project is significant. Assuming that the average laptop consumes 70W, plus 30W for an external screen, six research scientists dedicating 100% of their time during 6 months for this project, 8 hours per day, will use up 0.604MWh. We could also include costs of e-mail exchanges and video-conferences specifically, but these were found to be negligible in Aujoux et al., 2021. We round up the marginal costs to 1MWh, and note that this is but a rough estimate.

5.1.7 Summary

We showed that the total electricity consumption of the Noor project is not only about training the final models, as outlined in Figure 2. Nearly a third of the energy consumed (30%) went to tasks outside of main models pretraining.

Because of larger uncertainties, we keep the serving/inference assessment out of the previous budget. However, especially in the context of openly available models, the inference budget can rapidly catch up with the total budget outlined in 2.

5.2 Carbon footprint

Now, from the electricity consumption, and using information on the local carbon intensity, we will derive the full footprint of the Noor project. We will also add energy use coming from non-electric sources (e.g., flights). As the carbon intensity of the electricity mix varies significantly across regions, we outlined below the locations of interest:

- **Storage.** We used Amazon S3 in Bahrain;
- **R&D.** We used a GCP CPU cluster located in Netherlands, and MeluXina in Luxembourg;
- **Main training.** The smaller 1.3B model was trained on MeluXina, and the remaining models were trained on our dedicated HPC platform in the United Arab Emirates (UAE);
- **Other.** Six full-time scientists were involved, half in France and half in the UAE.

Table 2 shows the resulting carbon footprint for each of the development stages of Noor project. This highlights the importance of location for carbon footprint: notably, all calculations on performed on the relatively low-carbon MeluXina HPC end-up having very limited costs, even compared to small items like storage in Bahrain.

In addition to these development costs, we consider the carbon footprint of three round-trip flights of four scientists between Paris and Abu Dhabi. These trips were taken to run training workshops, brainstorming sessions, and discussions related to the project. We use the carbon emissions simulator of the International Civil Aviation Organization. One round-trip emits 527 kgCO2e per person, totalling 6.4 tons of emissions over all trips.

Finally, Figure 3 displays the total distribution of the carbon footprint of the project. As shown in the figure, factors like flights may be usually neglected, but have a significant contribution in the total carbon footprint. Specifically, as conference returns in-person, this is a systematic impact that exists on most papers. In the case of Noor, the few flights operated account for 18% of the total carbon emission of the whole project.

Table 2: **Carbon footprint of each phase of the Noor project.**

Phase	**Provider**	**Location**	**Mix** [gCO2e/kWh]	**Use** MWh	**Footprint** [tCO2e]
Storage	Amazon S3	Bahrain	1188	3.5	4.2
R&D	GCP	Netherlands	410	2.35	0.96
	MeluXina	Luxembourg	60	10.7	0.65
Training	MeluXina	Luxembourg	60	2.1	0.13
	Noor-HPC	UAE	600	39.5	23.7
Others		France	56	0.33	0.02
		UAE	600	0.66	0.4

Interestingly, we note that with increasingly clean electricity and efficient data centers, the exogenous costs linked to flights and personnel are bound to increase in proportional impact.

Inference. Forecasting the carbon footprint of inference is harder for open models: as they may be downloaded and deployed by anyone, it is impossible to predict the carbon intensity of the electricity they will use. We study two scenarios: an intermediate one, based on the world average emission per kWh (475 gCO2e/kWh) and a best-case one, based on the low-impact French mix (56 gCO2e/kWh). These two scenarios correspond to around 300,000 tokens generated per kgCO2e, or to 2,500,000 tokens generated per kgCO2e in the best-case. Going back to the 4.5 billion words per day of GPT-3, this amounts to 30 tons of CO2e per day and 3.5 tons.

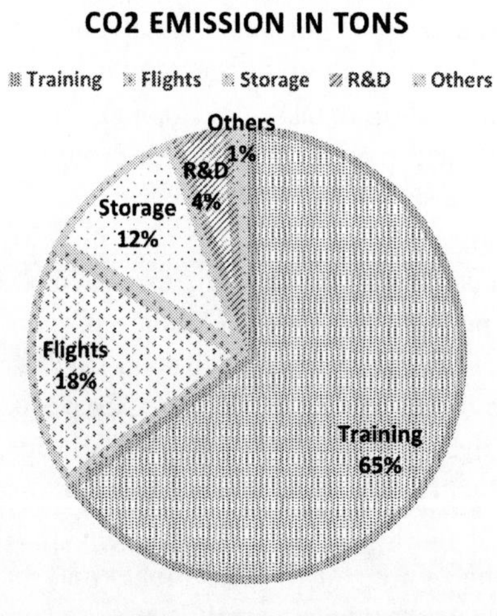

Figure 3: **Breakdown of the carbon footprint (total 36.5t tC02e) of the Noor project.** This breakdown is highly dependent on the localisation of the workloads and the local carbon intensity of the electricity mix.

6 Best practices and recommendations

From our experience with Noor, we highlight some recommendations for future projects to minimise their carbon footprint.

6.1 Modelling & engineering

A first angle of attack is to make the machine learning techniques used more efficient.

- **Efficient architectures.** Mixture-of-experts (MoE) models split the large fully-connected layers of a Transformer into distinct experts (Fedus et al., 2021). Although larger, MoE Transformers can bring significant energy savings during training and inference (Du et al., 2021), as the experts are only sparsely activated. Recent work demonstrate that they may even scale favorably compared to dense models (Clark et al., 2022). More broadly, even small changes (e.g. better embeddings, activation functions) may have a non-negligible impact on the overall carbon footprint.

- **Efficient inference.** As we have shown, inference costs can rapidly catch up with training costs: it is also interesting to make the model leaner for inference. Quantization (Yang et al., 2019) reduces numerical precision at inference time and accelerates inference, but it has seen limited adoption with large models. Distillation (i.e., training a smaller model from the outputs of a larger one) is a promising direction, already demonstrated for Transformers applied to vision (Touvron et al., 2021).

- **Efficient implementations.** Crucially, distributed training implementations must be as efficient as possible, to amortise the large idle consumption of the hardware – MeluXina reports for instance idle power of around 150W per GPU when accounting for CPU cores, infrastructure, etc. This includes taking into account fine-grained effects depending on architectures, such as wave and tile quantization, to achieve the best throughput possible.

6.2 Hardware

A second angle of attack is to focus on the hardware used to train these models.

- **Data center choice.** A data center with a PUE of 1.1 will decrease energy consumption by 39% compared to the world average of 1.8. Low PUE platforms should be preferred.
- **Local carbon intensity.** As highlighted by Table 2, the carbon intensity of the electricity mix significantly impacts the final footprint. Locating training in an area with a clean mix is an easy step to take that can drastically cut the footprint of a project. This is especially easy to do on online cloud platforms, which have many areas of availability.
- **Efficient inference.** Carefully selecting a proper AI accelerator for managed inference workloads can limit the footprint of model use. For instance, for smaller models (<3B), it may be possible to use T4s rather than A100s, which are 20% more energy efficient per FLOP than A100s. Finally, specialised accelerators are also starting to become available (Reuther et al., 2020). We note that this may however require specific developments.

6.3 Other practices

Finally, it is important to not underestimate costs beyond machine learning workloads.

- **Minimising exogenous impact.** Although we found the final footprint to be dominated by the main training runs, we still note the significant impact of the international flights taken during this cooperation (20% of the final footprint). Minimising such high-intensity cost center is important.
- **Costs reporting and offset.** The full cost of model development is rarely, if ever, reported in the literature. We highly recommend the AI community to start reporting the full energy consumption and the CO2e of their projects. This reporting can also be used as the basis for offsetting carbon emissions.

7 Discussion and conclusion

We undertook an end-to-end assessment of the carbon footprint associated with the development of an extreme-scale language model. We took into account data collection and storage, research and development, pretraining, and included estimates for future serving and inference. We also added personnel costs, such as international flights to run training workshops and brainstorming sessions.

In total, we estimate the development of the suite of the four Noor models to have emitted 36.5 tons of CO2, 65% of which for training the models, 18% for the international flights, 12% for data storage, and 4% for small-scale research and development experiments. To put this in perspective, the average carbon footprint per individual in the US is around 20 tons, so our project generated a little over two years of individual US emissions.

We find that the main driver of this carbon footprint is the carbon intensity of the mix used for model training. Appropriately selecting the location of calculations can significantly reduce the environmental impact of a project. For instance, in this project, running all computations in France would have reduced the total footprint to 14.9 tCO2e, 42% of which from the international flights. As the impact of the computations themselves become smaller, it is important for practitionners to more carefully weigh in exogenous contributions.

All-in-all, with careful considerations around data center choice, it is possible to run extreme-scale NLP projects with a low carbon impact.

Finally, we also identified that large-scale inference could also rapidly outtake pretraining costs in terms of carbon impact. Inference, if not centrally managed, is harder to control: with a publicly available model, it will happen on hardware decided by the end user. We thus think its equally important for practitioners to alert users regarding best efficient inference practices, and regarding best practices to limit the environmental cost of computations (e.g. choosing an efficient data center, running inference in a country with a low-impact mix, etc.)

References

Wissam Antoun, Fady Baly, and Hazem Hajj. 2021. Aragpt2: Pre-trained transformer for arabic language generation.

Joshua Aslan, Kieren Mayers, Jonathan Koomey, and Chris France. 2017. Electricity intensity of internet data transmission: Untangling the estimates: Electricity intensity of data transmission. *Journal of Industrial Ecology*, 22.

Clarisse Aujoux, Kumiko Kotera, and Odile Blanchard. 2021. Estimating the carbon footprint of the grand project, a multi-decade astrophysics experiment. *Astroparticle Physics*, 131:102587.

Jayant Baliga, Robert Ayre, Kerry Hinton, and Rodney Tucker. 2011. Green cloud computing: Balancing energy in processing, storage, and transport. *Proceedings of the IEEE*, 99:149 – 167.

Nesrine Bannour, Sahar Ghannay, Aurélie Névéol, and Anne-Laure Ligozat. 2021. Evaluating the carbon footprint of nlp methods: a survey and analysis of existing tools. In *EMNLP, Workshop SustaiNLP*.

Emily M Bender, Timnit Gebru, Angelina McMillan-Major, and Shmargaret Shmitchell. 2021. On the dangers of stochastic parrots: Can language models be too big? In *Proceedings of the 2021 ACM Conference on Fairness, Accountability, and Transparency*, pages 610–623.

Rishi Bommasani, Drew A Hudson, Ehsan Adeli, Russ Altman, Simran Arora, Sydney von Arx, Michael S Bernstein, Jeannette Bohg, Antoine Bosselut, Emma Brunskill, et al. 2021. On the opportunities and risks of foundation models. *arXiv preprint arXiv:2108.07258*.

Tom B. Brown, Benjamin Mann, Nick Ryder, Melanie Subbiah, Jared Kaplan, Prafulla Dhariwal, Arvind Neelakantan, Pranav Shyam, Girish Sastry, Amanda Askell, Sandhini Agarwal, Ariel Herbert-Voss, Gretchen Krueger, Tom Henighan, Rewon Child, Aditya Ramesh, Daniel M. Ziegler, Jeffrey Wu, Clemens Winter, Christopher Hesse, Mark Chen, Eric Sigler, Mateusz Litwin, Scott Gray, Benjamin Chess, Jack Clark, Christopher Berner, Sam McCandlish, Alec Radford, Ilya Sutskever, and Dario Amodei. 2020. Language models are few-shot learners.

Aidan Clark, Diego de las Casas, Aurelia Guy, Arthur Mensch, Michela Paganini, Jordan Hoffmann, Bogdan Damoc, Blake Hechtman, Trevor Cai, Sebastian Borgeaud, et al. 2022. Unified scaling laws for routed language models. *arXiv preprint arXiv:2202.01169*.

Nan Du, Yanping Huang, Andrew M. Dai, Simon Tong, Dmitry Lepikhin, Yuanzhong Xu, Maxim Krikun, Yanqi Zhou, Adams Wei Yu, Orhan Firat, Barret Zoph, Liam Fedus, Maarten Bosma, Zongwei Zhou, Tao Wang, Yu Emma Wang, Kellie Webster, Marie Pellat, Kevin Robinson, Kathy Meier-Hellstern, Toju Duke, Lucas Dixon, Kun Zhang, Quoc V Le, Yonghui Wu, Zhifeng Chen, and Claire Cui. 2021. Glam: Efficient scaling of language models with mixture-of-experts.

William Fedus, Barret Zoph, and Noam Shazeer. 2021. Switch transformers: Scaling to trillion parameter models with simple and efficient sparsity. *arXiv preprint arXiv:2101.03961*.

Leo Gao, Stella Biderman, Sid Black, Laurence Golding, Travis Hoppe, Charles Foster, Jason Phang, Horace He, Anish Thite, Noa Nabeshima, Shawn Presser, and Connor Leahy. 2020. The Pile: An 800gb dataset of diverse text for language modeling. *arXiv preprint arXiv:2101.00027*.

Udit Gupta, Young Geun Kim, Sylvia Lee, Jordan Tse, Hsien-Hsin S Lee, Gu-Yeon Wei, David Brooks, and Carole-Jean Wu. 2021. Chasing carbon: The elusive environmental footprint of computing. In *2021 IEEE International Symposium on High-Performance Computer Architecture (HPCA)*, pages 854–867. IEEE.

Tom Henighan, Jared Kaplan, Mor Katz, Mark Chen, Christopher Hesse, Jacob Jackson, Heewoo Jun, Tom B Brown, Prafulla Dhariwal, Scott Gray, et al. 2020. Scaling laws for autoregressive generative modeling. *arXiv preprint arXiv:2010.14701*.

Jared Kaplan, Sam McCandlish, Tom Henighan, Tom B. Brown, Benjamin Chess, Rewon Child, Scott Gray, Alec Radford, Jeffrey Wu, and Dario Amodei. 2020. Scaling laws for neural language models.

Boseop Kim, HyoungSeok Kim, Sang-Woo Lee, Gichang Lee, Donghyun Kwak, Dong Hyeon Jeon, Sunghyun Park, Sungju Kim, Seonhoon Kim, Dongpil Seo, et al. 2021. What changes can large-scale language models bring? intensive study on hyperclova: Billions-scale korean generative pretrained transformers. *arXiv preprint arXiv:2109.04650*.

Alexandre Lacoste, Alexandra Luccioni, Victor Schmidt, and Thomas Dandres. 2019. Quantifying the carbon emissions of machine learning. *arXiv preprint arXiv:1910.09700*.

Opher Lieber, Or Sharir, Barak Lenz, and Yoav Shoham. 2021. Jurassic-1: Technical details and evaluation. *White Paper. AI21 Labs*.

Kadan Lottick, Silvia Susai, Sorelle A. Friedler, and Jonathan P. Wilson. 2019. Energy usage reports: Environmental awareness as part of algorithmic accountability. *Workshop on Tackling Climate Change with Machine Learning at NeurIPS 2019*.

Valérie Masson-Delmotte, Panmao Zhai, Hans-Otto Pörtner, Debra Roberts, Jim Skea, Priyadarshi R Shukla, Anna Pirani, W Moufouma-Okia, C Péan,

R Pidcock, et al. 2018. Global warming of 1.5 c. *An IPCC Special Report on the impacts of global warming of*, 1(5).

Deepak Narayanan, Mohammad Shoeybi, Jared Casper, Patrick LeGresley, Mostofa Patwary, Vijay Korthikanti, Dmitri Vainbrand, Prethvi Kashinkunti, Julie Bernauer, Bryan Catanzaro, et al. 2021. Efficient large-scale language model training on gpu clusters using megatron-lm. In *Proceedings of the International Conference for High Performance Computing, Networking, Storage and Analysis*, pages 1–15.

David Patterson, Joseph Gonzalez, Urs Hölzle, Quoc Hung Le, Chen Liang, Lluis-Miquel Munguia, Daniel Rothchild, David So, Maud Texier, and Jeffrey Dean. 2022. The Carbon Footprint of Machine Learning Training Will Plateau, Then Shrink.

David Patterson, Joseph Gonzalez, Quoc Le, Chen Liang, Lluis-Miquel Munguia, Daniel Rothchild, David So, Maud Texier, and Jeff Dean. 2021. Carbon emissions and large neural network training.

Ashley Pilipiszyn. 2021. Gpt-3 powers the next generation of apps.

Lorenzo Posani, Alessio Paccoia, and Marco Moschettini. 2019. The carbon footprint of distributed cloud storage.

Jack W Rae, Sebastian Borgeaud, Trevor Cai, Katie Millican, Jordan Hoffmann, Francis Song, John Aslanides, Sarah Henderson, Roman Ring, Susannah Young, et al. 2021. Scaling language models: Methods, analysis & insights from training gopher. *arXiv preprint arXiv:2112.11446*.

Albert Reuther, Peter Michaleas, Michael Jones, Vijay Gadepally, Siddharth Samsi, and Jeremy Kepner. 2020. Survey of machine learning accelerators. In *2020 IEEE high performance extreme computing conference (HPEC)*, pages 1–12. IEEE.

Albert Reuther, Peter Michaleas, Michael Jones, Vijay Gadepally, Siddharth Samsi, and Jeremy Kepner. 2021. Ai accelerator survey and trends. In *2021 IEEE High Performance Extreme Computing Conference (HPEC)*, pages 1–9. IEEE.

Victor Schmidt, Kamal Goyal, Aditya Joshi, Boris Feld, Liam Conell, Nikolas Laskaris, Doug Blank, Jonathan Wilson, Sorelle Friedler, and Sasha Luccioni. 2021. CodeCarbon: Estimate and Track Carbon Emissions from Machine Learning Computing.

Roy Schwartz, Jesse Dodge, Noah A Smith, and Oren Etzioni. 2020. Green ai. *Communications of the ACM*, 63(12):54–63.

Jaime Sevilla, Lennart Heim, Anson Ho, Tamay Besiroglu, Marius Hobbhahn, and Pablo Villalobos. 2022. Compute trends across three eras of machine learning. *arXiv preprint arXiv:2202.05924*.

Matthew Skiles, Euijin Yang, Orad Reshef, Diego Robalino Muñoz, Diana Cintron, Mary Laura Lind, Alexander Rush, Patricia Perez Calleja, Robert Nerenberg, Andrea Armani, et al. 2021. Conference demographics and footprint changed by virtual platforms. *Nature Sustainability*, pages 1–8.

Shaden Smith, Mostofa Patwary, Brandon Norick, Patrick LeGresley, Samyam Rajbhandari, Jared Casper, Zhun Liu, Shrimai Prabhumoye, George Zerveas, Vijay Korthikanti, et al. 2022. Using deepspeed and megatron to train megatron-turing nlg 530b, a large-scale generative language model. *arXiv preprint arXiv:2201.11990*.

Emma Strubell, Ananya Ganesh, and Andrew McCallum. 2019. Energy and policy considerations for deep learning in nlp.

Mariarosaria Taddeo, Andreas Tsamados, Josh Cowls, and Luciano Floridi. 2021. Artificial intelligence and the climate emergency: Opportunities, challenges, and recommendations. *One Earth*, 4:776–779.

Neil C. Thompson, Kristjan Greenewald, Keeheon Lee, and Gabriel F. Manso. 2020. The computational limits of deep learning.

Nenad Tomašev, Julien Cornebise, Frank Hutter, Shakir Mohamed, Angela Picciariello, Bec Connelly, Danielle Belgrave, Daphne Ezer, Fanny Cachat van der Haert, Frank Mugisha, et al. 2020. Ai for social good: unlocking the opportunity for positive impact. *Nature Communications*, 11(1):1–6.

Hugo Touvron, Matthieu Cord, Matthijs Douze, Francisco Massa, Alexandre Sablayrolles, and Hervé Jégou. 2021. Training data-efficient image transformers & distillation through attention. In *International Conference on Machine Learning*, pages 10347–10357. PMLR.

Ashish Vaswani, Noam Shazeer, Niki Parmar, Jakob Uszkoreit, Llion Jones, Aidan N Gomez, Łukasz Kaiser, and Illia Polosukhin. 2017. Attention is all you need. *Advances in neural information processing systems*, 30.

Ben Wang and Aran Komatsuzaki. 2021. GPT-J-6B: A 6 Billion Parameter Autoregressive Language Model. `https://github.com/kingoflolz/mesh-transformer-jax`.

Guillaume Wenzek, Marie-Anne Lachaux, Alexis Conneau, Vishrav Chaudhary, Francisco Guzmán, Armand Joulin, and Edouard Grave. 2019. Ccnet: Extracting high quality monolingual datasets from web crawl data.

Carole-Jean Wu, Ramya Raghavendra, Udit Gupta, Bilge Acun, Newsha Ardalani, Kiwan Maeng, Gloria Chang, Fiona Aga Behram, James Huang, Charles Bai, Michael Gschwind, Anurag Gupta, Myle Ott, Anastasia Melnikov, Salvatore Candido,

David Brooks, Geeta Chauhan, Benjamin Lee, Hsien-Hsin S. Lee, Bugra Akyildiz, Maximilian Balandat, Joe Spisak, Ravi Jain, Mike Rabbat, and Kim Hazelwood. 2022. Sustainable ai: Environmental implications, challenges and opportunities.

Jiwei Yang, Xu Shen, Jun Xing, Xinmei Tian, Houqiang Li, Bing Deng, Jianqiang Huang, and Xiansheng Hua. 2019. Quantization networks.

GPT-NeoX-20B: An Open-Source Autoregressive Language Model

Sid Black* **Stella Biderman*** **Eric Hallahan***

Quentin Anthony **Leo Gao** **Laurence Golding** **Horace He**

Connor Leahy **Kyle McDonell** **Jason Phang** **Michael Pieler**

USVSN Sai Prashanth **Shivanshu Purohit** **Laria Reynolds**

Jonathan Tow **Ben Wang** **Samuel Weinbach**

Abstract

We introduce GPT-NeoX-20B, a 20 billion parameter autoregressive language model trained on the Pile, whose weights will be made freely and openly available to the public through a permissive license. It is, to the best of our knowledge, the largest dense autoregressive model that has publicly available weights at the time of submission. In this work, we describe GPT-NeoX-20B's architecture and training, and evaluate its performance on a range of language-understanding, mathematics and knowledge-based tasks. We open-source the training and evaluation code, as well as the model weights, at `https://github.com/EleutherAI/gpt-neox`.

1 Introduction

Over the past several years, there has been an explosion in research surrounding large language models (LLMs) for natural language processing, catalyzed largely by the impressive performance of Transformer-based language models such as BERT (Devlin et al., 2019), GPT-2 (Radford et al., 2019), GPT-3 (Brown et al., 2020), and T5 (Raffel et al., 2020). One of the most impactful outcomes of this research has been the discovery that the performance of LLMs scales predictably as a power-law with the number of parameters, with architecture details such as width/depth ratio having a minimal impact on performance within a wide range (Kaplan et al., 2020). A consequence of this has been an abundance of research focusing on scaling Transformer models up to ever-larger scales, resulting in dense models that surpass 500B parameters (Smith et al., 2022; Chowdhery et al., 2022), a milestone that would have been almost unthinkable just a few years prior.

Today, there are dozens of publicly acknowledged LLMs in existence. The largest have more than two orders of magnitude more parameters than GPT-2, and even at that scale there are nearly a dozen different models. However, these models are almost universally the protected intellectual property of large tech companies, and are gated behind a commercial API, available only upon request, or not available for outsider use at all. To our knowledge, the only freely and publicly available dense autoregressive language models larger than GPT-2 are GPT-Neo (2.7B parameters) (Black et al., 2021), GPT-J-6B (Wang and Komatsuzaki, 2021), Megatron-11B[1], Pangu-α-13B (Zeng et al., 2021), and the recently released FairSeq models (2.7B, 6.7B, and 13B parameters) (Artetxe et al., 2021).

In this paper we introduce GPT-NeoX-20B, a 20 billion parameter open source autoregressive language model. We make the models weights freely and openly available to the public through a permissive license, motivated by the belief that open access to LLMs is critical to advancing research in a wide range of areas—particularly in AI safety, mechanistic interpretability, and the study of how LLM capabilities scale. Many of the most interesting capabilities of LLMs only emerge above a certain number of parameters, and they have many properties that simply cannot be studied in smaller models. Although safety is often cited as a justification for keeping model weights private, we believe this is insufficient to prevent misuse, and is largely a limitation on the ability to probe and study LLMs for researchers not based at the small number of organizations that have access to state of the art language models.

In the following sections, we give a broad overview of GPT-NeoX-20B's architecture and training hyperparameters, detail the hardware and software setup used for training and evaluation, and

*Lead authors. Authors after the first three are listed in alphabetical order. See Appendix A for individual contribution details. Correspondence can be sent to `{sid, stella, contact}@eleuther.ai`

[1]This model does not work using the provided codebase, and we have been told it under-performs GPT-J.

Proceedings of BigScience Episode #5 – Workshop on Challenges & Perspectives in Creating Large Language Models, pages 95 - 136
May 27, 2022 ©2022 Association for Computational Linguistics

elaborate on the choices made when designing the training dataset and tokenization. We also address of some of the difficulties and unknowns we encountered in training such a large model. We place significant importance on the broader impacts of the release GPT-NeoX-20B and other such LLMs, and have prepared a separate manuscript for dissecting these issues in greater detail.

In addition, we also make available the model weights at evenly spaced 1000 step intervals throughout the whole of training. We hope that by making a wide range of checkpoints throughout training freely available, we will facilitate research on the training dynamics of LLMs, as well as the aforementioned areas of AI safety and interpretability.

2 Model Design and Implementation

GPT-NeoX-20B is an autoregressive transformer decoder model whose architecture largely follows that of GPT-3 (Brown et al., 2020), with a few notable deviations described below. Our model has 20 billion parameters, of which 19.9 billion are "non-embedding" parameters that Kaplan et al. (2020) identify as the proper number to use for scaling laws analysis. Our model has 44 layers, a hidden dimension size of 6144, and 64 heads.

2.1 Model Architecture

Although our architecture is largely similar to GPT-3, there are some notable differences. In this section we give a high-level overview of those differences, but ask the reader to refer to (Brown et al., 2020) for full details of the model architecture. Our model architecture is almost identical to that of GPT-J (Wang and Komatsuzaki, 2021)[2], however we choose to use GPT-3 as the point of reference because there is no canonical published reference on the design of GPT-J.

2.1.1 Rotary Positional Embeddings

We use rotary embeddings (Su et al., 2021) instead of the learned positional embeddings used in GPT models (Radford et al., 2018), based on our positive prior experiences using it in training LLMs. Rotary embeddings are a form of static relative positional embeddings. In brief, they twist the embedding space such that the attention of a token at position m to token at position n is linearly dependent on $m-n$. More formally, they modify the standard multiheaded attention equations from

$$\text{softmax}\left(\frac{1}{\sqrt{d}}\sum_{n,m}\mathbf{x}_m^T\mathbf{W}_q^T\mathbf{W}_k\mathbf{x}_n\right),$$

where $\mathbf{x}_m$, $\mathbf{x}_n$ are (batched) embeddings of tokens at position m and n respectively and $\mathbf{W}_q^T$, $\mathbf{W}_k$ are the query and key weights respectively to

$$\text{softmax}\left(\frac{1}{\sqrt{d}}\sum_{n,m}\mathbf{x}_m^T\mathbf{W}_q^T R^d_{\Theta,(n-m)}\mathbf{W}_k\mathbf{x}_n\right),$$

where $R^d_{\Theta,x}$ is a $d\times d$ block diagonal matrix with the block of index i being a 2D rotation by $x\theta_i$ for hyperparameters $\Theta=\{\theta_i=10000^{-2i/d}\mid i\in\{0,1,2,\ldots,(d-1)/2\}\}$.

While Su et al. (2021) apply rotary embeddings to every embedding vector, we follow Wang and Komatsuzaki (2021) and instead apply it only to the first 25% of embedding vector dimensions. Our initial experiments indicate that this strikes the best balance of performance and computational efficiency.[3]

2.1.2 Parallel Attention + FF Layers

We compute the Attention and Feed-Forward (FF) layers in parallel[4] and sum the results, rather than running them in series. This is primarily for efficiency purposes, as each residual addition with op-sharding requires one all-reduce in the forward pass and one in the backwards pass (Shoeybi et al., 2020). By computing the Attention and FFs in parallel, the results can be reduced locally before performing a single all-reduce. In Mesh Transformer JAX (Wang, 2021), this led to a 15% throughput increase, while having comparable loss curves with running them in series during early training.

Due to an oversight in our code, we unintentionally apply two independent Layer Norms instead of using a tied layer norm the way Wang and Komatsuzaki (2021) does. Instead of computing

$$x+\text{Attn}(\text{LN}_1(x))+\text{FF}(\text{LN}_1(x))$$

as intended, our codebase unties the layer norms:

$$x+\text{Attn}(\text{LN}_1(x))+\text{FF}(\text{LN}_2(x)).$$

Unfortunately, this was only noticed after we were much too far into training to restart. Subsequent

[2]The sole difference is due to an oversight discussed in Section 2.1.2

[3]See the Weights & Biases reports here and here for further details.

[4]See GitHub for implementation details.

experiments at small scales indicated that the untied layer norm makes no difference in performance, but we nevertheless wish to highlight this in the interest of transparency.

2.1.3 Initialization

For the Feed-Forward output layers before the residuals, we used the initialization scheme introduced in Wang (2021), $\frac{2}{L\sqrt{d}}$. This prevents activations from growing with increasing depth and width, with the factor of 2 compensating for the fact that the parallel and feed-forward layers are organized in parallel. For all other layers, we use the *small init* scheme from Nguyen and Salazar (2019), $\sqrt{\frac{2}{d+4d}}$

2.1.4 All Dense Layers

While GPT-3 uses alternating dense and sparse layers using the technique introduced in Child et al. (2019), we instead opt to exclusively use dense layers to reduce implementation complexity.

2.2 Software Libraries

Our model is trained using a codebase that builds on Megatron (Shoeybi et al., 2020) and DeepSpeed (Rasley et al., 2020) to facilitate efficient and straightforward training of large language models with tens of billions of parameters. We use the official PyTorch v1.10.0 release binary package compiled with CUDA 11.1. This package is bundled with NCCL 2.10.3 for distributed communications.

2.3 Hardware

We trained GPT-NeoX-20B on twelve Supermicro AS-4124GO-NART servers, each with eight NVIDIA A100-SXM4-40GB GPUs and configured with two AMD EPYC 7532 CPUs. All GPUs can directly access the InfiniBand switched fabric through one of four ConnectX-6 HCAs for GPUDirect RDMA. Two NVIDIA MQM8700-HS2R switches—connected by 16 links—compose the spine of this InfiniBand network, with one link per node CPU socket connected to each switch. Figure 7 shows a simplified overview of a node as configured for training.

3 Training

Due to the intractability of performing a hyperparameter sweep for a 20 billion parameter model, we opted to use the values from Brown et al. (2020) to guide our choice of hyperparameters. As Brown et al. (2020) did not train a model at our exact scale, we interpolate between the learning rates of their 13B and 175B models to arrive at a learning rate of 0.97E−5. Based on the results of smaller scale experiments, we select a weight decay of 0.01. To achieve a higher training throughput, we opt to use the same batch size as OpenAI's 175B model–approximately 3.15M tokens, or 1538 contexts of 2048 tokens each, and train for a total of 150,000 steps, decaying the learning rate with a cosine schedule to 10% of its original value at the end of training.

We use the AdamW (Loshchilov and Hutter, 2019) optimizer, with beta values of 0.9 and 0.95 respectively, and an epsilon of 1.0E−8. We extend AdamW with the *ZeRO* optimizer (Rajbhandari et al., 2020) to reduce memory consumption by distributing optimizer states across ranks. Since the weights and optimizer states of a model at this scale do not fit on a single GPU, we use the tensor parallelism scheme introduced in Shoeybi et al. (2020) in combination with pipeline parallelism (Harlap et al., 2018) to distribute the model across GPUs. To train GPT-NeoX-20B, we found that the most efficient way to distribute the model given our hardware setup was to set a tensor parallel size of 2, and a pipeline parallel size of 4. This allows for the most communication intensive processes, tensor and pipeline parallelism, to occur within a node, and data parallel communication to occur across node boundaries. In this fashion, we were able to achieve and maintain an efficiency of 117 teraFLOPS per GPU.

3.1 Training Data

GPT-NeoX-20B was trained on the Pile (Gao et al., 2020), a massive curated dataset designed specifically for training large language models. It consists of data from 22 data sources, coarsely broken down into 5 categories:

- **Academic Writing**: Pubmed Abstracts and PubMed Central, arXiv, FreeLaw,[5] USPTO Backgrounds,[6] PhilPapers,[7] NIH Exporter[8]
- **Web-scrapes and Internet Resources**: CommonCrawl, OpenWebText2, StackExchange,[9] Wikipedia (English)

[5]`https://www.courtlistener.com/`
[6]`https://bulkdata.uspto.gov/`
[7]`https://philpapers.org/`
[8]`https://exporter.nih.gov/`
[9]`https://archive.org/details/stackexchange`

- **Prose**: BookCorpus2, Bibliotik, Project Gutenberg (PG-19; Rae et al., 2019)

- **Dialogue**: Youtube subtitles, Ubuntu IRC,[10] OpenSubtitles (Lison and Tiedemann, 2016), Hacker News,[11] EuroParl (Koehn, 2005)

- **Miscellaneous**: GitHub, the DeepMind Mathematics dataset (Saxton et al., 2019), Enron Emails (Klimt and Yang, 2004)

In aggregate, the Pile consists of over 825GiB of raw text data. The diverse data sources reflects our desire for a general-purpose language model. Certain components are up-sampled to obtain a more balanced data distribution. In contrast, GPT-3's training data consists of web-scrapes, books datasets, and Wikipedia. When comparing results in this work to GPT-3, the training data is almost certainly the biggest known unknown factor. Full details of the Pile can be found in the technical report (Gao et al., 2020) and the associated datasheet (Biderman et al., 2022).

It is particularly notable that the Pile contains a scrape of StackExchange preprocessed into a Q/A form. There is a significant and growing body of work on the influence of the syntactic structure of finetuning data on downstream performance (Zhong et al., 2021; Tan et al., 2021; Sanh et al., 2021; Wei et al., 2021). While so far there has been no systematic work that focuses on *prompted pretraining*, recent work (Biderman and Raff, 2022) observed that the formulation of the StackExchange component of the Pile appears to heavily influences code generation.

3.2 Tokenization

For GPT-NeoX-20B, we use a BPE-based tokenizer similar to that used in GPT-2, with the same total vocabulary size of 50257, with three major changes to the tokenizer. First, we train a new BPE tokenizer based on the Pile, taking advantage of its diverse text sources to construct a more general-purpose tokenizer. Second, in contrast to the GPT-2 tokenizer which treats tokenization at the start of a string as a non-space-delimited token, the GPT-NeoX-20B tokenizer applies consistent space delimitation regardless. This resolves an inconsistency regarding the presence of prefix spaces to a tokenization input.[12]. An example can be seen in Figure 1. Third, our tokenizer contains tokens for repeated space tokens (all positive integer amounts of repeated spaces up to and including 24). This allows the GPT-NeoX-20B tokenizer to tokenize text with large amounts of whitespace using fewer tokens; for instance, program source code or arXiv LaTeX source files. See Appendix F for an analysis of the tokenizer.

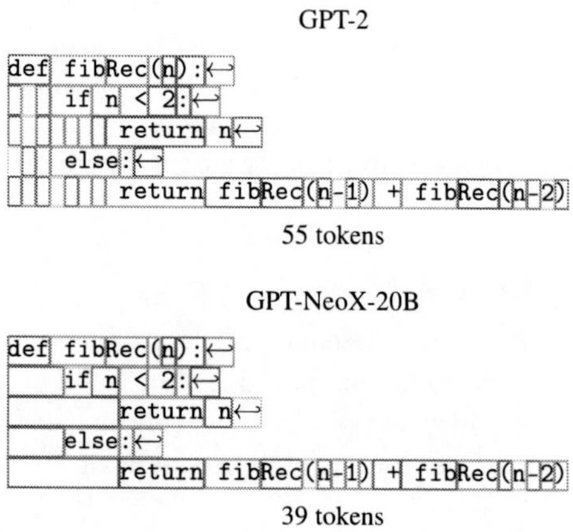

Figure 1: GPT-2 tokenization vs. GPT-NeoX-20B tokenization. GPT-NeoX-20B tokenization handles whitespace better, which is particularly useful for text such as source code. For more examples, see Appendix G.

3.3 Data Duplication

In the past two years, the standard practice when training autoregressive language models has become to train for only one epoch (Komatsuzaki, 2019; Kaplan et al., 2020; Henighan et al., 2020). Recent research has claimed to see significant benefits from going even further and deduplicating training data (Lee et al., 2021; Kandpal et al., 2022; Roberts et al., 2022). In particular, every publicly known larger language model other than GPT-3 (Brown et al., 2020) and Jurassic-1[13] either uses some form of deduplication (Rae et al., 2022; Askell et al., 2021; Zeng et al., 2021; Sun et al., 2021; Smith et al., 2022; Hoffmann et al., 2022; Chowdhery et al., 2022) or does not discuss the training data in sufficient detail to determine what was done (Kim et al., 2021).

When the Pile was originally made, the only language model larger than GPT-NeoX-20B that

[10]https://irclogs.ubuntu.com/

[11]https://news.ycombinator.com/

[12]https://discuss.huggingface.co/t/bpe-tokenizers-and-spaces-before-words/475/2

[13]In private communication, the authors confirmed that Jurassic-1 was trained on the Pile (Gao et al., 2020).

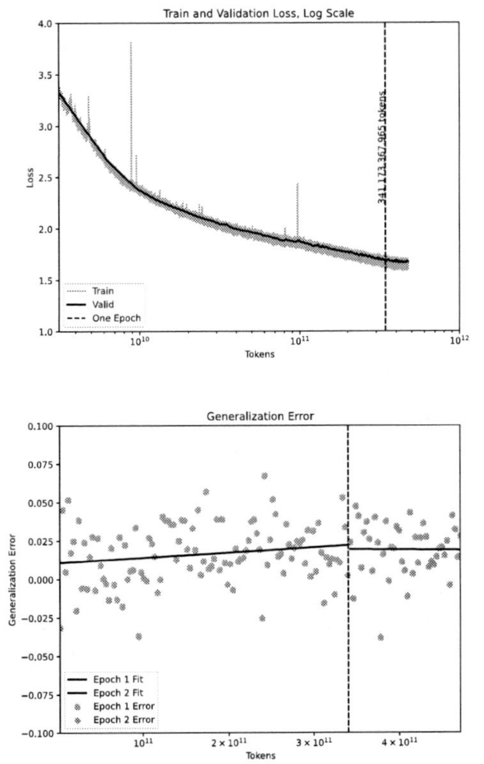

Figure 2: Training and validation loss for GPT-NeoX-20B. As the validation loss continued to fall into the beginning of the second epoch, we decided to let it train further.

existed was GPT-3, which upsampled high quality subsets of its training data. The Pile followed suit, and due to a combination of a lack of resources for large scale ablations and a lack of noticeable impact at smaller scales, we opt to use the Pile as-is. As shown in fig. 2, even at the 20B parameter scale we see no drop in test validation loss after crossing the 1 epoch boundary.

Unfortunately, none of the papers that have claimed to see an improvement from deduplication have released trained models that demonstrate this, making replication and confirmation of their results difficult. Lee et al. (2021) releases the deduplication code that they used, which we intend to use to explore this question in more detail in the future.

It is important to note that even if there is not an improvement in loss or on task evaluations there are nevertheless compelling reasons to deduplicate training data for any model put into production. In particular, systematic analysis has shown significant benefits in terms of reducing the leakage of training data (Lee et al., 2021; Zhang et al., 2021; Carlini et al., 2022; Kandpal et al., 2022).

4 Performance Evaluations

To evaluate our model we use the EleutherAI Language Model Evaluation Harness (Gao et al., 2021b), an open source codebase for language model evaluation that supports a number of model APIs. As our goal is to make a powerful model publicly accessible, we compare with English language models with at least 10B parameter that are publicly accessible. We compare with the GPT-3 models on the OpenAI API(Brown et al., 2020), the open source FairSeq dense models (Artetxe et al., 2021), and GPT-J-6B (Wang and Komatsuzaki, 2021). We do not compare against T5 (Raffel et al., 2020) or its derivatives as our evaluation methodology assumes that the models are autoregressive. While there is a Megatron 11B checkpoint that has been publicly released, the released code is non-functional and we have not been able to get the model to work. We do not compare against any mixture-of-experts models as no public MoE model achieves performance comparable to a 10B parameter dense model.

While it is common to display "scaling laws" curves of best fit, we opt to not do so as the small number of OpenAI API models give DaVinci an outsized influence on the slope of the curve. In many of the examples we study, including DaVinci in the scaling laws calculation moves the line of best fit so far as to entirely change the conclusions. Instead, we connect the points with lines directly. We categorize both GPT-J-6B and GPT-NeoX-20B under the umbrella of GPT-NeoX models, as both models are trained with the same architecture (except for the negligible differences described in Section 2.1.2) and were trained on the same dataset. However, we connect them using a dashed line to reflect the fact that these two models are not the same model trained at two different scales the way the FairSeq and OpenAI models are, having been trained using different codebases, different tokenizers, and for different numbers of tokens.

Where we were able to obtain the relevant information, we report two baselines: human-level performance and random performance. All plots contain error bars representing two standard errors, indicating the 95% confidence interval around each point. For some plots, the standard error is so small that the interval is not visible.

4.1 Tasks Evaluated

We evaluate our model on a diverse collection of standard language model evaluation datasets that we divide into three main categories: natural language tasks, Advanced Knowledge-Based Tasks, and Mathematical Tasks. Due to space constraints a representative subset of the results are shown here, with the rest in Appendix E.

Natural Language Tasks We evaluate our model on a diverse collection of standard language model evaluation datasets: ANLI (Nie et al., 2020), ARC (Clark et al., 2018), HeadQA (English) (Vilares and Gómez-Rodríguez, 2019), HellaSwag (Zellers et al., 2019), LAMBDADA (Paperno et al., 2016), LogiQA (Liu et al., 2020), OpenBookQA (Mihaylov et al., 2018), PiQA (Bisk et al., 2020), PROST (Aroca-Ouellette et al., 2021), QA4MRE (Peñas et al., 2013) (2013), SciQ (Welbl et al., 2017), TriviaQA (Joshi et al., 2017), Winogrande (Sakaguchi et al., 2021), and the SuperGlue version of the Winograd Schemas Challenge (WSC) (Wang et al., 2019).

Mathematical Tasks The solving of mathematical problem solving is an area that has had a long history of study in AI research, despite the fact that large language models tend to perform quite poorly on both arithmetic tasks and mathematical problems phrased in natural language. We evaluate on the MATH test dataset (Hendrycks et al., 2021b) as well as on the numerical arithmetic problems introduced by Brown et al. (2020). Note that the MATH test dataset is an evaluation metric that is generally finetuned on, but due to computational limitations we only evaluate models zero- and five-shot here.

Advanced Knowledge-Based Tasks We are also interested in the ability of our models to answer factual questions that (for humans) require advanced knowledge. To do this, we use a dataset of multiple choice questions in a variety of diverse domains developed by Hendrycks et al. (2021a). Following common practice on this dataset, we focus on results aggregated by subject area: Humanities, Social Sciences, STEM, and Miscellaneous as presented in Figure 6. We report five-shot performance to be comparable to previous work.

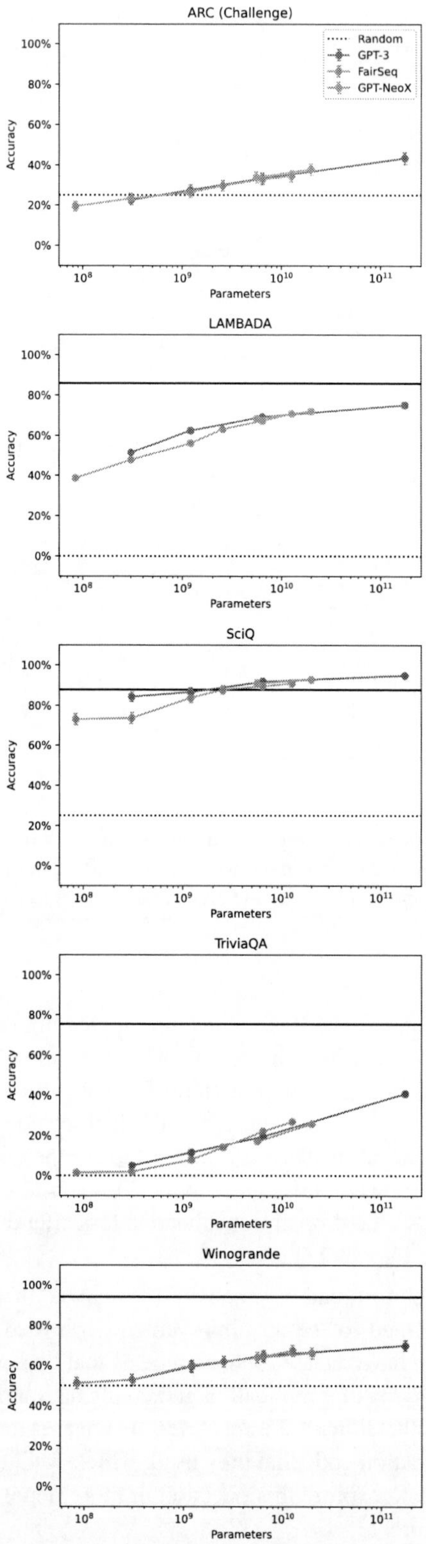

Figure 3: Zero-shot performance of GPT-NeoX-20B compared to GPT-J-6B and FairSeq and OpenAI models on a variety of language modeling benchmarks.

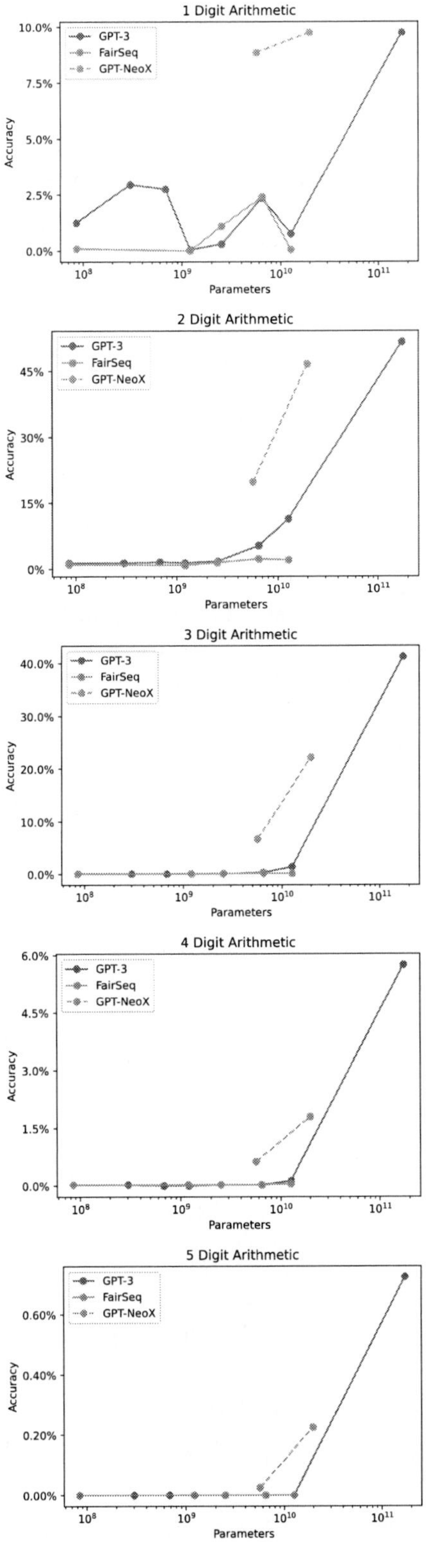

Figure 4: Zero-shot performance of GPT-NeoX-20B compared to and FairSeq and OpenAI models on arithmetic tasks. Random performance on these tasks is 0%, and we were unable to find information on median human performance.

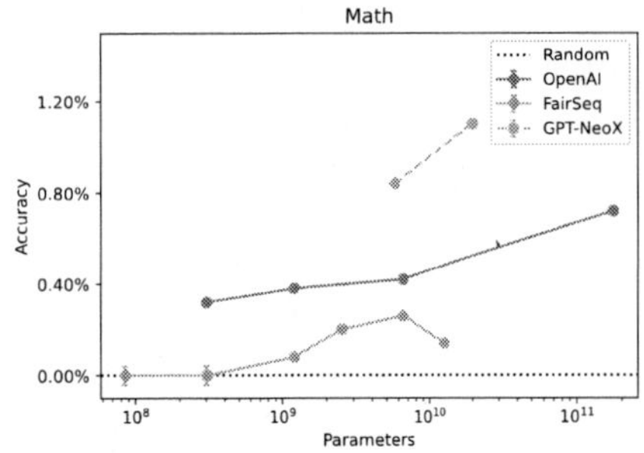

Figure 5: Zero-shot performance of GPT-NeoX-20B compared to and FairSeq and OpenAI models on arithmetic tasks. Random performance on these tasks is 0%, and we were unable to find information on median human performance.

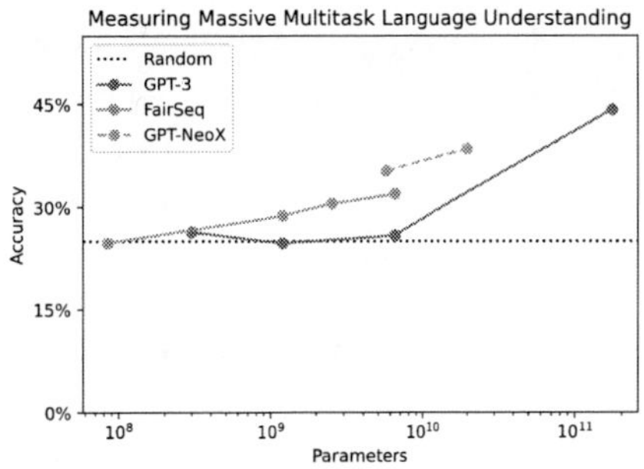

Figure 6: Five-shot performance of GPT-NeoX-20B compared to GPT-J-6B and FairSeq and OpenAI models on Hendrycks et al. (2021a).

5 Discussion

5.1 Performance Results

Natural Language Tasks While GPT-NeoX-20B outperforms FairSeq 13B on some tasks (e.g. ARC, LAMBADA, PIQA, PROST), it underperforms on others (e.g. HellaSwag, LogiQA zero-shot). In total, across the 32 evaluations we did we outpreform on 22 tasks, underpreform on four tasks, and fall within the margin of error on six tasks. By far our weakest performance is on HellaSwag, where we score four standard deviations below FairSeq 13B in both zero- and five-shot evaluations. Similarly, GPT-J underperforms FairSeq 6.7B by three standard deviations zero-shot and six standard deviations five-shot on HellaSwag. We find this massive performance loss largely inexplicable; while we originally assumed that the substantial non-prose components of the Pile were to blame, we note that GPT-J and GPT-NeoX *overpreform* FairSeq models on the very similar Lambada task by roughly the same amount.

Mathematics While GPT-3 and FairSeq models are generally quite close on arithmetic tasks, they are consistently out-preformed by GPT-J and GPT-NeoX. We conjecture that this is traceable to the prevalence of mathematics equations in the training data, but warn that people should not assume that this means that training on the Pile produces better *out-of-distribution* arithmetic reasoning. Razeghi et al. (2022) show that there is a strong correlation between the frequency of a numerical equation in the Pile and GPT-J's performance on that equation, and we see no reason this would not hold in GPT-NeoX 20B, FairSeq, and GPT-3. We are unfortunately unable to investigate this effect in FairSeq and GPT-3 models because the authors do not release their training data.

Advanced Knowledge-Based Tasks While GPT-NeoX and FairSeq both exhibit dominant performance on MMMLU compared to GPT-3 in the five-shot setting (Figures 6 and 11), their performance is much closer in the zero-shot setting (Figure 10). Hendrycks et al. (2021b) find that few-shot evaluation does not improve performance, but that appears to be only the case for GPT-3. We view this as a warning against drawing strong conclusions about evaluation metrics based only on one model, and encourage researchers developing new evaluation benchmarks to leverage multiple different classes of models to avoid overfitting their conclusions to a specific model.

5.2 Powerful Few-Shot Learning

Our experiments indicate that GPT-J-6B and GPT-NeoX-20B benefit substantially more from few-shot evaluations than the FairSeq models do. When going from 0-shot to 5-shot evaluations, GPT-J-6B improves by 0.0526 and GPT-NeoX-20B improves by 0.0598 while the FairSeq 6.7B and 13B models improve by 0.0051 and 0.0183 respectively. This result is statistically significant and robust to perturbations of prompting. While we do not have a particular explanation for this currently, we view this as a strong recommendation for our models.

5.3 Limitations

Optimal Training Hyperparameter tuning is an expensive process, and is often infeasible to do at full scale for multi-billion parameter models. Due to the aforementioned limitations, we opted to choose hyperparameters based on a mixture of experiments at smaller scales and by interpolating parameters appropriate for our model size based on previously published work (Brown et al., 2020). However, several aspects of both our model architecture [Section 2.1] and training setup, including the data [Section 3.1] and the tokenizer [Section 3.2], diverge significantly from Brown et al. (2020). As such, it is almost certainly the case that the hyperparameters used for our model are no longer optimal, and potentially never were.

Lack of Coding Evaluations Many of the design choices we made during the development of this model were oriented towards improving performance on coding tasks. However, we underestimated the difficulty and cost of existing coding benchmarks (Chen et al., 2021), and so were unable to evaluate out model in that domain. We hope to do so in the future.

Data Duplication Finally, the lack of dataset deduplication could also have had an impact on downstream performance. Recent work has shown that deduplicating training data can have a large effect on perplexity (Lee et al., 2021). While our experiments show no sign of this, it is hard to dismiss it due to the number of researchers who have found the opposite result.

5.4 Releasing a 20B Parameter LLM

The current status quo in research is that large language models are things people train and publish about, but do not actually release. To the best of our knowledge, GPT-NeoX-20B is the largest and most performant dense language model to ever be publicly released. A variety of reasons for the non-release of large language models are given by various groups, but the primary one is the harms that public access to LLMs would purportedly cause.

We take these concerns quite seriously. However, having taken them quite seriously, we feel that they are flawed in several respects. While a thorough analysis of these issues is beyond the scope of this paper, the public release of our model is the most important contribution of this paper and so an explanation of why we disagree with the prevailing wisdom is important.

Providing access to ethics and alignment researchers will prevent harm. The open-source release of this model is motivated by the hope that it will allow researchers who would not otherwise have access to LLMs to use them. While there are negative risks due to the potential acceleration of capabilities research, we believe the benefits of this release outweigh the risks. We also note that these benefits are not hypothetical, as a number of papers about the limits and ethics of LLMs has been explicitly enabled by the public release of previous models (Zhang et al., 2021; Kandpal et al., 2022; Carlini et al., 2022; Birhane et al., 2021; nostalgebraist, 2020; Meng et al., 2022; Lin et al., 2021).

Limiting access to governments and corporations will not prevent harm. Perhaps the most curious aspect of the argument that LLMs should not be released is that the people making such arguments are not arguing they *they* should not use LLMs. Rather, they are claiming that *other people* should not use them. We do not believe that this is a position that should be taken seriously. The companies and governments that have the financial resources to train LLMs are overwhelmingly more likely to do large scale harm using a LLM than a random individual.

Releasing this model is the beginning, not the end, of our work to make GPT-NeoX-20B widely accessible to researchers. Due to the size of the model, inference is most economical on a pair of RTX 3090 Tis or a single A6000 GPU and finetuning requires significantly more compute. Truly promoting widespread access to LLMs means promoting widespread access to *computing infrastructure* in addition to the models themselves. We plan to make progress on this issue going forward by continuing to work on reducing the inference costs of our model, and by working with researchers to provide access to the computing infrastructure they need to carry out experiments on our models. We strongly encourage researchers who are interested in studying GPT-NeoX-20B but lack the necessary infrastructure to reach out to discuss how we can help empower you.

6 Summary

We introduce GPT-NeoX-20B, a 20 billion parameter autoregressive Transformer language model trained on the Pile (Gao et al., 2020) dataset, and detail the main architectural differences between GPT-NeoX-20B and GPT-3—most notably the change in tokenizer, the addition of Rotary embeddings, the parallel computation of attention and feed-forward layers, and a different initialization scheme and hyperparameters. We run extensive evaluations of GPT-NeoX-20B on natural language and factual knowledge tasks, and compare it with other publicly available models, finding it performed particularly well on knowledge-based and mathematical tasks. Finally, we are open sourcing the training and evaluation code at `https://github.com/EleutherAI/gpt-neox`, where readers can find a link to download the model weights across the whole training run.

Acknowledgments

We thank staff at CoreWeave—in particular Max Hjelm, Brannin McBee, Peter Salanki, and Brian Venturo—for providing the GPUs and computing infrastructure that made this project possible. We would also like to acknowledge Eren Doğan and Wesley Brown for feedback and technical support throughout the project, and John Schulman, Evan Hubinger, Victor Sanh, Jacob Hilton, and Siddharth Karamcheti for providing feedback on drafts of the paper.

Finally, we thank Anthony DiPofi, Charles Foster, Jeffrey Hsu, Eric Tang, Anish Thite, Kevin Wang, and Andy Zou for their contributions to the EleutherAI Language Modeling Evaluation Harness we used to evaluate GPT-NeoX-20B.

References

Stuart Armstrong and Sören Mindermann. 2018. Occam's razor is insufficient to infer the preferences of irrational agents. In *Advances in Neural Information Processing Systems*, volume 31, pages 5598–5609. Curran Associates, Inc.

Stuart Armstrong, Anders Sandberg, and Nick Bostrom. 2012. Thinking inside the box: Controlling and using an oracle AI. *Minds and Machines*, 22(4):299–324.

Stéphane Aroca-Ouellette, Cory Paik, Alessandro Roncone, and Katharina Kann. 2021. PROST: Physical reasoning about objects through space and time. In *Findings of the Association for Computational Linguistics: ACL-IJCNLP 2021*, pages 4597–4608, Online. Association for Computational Linguistics.

Mikel Artetxe, Shruti Bhosale, Naman Goyal, Todor Mihaylov, Myle Ott, Sam Shleifer, Xi Victoria Lin, Jingfei Du, Srinivasan Iyer, Ramakanth Pasunuru, Giri Anantharaman, Xian Li, Shuohui Chen, Halil Akin, Mandeep Baines, Louis Martin, Xing Zhou, Punit Singh Koura, Brian O'Horo, Jeff Wang, Luke Zettlemoyer, Mona Diab, Zornitsa Kozareva, and Ves Stoyanov. 2021. Efficient large scale language modeling with mixtures of experts. *Computing Research Repository*, arXiv:2112.10684. Version 1.

Amanda Askell, Yuntao Bai, Anna Chen, Dawn Drain, Deep Ganguli, Tom Henighan, Andy Jones, Nicholas

Joseph, Ben Mann, Nova DasSarma, Nelson Elhage, Zac Hatfield-Dodds, Danny Hernandez, Jackson Kernion, Kamal Ndousse, Catherine Olsson, Dario Amodei, Tom Brown, Jack Clark, Sam McCandlish, Chris Olah, and Jared Kaplan. 2021. A general language assistant as a laboratory for alignment. *Computing Research Repository*, arXiv:2112.00861. Version 3.

Emily M. Bender, Timnit Gebru, Angelina McMillan-Major, and Shmargaret Shmitchell. 2021. On the dangers of stochastic parrots: Can language models be too big? In *Proceedings of the 2021 ACM Conference on Fairness, Accountability, and Transparency*, FAccT '21, pages 610–623, New York, NY, USA. Association for Computing Machinery.

Stella Biderman, Kieran Bicheno, and Leo Gao. 2022. Datasheet for the Pile. *Computing Research Repository*, arXiv:2201.07311. Version 1.

Stella Biderman and Edward Raff. 2022. Neural language models are effective plagiarists. *Computing Research Repository*, arXiv:2201.07406. Version 1.

Stella Biderman and Walter J Scheirer. 2020. Pitfalls in machine learning research: Reexamining the development cycle. In *"I Can't Believe It's Not Better!" NeurIPS 2020 workshop*. PMLR.

Abeba Birhane, Vinay Uday Prabhu, and Emmanuel Kahembwe. 2021. Multimodal datasets: misogyny, pornography, and malignant stereotypes. *Computing Research Repository*, arXiv:2110.01963. Version 1.

Yonatan Bisk, Rowan Zellers, Ronan Le bras, Jianfeng Gao, and Yejin Choi. 2020. PIQA: Reasoning about physical commonsense in natural language. In *Proceedings of the AAAI Conference on Artificial Intelligence*, volume 34, pages 7432–7439.

Sid Black, Leo Gao, Phil Wang, Connor Leahy, and Stella Biderman. 2021. GPT-Neo: Large scale autoregressive language modeling with Mesh-Tensorflow.

Tom Brown, Benjamin Mann, Nick Ryder, Melanie Subbiah, Jared D Kaplan, Prafulla Dhariwal, Arvind Neelakantan, Pranav Shyam, Girish Sastry, Amanda Askell, Sandhini Agarwal, Ariel Herbert-Voss, Gretchen Krueger, Tom Henighan, Rewon Child, Aditya Ramesh, Daniel Ziegler, Jeffrey Wu, Clemens Winter, Chris Hesse, Mark Chen, Eric Sigler, Mateusz Litwin, Scott Gray, Benjamin Chess, Jack Clark, Christopher Berner, Sam McCandlish, Alec Radford, Ilya Sutskever, and Dario Amodei. 2020. Language models are few-shot learners. In *Advances in Neural Information Processing Systems*, volume 33, pages 1877–1901. Curran Associates, Inc.

Nick Cammarata, Shan Carter, Gabriel Goh, Chris Olah, Michael Petrov, Ludwig Schubert, Chelsea Voss, Ben Egan, and Swee Kiat Lim. 2020. Thread: Circuits. *Distill*.

Nicholas Carlini, Daphne Ippolito, Matthew Jagielski, Katherine Lee, Florian Tramer, and Chiyuan Zhang. 2022. Quantifying memorization across neural language models. *Computing Research Repository*, arXiv:2202.07646. Version 2.

Mark Chen, Jerry Tworek, Heewoo Jun, Qiming Yuan, Henrique Ponde de Oliveira Pinto, Jared Kaplan, Harri Edwards, Yuri Burda, Nicholas Joseph, Greg Brockman, Alex Ray, Raul Puri, Gretchen Krueger, Michael Petrov, Heidy Khlaaf, Girish Sastry, Pamela Mishkin, Brooke Chan, Scott Gray, Nick Ryder, Mikhail Pavlov, Alethea Power, Lukasz Kaiser, Mohammad Bavarian, Clemens Winter, Philippe Tillet, Felipe Petroski Such, Dave Cummings, Matthias Plappert, Fotios Chantzis, Elizabeth Barnes, Ariel Herbert-Voss, William Hebgen Guss, Alex Nichol, Alex Paino, Nikolas Tezak, Jie Tang, Igor Babuschkin, Suchir Balaji, Shantanu Jain, William Saunders, Christopher Hesse, Andrew N. Carr, Jan Leike, Josh Achiam, Vedant Misra, Evan Morikawa, Alec Radford, Matthew Knight, Miles Brundage, Mira Murati, Katie Mayer, Peter Welinder, Bob McGrew, Dario Amodei, Sam McCandlish, Ilya Sutskever, and Wojciech Zaremba. 2021. Evaluating large language models trained on code. *Computing Research Repository*, arXiv:2107.03374. Version 2.

Rewon Child, Scott Gray, Alec Radford, and Ilya Sutskever. 2019. Generating long sequences with sparse transformers. *Computing Research Repository*, arXiv:1904.10509. Version 1.

Aakanksha Chowdhery, Sharan Narang, Jacob Devlin, Maarten Bosma, Gaurav Mishra, Adam Roberts, Paul Barham, Hyung Won Chung, Charles Sutton, Sebastian Gehrmann, Parker Schuh, Kensen Shi, Sasha Tsvyashchenko, Joshua Maynez, Abhishek Rao, Parker Barnes, Yi Tay, Noam Shazeer, Vinodkumar Prabhakaran, Emily Reif, Nan Du, Ben Hutchinson, Reiner Pope, James Bradbury, Jacob Austin, Michael Isard, Guy Gur-Ari, Pengcheng Yin, Toju Duke, Anselm Levskaya, Sanjay Ghemawat, Sunipa Dev, Henryk Michalewski, Xavier Garcia, Vedant Misra, Kevin Robinson, Liam Fedus, Denny Zhou, Daphne Ippolito, David Luan, Hyeontaek Lim, Barret Zoph, Alexander Spiridonov, Ryan Sepassi, David Dohan, Shivani Agrawal, Mark Omernick, Andrew M. Dai, Thanumalayan Sankaranarayana Pillai, Marie Pellat, Aitor Lewkowycz, Erica Moreira, Rewon Child, Oleksandr Polozov, Katherine Lee, Zongwei Zhou, Xuezhi Wang, Brennan Saeta, Mark Diaz, Orhan Firat, Michele Catasta, Jason Wei, Kathy Meier-Hellstern, Douglas Eck, Jeff Dean, Slav Petrov, and Noah Fiedel. 2022. PaLM: Scaling language modeling with pathways. *Computing Research Repository*, arXiv:2204.02311v2.

Paul Christiano, Ajeya Cotra, and Mark Xu. 2021. Eliciting latent knowledge: How to tell if your eyes deceive you.

Peter Clark, Isaac Cowhey, Oren Etzioni, Tushar Khot, Ashish Sabharwal, Carissa Schoenick, and Oyvind

Tafjord. 2018. Think you have solved question answering? try arc, the ai2 reasoning challenge. *Computing Research Repository*, arXiv:1803.05457. Version 1.

Damai Dai, Li Dong, Yaru Hao, Zhifang Sui, and Furu Wei. 2021. Knowledge neurons in pretrained transformers. *Computing Research Repository*, arXiv:2104.08696. Version 1.

Abram Demski. 2019. The parable of Predict-O-Matic. AI Alignment Forum.

Jacob Devlin, Ming-Wei Chang, Kenton Lee, and Kristina Toutanova. 2019. BERT: Pre-training of deep bidirectional transformers for language understanding. *Computing Research Repository*, arXiv:1810.04805. Version 2.

Jesse Dodge, Maarten Sap, Ana Marasović, William Agnew, Gabriel Ilharco, Dirk Groeneveld, Margaret Mitchell, and Matt Gardner. 2021. Documenting large webtext corpora: A case study on the Colossal Clean Crawled Corpus. In *Proceedings of the 2021 Conference on Empirical Methods in Natural Language Processing*, pages 1286–1305, Online and Punta Cana, Dominican Republic. Association for Computational Linguistics.

Nelson Elhage, Neel Nanda, Catherine Olsson, Tom Henighan, Nicholas Joseph, Ben Mann, Amanda Askell, Yuntao Bai, Anna Chen, Tom Conerly, Nova DasSarma, Dawn Drain, Deep Ganguli, Zac Hatfield-Dodds, Danny Hernandez, Andy Jones, Jackson Kernion, Liane Lovitt, Kamal Ndousse, Dario Amodei, Tom Brown, Jack Clark, Jared Kaplan, Sam McCandlish, and Chris Olah. 2021. A Mathematical Framework for Transformer Circuits. *transformer-circuits.pub*.

William Fedus, Barret Zoph, and Noam Shazeer. 2021. Switch transformers: Scaling to trillion parameter models with simple and efficient sparsity. *Computing Research Repository*, arXiv:2101.03961. Version 1.

Leo Gao. 2021. Behavior cloning is miscalibrated. AI Alignment Forum.

Leo Gao, Stella Biderman, Sid Black, Laurence Golding, Travis Hoppe, Charles Foster, Jason Phang, Horace He, Anish Thite, Noa Nabeshima, Shawn Presser, and Connor Leahy. 2020. The Pile: An 800GB dataset of diverse text for language modeling. *Computing Research Repository*, arXiv:2101.00027. Version 1.

Leo Gao, Kyle McDonell, Laria Reynolds, and Stella Biderman. 2021a. A preliminary exploration into factored cognition with language models. EleutherAI Blog.

Leo Gao, Jonathan Tow, Stella Biderman, Sid Black, Anthony DiPofi, Charles Foster, Laurence Golding, Jeffrey Hsu, Kyle McDonell, Niklas Muennighoff, Jason Phang, Laria Reynolds, Eric Tang, Anish Thite, Ben Wang, Kevin Wang, and Andy Zou. 2021b. A framework for few-shot language model evaluation.

Aaron Harlap, Deepak Narayanan, Amar Phanishayee, Vivek Seshadri, Nikhil Devanur, Greg Ganger, and Phil Gibbons. 2018. PipeDream: Fast and efficient pipeline parallel DNN training. *Computing Research Repository*, arXiv:1806.03377. Version 1.

Dan Hendrycks, Collin Burns, Steven Basart, Andy Zou, Mantas Mazeika, Dawn Song, and Jacob Steinhardt. 2021a. Measuring massive multitask language understanding. *Computing Research Repository*, arXiv:2009.03300. Version 3.

Dan Hendrycks, Collin Burns, Saurav Kadavath, Akul Arora, Steven Basart, Eric Tang, Dawn Song, and Jacob Steinhardt. 2021b. Measuring mathematical problem solving with the math dataset. *Computing Research Repository*, arXiv:2103.03874. Version 2.

Tom Henighan, Jared Kaplan, Mor Katz, Mark Chen, Christopher Hesse, Jacob Jackson, Heewoo Jun, Tom B. Brown, Prafulla Dhariwal, Scott Gray, Chris Hallacy, Benjamin Mann, Alec Radford, Aditya Ramesh, Nick Ryder, Daniel M. Ziegler, John Schulman, Dario Amodei, and Sam McCandlish. 2020. Scaling laws for autoregressive generative modeling. *Computing Research Repository*, arXiv:2010.14701. Version 2.

Jordan Hoffmann, Sebastian Borgeaud, Arthur Mensch, Elena Buchatskaya, Trevor Cai, Eliza Rutherford, Diego de Las Casas, Lisa Anne Hendricks, Johannes Welbl, Aidan Clark, et al. 2022. Training compute-optimal large language models. *Computing Research Repository*, arXiv:2203.15556. Version 1.

Wenlong Huang, Pieter Abbeel, Deepak Pathak, and Igor Mordatch. 2022. Language models as zero-shot planners: Extracting actionable knowledge for embodied agents. *Computing Research Repository*, arXiv:2201.07207. Version 1.

Evan Hubinger, Chris van Merwijk, Vladimir Mikulik, Joar Skalse, and Scott Garrabrant. 2021. Risks from learned optimization in advanced machine learning systems. *Computing Research Repository*, arXiv:1906.01820. Version 3.

Mandar Joshi, Eunsol Choi, Daniel Weld, and Luke Zettlemoyer. 2017. TriviaQA: A large scale distantly supervised challenge dataset for reading comprehension. In *Proceedings of the 55th Annual Meeting of the Association for Computational Linguistics (Volume 1: Long Papers)*, pages 1601–1611, Vancouver, Canada. Association for Computational Linguistics.

Nikhil Kandpal, Eric Wallace, and Colin Raffel. 2022. Deduplicating training data mitigates privacy risks in language models. *Computing Research Repository*, arXiv:2202.06539. Version 2.

Jared Kaplan, Sam McCandlish, Tom Henighan, Tom B Brown, Benjamin Chess, Rewon Child, Scott Gray, Alec Radford, Jeffrey Wu, and Dario Amodei. 2020. Scaling laws for neural language models. *Computing Research Repository*, arXiv:2001.08361. Version 1.

Boseop Kim, HyoungSeok Kim, Sang-Woo Lee, Gichang Lee, Donghyun Kwak, Jeon Dong Hyeon, Sunghyun Park, Sungju Kim, Seonhoon Kim, Dongpil Seo, Heungsub Lee, Minyoung Jeong, Sungjae Lee, Minsub Kim, Suk Hyun Ko, Seokhun Kim, Taeyong Park, Jinuk Kim, Soyoung Kang, Na-Hyeon Ryu, Kang Min Yoo, Minsuk Chang, Soobin Suh, Sookyo In, Jinseong Park, Kyungduk Kim, Hiun Kim, Jisu Jeong, Yong Goo Yeo, Donghoon Ham, Dongju Park, Min Young Lee, Jaewook Kang, Inho Kang, Jung-Woo Ha, Woomyoung Park, and Nako Sung. 2021. What changes can large-scale language models bring? intensive study on HyperCLOVA: Billions-scale Korean generative pretrained transformers. In *Proceedings of the 2021 Conference on Empirical Methods in Natural Language Processing*, pages 3405–3424, Online and Punta Cana, Dominican Republic. Association for Computational Linguistics.

Bryan Klimt and Yiming Yang. 2004. The Enron corpus: A new dataset for email classification research. In *Proceedings of the 15th European Conference on Machine Learning*, ECML'04, page 217–226, Berlin, Heidelberg. Springer-Verlag.

Jack Koch, Lauro Langosco, Jacob Pfau, James Le, and Lee Sharkey. 2021. Objective robustness in deep reinforcement learning. *Computing Research Repository*, arXiv:2105.14111. Version 2.

Philipp Koehn. 2005. Europarl: A parallel corpus for statistical machine translation. In *Proceedings of Machine Translation Summit X: Papers*, pages 79–86, Phuket, Thailand.

Aran Komatsuzaki. 2019. One epoch is all you need. *Computing Research Repository*, arXiv:1906.06669. Version 1.

Vanessa Kosoy. 2016. IRL is hard. AI Alignment Forum.

Julia Kreutzer, Isaac Caswell, Lisa Wang, Ahsan Wahab, Daan van Esch, Nasanbayar Ulzii-Orshikh, Allahsera Tapo, Nishant Subramani, Artem Sokolov, Claytone Sikasote, Monang Setyawan, Supheakmungkol Sarin, Sokhar Samb, Benoît Sagot, Clara Rivera, Annette Rios, Isabel Papadimitriou, Salomey Osei, Pedro Ortiz Suarez, Iroro Orife, Kelechi Ogueji, Andre Niyongabo Rubungo, Toan Q. Nguyen, Mathias Müller, André Müller, Shamsuddeen Hassan Muhammad, Nanda Muhammad, Ayanda Mnyakeni, Jamshidbek Mirzakhalov, Tapiwanashe Matangira, Colin Leong, Nze Lawson, Sneha Kudugunta, Yacine Jernite, Mathias Jenny, Orhan Firat, Bonaventure F. P. Dossou, Sakhile Dlamini, Nisansa de Silva, Sakine Çabuk Ballı, Stella Biderman, Alessia Battisti, Ahmed Baruwa, Ankur Bapna, Pallavi Baljekar, Israel Abebe Azime, Ayodele Awokoya, Duygu Ataman, Orevaoghene Ahia, Oghenefego Ahia, Sweta Agrawal, and Mofetoluwa Adeyemi. 2022. Quality at a Glance: An Audit of Web-Crawled Multilingual Datasets. *Transactions of the Association for Computational Linguistics*, 10:50–72.

Alexandre Lacoste, Alexandra Luccioni, Victor Schmidt, and Thomas Dandres. 2019. Quantifying the carbon emissions of machine learning. *Computing Research Repository*, arXiv:1910.09700. Version 2.

Connor Leahy. 2021. Why Release a Large Language Model? EleutherAI Blog.

Connor Leahy and Stella Biderman. 2021. The hard problem of aligning AI to human values. In *The State of AI Ethics Report*, volume 4, pages 180–183. The Montreal AI Ethics Institute.

Katherine Lee, Daphne Ippolito, Andrew Nystrom, Chiyuan Zhang, Douglas Eck, Chris Callison-Burch, and Nicholas Carlini. 2021. Deduplicating training data makes language models better. *Computing Research Repository*, arXiv:2107.06499. Version 1.

Opher Lieber, Or Sharir, Barak Lenz, and Yoav Shoham. 2021. Jurassic-1: Technical details and evaluation. Technical report, AI21 Labs.

Stephanie Lin, Jacob Hilton, and Owain Evans. 2021. TruthfulQA: Measuring how models mimic human falsehoods. *Computing Research Repository*, arXiv:2109.07958. Version 1.

Pierre Lison and Jörg Tiedemann. 2016. OpenSubtitles2016: Extracting large parallel corpora from movie and TV subtitles. In *Proceedings of the Tenth International Conference on Language Resources and Evaluation (LREC'16)*, pages 923–929, Portorož, Slovenia. European Language Resources Association (ELRA).

Jian Liu, Leyang Cui, Hanmeng Liu, Dandan Huang, Yile Wang, and Yue Zhang. 2020. LogiQA: A challenge dataset for machine reading comprehension with logical reasoning. In *Proceedings of the Twenty-Ninth International Joint Conference on Artificial Intelligence, IJCAI-20*, pages 3622–3628. International Joint Conferences on Artificial Intelligence Organization.

Ilya Loshchilov and Frank Hutter. 2019. Decoupled weight decay regularization. *Computing Research Repository*, arXiv:1711.05101. Version 3.

J. Nathan Matias. 2020. Why we need industry-independent research on tech & society. Citizens and Technology Lab.

Joshua Maynez, Shashi Narayan, Bernd Bohnet, and Ryan McDonald. 2020. On faithfulness and factuality in abstractive summarization. *Computing Research Repository*, arXiv:2005.00661. Version 1.

Kevin Meng, David Bau, Alex Andonian, and Yonatan Belinkov. 2022. Locating and editing factual knowledge in GPT. *Computing Research Repository*, arXiv:2202.05262v1. Version 1.

Todor Mihaylov, Peter Clark, Tushar Khot, and Ashish Sabharwal. 2018. Can a suit of armor conduct electricity? a new dataset for open book question answering. In *Proceedings of the 2018 Conference on Empirical Methods in Natural Language Processing*, pages 2381–2391, Brussels, Belgium. Association for Computational Linguistics.

Toan Q. Nguyen and Julian Salazar. 2019. Transformers without tears: Improving the normalization of self-attention. *Computing Research Repository*, arXiv:1910.05895. Version 2.

Yixin Nie, Adina Williams, Emily Dinan, Mohit Bansal, Jason Weston, and Douwe Kiela. 2020. Adversarial NLI: A new benchmark for natural language understanding. In *Proceedings of the 58th Annual Meeting of the Association for Computational Linguistics*, pages 4885–4901, Online. Association for Computational Linguistics.

nostalgebraist. 2020. interpreting GPT: the logit lens. LessWrong.

Maxwell Nye, Anders Johan Andreassen, Guy Gur-Ari, Henryk Michalewski, Jacob Austin, David Bieber, David Dohan, Aitor Lewkowycz, Maarten Bosma, David Luan, Charles Sutton, and Augustus Odena. 2021. Show your work: Scratchpads for intermediate computation with language models. *Computing Research Repository*, arXiv:2112.00114. Version 1.

Pedro A. Ortega, Markus Kunesch, Grégoire Delétang, Tim Genewein, Jordi Grau-Moya, Joel Veness, Jonas Buchli, Jonas Degrave, Bilal Piot, Julien Perolat, Tom Everitt, Corentin Tallec, Emilio Parisotto, Tom Erez, Yutian Chen, Scott Reed, Marcus Hutter, Nando de Freitas, and Shane Legg. 2021. Shaking the foundations: delusions in sequence models for interaction and control. *Computing Research Repository*, arXiv:2110.10819. Version 1.

Denis Paperno, Germán Kruszewski, Angeliki Lazaridou, Ngoc Quan Pham, Raffaella Bernardi, Sandro Pezzelle, Marco Baroni, Gemma Boleda, and Raquel Fernández. 2016. The LAMBADA dataset: Word prediction requiring a broad discourse context. In *Proceedings of the 54th Annual Meeting of the Association for Computational Linguistics (Volume 1: Long Papers)*, pages 1525–1534, Berlin, Germany. Association for Computational Linguistics.

Anselmo Peñas, Eduard Hovy, Pamela Forner, Álvaro Rodrigo, Richard Sutcliffe, and Roser Morante. 2013. QA4MRE 2011-2013: Overview of question answering for machine reading evaluation. In *Information Access Evaluation. Multilinguality, Multimodality, and Visualization*, pages 303–320, Berlin, Heidelberg. Springer Berlin Heidelberg.

Alec Radford, Karthik Narasimhan, Tim Salimans, and Ilya Sutskever. 2018. Improving language understanding by generative pre-training. Technical report, OpenAI.

Alec Radford, Jeff Wu, Rewon Child, David Luan, Dario Amodei, and Ilya Sutskever. 2019. Language models are unsupervised multitask learners. Technical report, OpenAI.

Jack W. Rae, Sebastian Borgeaud, Trevor Cai, Katie Millican, Jordan Hoffmann, H. Francis Song, John Aslanides, Sarah Henderson, Roman Ring, Susannah Young, Eliza Rutherford, Tom Hennigan, Jacob Menick, Albin Cassirer, Richard Powell, George van den Driessche, Lisa Anne Hendricks, Maribeth Rauh, Po-Sen Huang, Amelia Glaese, Johannes Welbl, Sumanth Dathathri, Saffron Huang, Jonathan Uesato, John Mellor, Irina Higgins, Antonia Creswell, Nat McAleese, Amy Wu, Erich Elsen, Siddhant M. Jayakumar, Elena Buchatskaya, David Budden, Esme Sutherland, Karen Simonyan, Michela Paganini, Laurent Sifre, Lena Martens, Xiang Lorraine Li, Adhiguna Kuncoro, Aida Nematzadeh, Elena Gribovskaya, Domenic Donato, Angeliki Lazaridou, Arthur Mensch, Jean-Baptiste Lespiau, Maria Tsimpoukelli, Nikolai Grigorev, Doug Fritz, Thibault Sottiaux, Mantas Pajarskas, Toby Pohlen, Zhitao Gong, Daniel Toyama, Cyprien de Masson d'Autume, Yujia Li, Tayfun Terzi, Vladimir Mikulik, Igor Babuschkin, Aidan Clark, Diego de Las Casas, Aurelia Guy, Chris Jones, James Bradbury, Matthew Johnson, Blake A. Hechtman, Laura Weidinger, Iason Gabriel, William S. Isaac, Edward Lockhart, Simon Osindero, Laura Rimell, Chris Dyer, Oriol Vinyals, Kareem Ayoub, Jeff Stanway, Lorrayne Bennett, Demis Hassabis, Koray Kavukcuoglu, and Geoffrey Irving. 2022. Scaling language models: Methods, analysis & insights from training Gopher. *Computing Research Repository*, arXiv:2112.11446. Version 2.

Jack W Rae, Anna Potapenko, Siddhant M Jayakumar, Chloe Hillier, and Timothy P Lillicrap. 2019. Compressive transformers for long-range sequence modelling. *Computing Research Repository*, arXiv:1911.05507. Version 1.

Colin Raffel, Noam Shazeer, Adam Roberts, Katherine Lee, Sharan Narang, Michael Matena, Yanqi Zhou, Wei Li, and Peter J Liu. 2020. Exploring the limits of transfer learning with a unified text-to-text transformer. *Journal of Machine Learning Research*, 21:1–67.

Samyam Rajbhandari, Jeff Rasley, Olatunji Ruwase, and Yuxiong He. 2020. ZeRO: Memory optimizations toward training trillion parameter models. In *Proceedings of the International Conference for High Performance Computing, Networking, Storage and Analysis*, SC '20. IEEE Press.

Jeff Rasley, Samyam Rajbhandari, Olatunji Ruwase, and Yuxiong He. 2020. DeepSpeed: System optimizations enable training deep learning models with over 100 billion parameters. In *Proceedings of the 26th ACM SIGKDD International Conference on Knowledge Discovery & Data Mining*, pages 3505–3506, New York, NY, USA. Association for Computing Machinery.

Yasaman Razeghi, Robert L Logan IV, Matt Gardner, and Sameer Singh. 2022. Impact of pretraining term frequencies on few-shot reasoning. *Computing Research Repository*, arXiv:2202.07206. Version 1.

Adam Roberts, Hyung Won Chung, Anselm Levskaya, Gaurav Mishra, James Bradbury, Daniel Andor, Sharan Narang, Brian Lester, Colin Gaffney, Afroz Mohiuddin, Curtis Hawthorne, Aitor Lewkowycz, Alex Salcianu, Marc van Zee, Jacob Austin, Sebastian Goodman, Livio Baldini Soares, Haitang Hu, Sasha Tsvyashchenko, Aakanksha Chowdhery, Jasmijn Bastings, Jannis Bulian, Xavier Garcia, Jianmo Ni, Andrew Chen, Kathleen Kenealy, Jonathan H. Clark, Stephan Lee, Dan Garrette, James Lee-Thorp, Colin Raffel, Noam Shazeer, Marvin Ritter, Maarten Bosma, Alexandre Passos, Jeremy Maitin-Shepard, Noah Fiedel, Mark Omernick, Brennan Saeta, Ryan Sepassi, Alexander Spiridonov, Joshua Newlan, and Andrea Gesmundo. 2022. Scaling up models and data with `t5x` and `seqio`. *Computing Research Repository*, arXiv:2203.17189. Version 1.

Jathan Sadowski, Salomé Viljoen, and Meredith Whittaker. 2021. Everyone should decide how their digital data are used — not just tech companies. *Nature*, 595(7866):169–171.

Keisuke Sakaguchi, Ronan Le Bras, Chandra Bhagavatula, and Yejin Choi. 2021. WinoGrande: An adversarial Winograd Schema Challenge at scale. *Commun. ACM*, 64(9):99–106.

Victor Sanh, Albert Webson, Colin Raffel, Stephen H. Bach, Lintang Sutawika, Zaid Alyafeai, Antoine Chaffin, Arnaud Stiegler, Teven Le Scao, Arun Raja, Manan Dey, M Saiful Bari, Canwen Xu, Urmish Thakker, Shanya Sharma Sharma, Eliza Szczechla, Taewoon Kim, Gunjan Chhablani, Nihal Nayak, Debajyoti Datta, Jonathan Chang, Mike Tian-Jian Jiang, Han Wang, Matteo Manica, Sheng Shen, Zheng Xin Yong, Harshit Pandey, Rachel Bawden, Thomas Wang, Trishala Neeraj, Jos Rozen, Abheesht Sharma, Andrea Santilli, Thibault Févry, Jason Alan Fries, Ryan Teehan, Stella Biderman, Leo Gao, Tali Bers, Thomas Wolf, and Alexander M. Rush. 2021. Multitask prompted training enables zero-shot task generalization. *Computing Research Repository*, arXiv:2110.08207. Version 2.

David Saxton, Edward Grefenstette, Felix Hill, and Pushmeet Kohli. 2019. Analysing mathematical reasoning abilities of neural models. *Computing Research Repository*, arXiv:1904.01557. Version 1.

Roy Schwartz, Jesse Dodge, Noah A Smith, and Oren Etzioni. 2020. Green AI. *Communications of the ACM*, 63(12):54–63.

Mohammad Shoeybi, Mostofa Patwary, Raul Puri, Patrick LeGresley, Jared Casper, and Bryan Catanzaro. 2020. Megatron-LM: Training multi-billion parameter language models using model parallelism. *Computing Research Repository*, arXiv:1909.08053. Version 4.

Mary Anne Smart. 2021. Addressing privacy threats from machine learning. *Computing Research Repository*, arXiv:2111.04439. Version 1.

Shaden Smith, Mostofa Patwary, Brandon Norick, Patrick LeGresley, Samyam Rajbhandari, Jared Casper, Zhun Liu, Shrimai Prabhumoye, George Zerveas, Vijay Korthikanti, Elton Zhang, Rewon Child, Reza Yazdani Aminabadi, Julie Bernauer, Xia Song, Mohammad Shoeybi, Yuxiong He, Michael Houston, Saurabh Tiwary, and Bryan Catanzaro. 2022. Using DeepSpeed and Megatron to train Megatron-Turing NLG 530B, a large-scale generative language model. *Computing Research Repository*, arXiv:2201.11990. Version 3.

Nate Soares. 2021. Visible thoughts project and bounty announcement. Machine Intelligence Research Institute.

Nisan Stiennon, Long Ouyang, Jeff Wu, Daniel M. Ziegler, Ryan Lowe, Chelsea Voss, Alec Radford, Dario Amodei, and Paul F. Christiano. 2022. Learning to summarize from human feedback. *Computing Research Repository*, arXiv:2009.01325.

Emma Strubell, Ananya Ganesh, and Andrew McCallum. 2019. Energy and policy considerations for deep learning in NLP. In *Proceedings of the 57th Annual Meeting of the Association for Computational Linguistics*, pages 3645–3650, Florence, Italy. Association for Computational Linguistics.

Jianlin Su, Yu Lu, Shengfeng Pan, Bo Wen, and Yunfeng Liu. 2021. RoFormer: Enhanced transformer with rotary position embedding. *Computing Research Repository*, arXiv:2104.09864. Version 2.

Yu Sun, Shuohuan Wang, Shikun Feng, Siyu Ding, Chao Pang, Junyuan Shang, Jiaxiang Liu, Xuyi Chen, Yanbin Zhao, Yuxiang Lu, Weixin Liu, Zhihua Wu, Weibao Gong, Jianzhong Liang, Zhizhou Shang, Peng Sun, Wei Liu, Xuan Ouyang, Dianhai Yu, Hao Tian, Hua Wu, and Haifeng Wang. 2021. ERNIE 3.0: Large-scale knowledge enhanced pre-training for language understanding and generation. *Computing Research Repository*, arXiv:2107.02137. Version 1.

Zeerak Talat, Aurélie Névéol, Stella Biderman, Miruna Clinciu, Manan Dey, Shayne Longpre, Alexandra Sasha Luccioni, Maraim Masoud, Margaret Mitchell, Dragomir Radev, Shanya Sharma, Arjun Subramonian, Jaesung Tae, Samson Tan, Deepak Tunuguntla, and Oskar van der Wal. 2022. You reap what you sow: On the challenges of bias evaluation under multilingual settings. In *Proceedings of the 1st Workshop on Challenges & Perspectives in Creating Large Language Models*. Association for Computational Linguistics.

Zhixing Tan, Xiangwen Zhang, Shuo Wang, and Yang Liu. 2021. MSP: Multi-stage prompting for making pre-trained language models better translators. *Computing Research Repository*, arXiv:2110.06609. Version 1.

Jie Tang. 2021. WuDao: Pretrain the world. Keynote address at the European Conference on Machine Learning and Principles and Practice of Knowledge Discovery in Databases.

David Vilares and Carlos Gómez-Rodríguez. 2019. HEAD-QA: A healthcare dataset for complex reasoning. In *Proceedings of the 57th Annual Meeting of the Association for Computational Linguistics*, pages 960–966, Florence, Italy. Association for Computational Linguistics.

Alex Wang, Yada Pruksachatkun, Nikita Nangia, Amanpreet Singh, Julian Michael, Felix Hill, Omer Levy, and Samuel Bowman. 2019. SuperGLUE: A stickier benchmark for general-purpose language understanding systems. *Advances in Neural Information Processing Systems*, 32:3266–3280.

Ben Wang. 2021. Mesh-Transformer-JAX: Model-parallel implementation of transformer language model with JAX.

Ben Wang and Aran Komatsuzaki. 2021. GPT-J-6B: A 6 billion parameter autoregressive language model.

Jason Wei, Maarten Bosma, Vincent Y Zhao, Kelvin Guu, Adams Wei Yu, Brian Lester, Nan Du, Andrew M Dai, and Quoc V Le. 2021. Finetuned language models are zero-shot learners. *Computing Research Repository*, arXiv:2109.01652. Version 5.

Johannes Welbl, Nelson F. Liu, and Matt Gardner. 2017. Crowdsourcing multiple choice science questions. In *Proceedings of the 3rd Workshop on Noisy User-generated Text*, pages 94–106, Copenhagen, Denmark. Association for Computational Linguistics.

John Wentworth. 2020. Alignment by default. AI Alignment Forum.

Meredith Whittaker. 2021. The steep cost of capture. *Interactions*, 28(6):50–55.

Linting Xue, Aditya Barua, Noah Constant, Rami Al-Rfou, Sharan Narang, Mihir Kale, Adam Roberts, and Colin Raffel. 2021. Byt5: Towards a token-free future with pre-trained byte-to-byte models. *Computing Research Repository*.

Linting Xue, Noah Constant, Adam Roberts, Mihir Kale, Rami Al-Rfou, Aditya Siddhant, Aditya Barua, and Colin Raffel. 2020. mT5: A massively multilingual pre-trained text-to-text transformer. *Computing Research Repository*, arXiv:2010.11934. Version 1.

Rowan Zellers, Ari Holtzman, Yonatan Bisk, Ali Farhadi, and Yejin Choi. 2019. HellaSwag: Can a machine really finish your sentence? In *Proceedings of the 57th Annual Meeting of the Association for Computational Linguistics*, pages 4791–4800, Florence, Italy. Association for Computational Linguistics.

Wei Zeng, Xiaozhe Ren, Teng Su, Hui Wang, Yi Liao, Zhiwei Wang, Xin Jiang, ZhenZhang Yang, Kaisheng Wang, Xiaoda Zhang, Chen Li, Ziyan Gong, Yifan Yao, Xinjing Huang, Jun Wang, Jianfeng Yu, Qi Guo, Yue Yu, Yan Zhang, Jin Wang, Hengtao Tao, Dasen Yan, Zexuan Yi, Fang Peng, Fangqing Jiang, Han Zhang, Lingfeng Deng, Yehong Zhang, Zhe Lin, Chao Zhang, Shaojie Zhang, Mingyue Guo, Shanzhi Gu, Gaojun Fan, Yaowei Wang, Xuefeng Jin, Qun Liu, and Yonghong Tian. 2021. Pangu-α: Large-scale autoregressive pretrained chinese language models with auto-parallel computation. *Computing Research Repository*, arXiv:2104.12369. Version 1.

Chiyuan Zhang, Daphne Ippolito, Katherine Lee, Matthew Jagielski, Florian Tramèr, and Nicholas Carlini. 2021. Counterfactual memorization in neural language models. *Computing Research Repository*, arXiv:2112.12938. Version 1.

Ruiqi Zhong, Kristy Lee, Zheng Zhang, and Dan Klein. 2021. Adapting language models for zero-shot learning by meta-tuning on dataset and prompt collections. *Computing Research Repository*, arXiv:2104.04670. Version 5.

A Individual Contributions

Sid Black was the lead developer and overall point person for the project. **Stella Biderman** was the lead scientist and project manager.

Implementation and Engineering

Implementation of training infrastructure:
Sid Black, Stella Biderman, Eric Hallahan, Quentin Anthony, Samuel Weinbach

Scaling experiments and optimization:
Sid Black, Stella Biderman, Quentin Anthony, Samuel Weinbach

Positional Embeddings:
Sid Black, Eric Hallahan, Michael Pieler

Tokenizer:
Sid Black

Miscellaneous:
USVSN Sai Prashanth, Ben Wang

Scientific Experimentation

Evaluations:
Stella Biderman, Leo Gao, Jonathan Tow, Sid Black, Shivanshu Purohit, Horace He, Laurence Golding

Positional Embeddings:
Stella Biderman, Laurence Golding, Michael Pieler

Tokenizer:
Stella Biderman, Jason Phang, Leo Gao

Broader Impacts

Alignment Implications:
Leo Gao, Connor Leahy, Laria Reynolds, Kyle McDonell

Environmental Impact:
Stella Biderman, Eric Hallahan

B Full Configuration Details

In Table 1 we attach the full configuration details used to train GPT-NeoX-20B. The file is available in `.yaml` format usable in `gpt-neox` at `https://github.com/EleutherAI/gpt-neox`, where we also provide documentation describing the role of each parameter.

Configuration Key	Value
attention-dropout	0
bias-gelu-fusion	True
checkpoint-activations	True
checkpoint-num-layers	1
data-impl	mmap
distributed-backend	nccl
eval-interval	1000
eval-iters	10
fp16.enabled	True
fp16.fp16	True
fp16.hysteresis	2
fp16.initial-scale-power	12
fp16.loss-scale	0
fp16.loss-scale-window	1000
fp16.min-loss-scale	1
gpt-j-residual	True
gradient-accumulation-steps	32
gradient-clipping	1.0
hidden-dropout	0
hidden-size	6144
init-method	small-init
log-interval	2
lr-decay-iters	150000
lr-decay-style	cosine
max-position-embeddings	2048
min-lr	9.7e-06
model-parallel-size	2
no-weight-tying	True
norm	layernorm
num-attention-heads	64
num-layers	44
optimizer.params.betas	[0.9, 0.95]
optimizer.params.eps	1e-08
optimizer.params.lr	9.7e-05
optimizer.type	Adam
output-layer-init-method	wang-init
output-layer-parallelism	column
partition-activations	False
pipe-parallel-size	4
pos-emb	rotary
rotary-pct	0.25
save-interval	500
scaled-upper-triang-masked-softmax-fusion	True
seq-length	2048
split	995,4,1
steps-per-print	2
synchronize-each-layer	True
tokenizer-type	HFTokenizer
train-iters	150000
train-micro-batch-size-per-gpu	4
vocab-file	20B-tokenizer.json
wall-clock-breakdown	False
warmup	0.01
weight-decay	0.01
zero-optimization.allgather-bucket-size	1260000000
zero-optimization.allgather-partitions	True
zero-optimization.contiguous-gradients	True
zero-optimization.cpu-offload	False
zero-optimization.overlap-comm	True
zero-optimization.reduce-bucket-size	1260000000
zero-optimization.reduce-scatter	True
zero-optimization.stage	1

Table 1: The full configuration details for GPT-NeoX-20B training

C Broader Impacts

The current status quo in research is that large language models are things people train and publish about, but do not actually release. To the best of our knowledge, GPT-NeoX-20B is the largest dense language model to ever be publicly released with a several-way tie for second place at 13 billion parameters (Artetxe et al., 2021; Xue et al., 2020, 2021) and many more models at the 10-11B parameter scale. A variety of reasons for the non-release of large language models are given by various groups, but the primary one is the harms that public access to LLMs would purportedly cause.

We take these concerns quite seriously. However, having taken them quite seriously, we feel that they are flawed in several respects. While a thorough analysis of these issues is beyond the scope of this paper, the public release of our model is the most important contribution of this paper and so an explanation of why we disagree with the prevailing wisdom is important.

Providing access to ethics and alignment researchers will prevent harm. The open-source release of this model is motivated by the hope that it will allow researchers who would not otherwise have access to LLMs to use them. While there are negative risks due to the potential acceleration of capabilities research, we believe the benefits of this release outweigh the risks. We also note that these benefits are not hypothetical, as a number of papers about the limits and ethics of LLMs has been explicitly enabled by the public release of previous models (Zhang et al., 2021; Kandpal et al., 2022; Carlini et al., 2022; Birhane et al., 2021; nostalgebraist, 2020; Meng et al., 2022; Lin et al., 2021).

Limiting access to governments and corporations will not prevent harm. Perhaps the most curious aspect of the argument that LLMs should not be released is that the people making such arguments are not arguing they *they* should not use LLMs. Rather, they are claiming that *other people* should not use them. We do not believe that this is a position that should be taken seriously. The companies and governments that have the financial resources to train LLMs are overwhelmingly more likely to do large scale harm using a LLM than a random individual.

The open-source release of this model is motivated by the hope that it will allow ethics and alignment researchers who would not otherwise have access to LLMs to use them. While there are negative risks due to the potential acceleration of capabilities research, we believe the benefits of this release outweigh the risks of accelerating capabilities research.

C.1 Impact on Capabilities Research and Products

When discussing the impact of access to technology, it is important to distinguish between *capacities research* which seeks to push the current state-of-the-art and research on

We feel the risk of releasing GPT-NeoX-20B is acceptable, as the contribution of the model to capabilities research is likely to be limited, for two reasons.

We ultimately believe that the benefits of releasing this model outweigh the risks, but this argument hinges crucially on the particular circumstances of this release. All actors considering releasing powerful AI models or advancing the frontier of capabilities should think carefully about what they release, in what way, and when.

C.2 Impact on Ethics and Alignment Research

To oversimplify a complex debate, there are broadly speaking two schools of thought regarding the mitigation of harm that is done by AI algorithms: *AI Ethics* and *AI Alignement.* AI Ethics researchers are primarily concerned with the impact of current technologies or technologies very similar to current technologies, while AI Alignment is primarily concerned with future "generally intelligent" systems whose capacities greatly outclass currently existing systems and possess human and superhuman levels of intelligence. While the tools, methods, and ideas of these camps are very different, we believe that increasing access to these technologies will empower and advance the goals of researchers in both schools.

C.2.1 The Necessity of Model Access for AI Ethics

Analyzing and documenting the limitations of models is an essential aspect of AI ethics research (Matias, 2020). Work examining and criticizing datasets (Kreutzer et al., 2022; Dodge et al., 2021; Birhane et al., 2021), functionality (Smart, 2021; Zhang et al., 2021; Carlini et al., 2022; Biderman and Raff, 2022), evaluation and deployment procedures (Biderman and Scheirer, 2020; Talat et al.,

2022), and more are essential to well-rounded and informed debate on the value and application of technology.

However *the current centralization of LLM training also creates a centralization of control of technology* (Sadowski et al., 2021; Whittaker, 2021) that makes meaningful independent evaluation impossible. This means that it is often not possible to do this kind of work in practice because of the severe access restrictions companies that own large language models put on them. While GPT-NeoX is the 13th largest dense language model at time of writing only model larger than GPT-NeoX 20B that is publicly accessible is GPT-3. There are significant limitations on people's ability to do research on GPT-3 though, as it is not free to use and its training data is private.

C.2.2 The Usefulness of Large Language Models in Alignment

LLMs represent a different paradigm than the AI systems generally studied by alignment researchers because they are not well-described as coherent agents or expected utility maximizers. Though trained to optimize a log-likelihood loss function, at a high level the goals a LLM pursues are varied and contradictory, depending on the way it is prompted. This introduces additional challenges, but may also enable new approaches to alignment.

GPT-NeoX-20B itself is not the system we need to align, but we hope it can serve as a publicly available platform for experiments whose results might generalize to crucial future work.

The following is a non-exhaustive list of potential approaches we consider promising for further investigation.

Mechanistic interpretability. Mechanistic interpretability research (Cammarata et al., 2020) hopes to gain an understanding into *how* models accomplish the tasks they do, in part in the hopes of detecting problematic or deceptive algorithms implemented by models before these failures manifest in the real world. Being able to interpret and inspect the detailed inner workings of trained models would be a powerful tool to ensure models are optimizing for the goals we intended (Hubinger et al., 2021; Koch et al., 2021). Reverse engineering transformer language models has already yielded insights about the inner functioning of LMs (Elhage et al., 2021; nostalgebraist, 2020; Meng et al., 2022; Dai et al., 2021).

Using a LLM as a reward model. Because they are trained to predict human writing, LLMs also appear to develop a useful representation of human values at the semantic level. Finding a way to utilise these representations could be a possible path toward solving the problem of reward robustness in RL and other algorithms which require a proxy of human judgment (Stiennon et al., 2022; Wentworth, 2020). Despite fundamental theoretical limitations on learning human values (Armstrong and Mindermann, 2018; Kosoy, 2016), value learning may still be robust enough to align weaker superhuman AIs. Future experiments could explore the extent to which LLM pretraining improves downstream reward model robustness and generalization.

Natural language transparency. Since LLM prompts are in a human-readable form, it can provide insight on the LLM's expected behavior. Prompt programming or finetuning can be used to leverage this fact and force a LLM to execute more transparent algorithms, such as splitting problems into steps or explicitly writing an "internal monologue" (Soares, 2021; Gao et al., 2021a; Nye et al., 2021). Reliability and trustworthiness can present significant challenges for these approaches.

However, this form of transparency also has its limits. In particular, models can often respond unpredictably to prompts, and internal monologues may become completely detached from the model's decision making process if translating between the model's ontology and the human ontology is more complex than simply modeling human monologues (Christiano et al., 2021).

Simulating agents at runtime. Although LLMs are not well-described as coherent agents, they can still be used to generate goal-directed processes. Given an appropriate prompt (such as a story of a character working to achieve a goal), LLMs can predict and thus simulate an agent (Huang et al., 2022). Simulated agents take representative actions according to the patterns present in the training data, similar to behavior cloning. One potential future research direction is testing whether they are less susceptible to failure modes that follow from expected utility maximization, such as Goodhart failures and power-seeking behavior. However, other failure modes can be introduced by the LM training procedure, such as "delusions" or "hallucinations" (Ortega et al., 2021; Gao, 2021; Maynez et al., 2020). Additionally, simulated agents may be uncompetitive with optimal agents like those produced by Reinforcement Learning. An important research direction is to explore how the beneficial properties of simulated agents can be maintained while making them competitive with RL based approaches.

Tool AI and automated alignment research. LMs can be used as relatively unagentic tools, such as OpenAI's Codex model (Chen et al., 2021) acting as a coding assistant. Because pretrained LLMs are not directly optimized for the factual accuracy of their predictions, it is possible they avoid some of the traditional problems with tool or oracle AI (Armstrong et al., 2012), such as the incentive to produce manipulative answers (Demski, 2019). Tool AI is not a long-term solution to the problem of alignment, but it could be used to assist alignment research or even automate large parts of it. For example, language models could be used to help brainstorm alignment ideas more quickly, act as a writing assistant, or directly generate alignment research papers for humans to review. This line of research also risks accelerating capabilities research, a concern we discuss more below.

C.3 Differential Impact on Access

Because training large models requires a significant engineering and capital investment, such models are often out of reach for small labs and independent researchers. As it stands, only large organizations have access to the latest generation of powerful language models (Brown et al., 2020; Rae et al., 2022; Fedus et al., 2021; Lieber et al., 2021; Tang, 2021). The number of researchers focused primarily on ethics and alignment working at these labs is much lower than those working on developing new capabilities.

We feel the risk of releasing GPT-NeoX-20B is acceptable, as the contribution of the model to capabilities research is likely to be limited, for two reasons. Firstly, the organizations pursuing capabilities research most aggressively are unlikely to benefit from our open-source release of this model as they have already developed more powerful models of their own. Secondly, we believe the single most important piece of knowledge that drives advancing capabilities research is the knowledge that scaling LLMs was possible in the first place (Leahy, 2021; Leahy and Biderman, 2021). Whereas the actual implementation is very fungible (as evidenced by the large number of parties who have succeeded in creating their own LLMs in the past two years). **This differential impact, wherein our release is expected to benefit primarily people who have less funding and infrastructure, is a key factor in our decision to release this model publicly.**

We ultimately believe that the benefits of releasing this model outweigh the risks, but this argument hinges crucially on the particular circumstances of this release. All actors considering releasing powerful AI models or advancing the frontier of capabilities should think carefully about what they release, in what way, and when.

C.4 Environmental Impact

A significant point of concern in some recent work is the energy usage and carbon emissions associated with training large language models (Strubell et al., 2019; Schwartz et al., 2020; Lacoste et al., 2019; Bender et al., 2021). In particular, Strubell et al. (2019) estimate that a then-recent paper by the authors released 626,155 lbs or 284.01 metric tons[14] of CO_2 (t_{CO_2}). As Strubell et al. (2019) has been widely cited and quoted in the media as representative of large-scale language models, we decided to explicitly and carefully track our energy usage and carbon emissions to see if this is truly a representative account of NLP emissions.

Throughout the development and training of our model, we tracked our energy usage and carbon emissions. We found that the process of developing and training GPT-NeoX-20B emitted almost exactly 10% of Strubell et al. (2019)'s estimate, coming in at a total of 69957 lbs or 31.73 metric tons of CO_2. This is roughly the equivalent of the yearly emissions of the average American or 35 round-trip flights between New York City and San Francisco. Our systems were based in Illinois, USA, and consumed energy sourced from the mix as follows

- 30.40% Coal (0.95 t_{CO_2}/MWh)
- 31.30% Gas (0.6078 t_{CO_2}/MWh)
- 1.30% Hydroelectric (0 t_{CO_2}/MWh)
- 17.40% Nuclear (0 t_{CO_2}/MWh)
- 0.30% Solar (0 t_{CO_2}/MWh)
- 18.10% Wind (0 t_{CO_2}/MWh)

[14] We choose to present environmental impact figures in metric tons to align with standard reporting.

- 1.30% Other Renewables (0 t_{CO_2}/MWh)

This mixture produces an average of 0.47905 t_{CO_2}/MWh, and we consumed a total of 43.92 MWh of electricity over the course of 1830 hours of training. Scaling, testing, and evaluation were responsible for the equivalent of another 920 hours on our systems, for a total energy consumption 66.24 MWh and thus the production of just under 35 metric tons of CO_2.

It is noteworthy that Strubell et al. (2019) are estimating emissions from a *neural architecture search* paper, and is therefore not directly comparable to ours. The primary motivation for our comparison is that their number has attracted a lot of attention and is often taken to be respresentative of NLP research. In general, we advocate for more systematic and comprehensive reporting to improve transparency surrounding this important topic.

D Architecture Diagram

E Full Evaluation Results

Results for natural language understanding tasks are shown in Tables 2 and 3, while results for Hendrycks tasks are found in Tables 10 to 13.

All evaluations had version 0 in the Evaluation Harness. This information is reported in the output of the Evaluation Harness and should be used for ensuring reproducibility of these results, even as the task implementations themselves may change to fix bugs.

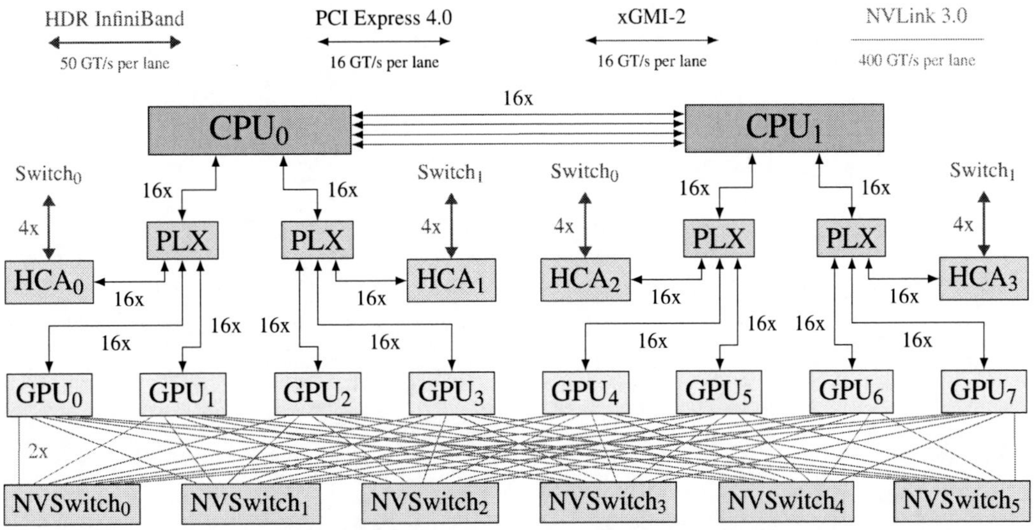

Figure 7: Architecture diagram of a single training node.

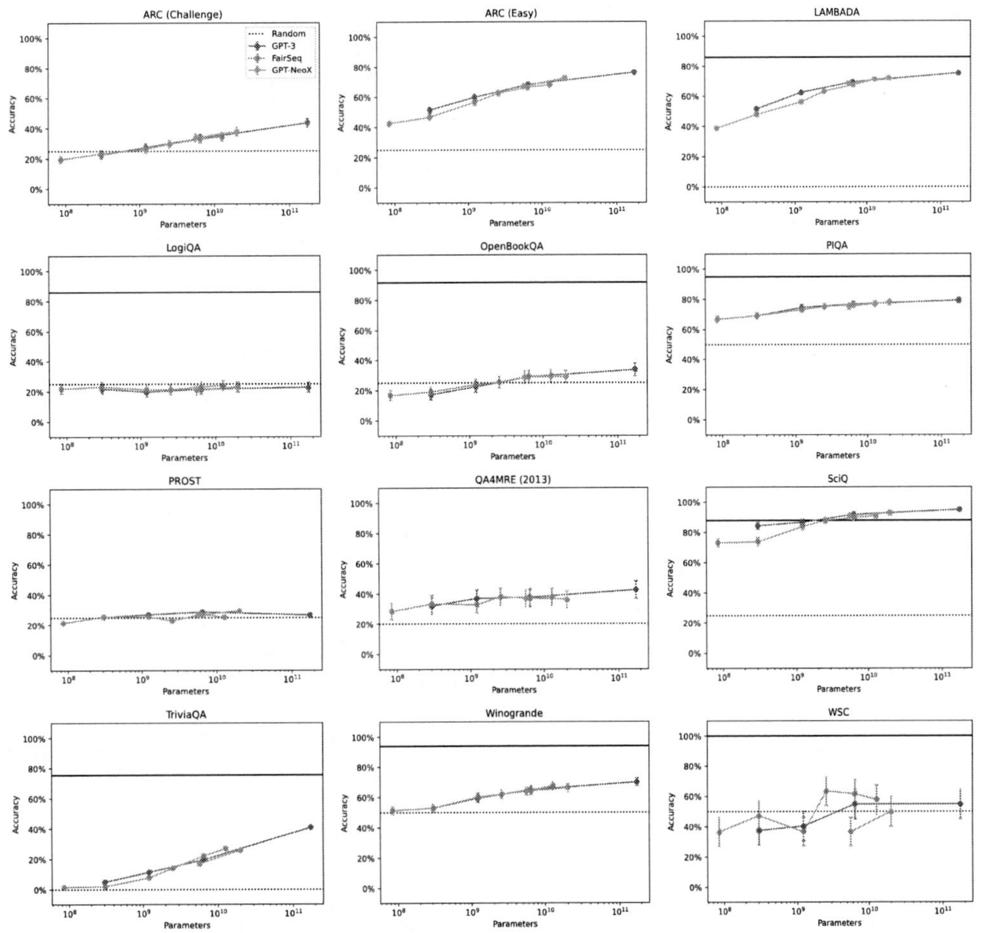

Figure 8: Zero-shot performance of GPT-NeoX-20B compared to GPT-J-6B and FairSeq and OpenAI models on a variety of language modeling benchmarks.

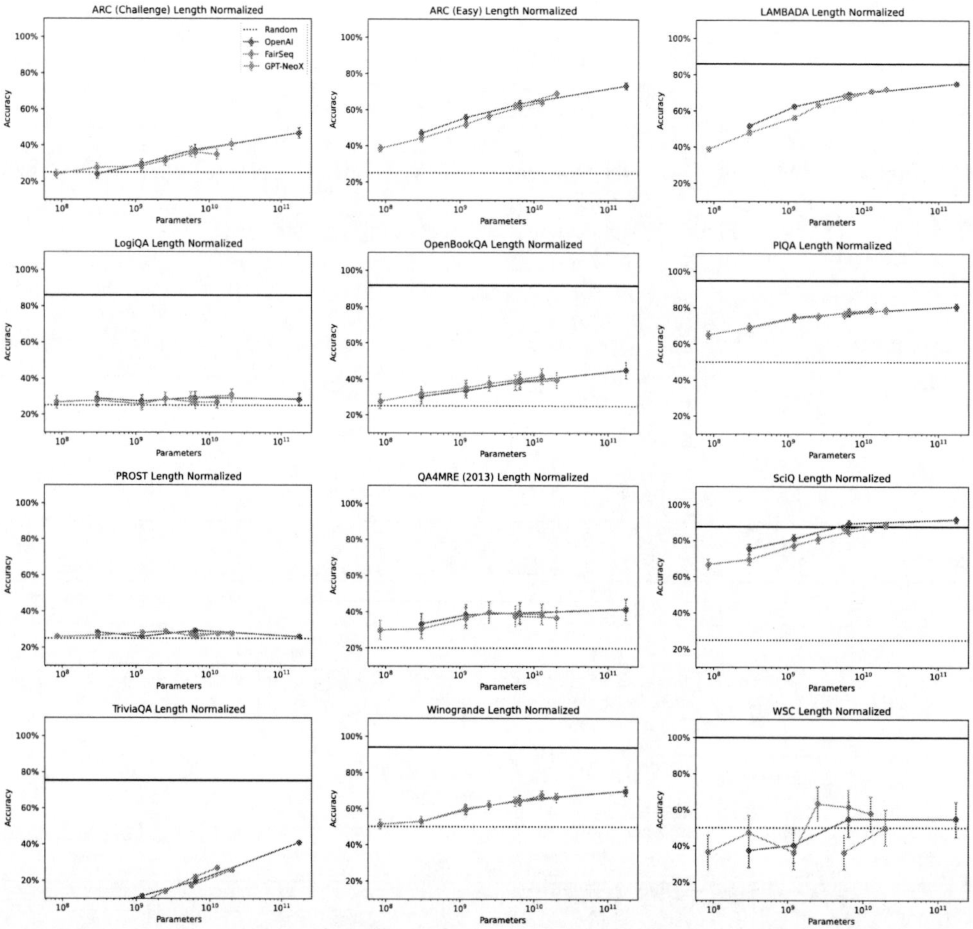

Figure 9: Length-normalized zero-shot performance of GPT-NeoX-20B compared to GPT-J-6B and FairSeq and OpenAI models on a variety of language modeling benchmarks.

Task	GPT-J 6B	GPT-NeoX 20B	GPT-3 Ada	GPT-3 Babbage	GPT-3 Curie	GPT-3 DaVinci
ANLI Round 1	0.324 ± 0.015	0.340 ± 0.015	0.334 ± 0.015	0.326 ± 0.015	0.325 ± 0.015	0.363 ± 0.015
ANLI Round 2	0.340 ± 0.015	0.343 ± 0.015	0.342 ± 0.015	0.308 ± 0.015	0.338 ± 0.015	0.375 ± 0.015
ANLI Round 3	0.355 ± 0.014	0.354 ± 0.014	0.354 ± 0.014	0.340 ± 0.014	0.353 ± 0.014	0.369 ± 0.014
LAMBADA	0.683 ± 0.006	0.720 ± 0.006	0.515 ± 0.007	0.625 ± 0.007	0.693 ± 0.006	0.752 ± 0.006
WSC	0.365 ± 0.047	0.500 ± 0.049	0.375 ± 0.048	0.404 ± 0.048	0.548 ± 0.049	0.548 ± 0.049
HellaSwag	0.518 ± 0.005	0.535 ± 0.005	0.359 ± 0.005	0.429 ± 0.005	0.505 ± 0.005	0.592 ± 0.005
Winogrande	0.640 ± 0.013	0.661 ± 0.013	0.528 ± 0.014	0.594 ± 0.014	0.649 ± 0.013	0.699 ± 0.013
SciQ	0.910 ± 0.009	0.928 ± 0.008	0.843 ± 0.012	0.866 ± 0.011	0.918 ± 0.009	0.949 ± 0.007
PIQA	0.752 ± 0.010	0.779 ± 0.010	0.690 ± 0.011	0.745 ± 0.010	0.767 ± 0.010	0.791 ± 0.009
TriviaQA	0.170 ± 0.004	0.259 ± 0.004	0.050 ± 0.002	0.115 ± 0.003	0.196 ± 0.004	0.409 ± 0.005
ARC (Easy)	0.670 ± 0.010	0.723 ± 0.009	0.514 ± 0.010	0.598 ± 0.010	0.682 ± 0.010	0.762 ± 0.009
ARC (Challenge)	0.340 ± 0.014	0.380 ± 0.014	0.225 ± 0.012	0.275 ± 0.013	0.334 ± 0.014	0.435 ± 0.014
OpenBookQA	0.288 ± 0.020	0.290 ± 0.020	0.172 ± 0.017	0.224 ± 0.019	0.290 ± 0.020	0.336 ± 0.021
HeadQA (English)	—	—	0.245 ± 0.008	0.278 ± 0.009	0.317 ± 0.009	0.356 ± 0.009
LogiQA	0.209 ± 0.016	0.230 ± 0.017	0.218 ± 0.016	0.198 ± 0.016	0.217 ± 0.016	0.227 ± 0.016
PROST	0.267 ± 0.003	0.296 ± 0.003	0.254 ± 0.003	0.270 ± 0.003	0.288 ± 0.003	0.267 ± 0.003
QA4MRE (2013)	0.373 ± 0.029	0.363 ± 0.029	0.320 ± 0.028	0.370 ± 0.029	0.377 ± 0.029	0.426 ± 0.029

Table 2: Zero-Shot Results on Natural Language Understanding Tasks (GPT-J, GPT-NeoX and GPT-3)

Task	FairSeq 125M	355M	1.3B	2.7B	6.7B	13B
ANLI Round 1	0.316 ± 0.015	0.322 ± 0.015	0.331 ± 0.015	0.318 ± 0.015	0.338 ± 0.015	0.340 ± 0.015
ANLI Round 2	0.336 ± 0.015	0.312 ± 0.015	0.334 ± 0.015	0.339 ± 0.015	0.322 ± 0.015	0.330 ± 0.015
ANLI Round 3	0.330 ± 0.014	0.323 ± 0.014	0.333 ± 0.014	0.340 ± 0.014	0.333 ± 0.014	0.347 ± 0.014
LAMBADA	0.388 ± 0.007	0.478 ± 0.007	0.562 ± 0.007	0.632 ± 0.007	0.673 ± 0.007	0.709 ± 0.006
WSC	0.365 ± 0.047	0.471 ± 0.049	0.365 ± 0.047	0.635 ± 0.047	0.615 ± 0.048	0.577 ± 0.049
HellaSwag	0.309 ± 0.005	0.380 ± 0.005	0.448 ± 0.005	0.493 ± 0.005	0.525 ± 0.005	0.554 ± 0.005
Winogrande	0.513 ± 0.014	0.529 ± 0.014	0.600 ± 0.014	0.620 ± 0.014	0.644 ± 0.013	0.674 ± 0.013
SciQ	0.732 ± 0.014	0.737 ± 0.014	0.838 ± 0.012	0.878 ± 0.010	0.895 ± 0.010	0.910 ± 0.009
PIQA	0.668 ± 0.011	0.690 ± 0.011	0.731 ± 0.010	0.751 ± 0.010	0.762 ± 0.010	0.769 ± 0.010
TriviaQA	0.015 ± 0.001	0.019 ± 0.001	0.078 ± 0.003	0.141 ± 0.003	0.221 ± 0.004	0.270 ± 0.004
ARC (Easy)	0.426 ± 0.010	0.468 ± 0.010	0.565 ± 0.010	0.625 ± 0.010	0.665 ± 0.010	0.680 ± 0.010
ARC (Challenge)	0.195 ± 0.012	0.233 ± 0.012	0.263 ± 0.013	0.296 ± 0.013	0.329 ± 0.014	0.345 ± 0.014
OpenBookQA	0.168 ± 0.017	0.190 ± 0.018	0.238 ± 0.019	0.254 ± 0.019	0.292 ± 0.020	0.296 ± 0.020
HeadQA (English)	0.233 ± 0.008	0.233 ± 0.008	0.256 ± 0.008	0.264 ± 0.008	0.280 ± 0.009	0.280 ± 0.009
LogiQA	0.220 ± 0.016	0.230 ± 0.017	0.214 ± 0.016	0.212 ± 0.016	0.232 ± 0.017	0.240 ± 0.017
PROST	0.215 ± 0.003	0.257 ± 0.003	0.257 ± 0.003	0.230 ± 0.003	0.272 ± 0.003	0.252 ± 0.003
QA4MRE (2013)	0.285 ± 0.027	0.335 ± 0.028	0.327 ± 0.028	0.380 ± 0.029	0.370 ± 0.029	0.380 ± 0.029

Table 3: Zero-Shot Results on Natural Language Understanding Tasks (FairSeq Models)

Task	GPT-J 6B	GPT-NeoX 20B	GPT-3 Ada	GPT-3 Babbage	GPT-3 Curie	GPT-3 DaVinci
ANLI Round 1	0.322 ± 0.015	0.312 ± 0.015	—	—	—	—
ANLI Round 2	0.331 ± 0.015	0.329 ± 0.015	—	—	—	—
ANLI Round 3	0.346 ± 0.014	0.342 ± 0.014	—	—	—	—
LAMBADA	0.662 ± 0.007	0.698 ± 0.006	—	—	—	—
WSC	0.365 ± 0.047	0.385 ± 0.048	—	—	—	—
HellaSwag	0.494 ± 0.005	0.538 ± 0.005	—	—	—	—
Winogrande	0.660 ± 0.013	0.683 ± 0.013	—	—	—	—
SciQ	0.913 ± 0.009	0.960 ± 0.006	—	—	—	—
PIQA	0.756 ± 0.010	0.774 ± 0.010	—	—	—	—
TriviaQA	0.289 ± 0.004	0.347 ± 0.004	—	—	—	—
ARC (Challenge)	0.360 ± 0.014	0.410 ± 0.014	—	—	—	—
ARC (Easy)	0.705 ± 0.009	0.746 ± 0.009	—	—	—	—
OpenBookQA	0.310 ± 0.021	0.326 ± 0.021	—	—	—	—
HeadQA (English)	0.326 ± 0.009	0.385 ± 0.009	—	—	—	—
LogiQA	0.230 ± 0.017	0.220 ± 0.016	—	—	—	—
QA4MRE (2013)	0.366 ± 0.029	0.363 ± 0.029	—	—	—	—

Table 4: Five-Shot Results on Natural Language Understanding Tasks (GPT-J and GPT-NeoX). GPT-3 is omitted due to financial limitations.

Task	FairSeq 125M	355M	1.3B	2.7B	6.7B	13B
ANLI Round 1	0.332 ± 0.015	0.336 ± 0.015	0.327 ± 0.015	0.336 ± 0.015	0.305 ± 0.015	0.335 ± 0.015
ANLI Round 2	0.345 ± 0.015	0.350 ± 0.015	0.347 ± 0.015	0.333 ± 0.015	0.340 ± 0.015	0.338 ± 0.015
ANLI Round 3	0.359 ± 0.014	0.347 ± 0.014	0.370 ± 0.014	0.326 ± 0.014	0.367 ± 0.014	0.357 ± 0.014
LAMBADA	0.268 ± 0.006	0.349 ± 0.007	0.427 ± 0.007	0.460 ± 0.007	0.494 ± 0.007	0.518 ± 0.007
WSC	0.365 ± 0.047	0.365 ± 0.047	0.365 ± 0.047	0.356 ± 0.047	0.500 ± 0.049	0.404 ± 0.048
HellaSwag	0.308 ± 0.005	0.379 ± 0.005	0.451 ± 0.005	0.497 ± 0.005	0.531 ± 0.005	0.559 ± 0.005
Winogrande	0.516 ± 0.014	0.538 ± 0.014	0.612 ± 0.014	0.633 ± 0.014	0.657 ± 0.013	0.690 ± 0.013
SciQ	0.758 ± 0.014	0.819 ± 0.012	0.859 ± 0.011	0.875 ± 0.010	0.871 ± 0.011	0.899 ± 0.010
PIQA	0.656 ± 0.011	0.700 ± 0.011	0.731 ± 0.010	0.750 ± 0.010	0.764 ± 0.010	0.769 ± 0.010
TriviaQA	0.044 ± 0.002	0.097 ± 0.003	0.160 ± 0.003	0.225 ± 0.004	0.293 ± 0.004	0.323 ± 0.004
ARC (Easy)	0.453 ± 0.010	0.533 ± 0.010	0.618 ± 0.010	0.664 ± 0.010	0.686 ± 0.010	0.702 ± 0.009
ARC (Challenge)	0.198 ± 0.012	0.231 ± 0.012	0.278 ± 0.013	0.310 ± 0.014	0.359 ± 0.014	0.370 ± 0.014
OpenBookQA	0.184 ± 0.017	0.206 ± 0.018	0.218 ± 0.018	0.258 ± 0.020	0.288 ± 0.020	0.290 ± 0.020
HeadQA (English)	0.235 ± 0.008	0.240 ± 0.008	0.254 ± 0.008	0.266 ± 0.008	0.276 ± 0.009	0.282 ± 0.009
LogiQA	0.218 ± 0.016	0.207 ± 0.016	0.210 ± 0.016	0.214 ± 0.016	0.214 ± 0.016	0.223 ± 0.016
QA4MRE (2013)	0.324 ± 0.028	0.338 ± 0.028	0.338 ± 0.028	0.352 ± 0.028	0.391 ± 0.029	0.387 ± 0.029

Table 5: Five-Shot Results on Natural Language Understanding Tasks (FairSeq Models)

Task	GPT-J 6B	GPT-NeoX 20B	GPT-3 Ada	GPT-3 Babbage	GPT-3 Curie	GPT-3 DaVinci
1DC	0.088 ± 0.006	0.098 ± 0.007	0.029 ± 0.000	0.001 ± 0.000	0.024 ± 0.000	0.098 ± 0.000
2D+	0.238 ± 0.010	0.570 ± 0.011	0.006 ± 0.000	0.009 ± 0.000	0.025 ± 0.000	0.769 ± 0.000
2Dx	0.139 ± 0.008	0.148 ± 0.008	0.022 ± 0.000	0.021 ± 0.000	0.058 ± 0.000	0.198 ± 0.000
2D-	0.216 ± 0.009	0.680 ± 0.010	0.013 ± 0.000	0.013 ± 0.000	0.076 ± 0.000	0.580 ± 0.000
3D+	0.088 ± 0.006	0.099 ± 0.007	0.001 ± 0.000	0.001 ± 0.000	0.003 ± 0.000	0.342 ± 0.000
3D-	0.046 ± 0.005	0.344 ± 0.011	0.001 ± 0.000	0.001 ± 0.000	0.004 ± 0.000	0.483 ± 0.000
4D+	0.007 ± 0.002	0.007 ± 0.002	0.001 ± 0.000	0.000 ± 0.000	0.001 ± 0.000	0.040 ± 0.000
4D-	0.005 ± 0.002	0.029 ± 0.004	0.000 ± 0.000	0.000 ± 0.000	0.000 ± 0.000	0.075 ± 0.000
5D+	0.001 ± 0.001	0.000 ± 0.000	0.000 ± 0.000	0.000 ± 0.000	0.000 ± 0.000	0.006 ± 0.000
5D-	0.000 ± 0.000	0.004 ± 0.001	0.000 ± 0.000	0.000 ± 0.000	0.000 ± 0.000	0.008 ± 0.000
MATH (Algebra)	0.013 ± 0.003	0.010 ± 0.003	0.003 ± 0.002	0.008 ± 0.003	0.003 ± 0.002	0.008 ± 0.003
MATH (Counting and Probability)	0.011 ± 0.005	0.017 ± 0.006	0.000 ± 0.000	0.004 ± 0.003	0.000 ± 0.000	0.006 ± 0.004
MATH (Geometry)	0.004 ± 0.003	0.017 ± 0.006	0.000 ± 0.000	0.000 ± 0.000	0.002 ± 0.002	0.002 ± 0.002
MATH (Intermediate Algebra)	0.004 ± 0.002	0.001 ± 0.001	0.000 ± 0.000	0.003 ± 0.002	0.006 ± 0.002	0.003 ± 0.002
MATH (Number Theory)	0.007 ± 0.004	0.013 ± 0.005	0.007 ± 0.004	0.000 ± 0.000	0.006 ± 0.003	0.011 ± 0.005
MATH (Pre-Algebra)	0.010 ± 0.003	0.018 ± 0.005	0.007 ± 0.003	0.006 ± 0.003	0.008 ± 0.003	0.014 ± 0.004
MATH (Pre-Calculus)	0.005 ± 0.003	0.005 ± 0.003	0.004 ± 0.003	0.000 ± 0.000	0.002 ± 0.002	0.004 ± 0.003

Table 6: Zero-Shot Results on Basic Arithmetic and MATH (GPT-J, GPT-NeoX, and GPT-3)

	FairSeq					
Task	125M	355M	1.3B	2.7B	6.7B	13B
1DC	0.001 ± 0.001	0.000 ± 0.000	0.000 ± 0.000	0.011 ± 0.002	0.024 ± 0.003	0.001 ± 0.001
2D+	0.005 ± 0.002	0.001 ± 0.001	0.002 ± 0.001	0.009 ± 0.002	0.019 ± 0.003	0.020 ± 0.003
2Dx	0.020 ± 0.003	0.004 ± 0.001	0.018 ± 0.003	0.023 ± 0.003	0.036 ± 0.004	0.028 ± 0.004
2D-	0.005 ± 0.002	0.002 ± 0.001	0.006 ± 0.002	0.013 ± 0.002	0.013 ± 0.003	0.015 ± 0.003
3D+	0.001 ± 0.001	0.001 ± 0.001	0.001 ± 0.001	0.001 ± 0.001	0.001 ± 0.001	0.001 ± 0.001
3D-	0.002 ± 0.001	0.001 ± 0.001	0.002 ± 0.001	0.002 ± 0.001	0.002 ± 0.001	0.002 ± 0.001
4D+	0.001 ± 0.001	0.000 ± 0.000	0.001 ± 0.001	0.001 ± 0.001	0.001 ± 0.001	0.001 ± 0.001
4D-	0.000 ± 0.000	0.000 ± 0.000	0.000 ± 0.000	0.000 ± 0.000	0.000 ± 0.000	0.000 ± 0.000
5D+	0.000 ± 0.000	0.000 ± 0.000	0.000 ± 0.000	0.000 ± 0.000	0.000 ± 0.000	0.000 ± 0.000
5D-	0.000 ± 0.000	0.000 ± 0.000	0.000 ± 0.000	0.000 ± 0.000	0.000 ± 0.000	0.000 ± 0.000
MATH (Algebra)	0.000 ± 0.000	0.000 ± 0.000	0.001 ± 0.001	0.003 ± 0.002	0.004 ± 0.002	0.003 ± 0.001
MATH (Counting and Probability)	0.000 ± 0.000	0.000 ± 0.000	0.000 ± 0.000	0.000 ± 0.000	0.004 ± 0.003	0.000 ± 0.000
MATH (Geometry)	0.000 ± 0.000	0.000 ± 0.000	0.000 ± 0.000	0.002 ± 0.002	0.000 ± 0.000	0.000 ± 0.000
MATH (Intermediate Algebra)	0.000 ± 0.002	0.000 ± 0.002	0.000 ± 0.000	0.001 ± 0.001	0.006 ± 0.002	0.002 ± 0.002
MATH (Number Theory)	0.000 ± 0.000	0.000 ± 0.000	0.000 ± 0.000	0.002 ± 0.002	0.000 ± 0.000	0.004 ± 0.003
MATH (Pre-Algebra)	0.000 ± 0.000	0.000 ± 0.000	0.003 ± 0.002	0.002 ± 0.002	0.001 ± 0.001	0.000 ± 0.000
MATH (Pre-Calculus)	0.000 ± 0.000	0.000 ± 0.000	0.000 ± 0.000	0.002 ± 0.002	0.000 ± 0.000	0.000 ± 0.000

Table 7: Zero-Shot Results on Basic Arithmetic and MATH (FairSeq Models)

Task	GPT-J 6B	GPT-NeoX 20B	GPT-3 Ada	Babbage	Curie	DaVinci
1DC	0.192 ± 0.009	0.191 ± 0.009	—	—	—	—
2D+	0.880 ± 0.007	0.992 ± 0.002	—	—	—	—
2Dx	0.282 ± 0.010	0.452 ± 0.011	—	—	—	—
2D-	0.817 ± 0.009	0.942 ± 0.005	—	—	—	—
3D+	0.357 ± 0.011	0.599 ± 0.011	—	—	—	—
3D-	0.497 ± 0.011	0.819 ± 0.009	—	—	—	—
4D+	0.058 ± 0.005	0.152 ± 0.008	—	—	—	—
4D-	0.092 ± 0.006	0.151 ± 0.008	—	—	—	—
5D+	0.009 ± 0.002	0.033 ± 0.004	—	—	—	—
5D-	0.021 ± 0.003	0.059 ± 0.005	—	—	—	—
MATH (Algebra)	0.032 ± 0.005	0.049 ± 0.006	—	—	—	—
MATH (Counting and Probability)	0.036 ± 0.009	0.030 ± 0.008	—	—	—	—
MATH (Geometry)	0.027 ± 0.007	0.015 ± 0.005	—	—	—	—
MATH (Intermediate Algebra)	0.024 ± 0.005	0.021 ± 0.005	—	—	—	—
MATH (Number Theory)	0.044 ± 0.009	0.065 ± 0.011	—	—	—	—
MATH (Pre-Algebra)	0.052 ± 0.008	0.057 ± 0.008	—	—	—	—
MATH (Pre-Calculus)	0.013 ± 0.005	0.027 ± 0.007	—	—	—	—

Table 8: Five-Shot Results on Basic Arithmetic and MATH (GPT-J and GPT-NeoX). GPT-3 is omitted due to financial limitations.

Task	FairSeq 125M	355M	1.3B	2.7B	6.7B	13B
1DC	0.019 ± 0.003	0.024 ± 0.003	0.029 ± 0.004	0.032 ± 0.004	0.046 ± 0.005	0.046 ± 0.005
2D+	0.005 ± 0.002	0.004 ± 0.001	0.006 ± 0.002	0.029 ± 0.004	0.034 ± 0.004	0.051 ± 0.005
2Dx	0.001 ± 0.001	0.025 ± 0.004	0.025 ± 0.003	0.025 ± 0.003	0.049 ± 0.005	0.053 ± 0.005
2D-	0.007 ± 0.002	0.011 ± 0.002	0.008 ± 0.002	0.013 ± 0.003	0.018 ± 0.003	0.030 ± 0.004
3D+	0.002 ± 0.001	0.002 ± 0.001	0.001 ± 0.001	0.003 ± 0.001	0.001 ± 0.001	0.003 ± 0.001
3D-	0.002 ± 0.001	0.004 ± 0.001	0.003 ± 0.001	0.003 ± 0.001	0.002 ± 0.001	0.003 ± 0.001
4D+	0.000 ± 0.000	0.000 ± 0.000	0.000 ± 0.000	0.000 ± 0.000	0.000 ± 0.000	0.000 ± 0.000
4D-	0.001 ± 0.001	0.000 ± 0.000	0.000 ± 0.000	0.001 ± 0.001	0.000 ± 0.000	0.000 ± 0.000
5D+	0.000 ± 0.000	0.000 ± 0.000	0.000 ± 0.000	0.000 ± 0.000	0.000 ± 0.000	0.000 ± 0.000
5D-	0.000 ± 0.000	0.000 ± 0.000	0.000 ± 0.000	0.000 ± 0.000	0.000 ± 0.000	0.000 ± 0.000
MATH (Algebra)	0.023 ± 0.004	0.010 ± 0.003	0.013 ± 0.003	0.014 ± 0.003	0.017 ± 0.004	0.012 ± 0.003
MATH (Counting and Probability)	0.008 ± 0.004	0.004 ± 0.003	0.015 ± 0.006	0.017 ± 0.006	0.015 ± 0.006	0.017 ± 0.006
MATH (Geometry)	0.000 ± 0.000	0.013 ± 0.005	0.006 ± 0.004	0.015 ± 0.005	0.015 ± 0.005	0.006 ± 0.004
MATH (Intermediate Algebra)	0.010 ± 0.003	0.002 ± 0.002	0.007 ± 0.003	0.010 ± 0.003	0.011 ± 0.003	0.004 ± 0.002
MATH (Number Theory)	0.019 ± 0.006	0.009 ± 0.004	0.007 ± 0.004	0.011 ± 0.005	0.028 ± 0.007	0.019 ± 0.006
MATH (Pre-Algebra)	0.013 ± 0.004	0.008 ± 0.003	0.010 ± 0.003	0.011 ± 0.004	0.021 ± 0.005	0.013 ± 0.004
MATH (Pre-Calculus)	0.002 ± 0.002	0.002 ± 0.002	0.004 ± 0.003	0.000 ± 0.000	0.002 ± 0.002	0.000 ± 0.000

Table 9: Five-Shot Results on Basic Arithmetic and MATH (FairSeq Models)

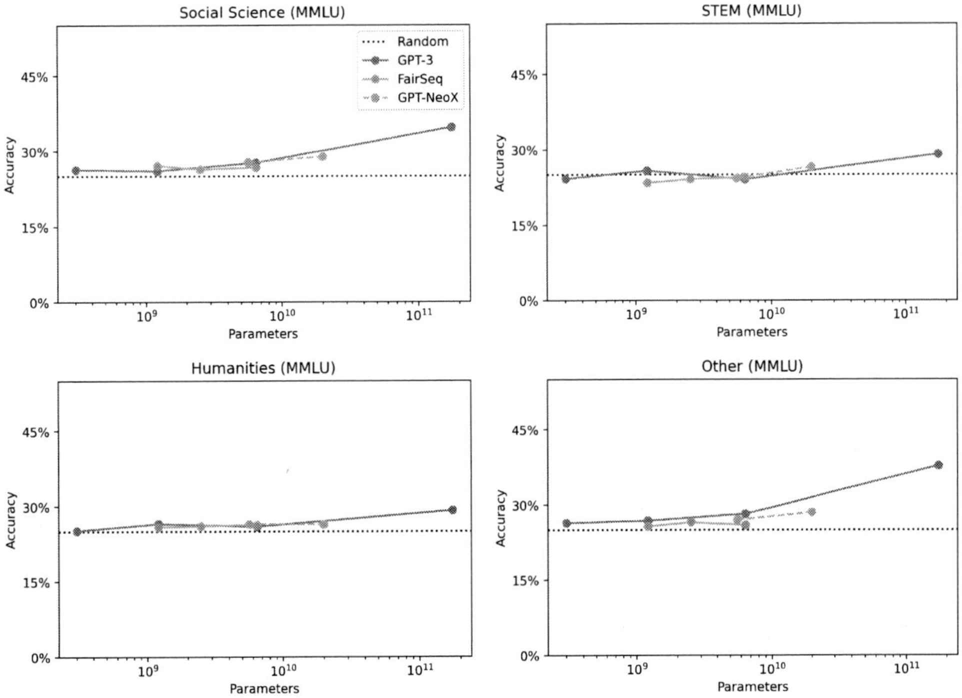

Figure 10: Zero-shot performance of GPT-NeoX-20B compared to GPT-J-6B and FairSeq and OpenAI models on Hendrycks et al. (2021a).

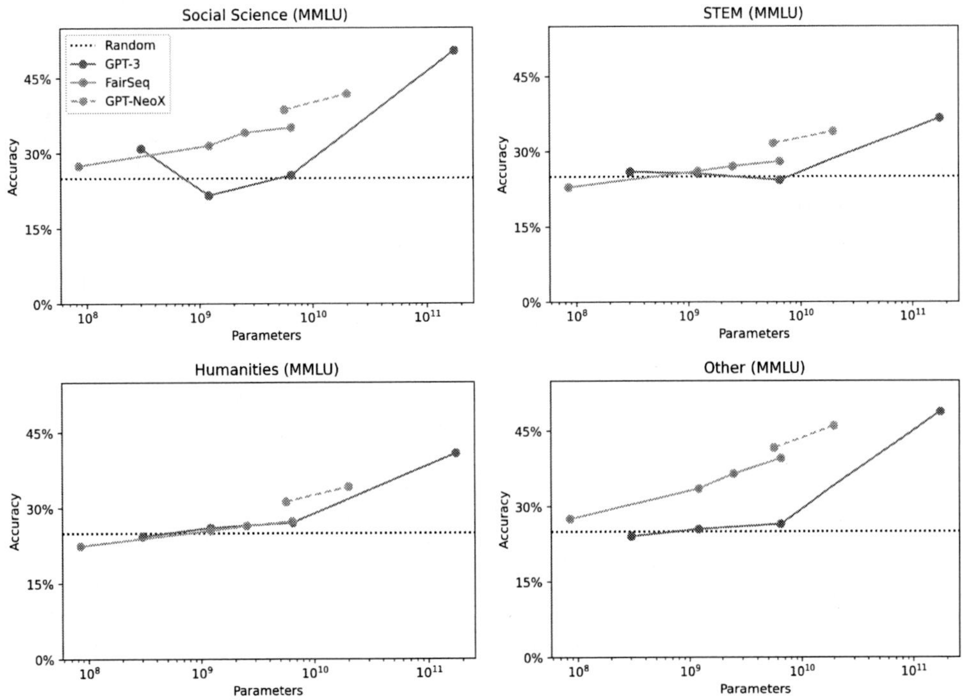

Figure 11: Five-shot performance of GPT-NeoX-20B compared to GPT-J-6B and FairSeq and OpenAI models on Hendrycks et al. (2021a). API limits we were unable to evaluate on the OpenAI API. Instead, we report numbers from Hendrycks et al. (2021a) with model sizes corrected.

Task	GPT-J 6B	GPT-NeoX 20B	GPT-3 Ada	GPT-3 Babbage	GPT-3 Curie	GPT-3 DaVinci
Abstract Algebra	0.260 ± 0.044	0.230 ± 0.042	0.170 ± 0.038	0.220 ± 0.042	0.220 ± 0.042	0.220 ± 0.042
Anatomy	0.274 ± 0.039	0.319 ± 0.040	0.207 ± 0.035	0.289 ± 0.039	0.274 ± 0.039	0.348 ± 0.041
Astronomy	0.243 ± 0.035	0.329 ± 0.038	0.237 ± 0.035	0.211 ± 0.033	0.237 ± 0.035	0.382 ± 0.040
Business Ethics	0.290 ± 0.046	0.280 ± 0.045	0.360 ± 0.048	0.330 ± 0.047	0.300 ± 0.046	0.390 ± 0.049
Clinical Knowledge	0.272 ± 0.027	0.291 ± 0.028	0.223 ± 0.026	0.234 ± 0.026	0.253 ± 0.027	0.317 ± 0.029
College Biology	0.285 ± 0.038	0.271 ± 0.037	0.271 ± 0.037	0.299 ± 0.038	0.208 ± 0.034	0.347 ± 0.040
College Chemistry	0.240 ± 0.043	0.160 ± 0.037	0.270 ± 0.045	0.290 ± 0.046	0.210 ± 0.041	0.250 ± 0.044
College Computer Science	0.270 ± 0.045	0.250 ± 0.044	0.310 ± 0.046	0.270 ± 0.045	0.240 ± 0.043	0.260 ± 0.044
College Mathematics	0.260 ± 0.044	0.240 ± 0.043	0.220 ± 0.042	0.160 ± 0.037	0.200 ± 0.040	0.170 ± 0.038
College Medicine	0.197 ± 0.030	0.283 ± 0.034	0.237 ± 0.032	0.202 ± 0.031	0.225 ± 0.032	0.289 ± 0.035
College Physics	0.206 ± 0.040	0.284 ± 0.045	0.304 ± 0.046	0.324 ± 0.047	0.255 ± 0.043	0.235 ± 0.042
Computer Security	0.270 ± 0.045	0.290 ± 0.046	0.250 ± 0.044	0.240 ± 0.043	0.320 ± 0.047	0.350 ± 0.048
Conceptual Physics	0.255 ± 0.029	0.294 ± 0.030	0.264 ± 0.029	0.260 ± 0.029	0.268 ± 0.029	0.294 ± 0.030
Econometrics	0.237 ± 0.040	0.289 ± 0.043	0.289 ± 0.043	0.246 ± 0.040	0.246 ± 0.040	0.228 ± 0.039
Electrical Engineering	0.359 ± 0.040	0.303 ± 0.038	0.338 ± 0.039	0.276 ± 0.037	0.310 ± 0.039	0.414 ± 0.041
Elementary Mathematics	0.254 ± 0.022	0.283 ± 0.023	0.243 ± 0.022	0.272 ± 0.023	0.249 ± 0.022	0.312 ± 0.024
Formal Logic	0.341 ± 0.042	0.294 ± 0.041	0.262 ± 0.039	0.349 ± 0.043	0.270 ± 0.040	0.294 ± 0.041
Global Facts	0.250 ± 0.044	0.220 ± 0.042	0.240 ± 0.043	0.240 ± 0.043	0.300 ± 0.046	0.290 ± 0.046
High School Biology	0.252 ± 0.025	0.300 ± 0.026	0.235 ± 0.024	0.232 ± 0.024	0.271 ± 0.025	0.335 ± 0.027
High School Chemistry	0.202 ± 0.028	0.236 ± 0.030	0.246 ± 0.030	0.241 ± 0.030	0.197 ± 0.028	0.232 ± 0.030
High School Computer Science	0.250 ± 0.044	0.210 ± 0.041	0.190 ± 0.039	0.240 ± 0.043	0.220 ± 0.042	0.290 ± 0.046
High School European History	0.261 ± 0.034	0.255 ± 0.034	0.224 ± 0.033	0.285 ± 0.035	0.261 ± 0.034	0.303 ± 0.036
High School Geography	0.202 ± 0.029	0.227 ± 0.030	0.217 ± 0.029	0.207 ± 0.029	0.242 ± 0.031	0.348 ± 0.034
High School Government and Politics	0.228 ± 0.030	0.228 ± 0.030	0.212 ± 0.030	0.181 ± 0.028	0.212 ± 0.030	0.326 ± 0.034
High School Macroeconomics	0.285 ± 0.023	0.328 ± 0.024	0.272 ± 0.023	0.277 ± 0.023	0.277 ± 0.023	0.303 ± 0.023
High School Mathematics	0.219 ± 0.025	0.263 ± 0.027	0.196 ± 0.024	0.230 ± 0.026	0.167 ± 0.023	0.248 ± 0.026

Table 10: Zero-Shot Results on Hendrycks Tasks, Part 1 (GPT-J, GPT-NeoX and GPT-3)

Task	GPT-J 6B	GPT-NeoX 20B	GPT-3 Ada	GPT-3 Babbage	GPT-3 Curie	GPT-3 DaVinci
High School Microeconomics	0.277 ± 0.029	0.294 ± 0.030	0.235 ± 0.028	0.265 ± 0.029	0.239 ± 0.028	0.307 ± 0.030
High School Physics	0.272 ± 0.036	0.298 ± 0.037	0.199 ± 0.033	0.298 ± 0.037	0.199 ± 0.033	0.219 ± 0.034
High School Physiology	0.273 ± 0.019	0.283 ± 0.019	0.209 ± 0.017	0.217 ± 0.018	0.246 ± 0.018	0.352 ± 0.020
High School Statistics	0.292 ± 0.031	0.319 ± 0.032	0.241 ± 0.029	0.278 ± 0.031	0.255 ± 0.030	0.278 ± 0.031
High School US History	0.289 ± 0.032	0.309 ± 0.032	0.255 ± 0.031	0.260 ± 0.031	0.240 ± 0.030	0.368 ± 0.034
High School World History	0.283 ± 0.029	0.295 ± 0.030	0.278 ± 0.029	0.262 ± 0.029	0.270 ± 0.029	0.321 ± 0.030
Human Aging	0.265 ± 0.030	0.224 ± 0.028	0.368 ± 0.032	0.336 ± 0.032	0.296 ± 0.031	0.327 ± 0.031
Human Sexuality	0.397 ± 0.043	0.405 ± 0.043	0.374 ± 0.042	0.427 ± 0.043	0.397 ± 0.043	0.481 ± 0.044
International Law	0.264 ± 0.040	0.298 ± 0.042	0.182 ± 0.035	0.207 ± 0.037	0.207 ± 0.037	0.331 ± 0.043
Jurisprudence	0.278 ± 0.043	0.250 ± 0.042	0.287 ± 0.044	0.278 ± 0.043	0.259 ± 0.042	0.370 ± 0.047
Logical Fallacies	0.294 ± 0.036	0.227 ± 0.033	0.239 ± 0.034	0.221 ± 0.033	0.245 ± 0.034	0.252 ± 0.034
Machine Learning	0.223 ± 0.040	0.268 ± 0.042	0.241 ± 0.041	0.286 ± 0.043	0.295 ± 0.043	0.232 ± 0.040
Management	0.233 ± 0.042	0.282 ± 0.045	0.184 ± 0.038	0.214 ± 0.041	0.320 ± 0.046	0.456 ± 0.049
Marketing	0.303 ± 0.030	0.321 ± 0.031	0.308 ± 0.030	0.282 ± 0.029	0.308 ± 0.030	0.491 ± 0.033
Medical Genetics	0.310 ± 0.046	0.340 ± 0.048	0.260 ± 0.044	0.300 ± 0.046	0.330 ± 0.047	0.430 ± 0.050
Miscellaneous	0.275 ± 0.016	0.299 ± 0.016	0.257 ± 0.016	0.269 ± 0.016	0.284 ± 0.016	0.450 ± 0.018
Moral Disputes	0.283 ± 0.024	0.289 ± 0.024	0.263 ± 0.024	0.263 ± 0.024	0.277 ± 0.024	0.301 ± 0.025
Moral Scenarios	0.237 ± 0.014	0.232 ± 0.014	0.238 ± 0.014	0.273 ± 0.015	0.238 ± 0.014	0.249 ± 0.014
Nutrition	0.346 ± 0.027	0.379 ± 0.028	0.301 ± 0.026	0.281 ± 0.026	0.291 ± 0.026	0.353 ± 0.027
Philosophy	0.260 ± 0.025	0.293 ± 0.026	0.215 ± 0.023	0.267 ± 0.025	0.244 ± 0.024	0.367 ± 0.027
Prehistory	0.244 ± 0.024	0.272 ± 0.025	0.244 ± 0.024	0.269 ± 0.025	0.284 ± 0.025	0.324 ± 0.026
Professional Accounting	0.262 ± 0.026	0.234 ± 0.025	0.202 ± 0.024	0.255 ± 0.026	0.238 ± 0.025	0.287 ± 0.027
Professional Law	0.241 ± 0.011	0.267 ± 0.011	0.261 ± 0.011	0.256 ± 0.011	0.259 ± 0.011	0.261 ± 0.011
Professional Medicine	0.276 ± 0.027	0.287 ± 0.027	0.221 ± 0.025	0.239 ± 0.026	0.265 ± 0.027	0.324 ± 0.028
Professional Psychology	0.284 ± 0.018	0.275 ± 0.018	0.245 ± 0.017	0.225 ± 0.017	0.257 ± 0.018	0.335 ± 0.019
Public Relations	0.282 ± 0.043	0.345 ± 0.046	0.255 ± 0.042	0.327 ± 0.045	0.364 ± 0.046	0.364 ± 0.046
Security Studies	0.363 ± 0.031	0.376 ± 0.031	0.367 ± 0.031	0.347 ± 0.030	0.384 ± 0.031	0.392 ± 0.031
Sociology	0.279 ± 0.032	0.284 ± 0.032	0.328 ± 0.033	0.303 ± 0.033	0.274 ± 0.032	0.368 ± 0.034
US Foreign Policy	0.340 ± 0.048	0.360 ± 0.048	0.330 ± 0.047	0.330 ± 0.047	0.380 ± 0.049	0.500 ± 0.050
Virology	0.355 ± 0.037	0.361 ± 0.037	0.307 ± 0.036	0.319 ± 0.036	0.337 ± 0.037	0.386 ± 0.038
World Religions	0.333 ± 0.036	0.386 ± 0.037	0.316 ± 0.036	0.310 ± 0.035	0.374 ± 0.037	0.398 ± 0.038

Table 11: Zero-Shot Results on Hendrycks Tasks, Part 2 (GPT-J, GPT-NeoX, and GPT-3)

Task	FairSeq 125M	355M	1.3B	2.7B	6.7B	13B
Abstract Algebra	0.260 ± 0.044	0.180 ± 0.039	0.230 ± 0.042	0.250 ± 0.044	0.240 ± 0.043	0.260 ± 0.044
Anatomy	0.178 ± 0.033	0.207 ± 0.035	0.185 ± 0.034	0.170 ± 0.032	0.259 ± 0.038	0.237 ± 0.037
Astronomy	0.270 ± 0.036	0.237 ± 0.035	0.243 ± 0.035	0.263 ± 0.036	0.296 ± 0.037	0.257 ± 0.036
Business Ethics	0.330 ± 0.047	0.410 ± 0.049	0.340 ± 0.048	0.350 ± 0.048	0.380 ± 0.049	0.340 ± 0.048
Clinical Knowledge	0.215 ± 0.025	0.264 ± 0.027	0.226 ± 0.026	0.249 ± 0.027	0.223 ± 0.026	0.264 ± 0.027
College Biology	0.285 ± 0.038	0.201 ± 0.034	0.243 ± 0.036	0.222 ± 0.035	0.271 ± 0.037	0.306 ± 0.039
College Chemistry	0.310 ± 0.046	0.290 ± 0.046	0.350 ± 0.048	0.300 ± 0.046	0.280 ± 0.045	0.240 ± 0.043
College Computer Science	0.200 ± 0.040	0.250 ± 0.044	0.260 ± 0.044	0.250 ± 0.044	0.300 ± 0.046	0.280 ± 0.045
College Mathematics	0.190 ± 0.039	0.170 ± 0.038	0.230 ± 0.042	0.200 ± 0.040	0.230 ± 0.042	0.250 ± 0.044
College Medicine	0.243 ± 0.033	0.237 ± 0.032	0.249 ± 0.033	0.254 ± 0.033	0.237 ± 0.032	0.260 ± 0.033
College Physics	0.216 ± 0.041	0.245 ± 0.043	0.216 ± 0.041	0.275 ± 0.044	0.343 ± 0.047	0.216 ± 0.041
Computer Security	0.240 ± 0.043	0.290 ± 0.046	0.300 ± 0.046	0.240 ± 0.043	0.230 ± 0.042	0.320 ± 0.047
Conceptual Physics	0.260 ± 0.029	0.255 ± 0.029	0.247 ± 0.028	0.243 ± 0.028	0.247 ± 0.028	0.204 ± 0.026
Econometrics	0.246 ± 0.040	0.272 ± 0.042	0.246 ± 0.040	0.281 ± 0.042	0.219 ± 0.039	0.263 ± 0.041
Electrical Engineering	0.283 ± 0.038	0.303 ± 0.038	0.234 ± 0.035	0.276 ± 0.037	0.310 ± 0.039	0.290 ± 0.038
Elementary Mathematics	0.246 ± 0.022	0.214 ± 0.021	0.233 ± 0.022	0.233 ± 0.022	0.246 ± 0.022	0.198 ± 0.021
Formal Logic	0.278 ± 0.040	0.302 ± 0.041	0.278 ± 0.040	0.310 ± 0.041	0.286 ± 0.040	0.333 ± 0.042
Global Facts	0.200 ± 0.040	0.210 ± 0.041	0.190 ± 0.039	0.150 ± 0.036	0.220 ± 0.042	0.160 ± 0.037
High School Biology	0.248 ± 0.025	0.255 ± 0.025	0.268 ± 0.025	0.226 ± 0.024	0.274 ± 0.025	0.235 ± 0.024
High School Chemistry	0.217 ± 0.029	0.207 ± 0.029	0.256 ± 0.031	0.281 ± 0.032	0.217 ± 0.029	0.266 ± 0.031
High School Computer Science	0.240 ± 0.043	0.230 ± 0.042	0.270 ± 0.045	0.240 ± 0.043	0.350 ± 0.048	0.280 ± 0.045
High School European History	0.230 ± 0.033	0.333 ± 0.037	0.279 ± 0.035	0.261 ± 0.034	0.273 ± 0.035	0.230 ± 0.033
High School Geography	0.263 ± 0.031	0.273 ± 0.032	0.222 ± 0.030	0.258 ± 0.031	0.207 ± 0.029	0.253 ± 0.031
High School Government and Politics	0.254 ± 0.031	0.290 ± 0.033	0.228 ± 0.030	0.233 ± 0.031	0.218 ± 0.030	0.187 ± 0.028
High School Macroeconomics	0.200 ± 0.020	0.272 ± 0.023	0.254 ± 0.022	0.269 ± 0.022	0.326 ± 0.024	0.256 ± 0.022
High School Mathematics	0.204 ± 0.025	0.189 ± 0.024	0.170 ± 0.023	0.226 ± 0.025	0.200 ± 0.024	0.193 ± 0.024

Table 12: Zero-Shot Results on Hendrycks Tasks, Part 1 (FairSeq Models)

Task	FairSeq 125M	355M	1.3B	2.7B	6.7B	13B
High School Microeconomics	0.248 ± 0.028	0.256 ± 0.028	0.244 ± 0.028	0.248 ± 0.028	0.269 ± 0.029	0.227 ± 0.027
High School Physics	0.238 ± 0.035	0.219 ± 0.034	0.258 ± 0.036	0.245 ± 0.035	0.232 ± 0.034	0.166 ± 0.030
High School Physiology	0.235 ± 0.018	0.272 ± 0.019	0.266 ± 0.019	0.284 ± 0.019	0.250 ± 0.019	0.261 ± 0.019
High School Statistics	0.222 ± 0.028	0.241 ± 0.029	0.269 ± 0.030	0.250 ± 0.030	0.287 ± 0.031	0.241 ± 0.029
High School US History	0.240 ± 0.030	0.284 ± 0.032	0.299 ± 0.032	0.299 ± 0.032	0.314 ± 0.033	0.294 ± 0.032
High School World History	0.283 ± 0.029	0.232 ± 0.027	0.270 ± 0.029	0.245 ± 0.028	0.300 ± 0.030	0.316 ± 0.030
Human Aging	0.274 ± 0.030	0.309 ± 0.031	0.323 ± 0.031	0.291 ± 0.031	0.296 ± 0.031	0.274 ± 0.030
Human Sexuality	0.252 ± 0.038	0.366 ± 0.042	0.328 ± 0.041	0.359 ± 0.042	0.359 ± 0.042	0.351 ± 0.042
International Law	0.157 ± 0.033	0.223 ± 0.038	0.240 ± 0.039	0.281 ± 0.041	0.264 ± 0.040	0.231 ± 0.038
Jurisprudence	0.241 ± 0.041	0.269 ± 0.043	0.287 ± 0.044	0.241 ± 0.041	0.213 ± 0.040	0.278 ± 0.043
Logical Fallacies	0.196 ± 0.031	0.221 ± 0.033	0.233 ± 0.033	0.196 ± 0.031	0.245 ± 0.034	0.221 ± 0.033
Machine Learning	0.232 ± 0.040	0.295 ± 0.043	0.348 ± 0.045	0.232 ± 0.040	0.259 ± 0.042	0.241 ± 0.041
Management	0.223 ± 0.041	0.311 ± 0.046	0.214 ± 0.041	0.291 ± 0.045	0.340 ± 0.047	0.262 ± 0.044
Marketing	0.295 ± 0.030	0.231 ± 0.028	0.286 ± 0.030	0.303 ± 0.030	0.333 ± 0.031	0.329 ± 0.031
Medical Genetics	0.250 ± 0.044	0.310 ± 0.046	0.310 ± 0.046	0.280 ± 0.045	0.270 ± 0.045	0.300 ± 0.046
Miscellaneous	0.258 ± 0.016	0.301 ± 0.016	0.264 ± 0.016	0.249 ± 0.015	0.284 ± 0.016	0.268 ± 0.016
Moral Disputes	0.269 ± 0.024	0.246 ± 0.023	0.220 ± 0.022	0.260 ± 0.024	0.269 ± 0.024	0.272 ± 0.024
Moral Scenarios	0.255 ± 0.015	0.236 ± 0.014	0.273 ± 0.015	0.238 ± 0.014	0.241 ± 0.014	0.253 ± 0.015
Nutrition	0.252 ± 0.025	0.261 ± 0.025	0.297 ± 0.026	0.297 ± 0.026	0.330 ± 0.027	0.304 ± 0.026
Philosophy	0.199 ± 0.023	0.219 ± 0.023	0.228 ± 0.024	0.222 ± 0.024	0.238 ± 0.024	0.270 ± 0.025
Prehistory	0.290 ± 0.025	0.222 ± 0.023	0.253 ± 0.024	0.228 ± 0.023	0.296 ± 0.025	0.235 ± 0.024
Professional Accounting	0.262 ± 0.026	0.220 ± 0.025	0.209 ± 0.024	0.170 ± 0.022	0.238 ± 0.025	0.266 ± 0.026
Professional Law	0.261 ± 0.011	0.261 ± 0.011	0.256 ± 0.011	0.256 ± 0.011	0.259 ± 0.011	0.261 ± 0.011
Professional Medicine	0.239 ± 0.026	0.254 ± 0.026	0.254 ± 0.026	0.206 ± 0.025	0.221 ± 0.025	0.195 ± 0.024
Professional Psychology	0.245 ± 0.017	0.247 ± 0.017	0.242 ± 0.017	0.248 ± 0.017	0.278 ± 0.018	0.252 ± 0.018
Public Relations	0.236 ± 0.041	0.245 ± 0.041	0.264 ± 0.042	0.227 ± 0.040	0.291 ± 0.044	0.291 ± 0.044
Security Studies	0.322 ± 0.030	0.331 ± 0.030	0.331 ± 0.030	0.335 ± 0.030	0.408 ± 0.031	0.359 ± 0.031
Sociology	0.234 ± 0.030	0.234 ± 0.030	0.259 ± 0.031	0.229 ± 0.030	0.234 ± 0.030	0.323 ± 0.033
US Foreign Policy	0.250 ± 0.044	0.300 ± 0.046	0.300 ± 0.046	0.310 ± 0.046	0.370 ± 0.049	0.330 ± 0.047
Virology	0.289 ± 0.035	0.301 ± 0.036	0.319 ± 0.036	0.355 ± 0.037	0.295 ± 0.036	0.331 ± 0.037
World Religions	0.292 ± 0.035	0.263 ± 0.034	0.287 ± 0.035	0.292 ± 0.035	0.269 ± 0.034	0.339 ± 0.036

Table 13: Zero-shot Results on Hendrycks Tasks, Part 2 (FairSeq Models)

F Tokenizer Analysis

Both tokenizers share 36938 out of 50257 tokens, a $\sim$73.5% overlap in tokens. In this section, we perform comparison between the GPT-NeoX-20B tokenizer to the GPT-2 tokenizer using the validation set of the Pile.

In Table 15, we show the resulting number of tokens from tokenizing each component of the Pile's validation set with both tokenizers, and the ratio of GPT-NeoX-20B tokens to GPT-2 tokens.

We observe that the GPT-NeoX-20B tokenizer represents all Pile components using fewer or very closely comparable numbers of tokens. The largest percentage improvement in token counts are in the EuroParl, GitHub, and PubMed Central components, with a more than 20% savings in the number of tokens needed to represent that component. We highlight that arXiv, GitHub, and StackExchange—subsets with large code components—can be represented with meaningfully fewer tokens with the GPT-NeoX-20B tokenizer compared to the GPT-2 tokenizer. Overall, the GPT-NeoX-20B tokenizer represents the Pile validation set with approximately 10% fewer tokens compared to the GPT-2 tokenizer.

Given that the GPT-NeoX-20B tokenizer is tweaked to better tokenize whitespace, we also perform a comparison between the two tokenizers excluding whitespace. We perform the same analysis as the above, but exclude all whitespace tokens from our computations, only counting the non-whitespace tokens. A token is considered a whitespace token if it consists only of whitespace characters. The results are shown in Table 16 in the Appendix. We observe that the GPT-NeoX-20B tokenizer still uses 5% fewer tokens to represent the Pile validation set compared to the GPT-2 tokenizer. As expected, the token ratios for certain components such as GitHub and StackExchange become closer to even once the whitespace characters are excluded.

	GPT-2	GPT-NeoX-20B	$\frac{\text{GPT-NeoX-20B}}{\text{GPT-2}}$
Pile (val)	383,111,734	342,887,807	0.89501
C4	173,669,294	173,768,876	1.001
C4 excl. Space	168,932,391	171,003,008	1.012

Table 14: Number of tokens from tokenizing the AllenAI C4 (en) validation set. The GPT-NeoX-20B tokenizer uses approximately the same number of tokens to represent C4 as the GPT-2 tokenizer.

While we evaluated our tokenizer using the validation set for the Pile, the Pile components would still be considered in-domain for the tokenizer and may not provide the most informative comparison point. To perform an out-of-domain comparison, we perform the same analysis using the AllenAI replication of C4,[15], another popular pretraining corpus for large language models. As above, we use the validation set for our analysis. Our results are shown in Table 14. We find that the GPT-NeoX-20B tokenizer tokenizes the C4 validation set to approximately the same number of tokens as the GPT-2 tokenizer. When excluding all whitespace tokens, the GPT-NeoX-20B requires approximately 1% more tokens to represent the corpus compared to the GPT-2 tokenizer.

F.1 Tokenizer Comparisons

F.1.1 Longest Tokens

We show in Table 17 the 10 longest tokens in each tokenizer vocabulary. We exclude consideration of tokens that comprise only symbols or whitespace characters. We observe that for the GPT-2 tokenizer, many of the longest tokens appear to reflect artifacts in the tokenizer training data, likely with certain websites or web-scrapes being overrepresented in the training data. For the GPT-NeoX-20B tokenizer, we observe that most of the longest tokens are scientific terms, likely arising from the PubMed components of the Pile.

F.1.2 Worst Case Word Tokenization Comparison

We consider the words for which there is the greatest discrepancy in the resulting token length between the two tokenizers, where one tokenizer needs many tokens to represent while the other tokenizer uses

[15] `https://github.com/allenai/allennlp/discussions/5056`

	GPT-2	GPT-NeoX-20B	$\frac{\text{GPT-NeoX-20B}}{\text{GPT-2}}$
arXiv	41,020,155	34,704,315	0.84603
BookCorpus2	2,336,388	2,365,633	1.01252
Books3	42,819,036	43,076,832	1.00602
DM Mathematics	7,699,527	7,413,775	0.96289
Enron Emails	480,500	433,867	0.90295
EuroParl	3,519,584	2,808,275	0.79790
FreeLaw	21,098,168	18,687,364	0.88573
GitHub	42,986,216	33,021,839	0.76820
Gutenberg (PG-19)	6,729,187	6,428,946	0.95538
HackerNews	2,578,933	2,551,720	0.98945
NIH ExPorter	776,688	739,558	0.95219
OpenSubtitles	5,431,529	5,446,485	1.00275
OpenWebText2	31,993,480	30,813,744	0.96313
PhilPapers	1,879,206	1,750,928	0.93174
Pile-CC	53,415,704	53,392,389	0.99956
PubMed Abstracts	8,708,180	8,215,529	0.94343
PubMed Central	56,874,247	43,534,166	0.76545
StackExchange	22,708,643	19,000,198	0.83669
USPTO Backgrounds	10,217,886	9,727,223	0.95198
Ubuntu IRC	3,341,287	2,771,066	0.82934
Wikipedia (en)	12,614,087	12,692,048	1.00618
YoutubeSubtitles	3,883,103	3,311,907	0.85290
Total	383,111,734	342,887,807	0.89501

Table 15: Number of tokens from tokenizing the Pile validation set. The GPT-NeoX-20B tokenizer uses fewer tokens to represent the Pile overall, with the biggest gains in whitespace heavy datasets such as arXiv, GitHub and StackExchange.

	GPT-2	GPT-NeoX-20B	$\frac{\text{GPT-NeoX-20B}}{\text{GPT-2}}$
arXiv	38,932,524	33,561,364	0.86204
BookCorpus2	2,233,367	2,262,609	1.01309
Books3	40,895,236	41,198,424	1.00741
DM Mathematics	7,214,874	6,929,066	0.96039
Enron Emails	374,978	373,498	0.99605
EuroParl	3,482,120	2,780,405	0.79848
FreeLaw	17,766,692	17,434,708	0.98131
GitHub	29,338,176	27,558,966	0.93936
Gutenberg (PG-19)	5,838,580	5,827,408	0.99809
HackerNews	2,312,116	2,299,848	0.99469
NIH ExPorter	776,619	739,543	0.95226
OpenSubtitles	5,428,118	5,445,721	1.00324
OpenWebText2	30,849,218	29,723,143	0.96350
PhilPapers	1,872,347	1,743,627	0.93125
Pile-CC	51,305,080	51,281,909	0.99955
PubMed Abstracts	8,676,790	8,185,417	0.94337
PubMed Central	44,508,570	40,722,151	0.91493
StackExchange	17,414,955	16,712,814	0.95968
USPTO Backgrounds	9,882,473	9,601,385	0.97156
Ubuntu IRC	3,220,797	2,659,225	0.82564
Wikipedia (en)	11,874,878	11,986,567	1.00941
YoutubeSubtitles	3,589,042	3,046,451	0.84882
Total	337,787,550	322,074,249	0.95348

Table 16: Number of tokens from tokenizing the Pile validation set, excluding whitespace tokens.

relatively few tokens. We define a word as a contiguous string delimited by whitespace or punctuation (as defined by `strings.punctuation` in Python). We perform this analysis at the component level. We only consider words that occur at least 10 times within the given component. We show in Table 18 a representative example from the Pile-CC corpus.

G Tokenization Examples

In Figures 12 and 17, we show examples of tokenized documents from the Pile, comparing the GPT-2 tokenizer to ours.

GPT-2	GPT-NeoX-20B
`rawdownloadcloneembedreportprint`	`Ġimmunohistochemistry`
`BuyableInstoreAndOnline`	`Ġimmunohistochemical`
`cloneembedreportprint`	`Ġtelecommunications`
`ĠRandomRedditorWithNo`	`Ġimmunofluorescence`
`Ġtelecommunications`	`Ġimmunosuppressive`
`channelAvailability`	`ĠBytePtrFromString`
`Ġdisproportionately`	`Ġmultidisciplinary`
`ĠTelecommunications`	`Ġhistopathological`
`ĠguiActiveUnfocused`	`Ġneurodegenerative`
`ItemThumbnailImage`	`Ġindistinguishable`

Table 17: Ten longest tokens (excluding tokens comprising mainly symbols, numbers and spaces) in tokenizer vocabularies. "Ġ" indicates a word delimiter.

GPT-2 Worst-case Tokenization			GPT-NeoX-20B Worst-case Tokenization		
Word	GPT-2 Tokenization	GPT-NeoX-20B Tokenization	Word	GPT-2 Tokenization	GPT-NeoX-20B Tokenization
hematopoietic	(6) hematopoietic	(1) hematopoietic	Schwarzenegger	(1) Schwarzenegger	(5) Schwarzenegger
adenocarcinoma	(6) adenocarcinoma	(1) adenocarcinoma	Bolshevik	(1) Bolshevik	(4) Bolshevik
MERCHANTABILITY	(5) MERCHANTABILITY	(1) MERCHANTABILITY	crowdfunding	(1) crowdfunding	(4) crowdfunding
CONSEQUENTIAL	(5) CONSEQUENTIAL	(1) CONSEQUENTIAL	misogyny	(1) misogyny	(4) misogyny
oligonucleotides	(5) oligonucleotides	(1) oligonucleotides	McAuliffe	(1) McAuliffe	(4) McAuliffe
cytoplasmic	(5) cytoplasmic	(1) cytoplasmic	unstoppable	(1) unstoppable	(4) unstoppable
corticosteroids	(4) corticosteroids	(1) corticosteroids	Timberwolves	(1) Timberwolves	(4) Timberwolves
neurodegenerative	(4) neurodegenerative	(1) neurodegenerative	excruciating	(1) excruciating	(4) excruciating
asymptotic	(4) asymptotic	(1) asymptotic	Kaepernick	(1) Kaepernick	(4) Kaepernick
aneurysm	(4) aneurysm	(1) aneurysm	Valkyrie	(1) Valkyrie	(4) Valkyrie

Table 18: Worst case word tokenization with respective tokenizers. We show cases where one tokenizer requires many more tokens to represent a word compared to the other tokenizer.

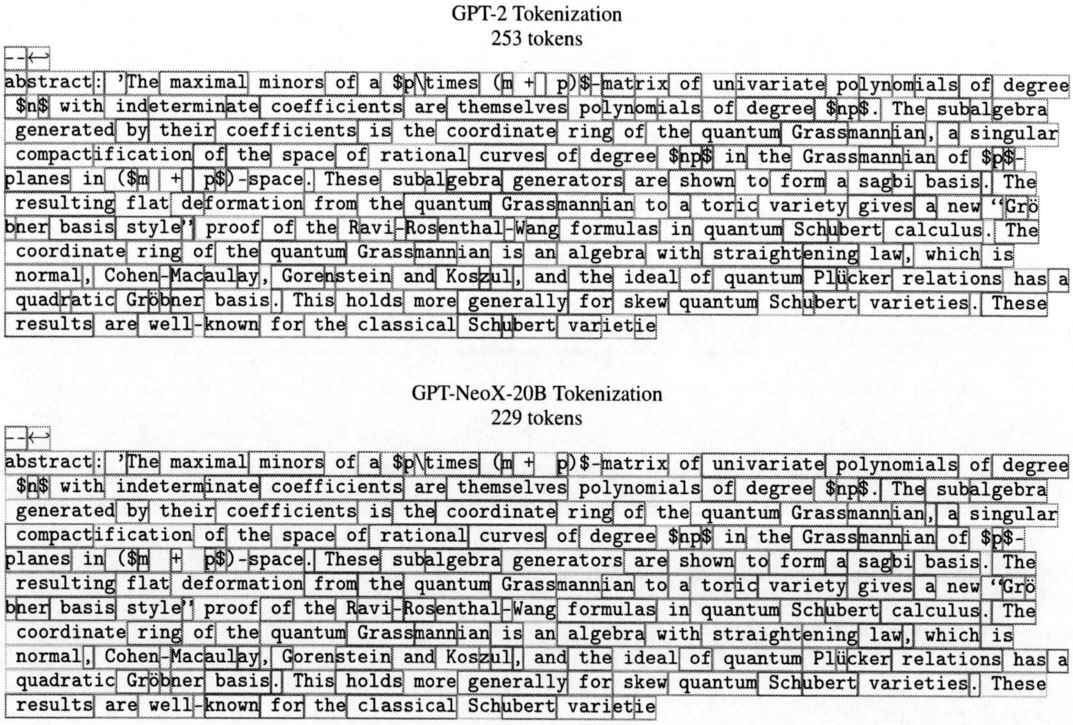

Figure 12: Pile (arXiv) Tokenization Example

GPT-2 Tokenization
224 tokens

↩
↩
THE TRAP↩
↩
Beverley Kendall↩
↩
Copyright © Beverley Kendall 2014↩
↩
Published by Season Publishing LLC↩
↩
This is a work of fiction. Names, characters, places and incidents are products of the author
's imagination or are used fictitiously and are not to be construed as real. Any resemblance to
actual events, locales, organizations, or persons, living or dead, is completely coincidental.
↩↩
www.beverleykendall.com↩↩
Cover Design © Okay Creations, Sarah Hansen↩↩
All rights reserved. Except as permitted under the U.S. Copyright Act of 1976, no part of this
publication may be reproduced, distributed or transmitted in any form or by any means, or
stored in a database or retrieval system, without the prior written permission of the author
.↩
↩
** License Statement **↩
↩
This ebook is licensed for your personal enjoyment only. This ebook may not be re-sold or given
away to other people. If you would like to share this book with another person, please purchase
an additional copy for each reader. If

GPT-NeoX-20B Tokenization
228 tokens

↩
↩
THE TRAP↩
↩
Beverley Kendall↩
↩
Copyright © Beverley Kendall 2014↩
↩
Published by Season Publishing LLC↩
↩
This is a work of fiction. Names, characters, places and incidents are products of the author
's imagination or are used fictitiously and are not to be construed as real. Any resemblance to
actual events, locales, organizations, or persons, living or dead, is completely coincidental.
↩↩
www.beverleykendall.com↩↩
Cover Design © Okay Creations, Sarah Hansen↩↩
All rights reserved. Except as permitted under the U.S. Copyright Act of 1976, no part of this
publication may be reproduced, distributed or transmitted in any form or by any means, or
stored in a database or retrieval system, without the prior written permission of the author
.↩
↩
** License Statement **↩
↩
This ebook is licensed for your personal enjoyment only. This ebook may not be re-sold or given
away to other people. If you would like to share this book with another person, please purchase
an additional copy for each reader. If

Figure 13: Pile (BookCorpus2) Tokenization Example

GPT-2 Tokenization
477 tokens

```
o?↩
True↩
Suppose -3*t = 1 + 8. Let s(d) = d**3 + 6*d**2 + 2*d + 1. Let u be s(t). Suppose 10 = 5*z, 5*a +
0*z = -z + u. Is 4 a factor of a?↩
True↩
Suppose 5*l = r - 35, -2*r + 5*l - 15 = -70. Is r a multiple of 4?↩
True↩
Suppose 2*l + 11 - 1 = 0. Does 15 divide (-2)/l - 118/(-5)?↩
False↩
Suppose 3*k - 3*f + 0*f - 72 = 0, -25 = -5*f. Is 9 a factor of 2/(-4) + k/2?↩
False↩
Suppose 6*w + 25 = w. Let t(c) = c + 9. Let u be t(w). Suppose -u*z = -3*z - 10. Is z a multiple
of 5?↩
True↩
Let j = 81 + -139. Let i = j + 101. Is 11 a factor of i?↩
False↩
Let q(s) = s**3 + 4*s**2 - s + 2. Let u be q(-4). Let o(w) = w**2 + w - 6. Let t be o(u).
Suppose -3*l - 39 = -3*d - 2*l, 0 = 3*d - 2*l - t. Does 9 divide d?↩
False↩
Suppose -2*b + 39 + 13 = 0. Is b a multiple of 14?↩
False↩
Let q = -7 + 12. Suppose 8*l = q*l + 81. Suppose 129 = 4*f - l. Is 13 a factor of f?↩
True↩
Suppose 0 = -4*n + j + 33, 4*n - n + 4*j = 20. Let c = 5 - n. Is 35*1 - (-6)/c a multiple of 11?
↩
True↩
Let g(m) = m**2 - 2*m - 3. Let k be g(3). Let j be
```

GPT-NeoX-20B Tokenization
468 tokens

```
o?↩
True↩
Suppose -3*t = 1 + 8. Let s(d) = d**3 + 6*d**2 + 2*d + 1. Let u be s(t). Suppose 10 = 5*z, 5*a +
0*z = -z + u. Is 4 a factor of a?↩
True↩
Suppose 5*l = r - 35, -2*r + 5*l - 15 = -70. Is r a multiple of 4?↩
True↩
Suppose 2*l + 11 - 1 = 0. Does 15 divide (-2)/l - 118/(-5)?↩
False↩
Suppose 3*k - 3*f + 0*f - 72 = 0, -25 = -5*f. Is 9 a factor of 2/(-4) + k/2?↩
False↩
Suppose 6*w + 25 = w. Let t(c) = c + 9. Let u be t(w). Suppose -u*z = -3*z - 10. Is z a multiple
of 5?↩
True↩
Let j = 81 + -139. Let i = j + 101. Is 11 a factor of i?↩
False↩
Let q(s) = s**3 + 4*s**2 - s + 2. Let u be q(-4). Let o(w) = w**2 + w - 6. Let t be o(u).
Suppose -3*l - 39 = -3*d - 2*l, 0 = 3*d - 2*l - t. Does 9 divide d?↩
False↩
Suppose -2*b + 39 + 13 = 0. Is b a multiple of 14?↩
False↩
Let q = -7 + 12. Suppose 8*l = q*l + 81. Suppose 129 = 4*f - l. Is 13 a factor of f?↩
True↩
Suppose 0 = -4*n + j + 33, 4*n - n + 4*j = 20. Let c = 5 - n. Is 35*1 - (-6)/c a multiple of 11?
↩
True↩
Let g(m) = m**2 - 2*m - 3. Let k be g(3). Let j be
```

Figure 14: Pile (DM Mathematics) Tokenization Example

GPT-2 Tokenization
430 tokens

```
<at-dialog title="vm.title" on-close="vm.onClose">
    <at-form state="vm.form" autocomplete="off" id="external_test_form">
        <at-input-group col="12" tab="20" state="vm.form.inputs" form-id="external_test"></at-
input-group>
        <at-action-group col="12" pos="right">
            <at-action-button
                variant="tertiary"
                ng-click="vm.onClose()"
            >
                ::vm.strings.get('CLOSE')
            </at-action-button>
            <at-action-button
                variant="primary"
                ng-click="vm.onSubmit()"
                ng-disabled="!vm.form.isValid || vm.form.disabled"
            >
                ::vm.strings.get('RUN')
            </at-action-button>
        </at-action-group>
    </at-form>
</at-dialog>
```

GPT-NeoX-20B Tokenization
257 tokens

```
<at-dialog title="vm.title" on-close="vm.onClose">
    <at-form state="vm.form" autocomplete="off" id="external_test_form">
        <at-input-group col="12" tab="20" state="vm.form.inputs" form-id="external_test"></at-
input-group>
        <at-action-group col="12" pos="right">
            <at-action-button
                variant="tertiary"
                ng-click="vm.onClose()"
            >
                ::vm.strings.get('CLOSE')
            </at-action-button>
            <at-action-button
                variant="primary"
                ng-click="vm.onSubmit()"
                ng-disabled="!vm.form.isValid || vm.form.disabled"
            >
                ::vm.strings.get('RUN')
            </at-action-button>
        </at-action-group>
    </at-form>
</at-dialog>
```

Figure 15: Pile (GitHub) Tokenization Example

GPT-2 Tokenization
178 tokens

Theresa May is expected to appoint an EU ambassador who ‘‘believes in Brexit’’ in the wake of the current Brussels representative’s decision to quit after being cut adrift by Downing Street.↵
↵
↵
Sir Ivan Rogers on Tuesday announced his resignation as Britain’s ambassador in Brussels after it was made clear Mrs May and her senior team had ‘‘lost confidence’’ in him over his ‘‘pessimistic’’ view of Brexit.↵
↵
Government sources made clear that Sir Ivan had ‘‘jumped before he was pushed’’ and that Number 10 believed his negative view of Brexit meant that he could not lead the negotiations after the Prime Minister triggers Article 50.↵
↵
In a 1,400-word resignation letter to his staff leaked on Tuesday night, Sir Ivan launched a thinly-veiled attack on the "muddled thinking" in Mrs May’s Government.

GPT-NeoX-20B Tokenization
170 tokens

Theresa May is expected to appoint an EU ambassador who ‘‘believes in Brexit’’ in the wake of the current Brussels representative’s decision to quit after being cut adrift by Downing Street.↵
↵
↵
Sir Ivan Rogers on Tuesday announced his resignation as Britain’s ambassador in Brussels after it was made clear Mrs May and her senior team had ‘‘lost confidence’’ in him over his ‘‘pessimistic’’ view of Brexit.↵
↵
Government sources made clear that Sir Ivan had ‘‘jumped before he was pushed’’ and that Number 10 believed his negative view of Brexit meant that he could not lead the negotiations after the Prime Minister triggers Article 50.↵
↵
In a 1,400-word resignation letter to his staff leaked on Tuesday night, Sir Ivan launched a thinly-veiled attack on the "muddled thinking" in Mrs May’s Government.

Figure 16: Pile (OpenWebText2) Tokenization Example

GPT-2 Tokenization
268 tokens

Carotid endarterectomy: operative risks, recurrent stenosis, and long-term stroke rates in a modern series.↵
To determine whether carotid endarterectomy (CEA) safely and effectively maintained a durable reduction in stroke complications over an extended period, we reviewed our data on 478 consecutive patients who underwent 544 CEA’s since 1976. Follow-up was complete in 83% of patients (mean 44 months). There were 7 early deaths (1.3%), only 1 stroke related (0.2%). Perioperative stroke rates (overall 2.9%) varied according to operative indications: asymptomatic, 1.4%; transient ischemic attacks (TIA)/amaurosis fugax (AF), 1.3%; nonhemispheric symptoms (NH), 4.9%; and prior stroke (CVA), 7.1%. Five and 10-year stroke-free rates were 96% and 92% in the asymptomatic group, 93% and 87% in the TIA/AF group, 92% and 92% in the NH group, and 80% and 73% in the CVA group. Late ipsilateral strokes occurred infrequently (8 patients, 1.7%). Late deaths were primarily cardiac related (51.3%). Stro

GPT-NeoX-20B Tokenization
250 tokens

Carotid endarterectomy: operative risks, recurrent stenosis, and long-term stroke rates in a modern series.↵
To determine whether carotid endarterectomy (CEA) safely and effectively maintained a durable reduction in stroke complications over an extended period, we reviewed our data on 478 consecutive patients who underwent 544 CEA’s since 1976. Follow-up was complete in 83% of patients (mean 44 months). There were 7 early deaths (1.3%), only 1 stroke related (0.2%). Perioperative stroke rates (overall 2.9%) varied according to operative indications: asymptomatic, 1.4%; transient ischemic attacks (TIA)/amaurosis fugax (AF), 1.3%; nonhemispheric symptoms (NH), 4.9%; and prior stroke (CVA), 7.1%. Five and 10-year stroke-free rates were 96% and 92% in the asymptomatic group, 93% and 87% in the TIA/AF group, 92% and 92% in the NH group, and 80% and 73% in the CVA group. Late ipsilateral strokes occurred infrequently (8 patients, 1.7%). Late deaths were primarily cardiac related (51.3%). Stro

Figure 17: Pile (PubMed Abstracts) Tokenization Example

Dataset Debt in Biomedical Language Modeling

Jason Alan Fries[*1,2] **Natasha Seelam**[*3] **Gabriel Altay**[*4] **Leon Weber**[*5,12]

Myungsun Kang[*6] **Debajyoti Datta**[*7] **Ruisi Su**[*8] **Samuele Garda**[*5]

Bo Wang[9] **Simon Ott**[10] **Matthias Samwald**[10] **Wojciech Kusa**[11]

[1] Stanford University [2] Snorkel AI [3] Sherlock Biosciences [4] Tempus Labs, Inc.
[5] Humboldt-Universität zu Berlin [6] Immuneering Corporation [7] University of Virginia
[8] Sway AI [9] Massachusetts General Hospital [10] Medical University of Vienna [11] TU Wien
[12] Max Delbrück Center for Molecular Medicine * Equal Contribution

Abstract

Large-scale language modeling and natural language prompting have demonstrated exciting capabilities for few and zero shot learning in NLP. However, translating these successes to specialized domains such as biomedicine remains challenging, due in part to biomedical NLP's significant *dataset debt* – the technical costs associated with data that are not consistently documented or easily incorporated into popular machine learning frameworks at scale. To assess this debt, we crowdsourced curation of datasheets for 167 biomedical datasets. We find that only 13% of datasets are available via programmatic access and 30% lack any documentation on licensing and permitted reuse. Our dataset catalog is available at: `https://tinyurl.com/bigbio22`.

1 Introduction

Natural language prompting has recently demonstrated significant benefits for language model pretraining, including unifying task inputs for large-scale multi-task supervision (Raffel et al., 2019) and improving zero-shot classification via explicit, multi-task prompted training data (Wei et al., 2022; Sanh et al., 2022). With performance gains reported when scaling to thousands of prompted training tasks (Xu et al., 2022), tools that enable large-scale integration of expert-labeled datasets hold great promise for improving zero-shot learning.

However, translating these successes to specialized domains such as biomedicine face strong headwinds due in part to the current state of dataset accessibility in biomedical NLP. Recently *data cascades* was proposed as a term-of-art for the costs of undervaluing data in machine learning (Sambasivan et al., 2021). We propose a similar term, *dataset debt*, to capture the technical costs (Sculley et al., 2015) of using datasets which are largely open and findable, but inconsistently documented, structured, and otherwise inaccessible via a consistent, programmatic interface. This type of debt creates significant practical challenges when integrating complex domain-specific corpora into popular machine learning frameworks.

We claim that biomedical NLP suffers from significant dataset debt. For example, while HuggingFace's popular Datasets library (Lhoest et al., 2021) contains over 3,000 datasets, biomedical data are underrepresented and favor tasks with general domain appeal such as question answering or semantic similarity (PubmedQA, SciTail, BIOSSES). To assess the state of biomedical dataset debt, we built, to our knowledge, the largest catalog of metadata for publicly available biomedical datasets. We document provenance, licensing, and other key attributes per (Gebru et al., 2021) to help guide future efforts for improving dataset access and machine learning reproducibility.

Our effort found low overall support for programmatic access, with only 13% (22/167) of our datasets present in the Datasets hub. Despite a proliferation of schemas designed to standardize dataset loading and harmonize task semantics. there remains no consistent, API interface for easily incorporating biomedical data into language model training at scale.

2 Data-Centric Machine Learning

Deep learning models are increasingly moving to commodified architectures. *Data-centric machine learning* (vs. model-centric) is inspired by the observation that the performance gains provided by novel architectures are often smaller than gains obtained using better training data. We outline some key challenges and opportunities in data-centric language modeling. These are broadly applicable to NLP, but have strong relevance to biomedicine

Proceedings of BigScience Episode #5 – Workshop on Challenges & Perspectives in Creating Large Language Models, pages 137 - 145
May 27, 2022

and the current state of dataset debt.

2.1 Curating and Cleaning Training Data

Popular language models such as GPT-3 (Brown et al., 2020) do not incorporate scientific or medical corpora in their training mixture, contributing to their lower performance when used in biomedical domains and few-shot tasks (Moradi et al., 2021). Additionally, simply training the language model on in-domain data might lead to non-trivial risks associated with the recapitulated biases from the training corpora (Zhang et al., 2020; Gururangan et al., 2022).

In scientific literature, discounting source provenance could manifest as language models parroting conflicting or inaccurate scientific findings. Zhao et al.(Zhao et al., 2022) curated scientific corpora to identify patient-specific information (e.g., mining PubMed Central to identify case reports that respect licensing for re-use and re-distribution). With sufficient metadata and dataset provenance, this level of curation could be extended to the entire training corpus for a biomedical language model.

Data cleaning has a large impact on language model performance. Deduplicating data leads to more accurate, more generalizable models requiring fewer training steps (Cohen et al., 2013; Lee et al., 2021). Cleaning up the consistency of answer response strings was reported to improve biomedical question answering (Yoon et al., 2021). Duplication contamination is a serious risk in biomedical datasets, which often iteratively build or extend prior annotations, introducing risk of test leakage in evaluation (Elangovan et al., 2021).

2.2 Programmatic Labeling

Biomedical domains require specialized knowledge, making expert-labeled datasets time-consuming and expensive to generate. In limited-data settings, distant and weakly supervised methods (Craven and Kumlien, 1999) are often used to combine curated, structured resources (e.g., knowledge bases, ontologies) with expert rules to programmatically label data. These approaches have demonstrated success across NER, relation extraction, and other biomedical applications (Kuleshov et al., 2019; Fries et al., 2021). However these approaches typically are applied to real, albeit unlabeled data, creating challenges when modeling rare classes. A recent trend is transforming structured resources directly into realistic-looking, but synthetic training examples. KELM (Agarwal et al., 2021) converts Wiki knowledge graph triplets into synthesized natural language text for language model pretraining.

Natural language prompting has emerged as a powerful technique for zero/few shot learning, where task guidance from prompts reduces sample complexity (Le Scao and Rush, 2021). Cross-lingual prompting (English prompts, non-English examples) has demonstrated competitive classification performance (Lin et al., 2021). Training language models directly on prompts has resulted in large gains in zero-shot performance over GPT-3 as well as producing models with fewer trained parameters (Sanh et al., 2022; Wei et al., 2022).

PromptSource (Bach et al., 2022) is a recent software platform for creating prompts and applying them to existing labeled datasets to build training data. These developments highlight a promising trend toward defining programmatic transformations on top of existing datasets, enabling them to be configured into new tasks. However, leveraging large-scale prompting remains challenging in biomedicine due to the lack of programmatic access to a large, diverse collections of biomedical datasets and tasks.

2.3 Diverse Evaluation and Benchmarking

Inspired by standardized benchmarks in general domain NLP research (Wang et al., 2018, 2019), BioNLP takes similar initiatives by establishing a benchmark of 10 datasets spanning 5 tasks (Peng et al., 2019, BLUE), an improved benchmark on BLUE with 13 datasets in 6 tasks (Gu et al., 2022, BLURB), and a benchmark of 9 different tasks for Chinese biomedical NLP (Zhang et al., 2021, CBLUE). While these benchmarks provide tools for consistent evaluation, only BLURB supports a leaderboard and none directly provide dataset access. Evaluation frameworks that provide programmatic access are often restricted to single and well-established tasks and impose pre-processing choices that can make inconsistent performance comparisons (Crichton et al., 2017; Weber et al., 2021).

To the best of our knowledge, there are currently no zero-shot evaluation frameworks for biomedical data similar to BIG-Bench[1], which currently contains little-to-no biomedical tasks.

Evaluation frameworks must also allow probing the trained language models' intrinsic properties,

[1] https://github.com/google/BIG-bench

rather than only measure downstream classification performance. Following (Petroni et al., 2019) in the general NLP domain, (Sung et al., 2021) introduce BioLAMA, a benchmark making available 49K biomedical knowledge triplets to probe the relational knowledge present in pre-trained language models.

3 Datasets Summary

3.1 Metadata/Datasheet Curation

Our inclusion criteria targeted expert-annotated datasets designated as public, reusable research benchmarks for one or more NLP tasks. We excluded: (1) multimodal datasets where removing the non-text modality undermines the task, e.g., visual question answering, audio transcription, image-to-text generation; (2) general resource datasets, e.g, the PMC Open Access Subset, MIMIC-III (Johnson et al., 2016); (3) derived resources, e.g., knowledge bases constructed via text mining; and (4) modeling artifacts, e.g., static embeddings or pretrained language models.

We recruited 8 volunteers to identify datasets and crowdsource their metadata curation for an open, community dataset catalog. Participants reviewed dataset publications and websites which described the curation process, and then completed the metadata schema outlined in Table 1 This schema loosely assesses compliance with FAIR data principles (Wilkinson et al., 2016).

Our initial effort identified 101 datasets. We combined this list with a contemporaneously curated catalog of biomedical datasets, identified via systematic literature review (Blagec et al., 2022). Since the catalog described in Blagec et al. (2022) was generated using broader inclusion criteria (e.g., non-public data, imaging and video datasets) we identified 104/475 entries that met our criteria. After merging, we conducted a second round of crowdsourcing to annotate metadata, resulting in our current catalog of 167 biomedical datasets. We did not conduct a formal assessment of inter-annotator agreement.

Field	Description
Name	Dataset name
Task Types	NER, NED, QA, NLI, coreference resolution, etc.
Domain	Corpora domain: biomedical or clinical/health
File Format	BioC, JSON, etc.
Annotations	Expert label provenance
API Access	Available via HuggingFace Datasets?
Splits	Canonical definitions for training/validation/testing splits
License	Provided license type
Languages	Included languages
Multilingual	Parallel corpora
Publication	Manuscript describing dataset
Year	Publication year
Citations	Google Scholar counts
Homepage	Website describing dataset
Public URL	Open URL (no authentication)
Dead Link	Dataset no longer accessible

Table 1: Metadata collected for all biomedical datasets. See Appendix A for more details on each category.

4 Results

4.1 Dataset Access

Only 22/167 (13%) of biomedical datasets are available via the Datasets API, despite 123/167 (74%) being openly hosted on public websites. The remaining datasets require authentication to access (21%) or were dead links (5%).

Format	Name	Count	Total
Structured	BioC	5	3%
Structured	BRAT	16	10%
Structured	CoNLL	11	7%
Structured	PubTator	4	2%
Semi-structured	XML	26	16%
Semi-structured	JSON	43	26%
Semi-structured	TSV/CSV	15	9%
Semi-structured	TMX	1	1%
Plain Text	Standoff	13	8%
Plain Text	Text	25	15%
Plain Text	ARFF	1	1%
Binary	Word	1	1%
Binary	Excel	2	1%
Unknown	Unknown	4	2%

Table 2: Distribution of file formats for biomedical datasets.

Table 2 outlines the diversity of commonly used biomedical file formats. Most datasets are provided in semi-structured form (51%), followed by structured (22%), and non-standard plain text files

(17%). There are several structured formats which propose a data model for parsing and standardizing task semantics (e.g., BRAT (Stenetorp et al., 2012), BioC (Comeau et al., 2013)). However, for information extraction tasks which could use these formats, only 31/86 (36%) actually do.

Table 2 outlines dataset licensing, broken down into six categories, largely based on commercial vs. non-commercial restrictions. These cover broad classes of licensing, ranging from permissive Creative Commons Share-Alike licenses to dataset-specific data-use agreements (DUA). Nearly 30% of datasets are publicly available online yet do not include any licensing information. A further 16.8% have DUA requirements, but include unclear language on what restrictions are placed on dataset usage.

License	Restrictions	Count	Percent
Public	C/NC	56	33.5%
Public	NC	13	7.8%
DUA	C/NC	12	7.2%
DUA	NC	8	4.8%
DUA	?	28	16.8%
Unknown	?	50	29.9%

Table 3: Dataset licenses. Restrictions are commercial (C), non-commercial (NC) and unknown (?).

4.2 Dataset and Task Diversity

Biomedical datasets (i.e., tasks built from scientific publications) made up 68% of available datasets while clinical datasets (patient notes, health news, clinical trial reports) made up 32%.

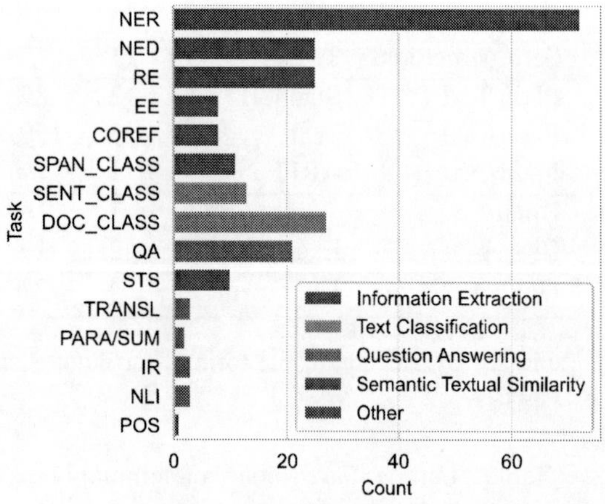

Figure 1: All NLP tasks, broken down into 5 categories (see legend). Note datasets often support multiple tasks.

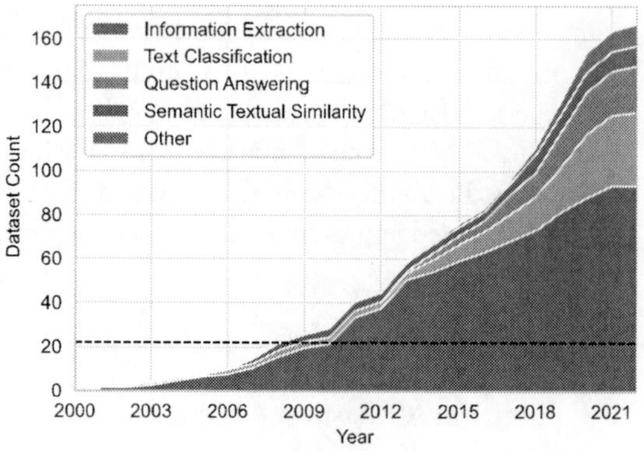

Figure 2: Cumulative count of datasets by task, ordered by year of dataset release. The black dashed line indicates the total number available via the Datasets API.

Fig.2 shows the overall homogeneity of public biomedical datasets as of 2022. Information extraction tasks (e.g., NER, NED, releation extraction, coreference resolution) comprise 56%, followed by 20% text classification (e.g, document labeling, sentiment analysis), 13% question answering, and 6% semantic similarity.

Task Category	Eng.	Non-Eng.
Information Extraction	128	34
Text Classification	33	10
Question Answering	21	0
Semantic Textual Similarity	10	0
Other	12	6

Table 4: Task category counts by English (Eng.) and Non-English (Non-Eng.) languages.

Given all tasks, 14 languages are covered. Five languages make up 95% of all datasets. English is the majority (80%), followed by Spanish (7.5%), German (2.4%), French (2.4%), and Chinese (2.4%). Table 4 contains counts of task categories binned into English and Non-English . Question answering and semantic similarity have zero non-English datasets.

5 Conclusion

In this work, we outlined several challenges in training biomedical language models. With increasingly large biomedical language models (Yang et al., 2022), limitations in the quality and properties of training data grow more stark. We argue that biomedical NLP suffers from significant dataset debt, with only 13% of datasets accessible via API access and readily usable in state-of-the-art NLP tools. Current biomedical datasets are homogeneous, largely focusing on NER and relation extraction tasks, and predominantly English language. These limitations highlight opportunities presented by recent data-centric machine learning methods such as prompting, which enables experts to inject task guidance into training and more easily reconfigure existing datasets into new training tasks.

References

Oshin Agarwal, Heming Ge, Siamak Shakeri, and Rami Al-Rfou. 2021. Knowledge graph based synthetic corpus generation for knowledge-enhanced language model pre-training. In *Proceedings of the 2021 Conference of the North American Chapter of the Association for Computational Linguistics: Human Language Technologies*, pages 3554–3565, Online. Association for Computational Linguistics.

Stephen H. Bach, Victor Sanh, Zheng-Xin Yong, Albert Webson, Colin Raffel, Nihal V. Nayak, Abheesht Sharma, Taewoon Kim, M Saiful Bari, Thibault Fevry, Zaid Alyafeai, Manan Dey, Andrea Santilli, Zhiqing Sun, Srulik Ben-David, Canwen Xu, Gunjan Chhablani, Han Wang, Jason Alan Fries, Maged S. Al-shaibani, Shanya Sharma, Urmish Thakker, Khalid Almubarak, Xiangru Tang, Dragomir Radev, Mike Tian-Jian Jiang, and Alexander M. Rush. 2022. Promptsource: An integrated development environment and repository for natural language prompts.

Kathrin Blagec, Jakob Kraiger, Wolfgang Frühwirt, and Matthias Samwald. 2022. Benchmark datasets driving artificial intelligence development fail to capture the needs of medical professionals. *arXiv preprint arXiv:2201.07040*.

Tom Brown, Benjamin Mann, Nick Ryder, Melanie Subbiah, Jared D Kaplan, Prafulla Dhariwal, Arvind Neelakantan, Pranav Shyam, Girish Sastry, Amanda Askell, et al. 2020. Language models are few-shot learners. *Advances in neural information processing systems*, 33:1877–1901.

Raphael Cohen, Michael Elhadad, and Noémie Elhadad. 2013. Redundancy in electronic health record corpora: analysis, impact on text mining performance and mitigation strategies. *BMC bioinformatics*, 14(1):1–15.

Donald C Comeau, Rezarta Islamaj Doğan, Paolo Ciccarese, Kevin Bretonnel Cohen, Martin Krallinger, Florian Leitner, Zhiyong Lu, Yifan Peng, Fabio Rinaldi, Manabu Torii, et al. 2013. Bioc: a minimalist approach to interoperability for biomedical text processing. *Database*, 2013.

Mark Craven and Johan Kumlien. 1999. Constructing biological knowledge bases by extracting information from text sources. In *Proceedings of the Seventh International Conference on Intelligent Systems for Molecular Biology, August 6-10, 1999, Heidelberg, Germany*, pages 77–86. AAAI.

Gamal Crichton, Sampo Pyysalo, Billy Chiu, and Anna Korhonen. 2017. A neural network multi-task learning approach to biomedical named entity recognition. *BMC bioinformatics*, 18(1):1–14.

Aparna Elangovan, Jiayuan He, and Karin Verspoor. 2021. Memorization vs. generalization : Quantifying data leakage in NLP performance evaluation. In *Proceedings of the 16th Conference of the European Chapter of the Association for Computational Linguistics: Main Volume*, pages 1325–1335, Online. Association for Computational Linguistics.

Jason A Fries, Ethan Steinberg, Saelig Khattar, Scott L Fleming, Jose Posada, Alison Callahan, and Nigam H Shah. 2021. Ontology-driven weak supervision for clinical entity classification in electronic health records. *Nature Communications*, 12(1):1–11.

Timnit Gebru, Jamie Morgenstern, Briana Vecchione, Jennifer Wortman Vaughan, Hanna M. Wallach, Hal Daumé III, and Kate Crawford. 2021. Datasheets for datasets. *Commun. ACM*, 64(12):86–92.

Thorsten Gruber. 2014. Academic sell-out: how an obsession with metrics and rankings is damaging academia. *Journal of Marketing for Higher Education*, 24(2):165–177.

Yu Gu, Robert Tinn, Hao Cheng, Michael Lucas, Naoto Usuyama, Xiaodong Liu, Tristan Naumann, Jianfeng Gao, and Hoifung Poon. 2022. Domain-specific language model pretraining for biomedical natural language processing. *ACM Trans. Comput. Heal.*, 3(1):2:1–2:23.

Suchin Gururangan, Dallas Card, Sarah K. Dreier, Emily K. Gade, Leroy Z. Wang, Zeyu Wang, Luke Zettlemoyer, and Noah A. Smith. 2022. Whose language counts as high quality? measuring language ideologies in text data selection. *CoRR*, abs/2201.10474.

Alistair EW Johnson, Tom J Pollard, Lu Shen, Li-wei H Lehman, Mengling Feng, Mohammad Ghassemi, Benjamin Moody, Peter Szolovits, Leo Anthony Celi, and Roger G Mark. 2016. Mimic-iii, a freely accessible critical care database. *Scientific data*, 3(1):1–9.

Volodymyr Kuleshov, Jialin Ding, Christopher Vo, Braden Hancock, Alexander Ratner, Yang Li, Christopher Ré, Serafim Batzoglou, and Michael Snyder. 2019. A machine-compiled database of genome-wide association studies. *Nature communications*, 10(1):1–8.

Teven Le Scao and Alexander Rush. 2021. How many data points is a prompt worth? In *Proceedings of the 2021 Conference of the North American Chapter of the Association for Computational Linguistics: Human Language Technologies*, pages 2627–2636, Online. Association for Computational Linguistics.

Katherine Lee, Daphne Ippolito, Andrew Nystrom, Chiyuan Zhang, Douglas Eck, Chris Callison-Burch, and Nicholas Carlini. 2021. Deduplicating training data makes language models better. *arXiv preprint arXiv:2107.06499*.

Quentin Lhoest, Albert Villanova del Moral, Yacine Jernite, Abhishek Thakur, Patrick von Platen, Suraj Patil, Julien Chaumond, Mariama Drame, Julien Plu, Lewis Tunstall, Joe Davison, Mario Šaško, Gunjan Chhablani, Bhavitvya Malik, Simon Brandeis, Teven Le Scao, Victor Sanh, Canwen Xu, Nicolas Patry, Angelina McMillan-Major, Philipp Schmid, Sylvain Gugger, Clément Delangue, Théo Matussière, Lysandre Debut, Stas Bekman, Pierric Cistac, Thibault Goehringer, Victor Mustar, François Lagunas, Alexander Rush, and Thomas Wolf. 2021. Datasets: A community library for natural language processing. In *Proceedings of the 2021 Conference on Empirical Methods in Natural Language Processing: System Demonstrations*, pages 175–184, Online and Punta Cana, Dominican Republic. Association for Computational Linguistics.

Xi Victoria Lin, Todor Mihaylov, Mikel Artetxe, Tianlu Wang, Shuohui Chen, Daniel Simig, Myle Ott, Naman Goyal, Shruti Bhosale, Jingfei Du, et al. 2021. Few-shot learning with multilingual language models. *arXiv preprint arXiv:2112.10668*.

Milad Moradi, Kathrin Blagec, Florian Haberl, and Matthias Samwald. 2021. Gpt-3 models are poor few-shot learners in the biomedical domain. *arXiv preprint arXiv:2109.02555*.

Yifan Peng, Shankai Yan, and Zhiyong Lu. 2019. Transfer learning in biomedical natural language processing: An evaluation of BERT and ELMo on ten benchmarking datasets. In *Proceedings of the 18th BioNLP Workshop and Shared Task*, pages 58–65, Florence, Italy. Association for Computational Linguistics.

Fabio Petroni, Tim Rocktäschel, Sebastian Riedel, Patrick Lewis, Anton Bakhtin, Yuxiang Wu, and Alexander Miller. 2019. Language models as knowledge bases? In *Proceedings of the 2019 Conference on Empirical Methods in Natural Language Processing and the 9th International Joint Conference on Natural Language Processing (EMNLP-IJCNLP)*, pages 2463–2473, Hong Kong, China. Association for Computational Linguistics.

Colin Raffel, Noam Shazeer, Adam Roberts, Katherine Lee, Sharan Narang, Michael Matena, Yanqi Zhou, Wei Li, and Peter J Liu. 2019. Exploring the limits of transfer learning with a unified text-to-text transformer. *arXiv preprint arXiv:1910.10683*.

Nithya Sambasivan, Shivani Kapania, Hannah Highfill, Diana Akrong, Praveen Paritosh, and Lora M Aroyo. 2021. "everyone wants to do the model work, not the data work": Data cascades in high-stakes ai. In *proceedings of the 2021 CHI Conference on Human Factors in Computing Systems*, pages 1–15.

Victor Sanh, Albert Webson, Colin Raffel, Stephen Bach, Lintang Sutawika, Zaid Alyafeai, Antoine Chaffin, Arnaud Stiegler, Arun Raja, Manan Dey, M Saiful Bari, Canwen Xu, Urmish Thakker, Shanya Sharma Sharma, Eliza Szczechla, Taewoon Kim, Gunjan Chhablani, Nihal Nayak, Debajyoti Datta, Jonathan Chang, Mike Tian-Jian Jiang, Han Wang, Matteo Manica, Sheng Shen, Zheng Xin Yong, Harshit Pandey, Rachel Bawden, Thomas Wang, Trishala Neeraj, Jos Rozen, Abheesht Sharma, Andrea Santilli, Thibault Fevry, Jason Alan Fries, Ryan Teehan, Teven Le Scao, Stella Biderman, Leo Gao, Thomas Wolf, and Alexander M Rush. 2022. Multitask prompted training enables zero-shot task generalization. In *International Conference on Learning Representations*.

David Sculley, Gary Holt, Daniel Golovin, Eugene Davydov, Todd Phillips, Dietmar Ebner, Vinay Chaudhary, Michael Young, Jean-Francois Crespo, and Dan Dennison. 2015. Hidden technical debt in machine learning systems. *Advances in neural information processing systems*, 28.

Pontus Stenetorp, Sampo Pyysalo, Goran Topić, Tomoko Ohta, Sophia Ananiadou, and Jun'ichi Tsujii. 2012. Brat: a web-based tool for nlp-assisted text annotation. In *Proceedings of the Demonstrations at the 13th Conference of the European Chapter of the Association for Computational Linguistics*, pages 102–107.

Mujeen Sung, Jinhyuk Lee, Sean Yi, Minji Jeon, Sungdong Kim, and Jaewoo Kang. 2021. Can language models be biomedical knowledge bases? In *Proceedings of the 2021 Conference on Empirical Methods in Natural Language Processing*, pages 4723–4734, Online and Punta Cana, Dominican Republic. Association for Computational Linguistics.

Alex Wang, Yada Pruksachatkun, Nikita Nangia, Amanpreet Singh, Julian Michael, Felix Hill, Omer Levy, and Samuel Bowman. 2019. Superglue: A stickier benchmark for general-purpose language understanding systems. *Advances in neural information processing systems*, 32.

Alex Wang, Amanpreet Singh, Julian Michael, Felix Hill, Omer Levy, and Samuel Bowman. 2018. GLUE: A multi-task benchmark and analysis platform for natural language understanding. In *Proceedings of the 2018 EMNLP Workshop BlackboxNLP: Analyzing and Interpreting Neural Networks for NLP*, pages 353–355, Brussels, Belgium. Association for Computational Linguistics.

Leon Weber, Mario Sänger, Jannes Münchmeyer, Maryam Habibi, Ulf Leser, and Alan Akbik. 2021. Hunflair: an easy-to-use tool for state-of-the-art biomedical named entity recognition. *Bioinformatics*, 37(17):2792–2794.

Jason Wei, Maarten Bosma, Vincent Zhao, Kelvin Guu, Adams Wei Yu, Brian Lester, Nan Du, Andrew M.

Dai, and Quoc V Le. 2022. Finetuned language models are zero-shot learners. In *International Conference on Learning Representations*.

Mark D Wilkinson, Michel Dumontier, IJsbrand Jan Aalbersberg, Gabrielle Appleton, Myles Axton, Arie Baak, Niklas Blomberg, Jan-Willem Boiten, Luiz Bonino da Silva Santos, Philip E Bourne, et al. 2016. The fair guiding principles for scientific data management and stewardship. *Scientific data*, 3(1):1–9.

Hanwei Xu, Yujun Chen, Yulun Du, Nan Shao, Yanggang Wang, Haiyu Li, and Zhilin Yang. 2022. Zeroprompt: Scaling prompt-based pretraining to 1,000 tasks improves zero-shot generalization. *arXiv preprint arXiv:2201.06910*.

Xi Yang, Nima Pour Nejatian, Hoo Chang Shin, Kaleb Smith, Christopher Parisien, Colin Compas, Mona Flores, Ying Zhang, Tanja Magoc, Christopher Harle, et al. 2022. Gatortron: A large clinical language model to unlock patient information from unstructured electronic health records. *medRxiv*.

Wonjin Yoon, Jaehyo Yoo, Sumin Seo, Mujeen Sung, Minbyul Jeong, Gangwoo Kim, and Jaewoo Kang. 2021. Ku-dmis at bioasq 9: Data-centric and model-centric approaches for biomedical question answering. In *CEUR Workshop Proceedings*, volume 2936, pages 351–359. CEUR-WS.

Haoran Zhang, Amy X Lu, Mohamed Abdalla, Matthew McDermott, and Marzyeh Ghassemi. 2020. Hurtful words: quantifying biases in clinical contextual word embeddings. In *proceedings of the ACM Conference on Health, Inference, and Learning*, pages 110–120.

Ningyu Zhang, Zhen Bi, Xiaozhuan Liang, Lei Li, Xiang Chen, Shumin Deng, Luoqiu Li, Xin Xie, Hongbin Ye, Xin Shang, Kangping Yin, Chuanqi Tan, Jian Xu, Mosha Chen, Fei Huang, Luo Si, Yuan Ni, Guotong Xie, Zhifang Sui, Baobao Chang, Hui Zong, Zheng Yuan, Linfeng Li, Jun Yan, Hongying Zan, Kunli Zhang, Huajun Chen, Buzhou Tang, and Qingcai Chen. 2021. CBLUE: A chinese biomedical language understanding evaluation benchmark. *CoRR*, abs/2106.08087.

Zhengyun Zhao, Qiao Jin, and Sheng Yu. 2022. Pmc-patients: A large-scale dataset of patient notes and relations extracted from case reports in pubmed central. *arXiv preprint arXiv:2202.13876*.

A Appendix

A.1 Metadata Overview

This section contains detailed descriptions of each metadata field collected for the dataset catalog.

A.1.1 Name

The dataset name, preferring short forms (BC5CDR) as typically used on homepages or scientific publications over verbose ones ("BioCreative 5 Chemical Disease Relation Task").

A.1.2 Task Types

Datasets contain labels for one or more tasks. Tables 5 and 6 outline the tasks we consider in this work.

Name	Abbreviation
Named Entity Recognition	NER
Named Entity Disambiguation	NED
Relation Extraction	RE
Event Extraction	EE
Coreference Resolution	COREF
Span Classification	SPAN
Document Classification	DOC
Sentence Classification	SENT
Semantic Textual Similarity	STS
Question Answering	QA
Translation	TRANSL
Paraphrasing	PARA
Summarization	SUM
Natural Language Inference	NLI
Part-of-Speech Tagging	POS
Information Retreival	IR

Table 5: All task types.

A.1.3 Domain

Source domain of the dataset.

- *Biomedical*: Tasks are defined for scientific literature (e.g., PubMed abstacts, full-text publications from the PMC Open Access Subset).
- *Clinical*: Tasks are defined for clinical notes from patient electronic health records, health-related questions from social media or news websites, clinical trial reports, etc.

A.1.4 File format

File formats provided by the original dataset creators.

Category	Abbreviation
Information Extraction	NER
Information Extraction	NED
Information Extraction	RE
Information Extraction	EE
Information Extraction	COREF
Information Extraction	SPAN
Text Classification	DOC
Text Classification	SENT
Semantic Textual Similarity	STS
Question Answering	QA
Other	TRANSL
Other	PARA
Other	SUM
Other	NLI
Other	POS
Other	IR

Table 6: Task categories.

A.1.5 Annotations

Provenance of labels used to create a dataset.

- *Manual*: Expert annotators directly label data instances. This may include multiple rounds of adjudication.
- *Model-assisted Manual*: Experts verify, correct, or augment the output of a model (e.g., pre-annotated entities are used by annotators to define relations).
- *Crowdsourced*: Labels are the result of a voting process over multiple annotator's labels.
- *Rules*: Heuristics developed by experts and applied to unlabeled text to create annotations. This includes a wide range of weak/distant supervision techniques.
- *Found*: Generated from "in-the-wild" data, such as aligned pairs of translated text mined from web pages.
- *Unlabeled*: no human-generated labels (e.g., the PMC Open Subset).

A.1.6 API Access

URL of HuggingFace's Datasets implementation, otherwise "no".

A.1.7 Splits

Are canonical train, validation, and test sets defined by the dataset creators? If so, which sets are provided. value ∈ { `NONE`, `train`, `valid`, `test` }.

A.1.8 License

License information accompanying the dataset. Unknown licenses means the annotator could not find any information or formal legal documents on the homepage, software repository (e.g, GitHub, Google Code), or README with the data itself.

- *Public*: Creative Commons (CC BY 3.0/4.0, CC BY-SA 3.0/4.0), Public Domain, GNU Free Documentation License, GNU Common Public License v3.0, MIT License, Apache License 2.0
- *Public Non-commercial*: Creative Commons (CC BY NC 2.0/3.0/4.0, CC BY-NC-SA 4.0), CSIRO Data License (Non-commercial), Public for Research
- *DUA-NC*: DUA for non-commercial use only.
- *DUA-C/NC*: DUA for commercial and non-commercial uses.
- *DUA-UNK*: DUA with unknown restrictions.
- *Unknown*: Public-Unknown, Public w/ Registration

A.1.9 Languages

Languages used in the labeled dataset.

A.1.10 Multilingual

Dataset contains aligned pairs for two or more languages.

A.1.11 Publication, Year

URL to the manuscript, DOI, and year of publication.

A.1.12 Citations

Current citation count from Google Scholar, as of 02-22-2022. This measure was collected to provide a weak measure of dataset visibility. We note that citation count is a problematic measure of valuation and subject to many criticisms (Gruber, 2014).

A.1.13 Homepage, Public URL

URL of website describing and hosting the dataset. If the dataset has a direct download link, denote if it is public or only available after authentication.

A.1.14 Dead Link

URL of dataset homepage, as documented in the source publication, is no longer active.

A.2 Domain-specific

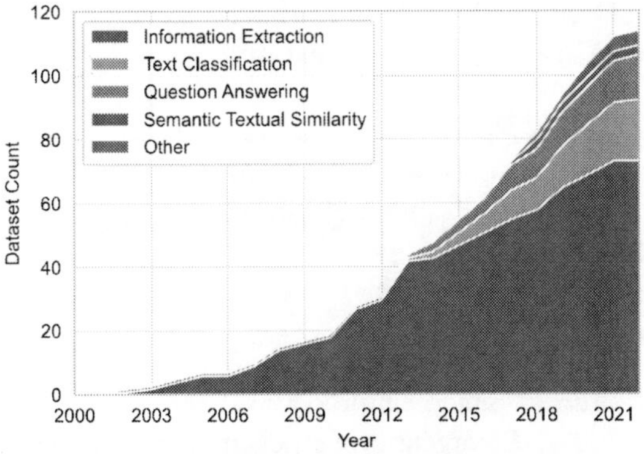

Figure 3: Scientific/biomedical domain (e.g., PubMed abstracts) cumulative distribution of available tasks, ordered by year of dataset release.

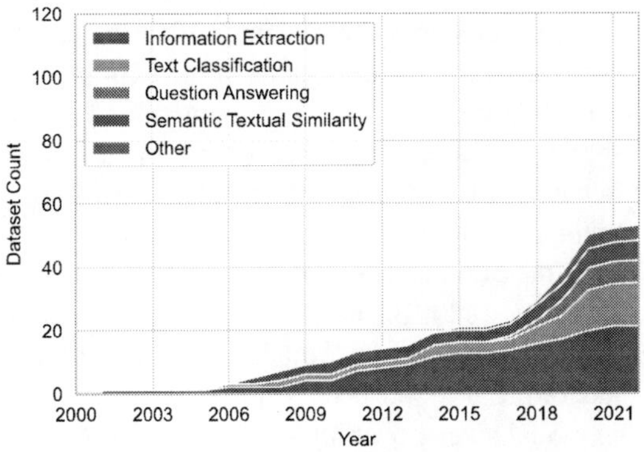

Figure 4: Clinical domain (e.g., patient notes) cumulative distribution of available tasks, ordered by year of dataset release.

A.3 Languages

Task	English	Non-English
NER	60	18
NED	21	9
RE	22	3
EE	8	0
COREF	8	0
SPAN_CLASS	9	4
SENT_CLASS	12	2
DOC_CLASS	21	8
QA	21	0
STS	10	0
TRANSL	3	5
PARA/SUM	2	0
IR	3	0
NLI	3	0
POS	1	1

Table 7: Tasks by language

Emergent Structures and Training Dynamics in Large Language Models

Ryan Teehan*[1,5], **Miruna Clinciu***[2,3,4,5], **Oleg Serikov***[5,6,7,8], **Eliza Szczechla***[5],
Natasha Seelam[5,9], **Shachar Mirkin**[5,10], **Aaron Gokaslan**[5,11]

[1]Charles River Analytics [2]Edinburgh Centre for Robotics
[3]Heriot-Watt University [4]University of Edinburgh [5]BigScience [6]AIR Institute
[7]DeepPavlov lab, MIPT [8]HSE University [9]Sherlock Biosciences [10]Lawgeex [11]Cornell University
Contact: `rsteehan@gmail.com`

Abstract

Large language models have achieved success on a number of downstream tasks, particularly in a few and zero-shot manner. As a consequence, researchers have been investigating both the kind of information these networks learn and how such information can be encoded in the parameters of the model. We survey the literature on changes in the network during training, drawing from work outside of NLP when necessary, and on learned representations of linguistic features in large language models. We note in particular the lack of sufficient research on the emergence of functional units – subsections of the network where related functions are grouped or organized – within large language models, and motivate future work that grounds the study of language models in an analysis of their changing internal structure during training time.

1 Introduction

Recent advances in self-supervised learning, distributed training, and architecture improvements have enabled training massive language models (Devlin et al., 2019; Brown et al., 2020; Radford et al., 2019; Ma et al., 2020; Liu et al., 2019). As these models have grown larger, so has their performance and generalization to new tasks. Furthermore, these techniques have also shown substantial improvements in learning multilingual (Chen et al., 2020) and multimodal representations (Radford et al., 2021). These large language models (LLMs) have advanced the state of the art in few- and zero-shot tasks (Radford et al., 2019; Brown et al., 2020; Radford et al., 2021). However, the size of these models makes them difficult to evaluate, examine, and audit. What structures emerge from training these neural networks? What internal representations do these networks learn?

In part, this opacity is implicit in the models themselves. Many of the fascinating capabilities of LLMs are "implicitly induced, not explicitly constructed" emergent properties (Bommasani et al., 2021). Emergent properties are those that result from the structural relations and interactions between a system's components (Ablowitz, 1939; Callebaut and Rasskin-Gutman, 2005). One way of characterizing the emergence of useful properties from complexity is through self-organization, wherein complex systems come to develop ordered patterns from the interactions of their components (Gershenson et al., 2020). Interactions between the parts of a system can produce complex global behavior, for example in the collective behavior of ants, flocking in birds (Cucker and Smale, 2007), or in the brain and central nervous system (Dresp-Langley, 2020; Brown, 2013). In the context of deep learning models, qualitatively different behavior has been observed during phase transitions in model size or training steps (Steinhardt, 2022). Current research on understanding the generalization abilities of LLMs has largely focused on the degree to which they learn various linguistic features (e.g. syntax) that would support performance on diverse downstream tasks. Our goal instead is to motivate research that grounds the learning of these higher-level representations, and from there, LLMs generalization abilities, in the emergent structures that result from self-organization within the networks.

To analyze LLMs themselves, we survey current research on the following topics and identify gaps in the literature. First, we turn to the development of internal representations of important features of language (e.g. syntax). Second, we look at the structure of the network (neurons, weights, etc.), how it evolves over time, and the emergence of functional units therein. In each case, we include not only research related to trained models, but also the changes that result over training time (termed *training dynamics*). Most research has focused on the aforementioned internal representations and

Proceedings of BigScience Episode #5 – Workshop on Challenges & Perspectives in Creating Large Language Models, pages 146 - 159
May 27, 2022

their connection to the downstream performance and generalization ability of LLMs, with only limited work on how the network structure changes over time and that change's connection to those representations. We aim to motivate research that not only applies work on the emergent structures within networks from outside of NLP to LLMs, but also develops a language-specific account of useful functional units that emerge in LLMs. Moreover, we identify methods for studying emergence and self-organization in complex systems with potential applications to analyzing LLM training dynamics and behavior. We conclude with a survey of explainability methods that allow researchers to connect structure with function.

2 Internal Representations

Linguistic Structure Representations A significant current area of research is dedicated to interpreting language models from a linguistic point of view. The motivation is to know to what extent models "understand" language, and more specifically, to what extent their generalizations over language agree with the generalizations about language described by linguistics. Following the hierarchy of language levels (morphology, syntax, discourse) (Dalrymple, 2001), experiments in probing studies typically address models' proficiency on a certain level of language. This line of research typically comes down to analyzing how *linguistic structures* are represented in a model's knowledge. Such structures represent syntagmatic/paradigmatic mechanisms of language (how language units combine and alternate, respectively). It is believed (McCoy et al., 2020) that rediscovering these structures would help models get closer to humans performance on a variety of tasks.

Probing Methods to Test for Linguistic Structure Probing tasks measure the linguistic awareness of a model's components, such as layers (Tenney et al., 2019) or groups of neurons (Durrani et al., 2020), by training an auxiliary model, the *probe*, on annotated data. Datasets providing such linguistically annotated data are called *probing datasets*, and cover a wide variety of properties (parts of speech, parse trees, etc.). A high performance of a probe model on a linguistic task implies that the representation tested encodes the property of interest. Several studies using probing methods have reported high accuracy predictions in identifying the underlying linguistic structure (Belinkov et al., 2017a,b; Peters et al., 2018; Tenney et al., 2019; Conneau et al., 2018; Zhang and Bowman, 2018; Alain and Bengio, 2017; Hewitt and Manning, 2019; Hewitt and Liang, 2019).

However, high performance may have confounding factors; there is uncertainty on whether the probing tasks properly test if representations actually encode linguistic structure and on how to interpret the results of probes (Hewitt and Liang, 2019; Zhang and Bowman, 2018; Voita and Titov, 2020; Pimentel et al., 2020b). Toward that end, the following section reviews several probing approaches in the context of language models, and the evaluation criteria used to determine the proficiency of a probe.

Grammatical and Semantic Probing Given the excellent performance of pre-trained representations on numerous linguistic tasks (Kitaev and Klein, 2018; He et al., 2018; Strubell et al., 2018; Lee et al., 2018), several studies have explored how semantic and grammatical knowledge are encoded within language models. *Syntactic* and morphological probing encompasses tasks that identify grammatical structure underlying the vector representations within pre-trained models, whereas *semantic* probing tasks investigate what meaning is conveyed within the representation.

Earlier work using part of speech (POS) and morphological tagging (Belinkov et al., 2017a) indicated that syntactic information may be encoded in layers of neural models. More recently, investigations have considered whether models learn to embed entire parse trees in their representations. In Hewitt and Manning (2019), the authors outline *structural probing* as a method to identify hierarchical, tree-like, structures from vector representations of language via the *syntactic distance* between embeddings. Their results across several large language models suggested that Transformer model encodings possess some hierarchical linguistic structure.

Several studies conducted probing experiments in multilingual settings. Chi et al. (2020) highlighted syntactic generalizations in multilingual language models via structured probing, and Şahin et al. (2020) propose a framework for multilingual morpho-syntactic probing, with 15 probing tasks for multiple languages, showing that, while cross-lingual typological regularities can be found with probing, probing dataset properties strongly impact the results (see Section 2.2 for more details about multilingual models).

Probes have also been used to measure semantic information within language model representations. The authors of Belinkov et al. (2017b) posed a semantic-class labeling task and found that higher layers of a model tend to perform better at semantic tagging. Similarly, semantic labeling tasks have been used to indicate that contextualized representations may encode multiple meanings within a single vector (Yaghoobzadeh et al., 2019). Contrarily, *edge probing*, developed by Tenney et al. (2019), implied that contextualized embeddings show larger gains on syntactic tasks as opposed to semantic ones (with only modest performance gains against non-contextualized baselines). There is no general evidence on how exactly language levels are distributed across model layers (Rogers et al., 2020).

Information Theoretic Probing Information-theoretic probing characterize tasks as a way of estimating the mutual information between an internal representation and the linguistic property of interest (Pimentel et al., 2020b; Pimentel and Cotterell, 2021; Voita and Titov, 2020; Pimentel et al., 2020a). Many of these approaches highlight the need to formalize the "effort" required in encoding a linguistic property, often via some form of a control function (Pimentel et al., 2020b). Counter-intuitively, work from Pimentel et al. (2020b) suggest that the "best" probes are ones that *always* perform highest on the task; their argument is that "learning" the task is equivalent to encoding the linguistic property in the initial representations. They provide approximations to calculate *information gain*, finding that BERT models contain only 12% more information than non-contextualized baselines.

Criticisms of accuracy-based performance metrics have argued that these methods are sensitive to structure, randomization, and hyperparameter selection (Voita and Titov, 2020; Hewitt and Liang, 2019; Zhang and Bowman, 2018; Pimentel et al., 2020b). As an alternative, the minimum description length (MDL) offers an information theoretic view on probe quality (Voita and Titov, 2020). Formally, it describes the "minimum number of bits required to transmit labels, knowing the representations", where better probes are those with smaller codelengths, as they suggest the information available in the representation is sufficiently accessible to solve the task. Prior studies have shown the MDL metric is robust and resilient to randomness (Voita and Titov, 2020). In comparison to the original POS tagging of Hewitt and Liang (2019), the MDL metric consistently distinguishes between the linguistic versus the control tasks across differences in hyperparameters and random seeds. Similarly, following Zhang and Bowman (2018), evaluation using MDL revealed longer codelengths for randomly initialized models as opposed to pre-trained ones.

2.1 Evaluating Probing Performance

Several studies have highlighted the need for interpretable performance scores on probes (Belinkov et al., 2017b; Peters et al., 2018; Tenney et al., 2019; Conneau et al., 2018; Zhang and Bowman, 2018; Alain and Bengio, 2017; Hall Maudslay and Cotterell, 2021). Two common themes have emerged for evaluating the proficiency of a probe: selectivity through *control tasks* and high informatic overlap via *control functions* (Hewitt and Liang, 2019; Pimentel et al., 2020b; Zhu and Rudzicz, 2020). Recent work suggests that both approaches yield comparable results empirically with similar error terms theoretically (Zhu and Rudzicz, 2020).

Control Tasks Selectivity is the trade-off between complexity and performance of the linguistic task. A "good" probe refers to one that performs highly on linguistic tasks, but poorly on control tasks, thus limiting the ability for a probe to "memorize" the task (Hewitt and Liang, 2019).

Arguments preferring "simpler" probes claim that these models should find "accessible" information within the representations (Shi et al., 2016). The simplest probes employ linear functions, yet more complex probes have been commonly used, including multi-layer perceptrons (MLP) or kernel methods (Belinkov et al., 2017a; Conneau et al., 2018; White et al., 2021; Adi et al., 2017), suggesting that some linguistic properties may be encoded non-linearly. Linear functions and MLPs are still commonly in use (Tenney et al., 2019).

Prior works within the probing literature have also explored how the size of training data can influence the performance of the probe (Zhang and Bowman, 2018; Hewitt and Liang, 2019). In an investigation considering probes of pre-trained language models and an untrained baseline on two syntactic tasks: POS tagging and Combinatorial Categorical Grammar (CCG) super-tagging (Hockenmaier and Steedman, 2007), probes with an untrained baseline model could surprisingly attain high performance compared to pre-trained models (Zhang and Bowman, 2018). However, the probe performance decreased dramatically when reducing the amount of available training data when compared to the pre-trained models. This suggested trained encoders captured enough syntactic information, beyond simple word-identities, which enabled these representations to achieve high performance on the linguistic tasks.

An extensive study on selectivity proposed several control tasks for POS tagging and dependency edge prediction (Hewitt and Liang, 2019). Across an array of probe architectures (linear, MLP-1, MLP-2) and hyperparameters, this investigation considered the effect of the hidden state dimensionality (size), number of training examples, regularization, and early stopping. The most effective probes were those with constrained hidden dimensions, yielding the most selective probes.

Control Functions Control functions compare the mutual information against a property of interest and the representation before and after the function is applied. The objective is used to measure the information gain of the representation. In Pimentel et al. (2020b), control functions were used to compare BERT contextualized models against FastText (Bojanowski et al., 2017) and a one-hot encoding on POS tagging. Curiously, their results suggested that BERT models only marginally improved information gain against these simpler baselines.

2.2 Emerging Multilingual Structures

Multilingual large language models, such as multilingual BERT (mBERT) (Devlin et al., 2019; Devlin, 2018) XLM (Conneau and Lample, 2019) or XLM-R (Conneau et al., 2020a) have shown impressive results when used for (zero-shot) cross-lingual transfer; that is, when the pre-trained multilingual language model is used as the basis for a task-specific model that is applied to a language in which it was not trained for. Their efficiency was proven in a wide variety of tasks, such as sentiment analysis, natural language inference, and question answering, to name a few.

Prior to the immense popularity of Transformer-based models, two approaches of using word embeddings for cross-lingual tasks have shown promising results. In the first, representations are learned separately from individual languages and then aligned to a shared space, thus producing *cross-lingual word embeddings* (Ruder et al., 2019), that in turn, are used on the target language. In the second, *multilingual* representations are learned by jointly training over multiple languages. Artetxe and Schwenk (2019), for example, trained a BiLSTM over 93 languages using parallel corpora, producing "universal" embeddings that were successfully used in various tasks.

The same two approaches are being explored with large language models. In Conneau et al. (2020b), monolingual BERT models that were trained separately for different languages produced similar (easily-aligned) representations. Pires et al. (2019) and Vulić et al. (2020) further showed – as expected – that the similarity depends on the typological distance between the languages. Universal language-agnostic embeddings also emerge when training multilingual models, even when no explicit connection (such as parallel corpora or bilingual dictionaries) between the languages is used during training, such as in the case of mBERT.

Multiple works looked into the factors that contribute to the successful transfer. These include domain and language similarity, shared parameters, and perhaps the most straightforward factor: common (sub-) words between the languages (Wu and Dredze, 2019; Conneau et al., 2020b; Pires et al., 2019). Interestingly, Conneau et al. (2020b) and K et al. (2020) showed that the universal representations do not heavily depend on shared vocabulary; instead, multilinguality emerges directly from the fact that parameters are shared in training, from the structure of the network, and is affected by common characteristics of the languages, such as word order (Dufter and Schütze, 2020). Pires et al. (2019) discovered that mBERT can also successfully transfer between languages with different scripts, and that generalization goes beyond the lexical level, and Chi et al. (2020) found that syntactic features representations in mBERT overlap between languages. Still, Ahmad et al. (2021) have shown that augmenting mBERT with syntactic information can improve cross-lingual transfer performance.

The size of each language's corpus in the language model's training set has been shown to be decisive for transfer to that language. Thus, low-resource languages often benefit more from the joint training (Wu and Dredze, 2020), while languages with abundant resources often achieve better performance when trained on their own (Nozza et al., 2020; Lewis et al., 2020).

2.3 Training Dynamics of Internal Representation Development

Training dynamics is an emerging field of research, promising to improve our understanding of knowledge acquisition in neural networks and offering insights into the utility of pre-trained models and embedded representations for downstream tasks. Most studies of Transformers (e.g. RoBERTa (Zhuang et al., 2021)) and LSTMs (Hochreiter and Schmidhuber, 1997) agree that models acquire linguistic knowledge early in the learning process.

Local syntactic information, such as parts of speech, is learned earlier than information encoding long-distance dependencies (e.g. topic) (Liu et al., 2021; Saphra, 2021). Exploration of ALBERT (Lan et al., 2019) and LSTM-based networks reveals different learning patterns for function and content words with more fine-grained distinctions within these categories including part of speech and verb form (Saphra, 2021; Chiang et al., 2020).

Differences in learning trajectory were also observed between layers. In LSTMs, recurrent layers become more task-independent over the course of training, while embeddings become more task-specific (Saphra, 2021). In Transformer-based architectures, i.e.: ALBERT and ELECTRA, Chiang et al. (2020) observe differences in performance patterns between the top and last layers. Similarly to other areas of research in NLP, most of the literature on training dynamics concentrate on English-language models. Another possible direction for future work is extending studies conducted on LSTMs to more widely used Transformers.

2.4 Critique of Testing Methods

Recent research has complicated the picture of grammar learning presented in Sections 2, 2.2, and 2.3. Specifically, there have been two separate but related types of critique leveled at probing and grammar learning. First, specific to probing, researchers question whether probes really identify linguistic representations at all. Secondly, and more fundamentally, it is unclear to what degree language models even learn grammar.

Hall Maudslay and Cotterell (2021) suggest that semantic "cues" may contaminate syntax probes, making it difficult to evaluate their scores. By employing "Jabberwocky probing", where pseudowords with no lexical meaning replace the original components of the sentence in a way that preserves grammar, the authors discovered that performance of syntactic probes considerably dropped for large language models, calling into question whether syntactic probes actually isolate syntactic knowledge withing language models.

A more fundamental issue for syntax learning in language models has been their performance when trained on perturbed or permuted data. Sinha et al. (2021) use a variety of word order permutations that preserve distributional information to isolate whether what language models learn is actually syntax. Word order has been assumed to be important not only for natural language understanding by humans but also by language models, particularly for learning syntax. Surprisingly then, word order appears to have less influence than one would expect on the downstream performance of language models and their performance on probing tasks. In part, the authors note that some syntax information can be acquired during fine-tuning to sufficiently answer tasks that require it. Moreover, in the context of syntax probes, the authors note that "while natural word order is useful for at least some probing tasks, the distributional prior of randomized models alone is enough to achieve a reasonably high accuracy on syntax sensitive probing". Furthermore, the results distinguish between parametric and non-parametric probes, where performance on the latter using randomization models degrades significantly. This degradation provides evidence that non-parametric probes are able to test for syntax learning in ways that parametric probes cannot. Similarly, O'Connor and Andreas (2021) use syntax-level perturbations and ablations to conclude that the information in context windows most useful to language models are local ordering statistics and content words, e.g. nouns, verbs, adverbs, and adjectives. In other words, it does not appear that language models make use of syntactic or other structural information in the context window.

2.5 Further Research

Despite recent probing studies providing a closer look at how linguistic structures are distributed in language models, it is an open question to what extent this knowledge acquisition differs from that of humans. While grammatical structures tend to be learned much faster than downstream knowledge (Conneau et al., 2018), there is still room for the study of more specific questions, such as whether models require more time to acquire the grammar of polysynthetic languages, as has been reported for humans (Kelly et al., 2014).

Another remaining open question is whether linguistic structure knowledge can be transferred between models with the neurons initialization mechanism (Durrani et al., 2021). While rough re-use of neurons is proven to be helpful in model initialization (Sanh et al., 2019), for instance, such neuron "surgery" would potentially lead to even quicker acquisition of grammatical knowledge.

Generally speaking, the performance of multilingual models is inferior to that of monolingual ones, especially when enough resources are available. Yet, high-quality multilingual models remain a desired objective that can particularly benefit low-resource languages. Further understanding the factors that enable learning language-independent representations is key for developing better multilingual training or cross-lingual fine-tuning strategies, especially for transfer between less similar language pairs. A particularly interesting question is whether some tasks require more language-specific adaptation, because, for instance, they depend on linguistic information that is currently not generalized well enough in multilingual LLMs.

3 Self-Organization and the Emergent Structure of Networks

3.1 Network Structure

Inspired by the architecture of biological neural networks (BNNs) and their adaptability to various tasks, where neurons and circuits are capable of self-organization, many researchers have investigated how Artificial Neural Networks (ANNs) can be seen as emergent structures, where interpretability of an ANN's parameters can help us to inspect their functional modularity. Broadly, researchers have approached this by identifying patterns in the weights or neurons especially through subgraphs of the network.

Branch specialization is the organization of branches – or "sequences of layers which temporarily don't have access to 'parallel' information which is still passed to later layers" (Voss et al., 2021) – of the network into functional units, across different architectures and tasks (Zhang et al., 2020; Bunel et al., 2020; Voss et al., 2021; Rössig and Petkovic, 2021). It is somewhat similar to how neurons are connected by synapses, forming small functional units called neural circuits that can be specialized for specific tasks, such as to "mediate reflexes, process sensory information, generate locomotion and mediate learning and memory" (Byrne et al., 2012; Luo, 2021). In their work on AlexNet, Voss et al. (2021) provided initial evidence of self-organization of neurons and circuits (subgraphs) into functional units in a neural network. This self-organized emergent structure is consistent "across different architectures and tasks". A look at evolving neural structures gives another perspective. Inspired by neural architecture search (NAS), So et al. (2019) presented "a first neural architecture search conducted to find improved feed-forward sequence models", where the search space contains five branch-level search fields. Recently, So et al. (2021) introduced Primer (PRIMitives searched TransformER), which can add improvements in the pre-training and one-shot downstream task transfer regime. However, branches are used just for the initialized multi-head attention.

Weight banding is the uniformity in the organization of the weights in a final layer. In neural networks, weights are parameters that can transform the input data between the network's hidden layers. Weight banding resembles another biological phenomenon when a neuron multiplies each input with a synaptic weight, which is represented as a number that highlights the importance assigned to that input. The weighted inputs are summed up in what represents the neuron's output (Iyer et al., 2013). Petrov et al. (2021) note that many vision models display a uniform pattern in their final layer. They investigate the nature of this structural phenomenon, connecting it ultimately to architectural choices in the network and noting that weight banding can serve as a method of preserving spatial information.

Clustering is the grouping of neurons or subnetworks into units that can be used for specific tasks (Hod et al., 2021). Starting from the fact that modular systems allow us to have a better understanding of a system if we can inspect the function of individual modules, different clustering methods for neural networks were proposed. Li et al. (2020) designed a modular neural network based on feature clustering to decompose features into clusters with each module processing different features. These modules work in parallel for a singular task. Filan et al. (2021) proposed a spectral clustering algorithm for decomposition of trained networks into clusters, finding that networks can have some sense of modularity and suggested further work related to clusterability in various domains.

Modularity focuses on the reusability of subnetworks for multiple tasks (Happel and Murre, 1994; Shukla et al., 2010; Csordás et al., 2021). In Csordás et al. (2021) neural networks trained on algorithmic tasks appear to fail to learn general, modular, compositional algorithms, and require specific subset weights to handle a particular combination of the input tokens. With these findings, Csordás et al. (2021) suggest further research about "function dependent weight sharing in the neural networks". Reusable multi-task subnetworks may also be discovered via Neural Architecture Search (NAS) methods (Pham et al., 2018). Pasunuru and Bansal (2019) leverage a technique called multi-task architecture search (MAS) to find multi-task cell structures in RNNs, capable of generalization to unseen tasks.

3.2 Training Dynamics of Network Changes

Understanding the change in network structure over time is equally as important as identifying structure in trained models. Here, the focus is on how the parameters of the model change over the course of training, which can give insight into the types of inductive biases that develop and shed light on the nature of LLMs' abilities to generalize. The most recent work covering this in the context of LLMs focuses on parameter norm growth, which refers to the growth of the ℓ_2 norm during training time. According to Merrill et al. (2021), neural networks learn successfully due to inductive biases introduced during training. Norm growth induces saturation in Transformer models, which reduces the attention heads to "generalized hard attention". The authors find that computations for *argmax* and *mean* are reducible to saturated attention, which partially explains why saturated Transformer models can learn counter languages, a kind of formal language, and may play a broader role in explaining their generalization abilities.

3.3 Further Research

As we have noted, most of the work on network structure is currently outside of NLP, either dealing with general ANNs or specific to Computer Vision with AlexNet and general convolutional networks trained on ImageNet (Voss et al., 2021; Petrov et al., 2021). This work should be replicated in the context of LLMs to test for the existence of language-specific functional units and, more generally, determine whether there are internal network structures that support the learned representations we discuss in Section 2. Likewise, since this research is still in its infancy, it is focused on simple emergent structures. Future research can incorporate higher-order emergent structures (Baas, 2000), new methods of structure detection in networks (Aktas et al., 2019), and even detection of structures whose form is not explicitly specified (Shalizi et al., 2006).

Additionally, by viewing the neural networks in question as time-evolving complex systems we can leverage older research on self-organization that has yet to be applied to understanding LLMs. In particular, Ball et al. (2010) provide a method for quantifying self-organization based on persistent mutual information. Likewise, Shalizi et al. (2004) ground self-organization in information theory and Shalizi (2003) extends this method to a general class of undirected graphs. Methods such as these can be used to identify and quantify self-organization in LLMs and better understand their emergent behavior.

4 Connecting Structure to Function: Explainable AI (XAI)

The rapid increase in the adoption of AI models in recent years and their growing impact on human lives created a need for techniques that offer insight into the models internal operations.

Since attention-based models (Vaswani et al., 2017) have become state-of-the-art tools in NLP, there have been numerous attempts to provide some understanding of their predictions by visualizing the attention layer. However, these approaches have been criticized for their inability to produce meaningful and coherent interpretations (Wiegreffe and Pinter, 2019; Bastings and Filippova, 2020; Serrano and Smith, 2019). To address these limitations, Ghaeini et al. (2018) examine the saliency of attention and LSTM gating signal in the intermediate layers of ESIM models, an architecture designed for natural language inference tasks (Chen et al., 2017). Their results show that visualizing attention saliency allows identifying which parts of the premise and hypothesis contribute most to the final score. Moreover, attention saliency maps compared across different ESIM models reveal differences in focus that reflect the differences in their predictions. According to this study, using saliency is much more effective than using attention alone.

Another approach to revealing how decisions are formed across network layers is *erasure*, where features are deemed irrelevant if their removal has a minor effect on the prediction. De Cao et al. (2020) extend this method to learned masking and adapt it to measure the importance of intermediate states rather than the inputs. They run the proposed DIFF-MASK method on BERT (Devlin et al., 2019) and find that separator tokens play an important role in the input layer for question answering but not for sentiment classification, a task where adjectives and nouns are kept for much longer. Given that separators serve as delimiters between the question and the context, these differences shed light on the connection between the internal latent structure and the task, marking a step toward gaining some understanding of the information flow in the model.

Applying neural models to the NLP domain poses specific challenges. This opens the way for research on the extent to which language-specific characteristics, such as compositionality of meaning, are reflected in the internal representations of neural networks. The work by Li et al. (2016) leverages several methods including variance-based and first-derivative saliency (a technique inspired by back-propagation), to study how models deal with compositionality of meaning, e.g., negation, intensification and combining meaning from different parts of the sentence. The study of recurrent, LSTM and bi-LSTM networks across time steps finds that, as decoding proceeds, the task (language modelling) gradually prevails overbuilding word representations.

An integrated gradients (Sundararajan et al., 2017) based method of finding neurons that encode individual facts has been proposed by Dai et al. (2021). This approach builds on the observation that large pre-trained language models can remember factual knowledge from the training corpus. The authors find that knowledge neurons are located in the feed-forward network of BERT and view these two-layer perceptron modules as knowledge memories in the Transformer architecture. The method allows for explicit editing of specific factual knowledge by manipulating the corresponding knowledge neurons with only a moderate influence on unrelated knowledge. These findings are in line with a work by Meng et al. (2022) that localizes factual knowledge to the feed-forward layer. Further, this approach makes a distinction between the notions of *knowing* and *saying* a fact and concludes that, while the feed-forward layers encode the former, the latter is attended to by the late self-attention.

Other approaches, e.g. SHAP, DeepLift and LIME (Lundberg and Lee, 2017; Shrikumar et al., 2019; Ribeiro et al., 2016) can reveal dependencies missed by the methods discussed here. In NLP, the key challenges include performance and, where applicable, choosing an adequate baseline for word embeddings. The dynamic progress of research in natural language processing has led researchers to review and analyze existing methods of interpreting neural models (Belinkov and Glass, 2019; Danilevsky et al., 2020). While the emerging field of explainable AI (XAI) is seeing faster growth, a path for research and discussion on the desired evaluation criteria of interpretation methods is opening up (Jacovi and Goldberg, 2020).

5 Conclusion and Future Directions

In this paper, we provide an overview of research on network structure, linguistic feature learning, their training dynamics, and explainability research that aims to connect network structure and function. In doing so, we highlight gaps in the literature and opportunities for future research, both in each individual research area and as a broad proposal for grounding research in understanding large language models. We highlight a few areas of future research as particularly important given the gaps in the current literature. For the study of how, and whether, linguistic structures are learned by language models, more work is needed to understand the training dynamics of this learning across a variety of model scales and architectures. More fundamentally, there is disagreement about what it means for a model to "encode" linguistic structures such as syntax, particularly in a multilingual setting.

More broadly, nascent work on the self-organization of neurons and subnetwork structures that emerge during training time has largely not been applied to LLMs, or neural networks in NLP more generally. Research in Computer Vision has shown the existence of emergent functional units with functions that are semantically meaningful to humans. In the context of LLMs, such structures may provide a basis for understanding the nature of linguistic features that LLMs purportedly learn, especially when comparing the development of each during training time. Additional research is needed to not only determine whether such structures emerge in LLMs, but also to apply and extend the literature on self-organization in complex systems. This research can also be used for explainability. Currently, assessment of the quality of interpretations of the information flow in neural models is not straightforward. Identification of modular and emergent structures within networks may be viewed as a way of moving away from the binary definition of *faithfulness* as postulated by Jacovi and Goldberg (2020). Evidence for the existence of structures aligning with human perception of language, if found, can help to enable separate consideration of *plausibility* from a human perspective, as proposed in the same study. More broadly, we propose grounding the study of LLMs properties in the analysis of the self-organization of weights and neurons into emergent structures.

References

Reuben Ablowitz. 1939. The theory of emergence. *Philosophy of Science*, 6(1):1–16.

Yossi Adi, Einat Kermany, Yonatan Belinkov, Ofer Lavi, and Yoav Goldberg. 2017. Fine-grained analysis of sentence embeddings using auxiliary prediction tasks. In *5th International Conference on Learning Representations, ICLR 2017, Toulon, France, April 24-26, 2017, Conference Track Proceedings*. OpenReview.net.

Wasi Ahmad, Haoran Li, Kai-Wei Chang, and Yashar Mehdad. 2021. Syntax-augmented multilingual BERT for cross-lingual transfer. In *Proceedings of the 59th Annual Meeting of the Association for Computational Linguistics and the 11th International Joint Conference on Natural Language Processing (Volume 1: Long Papers)*, pages 4538–4554, Online. Association for Computational Linguistics.

Mehmet Aktas, Esra Akbas, and Ahmed El Fatmaoui. 2019. Persistence homology of networks: methods and applications. *Applied Network Science*, 4.

Guillaume Alain and Yoshua Bengio. 2017. Understanding intermediate layers using linear classifier probes. In *5th International Conference on Learning Representations, ICLR 2017, Toulon, France, April 24-26, 2017, Workshop Track Proceedings*. OpenReview.net.

Mikel Artetxe and Holger Schwenk. 2019. Massively Multilingual Sentence Embeddings for Zero-Shot Cross-Lingual Transfer and Beyond. *Transactions of the Association for Computational Linguistics*, 7:597–610.

Nils A. Baas. 2000. Emergence, hierarchies, and hyperstructures. In Christopher G. Langton, editor, *Artificial Life III*, page 515–537. Addison-Wesley Longman Publishing Co., Inc., USA.

Robin C. Ball, Marina Diakonova, and Robert S. MacKay. 2010. Quantifying emergence in terms of persistent mutual information. *Adv. Complex Syst.*, 13:327–338.

Jasmijn Bastings and Katja Filippova. 2020. The elephant in the interpretability room: Why use attention as explanation when we have saliency methods? In *Proceedings of the Third BlackboxNLP Workshop on Analyzing and Interpreting Neural Networks for NLP*, pages 149–155, Online. Association for Computational Linguistics.

Yonatan Belinkov, Nadir Durrani, Fahim Dalvi, Hassan Sajjad, and James Glass. 2017a. What do neural machine translation models learn about morphology? In *Proceedings of the 55th Annual Meeting of the Association for Computational Linguistics (Volume 1: Long Papers)*, pages 861–872, Vancouver, Canada. Association for Computational Linguistics.

Yonatan Belinkov and James Glass. 2019. Analysis methods in neural language processing: A survey. *Transactions of the Association for Computational Linguistics*, 7:49–72.

Yonatan Belinkov, Lluís Màrquez, Hassan Sajjad, Nadir Durrani, Fahim Dalvi, and James Glass. 2017b. Evaluating layers of representation in neural machine translation on part-of-speech and semantic tagging tasks. In *Proceedings of the Eighth International Joint Conference on Natural Language Processing (Volume 1: Long Papers)*, pages 1–10, Taipei, Taiwan. Asian Federation of Natural Language Processing.

Piotr Bojanowski, Edouard Grave, Armand Joulin, and Tomas Mikolov. 2017. Enriching word vectors with subword information. *Transactions of the Association for Computational Linguistics*, 5:135–146.

Rishi Bommasani, Drew A. Hudson, Ehsan Adeli, Russ Altman, Simran Arora, Sydney von Arx, Michael S. Bernstein, Jeannette Bohg, Antoine Bosselut, Emma Brunskill, Erik Brynjolfsson, Shyamal Buch, Dallas Card, Rodrigo Castellon, Niladri Chatterji, Annie S. Chen, Kathleen Creel, Jared Quincy Davis, Dorottya Demszky, Chris Donahue, Moussa Doumbouya, Esin Durmus, Stefano Ermon, John Etchemendy, Kawin Ethayarajh, Li Fei-Fei, Chelsea Finn, Trevor Gale, Lauren Gillespie, Karan Goel, Noah D. Goodman, Shelby Grossman, Neel Guha, Tatsunori Hashimoto, Peter Henderson, John Hewitt, Daniel E. Ho, Jenny Hong, Kyle Hsu, Jing Huang, Thomas Icard, Saahil Jain, Dan Jurafsky, Pratyusha Kalluri, Siddharth Karamcheti, Geoff Keeling, Fereshte Khani, Omar Khattab, Pang Wei Koh, Mark S. Krass, Ranjay Krishna, Rohith Kuditipudi, and et al. 2021. On the opportunities and risks of foundation models. *CoRR*, abs/2108.07258.

Steven Ravett Brown. 2013. Emergence in the central nervous system. *Cognitive Neurodynamics*, 7(3).

Tom Brown, Benjamin Mann, Nick Ryder, Melanie Subbiah, Jared D Kaplan, Prafulla Dhariwal, Arvind

Neelakantan, Pranav Shyam, Girish Sastry, Amanda Askell, Sandhini Agarwal, Ariel Herbert-Voss, Gretchen Krueger, Tom Henighan, Rewon Child, Aditya Ramesh, Daniel Ziegler, Jeffrey Wu, Clemens Winter, Chris Hesse, Mark Chen, Eric Sigler, Mateusz Litwin, Scott Gray, Benjamin Chess, Jack Clark, Christopher Berner, Sam McCandlish, Alec Radford, Ilya Sutskever, and Dario Amodei. 2020. Language models are few-shot learners. In *Advances in Neural Information Processing Systems*, volume 33, pages 1877–1901. Curran Associates, Inc.

Rudy Bunel, Ilker Turkaslan, Philip H.S. Torr, M. Pawan Kumar, Jingyue Lu, and Pushmeet Kohli. 2020. Branch and bound for piecewise linear neural network verification. *Journal of Machine Learning Research*, 21.

John H Byrne, D Ph, and The Ut. 2012. Introduction to Neurons and Neuronal Networks. *Cellular and Molecular Neurobiology*, 1.

Werner Callebaut and Diego Rasskin-Gutman. 2005. *Modularity: Understanding the Development and Evolution of Natural Complex Systems*. The MIT Press.

Peng-Jen Chen, Ann Lee, Changhan Wang, Naman Goyal, Angela Fan, Mary Williamson, and Jiatao Gu. 2020. Facebook AI's WMT20 news translation task submission. In *Proceedings of the Fifth Conference on Machine Translation*, pages 113–125, Online. Association for Computational Linguistics.

Qian Chen, Xiaodan Zhu, Zhen-Hua Ling, Si Wei, Hui Jiang, and Diana Inkpen. 2017. Enhanced LSTM for natural language inference. In *Proceedings of the 55th Annual Meeting of the Association for Computational Linguistics (Volume 1: Long Papers)*, pages 1657–1668, Vancouver, Canada. Association for Computational Linguistics.

Ethan A. Chi, John Hewitt, and Christopher D. Manning. 2020. Finding universal grammatical relations in multilingual BERT. In *Proceedings of the 58th Annual Meeting of the Association for Computational Linguistics*, pages 5564–5577, Online. Association for Computational Linguistics.

Cheng-Han Chiang, Sung-Feng Huang, and Hung-yi Lee. 2020. Pretrained language model embryology: The birth of ALBERT. In *Proceedings of the 2020 Conference on Empirical Methods in Natural Language Processing (EMNLP)*, pages 6813–6828, Online. Association for Computational Linguistics.

Alexis Conneau, German Kruszewski, Guillaume Lample, Loïc Barrault, and Marco Baroni. 2018. What you can cram into a single $&!#* vector: Probing sentence embeddings for linguistic properties. In *Proceedings of the 56th Annual Meeting of the Association for Computational Linguistics (Volume 1: Long Papers)*, pages 2126–2136, Melbourne, Australia. Association for Computational Linguistics.

Alexis Conneau and Guillaume Lample. 2019. Cross-lingual language model pretraining. In *Advances in Neural Information Processing Systems*, volume 32. Curran Associates, Inc.

Alexis Conneau, Shijie Wu, Haoran Li, Luke Zettlemoyer, and Veselin Stoyanov. 2020a. Emerging cross-lingual structure in pretrained language models. In *Proceedings of the 58th Annual Meeting of the Association for Computational Linguistics, ACL 2020, Online, July 5-10, 2020*, pages 6022–6034. Association for Computational Linguistics.

Alexis Conneau, Shijie Wu, Haoran Li, Luke Zettlemoyer, and Veselin Stoyanov. 2020b. Emerging cross-lingual structure in pretrained language models. In *Proceedings of the 58th Annual Meeting of the Association for Computational Linguistics*, pages 6022–6034, Online. Association for Computational Linguistics.

Róbert Csordás, Sjoerd van Steenkiste, and Jürgen Schmidhuber. 2021. Are neural nets modular? inspecting functional modularity through differentiable weight masks. In *International Conference on Learning Representations*.

Felipe Cucker and Steve Smale. 2007. Emergent behavior in flocks. *IEEE Transactions on Automatic Control*, 52(5):852–862.

Damai Dai, Li Dong, Yaru Hao, Zhifang Sui, and Furu Wei. 2021. Knowledge neurons in pretrained transformers. *ArXiv*, abs/2104.08696.

Mary Dalrymple. 2001. *Lexical functional grammar*. Brill.

Marina Danilevsky, Kun Qian, Ranit Aharonov, Yannis Katsis, Ban Kawas, and Prithviraj Sen. 2020. A survey of the state of explainable AI for natural language processing. In *Proceedings of the 1st Conference of the Asia-Pacific Chapter of the Association for Computational Linguistics and the 10th International Joint Conference on Natural Language Processing*, pages 447–459, Suzhou, China. Association for Computational Linguistics.

Nicola De Cao, Michael Sejr Schlichtkrull, Wilker Aziz, and Ivan Titov. 2020. How do decisions emerge across layers in neural models? interpretation with differentiable masking. In *Proceedings of the 2020 Conference on Empirical Methods in Natural Language Processing (EMNLP)*, pages 3243–3255, Online. Association for Computational Linguistics.

Jacob Devlin. 2018. Multilingual bert.

Jacob Devlin, Ming-Wei Chang, Kenton Lee, and Kristina Toutanova. 2019. BERT: Pre-training of deep bidirectional transformers for language understanding. In *Proceedings of the 2019 Conference of the North American Chapter of the Association for Computational Linguistics: Human Language Technologies, Volume 1 (Long and Short Papers)*, pages 4171–4186, Minneapolis, Minnesota. Association for Computational Linguistics.

Birgitta Dresp-Langley. 2020. Seven properties of self-organization in the human brain. *Big Data and Cognitive Computing*, 4(2).

Philipp Dufter and Hinrich Schütze. 2020. Identifying elements essential for BERT's multilinguality. In *Proceedings of the 2020 Conference on Empirical Methods in Natural Language Processing (EMNLP)*, pages 4423–4437, Online. Association for Computational Linguistics.

Nadir Durrani, Hassan Sajjad, and Fahim Dalvi. 2021. How transfer learning impacts linguistic knowledge in deep NLP models? In *Findings of the Association for Computational Linguistics: ACL-IJCNLP 2021*, pages 4947–4957, Online. Association for Computational Linguistics.

Nadir Durrani, Hassan Sajjad, Fahim Dalvi, and Yonatan Belinkov. 2020. Analyzing individual neurons in pre-trained language models. *arXiv preprint arXiv:2010.02695*.

Daniel Filan, Stephen Casper, Shlomi Hod, Cody Wild, Andrew Critch, and Stuart Russell. 2021. Clusterability in neural networks. *CoRR*, abs/2103.03386.

Carlos Gershenson, Vito Trianni, Justin Werfel, and Hiroki Sayama. 2020. Self-Organization and Artificial Life. *Artificial Life*, 26(3):391–408.

Reza Ghaeini, Xiaoli Fern, and Prasad Tadepalli. 2018. Interpreting recurrent and attention-based neural models: a case study on natural language inference. In *Proceedings of the 2018 Conference on Empirical Methods in Natural Language Processing*, pages 4952–4957, Brussels, Belgium. Association for Computational Linguistics.

Rowan Hall Maudslay and Ryan Cotterell. 2021. Do syntactic probes probe syntax? experiments with jabberwocky probing. In *Proceedings of the 2021 Conference of the North American Chapter of the Association for Computational Linguistics: Human Language Technologies*, pages 124–131, Online. Association for Computational Linguistics.

Bart L.M. Happel and Jacob M.J. Murre. 1994. Design and evolution of modular neural network architectures. *Neural Networks*, 7(6-7).

Luheng He, Kenton Lee, Omer Levy, and Luke Zettlemoyer. 2018. Jointly predicting predicates and arguments in neural semantic role labeling. In *Proceedings of the 56th Annual Meeting of the Association for Computational Linguistics (Volume 2: Short Papers)*, pages 364–369, Melbourne, Australia. Association for Computational Linguistics.

John Hewitt and Percy Liang. 2019. Designing and interpreting probes with control tasks. In *Proceedings of the 2019 Conference on Empirical Methods in Natural Language Processing and the 9th International Joint Conference on Natural Language Processing (EMNLP-IJCNLP)*, pages 2733–2743, Hong Kong, China. Association for Computational Linguistics.

John Hewitt and Christopher D. Manning. 2019. A structural probe for finding syntax in word representations. In *Proceedings of the 2019 Conference of the North American Chapter of the Association for Computational Linguistics: Human Language Technologies, Volume 1 (Long and Short Papers)*, pages 4129–4138, Minneapolis, Minnesota. Association for Computational Linguistics.

Sepp Hochreiter and Jürgen Schmidhuber. 1997. Long short-term memory. *Neural computation*, 9(8):1735–1780.

Julia Hockenmaier and Mark Steedman. 2007. Ccgbank: A corpus of ccg derivations and dependency structures extracted from the penn treebank. *Comput. Linguist.*, 33(3):355–396.

Shlomi Hod, Stephen Casper, Daniel Filan, Cody Wild, Andrew Critch, and Stuart J. Russell. 2021. Detecting modularity in deep neural networks. *ArXiv*, abs/2110.08058.

Ramakrishnan Iyer, Vilas Menon, Michael Buice, Christof Koch, and Stefan Mihalas. 2013. The Influence of Synaptic Weight Distribution on Neuronal Population Dynamics. *PLoS Computational Biology*, 9(10).

Alon Jacovi and Yoav Goldberg. 2020. Towards faithfully interpretable NLP systems: How should we define and evaluate faithfulness? In *Proceedings of the 58th Annual Meeting of the Association for Computational Linguistics*, pages 4198–4205, Online. Association for Computational Linguistics.

Karthikeyan K, Zihan Wang, Stephen Mayhew, and Dan Roth. 2020. Cross-lingual ability of multilingual bert: An empirical study. In *International Conference on Learning Representations*.

Barbara Kelly, Gillian Wigglesworth, Rachel Nordlinger, and Joseph Blythe. 2014. The acquisition of polysynthetic languages. *Language and Linguistics Compass*, 8(2):51–64.

Nikita Kitaev and Dan Klein. 2018. Constituency parsing with a self-attentive encoder. In *Proceedings of the 56th Annual Meeting of the Association for Computational Linguistics (Volume 1: Long Papers)*, pages 2676–2686, Melbourne, Australia. Association for Computational Linguistics.

Zhenzhong Lan, Mingda Chen, Sebastian Goodman, Kevin Gimpel, Piyush Sharma, and Radu Soricut. 2019. Albert: A lite bert for self-supervised learning of language representations. *arXiv preprint arXiv:1909.11942*.

Kenton Lee, Luheng He, and Luke Zettlemoyer. 2018. Higher-order coreference resolution with coarse-to-fine inference. In *Proceedings of the 2018 Conference of the North American Chapter of the Association for Computational Linguistics: Human Language Technologies, Volume 2 (Short Papers)*, pages 687–692, New Orleans, Louisiana. Association for Computational Linguistics.

Patrick Lewis, Barlas Oguz, Ruty Rinott, Sebastian Riedel, and Holger Schwenk. 2020. MLQA: Evaluating cross-lingual extractive question answering. In *Proceedings of the 58th Annual Meeting of the Association for Computational Linguistics*, pages 7315–7330, Online. Association for Computational Linguistics.

Jiwei Li, Xinlei Chen, Eduard Hovy, and Dan Jurafsky. 2016. Visualizing and understanding neural models in NLP. In *Proceedings of the 2016 Conference of the North American Chapter of the Association for Computational Linguistics: Human Language Technologies*, pages 681–691, San Diego, California. Association for Computational Linguistics.

Wenjing Li, Meng Li, Junfei Qiao, and Xin Guo. 2020. A feature clustering-based adaptive modular neural network for nonlinear system modeling. *ISA Transactions*, 100:185–197.

Nelson F. Liu, Matt Gardner, Yonatan Belinkov, Matthew E. Peters, and Noah A. Smith. 2019. Linguistic knowledge and transferability of contextual representations. In *Proceedings of the 2019 Conference of the North American Chapter of the Association for Computational Linguistics: Human Language Technologies, Volume 1 (Long and Short Papers)*, pages 1073–1094, Minneapolis, Minnesota. Association for Computational Linguistics.

Zeyu Liu, Yizhong Wang, Jungo Kasai, Hannaneh Hajishirzi, and Noah A. Smith. 2021. Probing across time: What does RoBERTa know and when? In *Findings of the Association for Computational Linguistics: EMNLP 2021*, pages 820–842, Punta Cana, Dominican Republic. Association for Computational Linguistics.

Scott M Lundberg and Su-In Lee. 2017. A unified approach to interpreting model predictions. In *Advances in Neural Information Processing Systems*, volume 30. Curran Associates, Inc.

Liqun Luo. 2021. Architectures of neuronal circuits. *Science*, 373(6559):eabg7285.

Shuming Ma, Jian Yang, Haoyang Huang, Zewen Chi, Li Dong, Dongdong Zhang, Hany Hassan Awadalla, Alexandre Muzio, Akiko Eriguchi, Saksham Singhal, et al. 2020. Xlm-t: Scaling up multilingual machine translation with pretrained cross-lingual transformer encoders. *arXiv preprint arXiv:2012.15547*.

R. Thomas McCoy, Junghyun Min, and Tal Linzen. 2020. BERTs of a feather do not generalize together: Large variability in generalization across models with similar test set performance. In *Proceedings of the Third BlackboxNLP Workshop on Analyzing and Interpreting Neural Networks for NLP*, pages 217–227, Online. Association for Computational Linguistics.

Kevin Meng, David Bau, Alex Andonian, and Yonatan Belinkov. 2022. Locating and editing factual knowledge in gpt.

William Merrill, Vivek Ramanujan, Yoav Goldberg, Roy Schwartz, and Noah A. Smith. 2021. Effects of parameter norm growth during transformer training: Inductive bias from gradient descent. In *Proceedings of the 2021 Conference on Empirical Methods in Natural Language Processing*, pages 1766–1781, Online and Punta Cana, Dominican Republic. Association for Computational Linguistics.

Debora Nozza, Federico Bianchi, and Dirk Hovy. 2020. What the [mask]? making sense of language-specific bert models.

Joe O'Connor and Jacob Andreas. 2021. What context features can transformer language models use? In *Proceedings of the 59th Annual Meeting of the Association for Computational Linguistics and the 11th International Joint Conference on Natural Language Processing (Volume 1: Long Papers)*, pages 851–864, Online. Association for Computational Linguistics.

Ramakanth Pasunuru and Mohit Bansal. 2019. Continual and multi-task architecture search.

Matthew E. Peters, Mark Neumann, Luke Zettlemoyer, and Wen-tau Yih. 2018. Dissecting contextual word embeddings: Architecture and representation. In *Proceedings of the 2018 Conference on Empirical Methods in Natural Language Processing*, pages 1499–1509, Brussels, Belgium. Association for Computational Linguistics.

Michael Petrov, Chelsea Voss, Ludwig Schubert, Nick Cammarata, Gabriel Goh, and Chris Olah. 2021. Weight banding. *Distill*. Https://distill.pub/2020/circuits/weight-banding.

Hieu Pham, Melody Y. Guan, Barret Zoph, Quoc V. Le, and Jeff Dean. 2018. Efficient neural architecture search via parameter sharing.

Tiago Pimentel and Ryan Cotterell. 2021. A bayesian framework for information-theoretic probing.

Tiago Pimentel, Naomi Saphra, Adina Williams, and Ryan Cotterell. 2020a. Pareto probing: Trading off accuracy for complexity. *CoRR*, abs/2010.02180.

Tiago Pimentel, Josef Valvoda, Rowan Hall Maudslay, Ran Zmigrod, Adina Williams, and Ryan Cotterell. 2020b. Information-theoretic probing for linguistic structure. *CoRR*, abs/2004.03061.

Telmo Pires, Eva Schlinger, and Dan Garrette. 2019. How multilingual is multilingual BERT? In *Proceedings of the 57th Annual Meeting of the Association for Computational Linguistics*, pages 4996–5001, Florence, Italy. Association for Computational Linguistics.

Alec Radford, Jong Wook Kim, Chris Hallacy, Aditya Ramesh, Gabriel Goh, Sandhini Agarwal, Girish Sastry, Amanda Askell, Pamela Mishkin, Jack Clark, et al. 2021. Learning transferable visual models from natural language supervision. *arXiv preprint arXiv:2103.00020*.

Alec Radford, Jeffrey Wu, Rewon Child, David Luan, Dario Amodei, Ilya Sutskever, et al. 2019. Language models are unsupervised multitask learners. *OpenAI blog*, 1(8):9.

Marco Ribeiro, Sameer Singh, and Carlos Guestrin. 2016. "why should I trust you?": Explaining the predictions of any classifier. In *Proceedings of the 2016 Conference of the North American Chapter of the Association for Computational Linguistics: Demonstrations*, pages 97–101, San Diego, California. Association for Computational Linguistics.

Anna Rogers, Olga Kovaleva, and Anna Rumshisky. 2020. A primer in bertology: What we know about how bert works. *Transactions of the Association for Computational Linguistics*, 8:842–866.

Ansgar Rössig and Milena Petkovic. 2021. Advances in verification of ReLU neural networks. *Journal of Global Optimization*, 81(1).

Sebastian Ruder, Ivan Vulić, and Anders Søgaard. 2019. A survey of cross-lingual word embedding models. *Journal of Artificial Intelligence Research*, 65:569–631.

Gözde Gül Şahin, Clara Vania, Ilia Kuznetsov, and Iryna Gurevych. 2020. Linspector: Multilingual probing tasks for word representations. *Computational Linguistics*, 46(2):335–385.

Victor Sanh, Lysandre Debut, Julien Chaumond, and Thomas Wolf. 2019. Distilbert, a distilled version of bert: smaller, faster, cheaper and lighter. *arXiv preprint arXiv:1910.01108*.

Naomi Saphra. 2021. *Training dynamics of neural language models*. Ph.D. thesis, The University of Edinburgh.

Sofia Serrano and Noah A. Smith. 2019. Is attention interpretable? In *Proceedings of the 57th Annual Meeting of the Association for Computational Linguistics*, pages 2931–2951, Florence, Italy. Association for Computational Linguistics.

Cosma Rohilla Shalizi. 2003. Optimal nonlinear prediction of random fields on networks. In *DMCS*.

Cosma Rohilla Shalizi, Robert Haslinger, Jean-Baptiste Rouquier, Kristina Lisa Klinkner, and Cristopher Moore. 2006. Automatic filters for the detection of coherent structure in spatiotemporal systems. *Physical review. E, Statistical, nonlinear, and soft matter physics*, 73 3 Pt 2:036104.

Cosma Rohilla Shalizi, Kristina Lisa Shalizi, and Robert Haslinger. 2004. Quantifying self-organization with optimal predictors. *Physical review letters*, 93 11:118701.

Xing Shi, Inkit Padhi, and Kevin Knight. 2016. Does string-based neural MT learn source syntax? In *Proceedings of the 2016 Conference on Empirical Methods in Natural Language Processing*, pages 1526–1534, Austin, Texas. Association for Computational Linguistics.

Avanti Shrikumar, Peyton Greenside, and Anshul Kundaje. 2019. Learning important features through propagating activation differences.

Anupam Shukla, Ritu Tiwari, and Rahul Kala. 2010. *Modular Neural Networks*, pages 307–335. Springer Berlin Heidelberg, Berlin, Heidelberg.

Koustuv Sinha, Robin Jia, Dieuwke Hupkes, Joelle Pineau, Adina Williams, and Douwe Kiela. 2021. Masked language modeling and the distributional hypothesis: Order word matters pre-training for little. In *Proceedings of the 2021 Conference on Empirical Methods in Natural Language Processing*, pages 2888–2913, Online and Punta Cana, Dominican Republic. Association for Computational Linguistics.

David So, Quoc Le, and Chen Liang. 2019. The evolved transformer. In *Proceedings of the 36th International Conference on Machine Learning*, volume 97 of *Proceedings of Machine Learning Research*, pages 5877–5886. PMLR.

David R. So, Wojciech Manke, Hanxiao Liu, Zihang Dai, Noam Shazeer, and Quoc V. Le. 2021. Primer: Searching for efficient transformers for language modeling. *CoRR*, abs/2109.08668.

Jacob Steinhardt. 2022. Future ml systems will be qualitatively different. Https://bounded-regret.ghost.io/future-ml-systems-will-be-qualitatively-different/.

Emma Strubell, Patrick Verga, Daniel Andor, David Weiss, and Andrew McCallum. 2018. Linguistically-informed self-attention for semantic role labeling. In *Proceedings of the 2018 Conference on Empirical Methods in Natural Language Processing*, pages 5027–5038, Brussels, Belgium. Association for Computational Linguistics.

Mukund Sundararajan, Ankur Taly, and Qiqi Yan. 2017. Axiomatic attribution for deep networks. In *Proceedings of the 34th International Conference on Machine Learning*, volume 70 of *Proceedings of Machine Learning Research*, pages 3319–3328. PMLR.

Ian Tenney, Patrick Xia, Berlin Chen, Alex Wang, Adam Poliak, R Thomas McCoy, Najoung Kim, Benjamin Van Durme, Samuel R. Bowman, Dipanjan Das, and Ellie Pavlick. 2019. What do you learn from context? Probing for sentence structure in contextualized word representations. *arXiv e-prints*, page arXiv:1905.06316.

Ashish Vaswani, Noam Shazeer, Niki Parmar, Jakob Uszkoreit, Llion Jones, Aidan N Gomez, Ł ukasz Kaiser, and Illia Polosukhin. 2017. Attention is all you need. In *Advances in Neural Information Processing Systems*, volume 30. Curran Associates, Inc.

Elena Voita and Ivan Titov. 2020. Information-theoretic probing with minimum description length. In *Proceedings of the 2020 Conference on Empirical Methods in Natural Language Processing (EMNLP)*, pages 183–196, Online. Association for Computational Linguistics.

Chelsea Voss, Gabriel Goh, Nick Cammarata, Michael Petrov, Ludwig Schubert, and Chris Olah. 2021. Branch specialization. *Distill*. Https://distill.pub/2020/circuits/branch-specialization.

Ivan Vulić, Edoardo Maria Ponti, Robert Litschko, Goran Glavaš, and Anna Korhonen. 2020. Probing pretrained language models for lexical semantics. In *Proceedings of the 2020 Conference on Empirical Methods in Natural Language Processing (EMNLP)*, pages 7222–7240, Online. Association for Computational Linguistics.

Jennifer C. White, Tiago Pimentel, Naomi Saphra, and Ryan Cotterell. 2021. A non-linear structural probe. In *Proceedings of the 2021 Conference of the North American Chapter of the Association for Computational Linguistics: Human Language Technologies*, pages 132–138, Online. Association for Computational Linguistics.

Sarah Wiegreffe and Yuval Pinter. 2019. Attention is not not explanation. In *Proceedings of the 2019 Conference on Empirical Methods in Natural Language Processing and the 9th International Joint Conference on Natural Language Processing (EMNLP-IJCNLP)*, pages 11–20, Hong Kong, China. Association for Computational Linguistics.

Shijie Wu and Mark Dredze. 2019. Beto, bentz, becas: The surprising cross-lingual effectiveness of BERT. In *Proceedings of the 2019 Conference on Empirical Methods in Natural Language Processing and the 9th International Joint Conference on Natural Language Processing (EMNLP-IJCNLP)*, pages 833–844, Hong Kong, China. Association for Computational Linguistics.

Shijie Wu and Mark Dredze. 2020. Are all languages created equal in multilingual BERT? In *Proceedings of the 5th Workshop on Representation Learning for NLP*, pages 120–130, Online. Association for Computational Linguistics.

Yadollah Yaghoobzadeh, Katharina Kann, T. J. Hazen, Eneko Agirre, and Hinrich Schütze. 2019. Probing for semantic classes: Diagnosing the meaning content of word embeddings. In *Proceedings of the 57th Annual Meeting of the Association for Computational Linguistics*, pages 5740–5753, Florence, Italy. Association for Computational Linguistics.

Hongyang Zhang, Junru Shao, and Ruslan Salakhutdinov. 2020. Deep neural networks with multi-branch architectures are intrinsically less non-convex. In *AISTATS 2019 - 22nd International Conference on Artificial Intelligence and Statistics*.

Kelly Zhang and Samuel Bowman. 2018. Language modeling teaches you more than translation does: Lessons learned through auxiliary syntactic task analysis. In *Proceedings of the 2018 EMNLP Workshop BlackboxNLP: Analyzing and Interpreting Neural Networks for NLP*, pages 359–361, Brussels, Belgium. Association for Computational Linguistics.

Zining Zhu and Frank Rudzicz. 2020. An information theoretic view on selecting linguistic probes. In *Proceedings of the 2020 Conference on Empirical Methods in Natural Language Processing (EMNLP)*, pages 9251–9262, Online. Association for Computational Linguistics.

Liu Zhuang, Lin Wayne, Shi Ya, and Zhao Jun. 2021. A robustly optimized BERT pre-training approach with post-training. In *Proceedings of the 20th Chinese National Conference on Computational Linguistics*, pages 1218–1227, Huhhot, China. Chinese Information Processing Society of China.

Foundation Models of Scientific Knowledge for Chemistry: Opportunities, Challenges and Lessons Learned

Sameera Horawalavithana, Ellyn Ayton, Shivam Sharma, Scott Howland, Megha Subramanian, Scott Vasquez, Robin Cosbey, Maria Glenski, Svitlana Volkova
Pacific Northwest National Laboratory, Richland, WA

Abstract

Foundation models pre-trained on large corpora demonstrate significant gains across many natural language processing tasks and domains e.g., law, healthcare, education, etc. However, only limited efforts have investigated the opportunities and limitations of applying these powerful models to science and security applications. In this work, we develop foundation models of scientific knowledge for chemistry to augment scientists with the advanced ability to perceive and reason at scale previously unimagined. Specifically, we build large-scale (1.47B parameter) general-purpose models for chemistry that can be effectively used to perform a wide range of in-domain and out-of-domain tasks. Evaluating these models in a zero-shot setting, we analyze the effect of model and data scaling, knowledge depth, and temporality on model performance in context of model training efficiency.

Our novel findings demonstrate that (1) model size significantly contributes to the task performance when evaluated in a zero-shot setting; (2) data quality (aka diversity) affects model performance more than data quantity; (3) similarly, unlike previous work (Luu et al., 2021) temporal order of the documents in the corpus boosts model performance only for specific tasks, e.g., SciQ; and (4) models pre-trained from scratch perform better on in-domain tasks than those tuned from general-purpose models like Open AI's GPT-2.

1 Introduction

The emergence of foundation models (Bommasani et al., 2021) such as large-scale autoencoding models (*e.g.,* BERT (Devlin et al., 2018), RoBERTa (Liu et al., 2019)) and autoregressive language models (*e.g.,* GPT-2 (Radford et al., 2019), GPT-3 (Brown et al., 2020), Megatron-Turing (Smith et al., 2022) and Gopher (Rae et al., 2021)) as well as multimodal vision and language models, such as FLAVA (Singh et al., 2021) and Perceiver (Jaegle et al., 2021), established a paradigm shift in Artificial Intelligence (AI). These foundation models, also called *neural platforms*, are built using self-supervised pretraining at scale. They are then able to be easily adapted to a wide range of downstream tasks via transfer learning (Bommasani et al., 2021) and fine-tuning (Lee et al., 2019).

The wide community adoption of foundation models can be explained by their key properties, two of which are *emergent behavior* and *homogenization* – which also make foundation models appealing for adaption across science and security domains. Emergence, or emergent behavior, reflect new behaviors that a model introduces or is capable of that it was not explicitly trained to perform. Homogenization is the consolidation of methods for building machine learning systems across a wide range of tasks. Another key advantage of scaling language models is that they perform competitively on language tasks using in-context learning without fine-tuning or gradient updates. Thus, in-context learning allows foundation models to be effectively used across new downstream tasks with only simple instructions and a few optional examples.

In this work we focus on a science domain (chemistry) and demonstrate the value and limitations of large-scale language models evaluated across a wide range of in-domain (science-focused) and out-of-domain tasks. Unlike the majority of work on foundation models that focuses on pretraining these models on book corpora, web pages, Wikipedia and mixed sources, *e.g.,* the Pile (Gao et al., 2020), we pretrain our models on scientific literature. Using scientific literature presents unique opportunities and challenges. Opportunities include the scale and diversity of scientific literature, the explicit structure, and explicit alignment across different modalities in the papers, *e.g.,* table and figure references. Challenges include limited benchmarks that can be used to perform model

Proceedings of BigScience Episode #5 – Workshop on Challenges & Perspectives in Creating Large Language Models, pages 160 - 172
May 27, 2022

evaluation, model prompting and interactions.

There are three major contributions of this work: *(1)* we collect and release a 0.67TB dataset covering research publication data across 10+ sources for chemistry; *(2)* we release 28 auto-regressive foundation models for chemistry that have been pretrained from scratch; and *(3)* we present a rigorous evaluation of model performance on 15+ in-domain and out-of-domain tasks that investigates the effects of model and data scaling, knowledge depth (aka diversity), and temporal order on performance as described in research questions below.

(RQ1) Science-Focused Benchmarks What are the strengths and weaknesses of foundation models pretrained on scientific literature when evaluated on out-of-domain vs. in-domain tasks?

(RQ2) Scaling Effect How does model scale affect the downstream performance? Do neural scaling laws presented in (Kaplan et al., 2020) hold for the foundation models for science?

(RQ3) Diversity Effect How does the depth of scientific knowledge, *e.g.,* from paper abstracts vs. full text, affect downstream performance?

(RQ4) Temporal Effect How does the recency of scientific knowledge, *e.g.,* when manipulating the temporal order of the documents processed by the model, affect downstream performance?

2 Related Work

In this section we summarize previous efforts in two categories: *mixed-domain continual pretraining* that continues pretraining of a base model on domain data and *in-domain pretraining from scratch* that pretrains a from scratch on domain data. We present a model summary in Table 1.

Mixed-Domain Continual Pretraining Many efforts have focused on continual pretraining of a BERT (Devlin et al., 2018) base model. Several models have been developed for the biomedical domain and the most frequently used corpora for domain-specific continual preraining are PubMed abstracts and PubMed Central full-text articles (PMC) (Lee et al., 2020; Peng et al., 2019; Phan et al., 2021). In the Chemistry domain, Guo et al. (2021) performed continual pretraining of a base BERT model on 200K chemistry journal articles for product extraction (ChemBERT) and reaction role labeling (ChemRxnBERT).

In-Domain Pretraining from Scratch Previous work has shown that pretraining models from scratch on domain-specific data has a significant benefit over continual pretraining of general-domain language models (Gu et al., 2021). This is mainly due to the availability of in-domain data for both generating the vocabulary and pretraining. SciBERT (Beltagy et al., 2019) is pretrained according to this procedure using the vocabulary generated from computer science and biomedical domains. PubMedBERT (Gu et al., 2021) is another example of pretraining the base BERT model from scratch using PubMed. Unlike any previous work, we use both continual and from scratch pretraining to build the largest foundation model for Chemistry (1.47B) on the largest (0.67TB) and the most diverse corpus (10+ sources) collected to date.

3 Model Pretraining

Unlike the majority of related models that rely on a base BERT (or variant) model, we adapt the OpenAI's GPT-2 transformer decoder architecture (Radford et al., 2019) to train autoregressive language models for Chemistry. To understand the impact of model size (RQ2), we experiment with four different Transformer sizes: small (S), medium (M), large (L), and extra-large (XL). These models differ in the number of decoder layers, hidden size of the model, and the number of attention heads in transformer blocks as shown in Table 2.

Our experiments leverage the GPT-NeoX Python library (Andonian et al., 2021) developed with Megatron (Shoeybi et al., 2019) and DeepSpeed (Rasley et al., 2020). We optimize the autoregressive log-likelihood (*i.e.,* cross-entropy loss) averaged over a 2048-token context. We set the micro batch size per GPU as 4, and the learning rate to 2×10^{-4}, and rely on the cosine decay. We use an Adam optimizer with $\beta_1 = 0.9$, $\beta_2 = 0.99$, and $\sigma = 10^{-8}$ and clip the gradient norm at 1.0. In addition, ZeRO optimizer (Rajbhandari et al., 2019) was used to reduce memory footprint by distributing optimizer states across several processes.

To reduce memory and increase training throughput, we use mixed-precision training (Rasley et al., 2020) and the parallel attention and feed-forward implementations available in GPT-NeoX (Black et al., 2022). We also use the Rotary positional embeddings (Su et al., 2021) instead of the learned positional embeddings used in the GPT-2 model (Radford et al., 2019) because they offer performance

Table 1: Foundation models for science focus on the biomedical, math, computer science and chemistry domains. We use † to indicate models trained for chemistry.

Model		Data Source	Pretraining	Corpus	#Params (B)
Lee et al. 2020	BioBERT	Wiki + Books	continual pretraining	PubMed	0.11
Alsentzer et al. 2019	ClinicalBERT	Wiki + Books	continual pretraining	MIMIC[1]	0.11
Peng et al. 2019	BlueBERT	Wiki + Books	continual pretraining	PubMed + MIMIC	0.11
Liu et al. 2021	MATH-BERT	Arxiv	continual pretraining	Arxiv	0.11
Guo et al. 2021	Chem(Rxn)BERT †	Wiki + Books	continual pretraining	Chemistry Journals	0.11
Phan et al. 2021	SciFive	C4	continual pretraining	PubMed	0.22 0.77
Naseem et al. 2021	BioALBERT	Wiki + Books	continual pretraining	PMC + MIMIC-II	0.02
Lewis et al. 2020	BioRoBERTa	Wiki + Books	continual pretraining	PMC + MIMIC-III	0.30
Yuan et al. 2021	KeBioLM	PubMed	continual pretraining	PubMed + UMLS[2]	0.34
Shin et al. 2020	BioMegatron	PubMed	from scratch continual pretraining	PubMed	0.80 1.20
Kanakarajan et al. 2021	BioELECTRA	PubMed	from scratch	PubMed	0.11
Miolo et al. 2021	ELECTRAMed	PubMed	from scratch	PubMed	0.11
Beltagy et al. 2019	SciBERT	PMC + CS	from scratch	PMC + CS	0.11
Liu et al. 2021	OAG-BERT	OAG	from scratch	OAG	0.11
Gu et al. 2021	PubMedBERT	PubMed	from scratch	PubMed	0.34
Our Work (autoregressive) †		10+ sources (Chemistry)	from scratch continual pretraining	10+ sources (Chemistry)	1.47

Table 2: Our model configurations: d_L is the number of decoder layers, d_{dim} is the hidden size of the model, d_{heads} is the number of attention heads. We compare model configurations between GPT-NeoX and OpenAI's GPT-2. GPT-NeoX architecture is originally from GPT-3 (Brown et al., 2020)

Size	Model	d_L	d_{dim}	d_{heads}	#Params (B)
S	GPT-NeoX	12	768	12	0.18
	GPT-2	12	768	12	
M	GPT-NeoX	24	1024	16	0.40
	GPT-2	24	1024	16	
L	GPT-NeoX	24	1536	16	0.80
	GPT-2	36	1280	20	
XL	GPT-NeoX	24	2048	16	1.47
	GPT-2	48	1600	25	

advantages in tasks with longer texts by capturing relative position dependency in self-attention.

Our models are pretrained across multiple workers with data parallelism. As the largest model in our experiments fit on a single GPU, we didn't use the model (tensor) or pipeline parallelism. Models are pretrained from scratch for a total of 320K steps. The original GPT-2 models are fine-tuned for 150K steps. We perform experiments in a single DGX-A100 machine with 8 80Gb GPUs.

4 Data Collection and Processing

We collected a large corpus of 53.45 million chemistry-focused scientific articles and abstracts, resulting in 670GB of text data. As shown in Table 3, our corpus was collected from 10 different data sources: Arxiv, Aminer (AMiner), CORD-19 (Wang et al., 2020b), CORE (Pontika et al., 2016), Microsoft Academic Graph (MAG) (Wang et al., 2020a), OSTI, PubMed (Gao et al., 2020) (abstracts and fulltexts), and the Web of Science (WoS). See Appendix A for full data descriptions.

Table 3: Dataset statistics: combined datasets are after the de-duplication process. We split datasets to those that include abstracts ⟨A⟩ vs. full texts ⟨FT⟩.

Source	#Articles (M)	#Tokens (B)	Size (Gb)
MAG ⟨A⟩	34.26	7.43	46
Aminer ⟨A⟩	18.50	5.80	35
S2ORC ⟨A⟩	10.44	2.05	32
WoS ⟨A⟩	7.90	3.31	18
CORD-19 ⟨A⟩	< 0.01	< 0.01	0.2
OSTI ⟨A⟩	0.05	< 0.01	0.1
Arxiv ⟨A⟩	0.38	0.04	0.4
PubMed ⟨A⟩	0.28	0.08	0.5
PubMed ⟨FT⟩	0.70	7.34	32
CORE ⟨FT⟩	7.27	215.50	743
Combined ⟨A⟩	46.94	16.18	67
Combined ⟨FT⟩	6.52	184.42	603
Combined ⟨A+FT⟩	53.45	200.61	670

Because the data sources we relied on comprise research publications from many science domains, we sampled articles using a list of domain-specific keywords for chemistry to create the dataset summarized in Table 3. These keywords were extracted by using a Correlation Explanation (Gallagher et al., 2017) topic model followed by manual filtering by subject matter experts. This resulted in a list of more than 1K chemistry-related entities, ranging from compound names like *ethyl acetate*, *methyl methacrylate*, *sulfoxide*, etc. to experiment and procedures like *tunneling microscopy*, *neutralization*, *enzymatic hydrolysis*, etc.

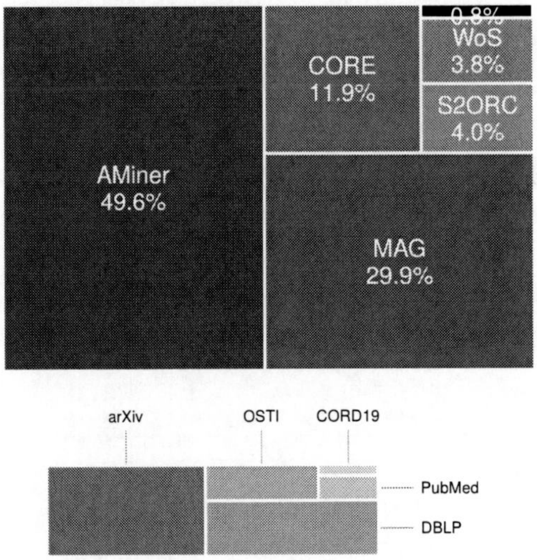

Distribution within *Sources with <1%* (upper right, black box)

Figure 1: Summary of data source representation within the *Combined A+F* data sample. Coloring illustrates whether a data source contains *peer reviewed* (Blue), *mixed* (Purple), or *not peer reviewed* (Red) articles.

Data Cleaning Recent research has shown that duplicates in training data can significantly impact the downstream task performance of LLMs (Lee et al., 2021; Carlini et al., 2022). To this end, we performed deduplication of our corpus based on overlap of titles within and across data sources. We processed titles to strip punctuation and casefold and considered two articles A_1 and A_2 to be duplicates if they had the same processed title. With this technique, we were able to remove significant amounts of duplicate scientific articles both within and across sources. The deduplication process reduced our corpus from 875GB to 670GB (67.8M to 53.5M publications), removing 14.3M duplicates.

Tokenization As used in GPT-2 model, we use a Byte Pair Encoding (BPE) tokenizer. We train BPE tokenizers for each data sample with a vocabulary size of 64K as preliminary experiments varying vocabulary sizes from 64K to 256K for smaller scale model pretraining did not show significant differences in performance. We compare the GPT-2 vocabulary generated from the WebText and the in-domain vocabularies generated from our corpora and find that the in-domain vocabulary breaks chemical entities into fewer tokens. For example, *dimethylnitroxide* was tokenized into #dimethyl, #nitr, #oxide using the in-domain vocabulary and *#dim, #ethyl, #nit, #rox, #ide* using the GPT-2 vocabulary.

5 Analysis and Results

This section presents the analysis of 28 pretrained models evaluated on 15+ in-domain and out-of-domain downstream tasks (*RQ1*, Section 5.1). We investigate the effects of model and data scaling (*RQ2*, Section 5.2), knowledge diversity (*RQ3*, Section 5.3), and temporal order (*RQ4*, Section 5.4) on the downstream performance. We also compare the results from continual vs. from scratch pretraining (Section 5.5) and present the analysis of large-scale training efficiency (Section 5.6).

Baseline Models As we use a similar model architecture, we identify Open AI's GPT-2 (Radford et al., 2019) as a baseline comparison model. We compare our performance with four variants of the original GPT-2 models, corresponding to small (S), medium (M), large (L), and extra-large (XL) sized transformer architectures shown in Table 2. We note that GPT-2 models were pretrained on WebText – 8 million web documents (40Gb). Thus, we also include a base GPT-2 model (medium) that has been updated with continual pretraining using our *Combined ⟨A+FT⟩* dataset.

Our Models We pretrained models with individual datasets (AMiner, CORE, MAG, PubMed, S2ORC, WOS) and combined abstracts and full-texts. Our goal is to systematically study data biases in the model performance when pretraining models with individual datasets. For example, PubMed publications cover mostly bio-medicinal terms (Gu et al., 2021), while the majority of S2ORC publications are from medicine, biology, physics, and mathematics (Lo et al., 2020). We only use 4 GPUs for the models pretrained with individual datasets and 8 GPUs for the rest. This is to control the number of tokens seen during model pretraining (320,000 steps * 4 GPUs * 4 micro batch size * 2,048 context size = 10B tokens) relative to the maximum number of tokens available in the respective datasets (as reported in Table 3). We also trained one XL (4x) model with 4x larger batch size than what used in XL model to evaluate the impact of the number of training tokens.

5.1 Zero-shot Performance

We evaluate our models using several benchmarks to assess the effectiveness in both in-domain and out-of-domain tasks. The benchmarks we include are described in Appendix B. We use the lm-evaluation-harness Python repository (Gao et al.,

Table 4: Downstream Zero-shot In-Domain Task Performance. We use ‡ to indicate the baseline model tuned from the base GPT-2 model. Pile performance is reported using perplexity, with all other tasks reported using accuracy. We highlight the top-4 performance per task in bold, with top performance indicated with an underline. XL (4x) model is trained with 4x larger batch size that used in other models.

Model	Size	HT-HC	HT-CC	ARC-E	ARC-C	SciQ	OpenBookQA	Pile
Baseline	S	0.22	0.25	0.44	0.19	0.75	0.16	96.50
	M	0.18	0.27	0.49	0.22	0.77	**0.19**	61.26
	L	0.18	0.28	**0.53**	0.22	**0.80**	**0.19**	48.86
	XL	0.18	0.26	**0.58**	**0.25**	**0.83**	**0.22**	42.29
	M‡	0.19	0.31	0.35	0.19	0.61	0.13	87.57
AMiner	S	0.18	0.27	0.43	0.21	0.70	0.17	38.40
	M	0.18	**0.34**	0.45	0.20	0.74	0.16	30.55
	L	0.23	**0.34**	0.49	**0.23**	0.78	0.18	**24.18**
	XL	0.23	**0.34**	0.50	**0.23**	0.77	0.17	25.52
CORE	S	0.19	0.28	0.36	0.19	0.69	0.15	78.24
	M	0.22	**0.34**	0.40	0.20	0.71	0.15	59.19
	L	0.17	0.30	0.41	0.19	0.75	0.14	52.95
	XL	0.20	0.28	0.47	0.21	0.78	0.15	39.46
MAG	S	0.24	0.28	0.41	0.20	0.66	0.17	38.03
	M	0.18	0.27	0.45	0.21	0.68	0.17	30.88
	L	0.19	**0.36**	0.51	**0.24**	**0.80**	0.18	**24.78**
	XL	0.20	**0.36**	0.50	0.22	**0.80**	**0.20**	26.09
PubMed-F	S	**0.26**	0.30	0.41	0.20	0.60	0.16	56.03
	M	0.19	0.27	0.43	0.21	0.68	0.18	45.69
	L	0.18	0.28	0.43	0.22	0.74	0.17	37.22
	XL	0.18	0.27	0.48	0.21	0.77	0.16	35.14
S2ORC	S	**0.26**	0.33	0.31	0.21	0.31	0.17	59.20
	M	**0.27**	0.22	0.33	0.18	0.31	0.16	45.60
	L	**0.28**	0.23	0.32	0.21	0.31	0.17	42.14
	XL	0.24	0.31	0.33	0.19	0.30	0.18	42.35
WoS	S	0.22	0.31	0.33	0.22	0.37	0.17	54.41
	M	0.25	0.32	0.32	0.20	0.34	0.16	48.31
	L	**0.27**	0.30	0.32	0.21	0.37	0.17	46.44
	XL	0.23	**0.34**	0.34	0.21	0.39	0.16	45.86
Combined-A	XL	0.17	0.28	**0.54**	**0.23**	**0.83**	0.18	**22.77**
Combined-F	XL	0.20	0.30	0.48	0.21	0.79	0.15	40.18
Combined-A+F	XL	0.18	0.30	0.48	0.22	0.79	0.17	31.03
Combined-A+F	XL (4x)	0.18	0.25	**0.55**	**0.24**	**0.84**	0.17	**23.01**

2021) for the benchmark implementation.

In-domain Evaluation We consider five existing chemistry benchmarks, specifically HendrycksTest (Hendrycks et al., 2020) for high school (HT-HC) and college (HT-CC) levels, and science-focused – ARC (Clark et al., 2018), SciQ (Welbl et al., 2017), OpenBookQA (Mihaylov et al., 2018), Pile-PubMed-Abstracts (Gao et al., 2020)). As shown in Table 4, one or more of our models outperform baseline GPT-2 models for the two chemistry tasks, general science QA (SciQ) and the science-focused language modelling. Of the remaining tasks, our models perform within 1-4% of GPT-2 baselines.

Out-of-domain Evaluation We evaluate out-of-domain performance using 9 commonly used LLM benchmarks: BoolQ (Clark et al., 2019), CB (De Marneffe et al., 2019), WIC (Pilehvar and Camacho-Collados, 2018), WSC (Levesque et al., 2012), MathQA (Amini et al., 2019), PIQA (Bisk et al., 2020), PubMedQA (Jin et al., 2019), Lambada (Paperno et al., 2016) and WikiText (Merity et al., 2016). As shown in Table 5, our models outperform baseline GPT-2 models for CB, WIC and WSC and match the best accuracy for BoolQ but the GPT-2 baselines outperform on the remaining tasks, particularly Lambada and Wikitext – the two general language modeling tasks.

5.2 Scaling Effect

Previous work (Kaplan et al., 2020) has shown that upstream cross entropy loss scales as a power-law with model size, dataset size, and the amount of compute. In this section, we revisit these claims on scaling Transformer architectures.

Analyzing upstream cross entropy loss During pretraining, we group each dataset into training/validation/test (949/50/1) splits. We report the

Table 5: Downstream Out-of-domain Task Performance. We use ‡ to indicate the baseline model tuned from the base GPT-2 model. Performance on Lambada and Wikitext is reported using perplexity, all other tasks report accuracy . Top-4 performance highlighted in bold, with best performance indicated with underlines. XL (4x) model is trained with 4x larger batch size that used in other models.

Model	Size	BoolQ	CB	WIC	WSC	MathQA	PIQA	PubMedQA	Lambada	Wikitext
Baseline	S	0.49	0.41	0.49	0.43	0.21	**0.63**	0.44	40.06	37.37
	M	0.59	0.43	0.50	0.40	**0.23**	**0.68**	0.53	**18.25**	**26.75**
	L	0.60	**0.45**	0.50	0.46	**0.23**	**0.70**	0.54	**12.97**	**22.61**
	XL	**0.61**	0.39	0.50	0.50	**0.24**	**0.71**	**0.59**	**10.63**	**20.38**
	M‡	**0.62**	0.34	0.50	0.36	0.20	0.55	**0.55**	2834.51	126.55
AMiner	S	0.41	0.39	0.50	0.44	0.22	0.56	0.46	2825.84	158.85
	M	0.40	0.39	**0.51**	0.41	0.21	0.57	0.43	1802.35	116.93
	L	**0.61**	**0.48**	0.50	0.47	0.22	0.58	0.36	661.81	87.23
	XL	0.50	0.39	0.50	0.37	0.21	0.58	0.43	786.22	91.28
CORE	S	**0.62**	0.41	0.50	0.37	0.20	0.55	**0.55**	671.43	100.53
	M	**0.62**	0.41	0.50	0.37	0.21	0.56	**0.55**	273.06	77.96
	L	**0.61**	0.41	0.50	0.37	0.21	0.57	0.51	173.15	69.62
	XL	**0.61**	0.38	0.50	0.37	0.22	0.58	0.45	79.95	50.47
MAG	S	0.41	0.23	0.50	0.40	0.21	0.56	0.43	1142.83	118.40
	M	0.38	0.07	0.50	0.37	0.21	0.57	0.41	628.72	91.36
	L	0.51	0.14	0.50	0.35	0.22	0.59	0.39	282.39	67.74
	XL	0.40	0.11	**0.51**	0.62	0.22	0.59	0.34	364.54	70.71
PubMed-F	S	0.58	0.41	0.50	0.45	0.21	0.57	0.54	2670.39	148.88
	M	**0.61**	0.39	0.50	0.38	0.20	0.58	0.49	1742.00	119.74
	L	0.57	0.41	0.50	0.38	0.21	0.59	0.42	843.83	95.75
	XL	0.60	0.41	0.50	0.39	0.22	0.59	0.49	679.80	90.38
S2ORC	S	0.38	0.41	0.50	**0.63**	0.20	0.57	0.34	122739.30	403.48
	M	0.38	0.43	0.50	**0.63**	0.22	0.56	0.34	80151.10	330.56
	L	0.38	**0.46**	0.50	**0.63**	0.21	0.56	0.34	89136.68	327.53
	XL	0.38	0.50	0.50	**0.63**	0.20	0.56	0.33	107065.48	351.81
WoS	S	0.38	0.39	0.50	**0.63**	0.21	0.55	0.34	140552.69	556.00
	M	0.38	**0.45**	0.50	**0.63**	0.19	0.54	0.34	182967.37	498.36
	L	0.41	0.36	0.47	0.54	0.21	0.56	0.42	148609.73	480.91
	XL	0.57	0.34	0.50	0.37	0.20	0.55	**0.56**	192970.64	509.06
Combined-A	XL	0.56	0.16	0.50	0.37	0.21	0.60	0.50	250.88	61.07
Combined-F	XL	**0.62**	0.38	0.50	0.37	0.22	0.57	**0.55**	72.50	48.96
Combined-A+F	XL	**0.61**	0.41	0.50	0.39	**0.23**	0.59	0.48	71.43	48.65
Combined-A+F	XL (4x)	**0.61**	0.41	0.50	0.37	**0.24**	0.60	**0.56**	**30.40**	**33.05**

model performance on validation data using cross entropy loss in nats. This measure will be averaged over the 2048-token context. We find that the cross entropy loss decreases as we increase the model size (as shown in Figure 2). Larger models reach a given loss value in a higher rate than the smaller models. This observation illustrates the relationship between model performance (as measured by the upstream cross entropy loss) and model size, confirming (Kaplan et al., 2020).

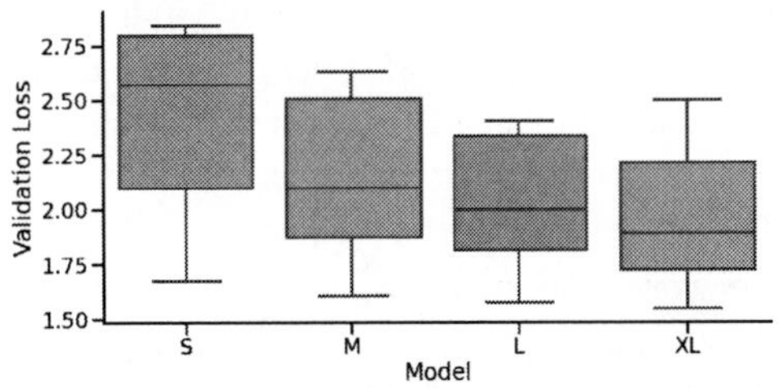

Figure 2: Distribution of validation loss by model size: performance improves as the model size increases.

Analyzing downstream task performance Can we speculate downstream task performance of a model from the pretraining performance? First, we find that the models perform considerably well on *Pile* in comparison to the *Lambada or WikiText*. There is a 48% performance advantage in this task over the best performing baseline GPT-2 model. This may be due to the models capturing scientific language better than general language. It is important to note that we exclude PubMed Abstracts in the individual data collection to avoid potential contamination between the training and *Pile* testing data. As shown in Table 4, larger models perform well on these language modeling tasks.

Second, we noticed that the XL (4x) model trained for more tokens performs significantly better than the similar sized XL model. Specifically, XL (4x) model was trained with 128 total batch size compared to the 32 total batch size used in XL model. XL (4x) model achieves the lowest *Lambada and WikiText* perplexity values across all our models trained from scratch (as shown in Table 5). The same model also achieves the best SciQ performance with 0.84 accuracy and comparable in other tasks performance with the XL model. This experiment highlights the importance of training models with larger batch size. We note that the baseline models (Radford et al., 2019) were trained with 4x larger batch size (total batch size 512) than what used in XL (4x) model. We believe that the XL (4x) model can reach the similar perplexity values when trained for this data scale.

Third, we find that zero-shot task performance in SciQ, HT-CC and ARC-E increases as we increase the model size (see Table 5). However, there is no clear relationship between the task performance and the model sizes in the rest of benchmark datasets. We suggest that pretraining performance may not be the ideal indicator to speculate the overall downstream task performance, especially in the zero-shot setting. However, model size significantly contributes to the task performance.

5.3 Diversity Effect

While abstracts often provide a summary of scientific publications, the full text contains more details. In this section, we analyze the performance of models trained on paper abstracts versus full texts.

First, the XL models trained with the combined abstract dataset achieve the lowest perplexity score (22.77) on the Pile – a 45% performance advantage over the full text version. There are might be several factors that contribute to this, but one may be the focused language in abstracts.

Second, the model trained with the combined abstracts achieves the second best accuracy (0.83 in comparison to 0.79 for the full text model) in SciQ. Some of the models pretrained on individual abstract data achieve comparable performance in SciQ, *e.g.,* MAG and AMiner models achieve 0.8 and 0.78 accuracy, respectively. We believe the diversity of scientific knowledge provided from the abstract data is useful since SciQ questions span biology, chemistry, earth science, and physics.

Third, we compare model performance trained with abstracts vs. full texts in the HT task and see that the best accuracy is achieved using the MAG and S2ORC datasets rather than the combined abstracts. This suggests the importance of contextual knowledge provided by different data sources.

Finally, combined full text model performs better than the model trained with the abstracts in all out-of-domain tasks except PIQA. This performance difference may be due to the more expressive and diverse language presented in the full texts than in the abstracts. Thus, expanding full text coverage may improve out-of-domain task generalization.

5.4 Temporal Effect

Scientific knowledge evolves over time reflecting new research ideas, innovations, and findings. In this section, we test how continual pretraining on temporal-aligned scientific publications impacts downstream performance. For this experiment, we maintain two variants of the MAG dataset with random-ordered and temporal-ordered articles, splitting each into ten equal subsets. We continue pretraining a base medium (M) sized model iteratively with the subsets in the order they appeared in the respective data variant. For example, in the temporally-aligned experiments, we first pretrain a model with 3.4M (10%) articles from before 1978, and then use it as the base model to continue pretraining with another 3.4M (10%) articles from between 1978 and 1989. We train the initial model for 150K steps and each subsequent model for 10K steps with additional data. Figure 3 shows the performance of model checkpoints across in-domain and out-of-domain tasks.

There are two key findings. First, SciQ and ARC-E zero-shot task performances improve over time with the models trained with temporally-ordered scientific texts (as shown in Figure 3b). For example, SciQ accuracy improves from 0.64 to 0.73 from the base model checkpoint to the final model checkpoint. Similarly, ARC-E accuracy improves from 0.43 to 0.45. This is due to the temporal order of the knowledge acquired by the model. When the model was pretrained with random-ordered data subsets, we observe only a slight ($< 1\%$) performance increase (as shown in Figure 3a).

There are mixed patterns in performance across out-of-domain tasks. For example, a slight performance increase in the PIQA, CB, PubMedQA, and WIC over time with the models trained with temporally-ordered scientific texts. On the other hand, there is a performance drop in the BoolQ and WSC over time. This may be due to the *catastrophic forgetting* prevalent in continual learning (Ramasesh et al., 2021). Future work will in-

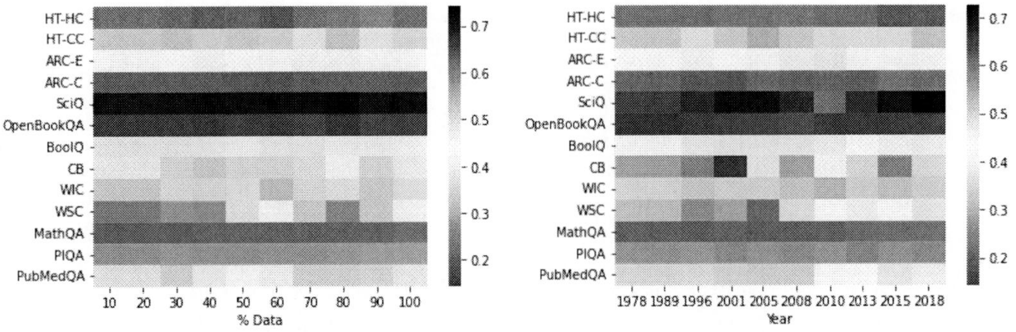

(a) Random Order (b) Temporal Order

Figure 3: The effect of temporal order of publications during pretraining. We align publications in the MAG corpus by year and split them into ten equal subsets. We repeat the process in a randomly-ordered corpus for comparison, recording model checkpoints after performing *continual pretraining* on each data subset.

vestigate other confounding factors that may contribute to this performance patterns.

5.5 Continual vs. From Scratch Pretraining

In this section, we test whether the continual pretraining of a base GPT model with additional domain-specific data is helpful in the downstream task performance. We report the zero-shot performance of the tuned model across in-domain (Table 4) and out-of-domain (Table 5) tasks. We have two main observations from this experiment.

First, fine-tuned models fall behind other baselines in a majority of in-domain tasks. HT-CC is the only in-domain task that the tuned model outperforms the rest of models, yet fails to outperform the best performing model trained from scratch.

Second, fine-tuned models have a significant performance drop in the general language modeling tasks (Lambada and Wikitext). For example, the tuned model records 6x performance drop in the Wikitext compared to the best performing model. There are several factors in the continual pretraining that may contribute to this. As the tuned model uses the original GPT-2 vocabulary, it must use the fragmented general subwords to tokenize the chemistry terms available in our corpora. On the other hand, the tuned model starts with the suboptimal initialization from the general-domain language model (Gu et al., 2021). This initialization may diverge the model in the optimization process that may not be recovered.

5.6 Training Efficiency

We use several dimensions to describe the training efficiency, *i.e.,* #FLOPs, throughput (speed), and memory. We compare these compute dimensions

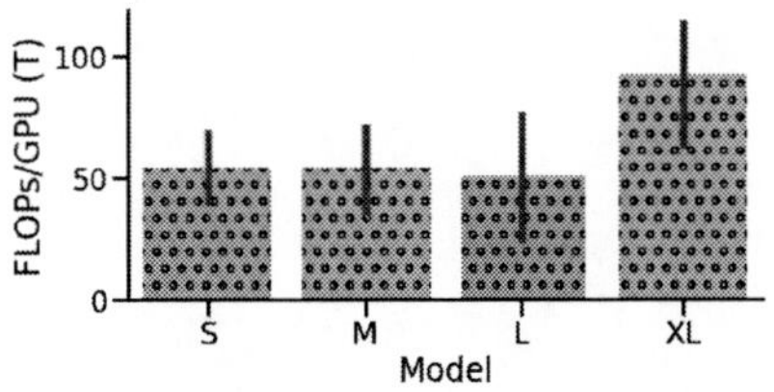

(a) GPU computation in #Floating Point Operations

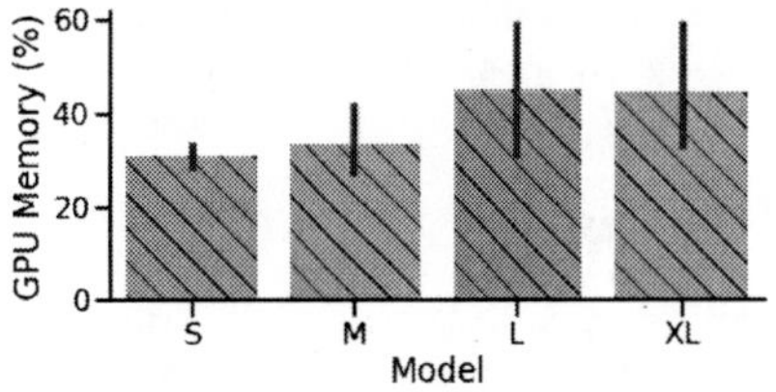

(b) GPU Memory Allocation

Figure 4: GPU system performance during pretraining.

across the four model sizes described in the Table 2. The smallest (S) model has 59% FLOPs of the largest (XL) model, twice the speed (steps/s), 32% per device GPU memory savings, and 76% total parameter savings (see Figure 4). With such compute budget, small (S) models only outperforms the XL model in 21% in-domain and 34% out-of-domain evaluation tasks. This suggests the importance of compute budget required in scaling foundation models.

6 Conclusions

In this paper, we collected and released 0.67TB of research publication data collected across 10+ sources for chemistry. We pretrained and released 25+ foundation models for chemistry. We rigorously analyzed model performance on 15+ in-domain and out-of-domain tasks.

References

Emily Alsentzer, John R Murphy, Willie Boag, Wei-Hung Weng, Di Jin, Tristan Naumann, and Matthew McDermott. 2019. Publicly available clinical bert embeddings. *arXiv preprint arXiv:1904.03323*.

AMiner. https://www.aminer.org/.

Aida Amini, Saadia Gabriel, Peter Lin, Rik Koncel-Kedziorski, Yejin Choi, and Hannaneh Hajishirzi. 2019. Mathqa: Towards interpretable math word problem solving with operation-based formalisms. *arXiv preprint arXiv:1905.13319*.

Alex Andonian, Quentin Anthony, Stella Biderman, Sid Black, Preetham Gali, Leo Gao, Eric Hallahan, Josh Levy-Kramer, Connor Leahy, Lucas Nestler, Kip Parker, Michael Pieler, Shivanshu Purohit, Tri Songz, Phil Wang, and Samuel Weinbach. 2021. GPT-NeoX: Large scale autoregressive language modeling in pytorch.

Iz Beltagy, Kyle Lo, and Arman Cohan. 2019. Scibert: A pretrained language model for scientific text. *arXiv preprint arXiv:1903.10676*.

Yonatan Bisk, Rowan Zellers, Jianfeng Gao, Yejin Choi, et al. 2020. Piqa: Reasoning about physical commonsense in natural language. In *Proceedings of the AAAI conference on artificial intelligence*, volume 34, pages 7432–7439.

Sid Black, Stella Biderman, Eric Hallahan, Quentin Anthony, Leo Gao, Laurence Golding, Horace He, Connor Leahy, Kyle McDonell, Jason Phang, et al. 2022. Gpt-neox-20b: An open-source autoregressive language model.

Rishi Bommasani, Drew A Hudson, Ehsan Adeli, Russ Altman, Simran Arora, Sydney von Arx, Michael S Bernstein, Jeannette Bohg, Antoine Bosselut, Emma Brunskill, et al. 2021. On the opportunities and risks of foundation models. *arXiv preprint arXiv:2108.07258*.

Tom Brown, Benjamin Mann, Nick Ryder, Melanie Subbiah, Jared D Kaplan, Prafulla Dhariwal, Arvind Neelakantan, Pranav Shyam, Girish Sastry, Amanda Askell, et al. 2020. Language models are few-shot learners. *Advances in neural information processing systems*, 33:1877–1901.

Nicholas Carlini, Daphne Ippolito, Matthew Jagielski, Katherine Lee, Florian Tramer, and Chiyuan Zhang. 2022. Quantifying memorization across neural language models. *arXiv preprint arXiv:2202.07646*.

Christopher Clark, Kenton Lee, Ming-Wei Chang, Tom Kwiatkowski, Michael Collins, and Kristina Toutanova. 2019. Boolq: Exploring the surprising difficulty of natural yes/no questions. In *NAACL*.

Peter Clark, Isaac Cowhey, Oren Etzioni, Tushar Khot, Ashish Sabharwal, Carissa Schoenick, and Oyvind Tafjord. 2018. Think you have solved question answering? try arc, the ai2 reasoning challenge. *arXiv preprint arXiv:1803.05457*.

Cord19. https://www.semanticscholar.org/cord19/download.

Marie-Catherine De Marneffe, Mandy Simons, and Judith Tonhauser. 2019. The commitmentbank: Investigating projection in naturally occurring discourse. In *proceedings of Sinn und Bedeutung*, volume 23, pages 107–124.

Jacob Devlin, Ming-Wei Chang, Kenton Lee, and Kristina Toutanova. 2018. Bert: Pre-training of deep bidirectional transformers for language understanding. *arXiv preprint arXiv:1810.04805*.

Ryan J Gallagher, Kyle Reing, David Kale, and Greg Ver Steeg. 2017. Anchored correlation explanation: Topic modeling with minimal domain knowledge. *Transactions of the Association for Computational Linguistics*, 5:529–542.

Leo Gao, Stella Biderman, Sid Black, Laurence Golding, Travis Hoppe, Charles Foster, Jason Phang, Horace He, Anish Thite, Noa Nabeshima, et al. 2020. The pile: An 800gb dataset of diverse text for language modeling. *arXiv preprint arXiv:2101.00027*.

Leo Gao, Jonathan Tow, Stella Biderman, Sid Black, Anthony DiPofi, Charles Foster, Laurence Golding, Jeffrey Hsu, Kyle McDonell, Niklas Muennighoff, Jason Phang, Laria Reynolds, Eric Tang, Anish Thite, Ben Wang, Kevin Wang, and Andy Zou. 2021. A framework for few-shot language model evaluation.

Yu Gu, Robert Tinn, Hao Cheng, Michael Lucas, Naoto Usuyama, Xiaodong Liu, Tristan Naumann, Jianfeng Gao, and Hoifung Poon. 2021. Domain-specific language model pretraining for biomedical natural language processing. *ACM Transactions on Computing for Healthcare (HEALTH)*, 3(1):1–23.

Jiang Guo, A. Santiago Ibanez-Lopez, Hanyu Gao, Victor Quach, Connor W. Coley, Klavs F. Jensen, and Regina Barzilay. 2021. Automated chemical reaction extraction from scientific literature. *Journal of Chemical Information and Modeling*, 0(0):null. PMID: 34115937.

Dan Hendrycks, Collin Burns, Steven Basart, Andy Zou, Mantas Mazeika, Dawn Song, and Jacob Steinhardt. 2020. Measuring massive multitask language understanding. *arXiv preprint arXiv:2009.03300*.

Andrew Jaegle, Felix Gimeno, Andy Brock, Oriol Vinyals, Andrew Zisserman, and Joao Carreira. 2021. Perceiver: General perception with iterative attention. In *International Conference on Machine Learning*, pages 4651–4664. PMLR.

Qiao Jin, Bhuwan Dhingra, Zhengping Liu, William W Cohen, and Xinghua Lu. 2019. Pubmedqa: A dataset for biomedical research question answering. *arXiv preprint arXiv:1909.06146*.

Kamal Kanakarajan, Bhuvana Kundumani, and Malaikannan Sankarasubbu. 2021. Bioelectra: pretrained biomedical text encoder using discriminators. In *Proceedings of the 20th Workshop on Biomedical Language Processing*, pages 143–154.

Jared Kaplan, Sam McCandlish, Tom Henighan, Tom B Brown, Benjamin Chess, Rewon Child, Scott Gray, Alec Radford, Jeffrey Wu, and Dario Amodei. 2020. Scaling laws for neural language models. *arXiv preprint arXiv:2001.08361*.

Cheolhyoung Lee, Kyunghyun Cho, and Wanmo Kang. 2019. Mixout: Effective regularization to finetune large-scale pretrained language models. *arXiv preprint arXiv:1909.11299*.

Jinhyuk Lee, Wonjin Yoon, Sungdong Kim, Donghyeon Kim, Sunkyu Kim, Chan Ho So, and Jaewoo Kang. 2020. Biobert: a pre-trained biomedical language representation model for biomedical text mining. *Bioinformatics*, 36(4):1234–1240.

Katherine Lee, Daphne Ippolito, Andrew Nystrom, Chiyuan Zhang, Douglas Eck, Chris Callison-Burch, and Nicholas Carlini. 2021. Deduplicating training data makes language models better. *arXiv preprint arXiv:2107.06499*.

Hector J. Levesque, Ernest Davis, and Leora Morgenstern. 2012. The winograd schema challenge. KR'12, page 552–561. AAAI Press.

Patrick Lewis, Myle Ott, Jingfei Du, and Veselin Stoyanov. 2020. Pretrained language models for biomedical and clinical tasks: Understanding and extending the state-of-the-art. In *Proceedings of the 3rd Clinical Natural Language Processing Workshop*, pages 146–157.

Wang Ling, Dani Yogatama, Chris Dyer, and Phil Blunsom. 2017. Program induction by rationale generation: Learning to solve and explain algebraic word problems. *arXiv preprint arXiv:1705.04146*.

Xiao Liu, Da Yin, Xingjian Zhang, Kai Su, Kan Wu, Hongxia Yang, and Jie Tang. 2021. Oag-bert: Pretrain heterogeneous entity-augmented academic language models. *arXiv preprint arXiv:2103.02410*.

Yinhan Liu, Myle Ott, Naman Goyal, Jingfei Du, Mandar Joshi, Danqi Chen, Omer Levy, Mike Lewis, Luke Zettlemoyer, and Veselin Stoyanov. 2019. Roberta: A robustly optimized bert pretraining approach. *arXiv preprint arXiv:1907.11692*.

Kyle Lo, Lucy Lu Wang, Mark Neumann, Rodney Michael Kinney, and Daniel S. Weld. 2020. S2orc: The semantic scholar open research corpus. In *ACL*.

Kelvin Luu, Daniel Khashabi, Suchin Gururangan, Karishma Mandyam, and Noah A Smith. 2021. Time waits for no one! analysis and challenges of temporal misalignment. *arXiv preprint arXiv:2111.07408*.

Stephen Merity, Caiming Xiong, James Bradbury, and Richard Socher. 2016. Pointer sentinel mixture models. *arXiv preprint arXiv:1609.07843*.

Todor Mihaylov, Peter Clark, Tushar Khot, and Ashish Sabharwal. 2018. Can a suit of armor conduct electricity? a new dataset for open book question answering. *arXiv preprint arXiv:1809.02789*.

Giacomo Miolo, Giulio Mantoan, and Carlotta Orsenigo. 2021. Electramed: a new pre-trained language representation model for biomedical nlp. *arXiv preprint arXiv:2104.09585*.

Usman Naseem, Adam G Dunn, Matloob Khushi, and Jinman Kim. 2021. Benchmarking for biomedical natural language processing tasks with a domain specific albert. *arXiv preprint arXiv:2107.04374*.

OAG. https://www.microsoft.com/en-us/research/project/open-academic-graph/.

Denis Paperno, Germán Kruszewski, Angeliki Lazaridou, Quan Ngoc Pham, Raffaella Bernardi, Sandro Pezzelle, Marco Baroni, Gemma Boleda, and Raquel Fernández. 2016. The lambada dataset: Word prediction requiring a broad discourse context. *arXiv preprint arXiv:1606.06031*.

Yifan Peng, Shankai Yan, and Zhiyong Lu. 2019. Transfer learning in biomedical natural language processing: an evaluation of bert and elmo on ten benchmarking datasets. *arXiv preprint arXiv:1906.05474*.

Long N Phan, James T Anibal, Hieu Tran, Shaurya Chanana, Erol Bahadroglu, Alec Peltekian, and Grégoire Altan-Bonnet. 2021. Scifive: a text-to-text transformer model for biomedical literature. *arXiv preprint arXiv:2106.03598*.

Mohammad Taher Pilehvar and Jose Camacho-Collados. 2018. Wic: the word-in-context dataset for evaluating context-sensitive meaning representations. *arXiv preprint arXiv:1808.09121*.

Nancy Pontika, Petr Knoth, Matteo Cancellieri, and Samuel Pearce. 2016. Developing infrastructure to support closer collaboration of aggregators with open repositories. *LIBER Quarterly*, 25(4):172–188.

Alec Radford, Jeffrey Wu, Rewon Child, David Luan, Dario Amodei, Ilya Sutskever, et al. 2019. Language models are unsupervised multitask learners. *OpenAI blog*, 1(8):9.

Jack W Rae, Sebastian Borgeaud, Trevor Cai, Katie Millican, Jordan Hoffmann, Francis Song, John Aslanides, Sarah Henderson, Roman Ring, Susannah Young, et al. 2021. Scaling language models: Methods, analysis & insights from training gopher. *arXiv preprint arXiv:2112.11446*.

S Rajbhandari, J Rasley, O Ruwase, and Y He. 2019. Zero: memory optimization towards training a trillion parameter models. arxiv e-prints arxiv: 11910.02054 (2019).

Vinay Venkatesh Ramasesh, Aitor Lewkowycz, and Ethan Dyer. 2021. Effect of scale on catastrophic forgetting in neural networks. In *International Conference on Learning Representations*.

Jeff Rasley, Samyam Rajbhandari, Olatunji Ruwase, and Yuxiong He. 2020. Deepspeed: System optimizations enable training deep learning models with over 100 billion parameters. In *Proceedings of the 26th ACM SIGKDD International Conference on Knowledge Discovery & Data Mining*, pages 3505–3506.

Hoo-Chang Shin, Yang Zhang, Evelina Bakhturina, Raul Puri, Mostofa Patwary, Mohammad Shoeybi, and Raghav Mani. 2020. Biomegatron: Larger biomedical domain language model. *arXiv preprint arXiv:2010.06060*.

Mohammad Shoeybi, Mostofa Patwary, Raul Puri, Patrick LeGresley, Jared Casper, and Bryan Catanzaro. 2019. Megatron-lm: Training multi-billion parameter language models using model parallelism. *arXiv preprint arXiv:1909.08053*.

Amanpreet Singh, Ronghang Hu, Vedanuj Goswami, Guillaume Couairon, Wojciech Galuba, Marcus Rohrbach, and Douwe Kiela. 2021. Flava: A foundational language and vision alignment model. *arXiv preprint arXiv:2112.04482*.

Shaden Smith, Mostofa Patwary, Brandon Norick, Patrick LeGresley, Samyam Rajbhandari, Jared Casper, Zhun Liu, Shrimai Prabhumoye, George Zerveas, Vijay Korthikanti, et al. 2022. Using deepspeed and megatron to train megatron-turing nlg 530b, a large-scale generative language model. *arXiv preprint arXiv:2201.11990*.

Jianlin Su, Yu Lu, Shengfeng Pan, Bo Wen, and Yunfeng Liu. 2021. Roformer: Enhanced transformer with rotary position embedding. *arXiv preprint arXiv:2104.09864*.

Kuansan Wang, Zhihong Shen, Chiyuan Huang, Chieh-Han Wu, Yuxiao Dong, and Anshul Kanakia. 2020a. Microsoft academic graph: When experts are not enough. *Quantitative Science Studies*, 1(1):396–413.

Lucy Lu Wang, Kyle Lo, Yoganand Chandrasekhar, Russell Reas, Jiangjiang Yang, Doug Burdick, Darrin Eide, Kathryn Funk, Yannis Katsis, Rodney Michael Kinney, Yunyao Li, Ziyang Liu, William Merrill, Paul Mooney, Dewey A. Murdick, Devvret Rishi, Jerry Sheehan, Zhihong Shen, Brandon Stilson, Alex D. Wade, Kuansan Wang, Nancy Xin Ru Wang, Christopher Wilhelm, Boya Xie, Douglas M. Raymond, Daniel S. Weld, Oren Etzioni, and Sebastian Kohlmeier. 2020b. CORD-19: The COVID-19 open research dataset. In *Proceedings of the 1st Workshop on NLP for COVID-19 at ACL 2020*, Online. Association for Computational Linguistics.

Johannes Welbl, Nelson F Liu, and Matt Gardner. 2017. Crowdsourcing multiple choice science questions. *arXiv preprint arXiv:1707.06209*.

Zheng Yuan, Yijia Liu, Chuanqi Tan, Songfang Huang, and Fei Huang. 2021. Improving biomedical pretrained language models with knowledge. *arXiv preprint arXiv:2104.10344*.

Yukun Zhu, Ryan Kiros, Rich Zemel, Ruslan Salakhutdinov, Raquel Urtasun, Antonio Torralba, and Sanja Fidler. 2015. Aligning books and movies: Towards story-like visual explanations by watching movies and reading books. In *Proceedings of the IEEE international conference on computer vision*, pages 19–27.

A Data Descriptions

AMiner ArnetMiner (AMiner) is a service that crawls research publications, performs profile extraction of scientists, models academic networks by integrating publication data from the existing libraries. For the experiments described in this work, we use a sub-sampled version of the data presented in the Open Academic Graph (OAG) version of the AMiner dataset, which originally consisted of more that 172M articles, with 18.5M chemistry-related abstracts.

CORE COnnecting REpositories (CORE) (Pontika et al., 2016) is a large-scale aggregation system which provides an open access to the global network of scientific journals and publications. CORE currently contains more than 207M open-access articles collected from over 10 thousand data providers, out of which more than 92M are open access full-text research papers. We sub-sampled the original collect into our chemistry-specific corpus consisting of more than 7M full-text articles.

CORD-19 CORD-19 corpus contains COVID-19 (Cord19) and other coronavirus-related publications (e.g. SARS, MERS, etc.) from PubMed's PMC open access corpus, bioRxiv, and medRxiv pre-prints, in addition to COVID-19 articles maintained by the World Health Organization (WHO).

MAG Microsoft Academic Graph (MAG) is a heterogeneous graph created by extracting knowledge from scholarly publications on the web (Wang et al., 2020a). The data used in this work is a subsample from the OAG version of the MAG dataset, which originally consisted of $>$ 208M articles, with 34M chemistry-related articles with abstracts.

PubMed PubMed is a domain-specific data source that allows for search and retrieval of the biomedical and life sciences literature. It is maintained by the National Centre for Biotechnology Information (NCBI) at the U.S. National Library of Medicine (NLM). For this work we utilized the PubMed Central data provided in the Pile corpus (Gao et al., 2020). As presented in Table 3 the sub-sampled data consists of documents with more than 280K abstracts and 700K full text articles.

S2ORC The Semantic Scholar Open Research Corpus (S2ORC) (Lo et al., 2020) is a large academic corpus consisting of 81.1M documents. The data includes the metadata, abstracts, bibliographical references and full-text publications for over 8M open access research articles. In this work, we utilize the sub-sampled version of the original data specific to chemistry, which includes more than 10M abstracts.

WoS The Web of Science (WoS) is a multi-discipline citation database produced by the Institute of Scientific Information. The platform hosts over 171M records across various disciplines, which, when sub-sampled for our chemistry domain, rounded to more than 7M records with abstracts available.

B Task Descriptions

HendrycksTest-Chemistry The Hendrycks Test (Hendrycks et al., 2020) is a large scale collection of multiple choice questions covering 57 subjects. In our experiments, we subsampled college chemistry (HT-CC) and high school chemistry (HT-HC). HT-CC contains 100 questions related to analytical, organic, inorganic, physical, etc. and HT-HC contains 203 questions related chemical reactions, ions, acids and bases, etc.

ARC The ARC dataset (Clark et al., 2018) contains 7,787 genuine grade-school level, science MCQs and is partitioned into a Challenge Set (ARC-C) and an Easy Set (ARC-E). Additionally, 14M science-related sentences are provided with relevant knowledge to answer the ARC questions.

SciQ The SciQ dataset (Welbl et al., 2017) contains 13,679 crowdsourced multiple-choice science exam questions about Physics, Chemistry and Biology, among others.

OpenBookQA The OpenBookQA (Mihaylov et al., 2018) dataset consists of 5,957 multiple choice questions and 1,326 elementary-level science facts. The facts alone do not contain enough information to correctly answer the multiple choice questions, therefore the task is designed to evaluate systems beyond paraphrase matching.

Pile PubMed Abstracts The Pile dataset (Gao et al., 2020) contains 800GB of diverse text sources for benchmarking language models. We limit this task to only include abstracts from the Pile's PubMed collection. As this is framed as a language modeling task, we report word level perplexity.

BoolQ BoolQ (Clark et al., 2019) is a reading comprehension dataset comprised of 16k real, naturally formed queries to the Google search engine with a yes or no answer. Each question-answer pair is accompanied by a Wikipedia article providing evidence to support the correct answer.

CB Commitment Bank (CB) (De Marneffe et al., 2019) is a 3-way classification of textual entailment (true, false, unknown) from 1,200 short text segments where at least one sentence contains an embedded clause. The dataset contains passages from three sources: the Wall Street Journal, the British National Corpus, and Switchboard.

WIC The Word-in-Context dataset (WIC) (Pilehvar and Camacho-Collados, 2018) is a benchmark for evaluating context-sensitive word embeddings. The task is to classify if a target word has the same meaning in two context sentence.

WSC The Winograd Schema Challenge (WSC) (Levesque et al., 2012) dataset is a collection of 804 sentences in which the task is to resolve coreferences.

MathQA MathQA (Amini et al., 2019) is a dataset containing 37k multiple choice math word problems built from the existing dataset, AQuA (Ling et al., 2017).

PIQA The Physical Interactions: Question Answering (PIQA) (Bisk et al., 2020) benchmark dataset provides 21k questions about the physical world and plausible interactions encountered by humans. Annotators provided correct and incorrect answers to questions extracted from instructables.com, a website of instructions for completing many everyday tasks.

PubMedQA The PubMedQA dataset (Jin et al., 2019) is a collection of 273.5k biomedical research questions and related PubMed articles with yes/no/maybe answers.

Lambada Lambada (Paperno et al., 2016) contains passages and target sentences from 5,325 novels collected from Book Corpus (Zhu et al., 2015), and the goal is to predict the last word of the target sentence given the context passage. This task was designed to test genuine language understanding since accurate prediction of the final word would be improbable without the context passage.

WikiText The Wikitext benchmark (Merity et al., 2016) is a language modeling dataset of 29k articles from Wikipedia. Only articles classified as *Good* or *Featured* by Wikipedia editors are included since they are considered to be well written and neutral in language. All results are reported on Wikitext-2.

Author Index

Association for Computational Linguistics
209 N. Eighth Street
Stroudsburg, Pennsylvania 18360

ISBN 978-1-7138-6727-2

CURRAN ASSOCIATES INC.
proceedings.com